4th edition

The Challenge of Third World Development

4th edition

The Challenge of Third World Development

HOWARD HANDELMAN
University of Wisconsin-Milwaukee

PEARSON

Prentice
Hall

Upper Saddle River, New Jersey 07458

Library of Congress Cataloging-in-Publication Data

Handelman, Howard
The challenge of Third World development / Howard Handelman.—4th ed.
  p. cm.
  Includes bibliographical references and index.
  ISBN 0-13-193070-2
    1. Developing countries—Economic conditions. 2. Developing countries—Economic policy.
  3. Developing countries—Politics and government. 4. Economic development. I. Title.

HC59.7.H299 2005
338.9'009172'4—dc22

                                                                                2005048920

Editorial Director: Charlyce Jones Owen
Director of Marketing: Heather Shelstad
Marketing Assistant: Jennifer Lang
Director of Production and Manufacturing: Barbara Kittle
Managing Editor: Lisa Iarkowski
Production Liaison: Joe Scordato
Production Assistant: Marlene Gassler
Manufacturing Buyer: Sherry Lewis
Manufacturing Manager: Nick Sklitsis
Cover Design: Bruce Kenselaar
Cover Art Director: Jayne Conte
Cover Illustration/Photo: Getty Images, Inc
Full Service Management: Andrea Clemente/Cadmus Professional Communications

This book was set in 10/11 Palatino by Cadmus Professional Communications and was printed by The Courier Companies, Inc. The cover was printed by The Courier Companies, Inc.

Credits and acknowledgments borrowed from other sources and reproduced, with permission, in this textbook appear on appropriate page within text.

Pearson Education Ltd
Pearson Education Singapore, Pte. Ltd
Pearson Education, Canada, Ltd
Pearson Education—Japan

Pearson Education Australia PTY, Limited
Pearson Education North Asia Ltd
Pearson Educacion de Mexico, S.A. de C.V.
Pearson Education Malaysia, Pte. Ltd

PEARSON
Prentice
Hall

10 9 8 7 6 5 4 3 2 1
ISBN 0-13-193070-2

TO MICHAEL, PHOEBE, AND ALICE

Contents

chapter 9
Soldiers and Politics   223

chapter 10
The Political Economy of Third World Development   253

Preface

While Americans and other Westerners often find the politics of developing areas (Africa, Asia, the Caribbean, Latin America, and the Middle East) difficult to comprehend, developments in those regions are an inescapable part of our lives. The recent wars in Iraq and Afghanistan, Islamic fundamentalism and the war on terrorism, genocidal activity in Sudan, rapid economic growth in China and India, and emigration from the developing world are but a few of the events which draw our attention. The purpose of this book is to better understand the dynamics and challenges of political and socioeconomic changes in these developing nations, which account for most of the world's population.

For want of a better term, I refer to the more than 150 disparate, developing nations as the Third World (the term is defined in Chapter 1). They include desperately poor countries such as Afghanistan and Ethiopia and rapidly developing industrial powers such as South Korea and Taiwan. Some, like Trinidad and Costa Rica, are stable democracies; others, such as Myanmar and Syria, suffer under highly repressive dictatorships. All of them, however, share at least some of the aspects of political, economic, and social underdevelopment that are analyzed in this book.

No text is capable of fully examining the political and economic systems of so many highly diverse countries. Instead, we will look for common issues, problems, and potential solutions. We start in Chapter 1 by exploring the nature of political and economic underdevelopment, and we then analyze the leading explanatory theories. The next chapter discusses what has been arguably the most important political change in world politics during the late twentieth and early twenty-first centuries—the wave of democratic change that has swept over the developing nations of Africa, Asia, Latin America, and the Middle East (as well as the former Soviet bloc of nations and southern Europe).

Because these often still-fragile transitions from authoritarian to democratic government are potentially so important, most of the chapters that follow contain discussion of how democratization is likely to influence issues such as the level of ethnic conflict, the role of women in the political system, and the proper path to economic development.

Chapters 3 to 5 on Religion and Politics, Cultural Pluralism and Ethnic Conflict, and Women and Development analyze broad social forces and gender issues that have often divided developing nations. Chapters 6 and 7 on Rural Change and Urbanization discuss the specific problems and challenges that many countries face in those two sectors of society. Next, Chapters 8 and 9 on Revolutionary Change and Soldiers and Politics consider the records of each of those regime types (e.g., revolutionary governments in China and Cuba and military regimes in Brazil and Indonesia) as alternative models of political and economic development. Finally, Chapter 10, dealing with Third World Political Economies, compares alternative paths to economic development and evaluates the relative effectiveness of each.

It is easy to despair when considering the tremendous obstacles facing most Third World nations and the failures of political leadership that so many of them have endured. Unfortunately, many of us in the First World have suffered from "compassion fatigue" or have become cynical about cooperative efforts with Third World countries. The assaults on the World Trade Center and the Pentagon in 2001 and the subsequent wars (and post-war conflicts) in Afghanistan and Iraq have reinforced many people's perception of the less developed nations (LDCs) as poor beyond redemption and saturated with fanaticism and authoritarian beliefs. Yet the recent trend toward democratization in the developing world (most notably in Latin America), the increased stability that has come to parts of Africa, and the enormous economic growth that has taken place in parts of Asia all provide new bases for hope. It is incumbent upon the West's next generation of citizens and leaders to renew efforts to understand the challenge of Third World development.

ACKNOWLEDGMENTS

Because of the broad geographic and conceptual scope of any book on Third World politics, I am particularly indebted to others for their kind help and advice.

First, I would like to thank St. Martin's Press for granting me permission to reproduce a portion of Chapter 1, which is incorporated from *Politics in a Changing World* by Marcus Ethridge and Howard Handelman (copyright 1993 by St. Martin's Press). Thanks also to the many people at Prentice Hall who have worked with me through four editions of this book.

Much of the original research took place during a sabbatical leave from the University of Wisconsin-Milwaukee. I am grateful to my own university for granting me that sabbatical support and to the University of Wisconsin-Madison, whose outstanding libraries, lectures, and other scholarly activities informed me during a wonderful year there.

Finally, my greatest debt is to the scholars who generously agreed to read portions of the manuscript of the first edition. They include Lourdes Benería (Cornell University), Josef Gugler (University of Connecticut), Stephan Haggard (University of California-San Diego), Kathleen Staudt (University of Texas-El Paso), Mark Tessler (University of Michigan), William Thiesenhusen (University of Wisconsin-Madison), and M. Crawford Young (University of Wisconsin-Madison). Thanks also to Prentice Hall's reviewers Robert Griffiths (University of North Carolina-Greensboro), Robert W. Hunt (Illinois State University), and Jamal R. Nassar (Illinois State University); the quality of the manuscript benefitted greatly from their many insights, suggestions, and corrections. The usual caveat, of course, applies: Any remaining errors of fact or interpretation are my own responsibility.

Howard Handelman
University of Wisconsin-Milwaukee

4th edition

The Challenge of Third World Development

chapter 1

Understanding Underdevelopment

To almost any observer, the problems plaguing Africa, Asia, Latin America, the Caribbean, and the Middle East today appear daunting. The most troubled countries in these regions are beset by warfare, internal violence, and massive human suffering: armed insurgency, terrorism, and ethnic tensions in Iraq; poverty and revolutionary conflict in Colombia and Nepal; ethnically based massacres in Sudan and Sri Lanka; and political repression in Syria, Zimbabwe, and Myanmar (Burma). Of course, many of those problems exist in industrialized democracies as well, though in a milder form. For example, in recent times both Northern Ireland and the Basque region of Spain have experienced ethnic violence and terrorism. Portions of Washington, D.C. have higher infant mortality rates than Cuba or Singapore. But it is the scope and persistence of the developing world's political, economic, and social challenges that ultimately draw our attention.

Understanding the nature and causes of underdevelopment is a complex task complicated by theoretical debates between scholars and a profusion of terminology. There is not even agreement on a collective name for the approximately 140 countries that constitute the developing world. At one time it was common to call these countries *underdeveloped nations*. But many found this title objectionable, suggesting, as it did, that those countries' political and economic systems were backward. Because of its pejorative connotations and implied inferiority, the adjective *underdeveloped* fell into disfavor. Instead, the term *developing nations (or areas)* has often been used in its place. Though clearly more positive, this term unfortunately suffers from the opposite problem—excessive optimism.

At various times during the 1970s and 1980s, most African and Latin American countries suffered from political and economic decay, and today many remain trapped on a political or economic treadmill. In the late 1990s, even the previously thriving economies of East Asia were plunged into a crisis from which some countries have yet to fully recover. And today, countries such as Congo, Nepal, and Haiti show few signs of forward progress. In short, for extended time periods, many of these so-called "developing countries" have shown few signs of political or economic development. Hence, the United Nations and many other international organizations favor the label *less developed countries* (or LDCs), an expression that escapes the normative flaws of its competitors.

The term *Third World countries* (or simply *the Third World*) is preferred by many social scientists and is the label most frequently employed in this book.[1] It has both the virtue and defect of being somewhat fuzzy. Simply put, Third World countries are the nations of Africa, Asia, the Middle East, Latin America, and the Caribbean that belong neither to the First World (Japan and the Western industrialized democracies, the first countries to develop advanced industrial economies and liberal democracies), nor to the now-defunct Second World (the bloc of former communist nations that included the Soviet Union and Eastern Europe).[2]

Thus, Third World is essentially a residual category. Countries fall under its banner not because of any specific quality, but simply because they are not members of either the First or Second Worlds.[3] Like the previously discussed classifications, Third World glosses over the many political and socioeconomic differences among its members, placing all of them under one big tent. Of course, in reality they differ considerably. A few (including Singapore, Taiwan, and Kuwait) are relatively affluent, while many others (such as Afghanistan, Cambodia, and Somalia) are desperately poor. Some (Barbados, Costa Rica, and India, for example) are stable democracies. Many others, however, suffer either from severe political instability, government repression, or other manifestations of political underdevelopment.

Therefore, like any residual category, the term *Third World* suffers from a degree of imprecision. Its virtue, however, is that unlike *underdeveloped nations* or *developing nations*, it makes no value judgment or predictions. As one author writes, paraphrasing Winston Churchill's comments on democracy, "It is the worst term we have, except for all the others."[4] With some irony, Christopher Clapham has written, "I have chosen to use the term [Third World] ... because of its meaninglessness. Its alternatives all carry conceptual overtones which are even more misleading, in that they imply positive elements of commonality rather than a simply negative residual category."[5] Taking a less cynical position than Clapham, I maintain in the next section that, despite their many differences, there are enough commonalities among Third World countries to make the category useful and usable. Of course, it may be argued that the collapse of Soviet communism has made the term *Third World* rather anachronistic. Since there no longer is a Second World (those nations are now called "postcommunist" countries), technically there cannot be a Third World. But like many political scientists, I continue to use the term in this book (and in the book's title) because I feel that it is conceptually useful and is still comprehensible to many readers.

In order to avoid repetitive usage of the term, throughout this book I alternately use the categories Third World, less developed countries (LDCs), developing countries, and developing world interchangeably.

THIRD WORLD COMMONALITIES: THE NATURE OF UNDERDEVELOPMENT

Despite the substantial differences among them, Third World nations still share a number of common characteristics. All of them suffer from some aspects of political, economic, or social underdevelopment. Although some of East Asia's newly industrializing countries (NICs)—South Korea, Singapore, and Taiwan— are no longer *economically* underdeveloped, they share a high vulnerability to global economic forces (as evidenced by East Asia's recent economic crisis) and continue to suffer from aspects of political underdevelopment. On the other hand, Costa Rica and Botswana are rather well developed politically and socially, but manifest the problems of economic underdevelopment. In short, while some Third World countries are underdeveloped in all major aspects of modernization, other LDCs are far more advanced in some areas of development than in others. As we shall see, economic, social, and political underdevelopment are closely related to each other, but they are by no means perfectly correlated.

Economic Underdevelopment

Perhaps the most salient characteristic of most Third World countries is their poverty. This is manifested at the national level by some combination of low per-capita income (technically expressed as low Gross Domestic Product [GDP] per capita), highly unequal income distribution, poor infrastructure (including communications and transportation), limited use of modern technology, and low consumption of energy.[6] At the individual level, economic underdevelopment connotes widespread poverty, including unemployment, substandard housing, poor health conditions, and inadequate nutrition.

Table 1.1 presents economic data comparing two wealthy countries (United States and Japan); one relatively affluent developing country (Hong Kong, now a part of China but with its own economy); two middle-income Latin American countries (Mexico and Brazil); three lower-income Asian and Middle Eastern nations (China, India, and Egypt); and one very impoverished African country (Nigeria).[7] The second column in the table, commonly referred to as *Per-Capita Income*, is, more precisely, the average dollar value of goods and services produced per person during the year 2003.[8] The data illustrate both the tremendous gap in living standards between most First and Third World countries and the considerable variation among Third World nations. On the one hand, the table reveals that the average American earns about *four to five* times as much as a typical Mexican or Brazilian. At the same time, however, Mexicans and Brazilians earn about *nine to ten* times more than the average Nigerian. On the other hand, residents of Hong Kong and a few other Third World nations (such as Singapore) now earn as much as the Japanese or Italians.

TABLE 1.1   Measures of Economic Development

Country	Per-Capita Income (PPP)	Share of the Poorest 20%	Share of the Richest 20%	Ratio of Richest 20% to Poorest 20%
United States	$35,750	5.4%	45.8%	8.4
Japan	$26,940	10.6	35.7	3.4
Hong Kong	$26,910	5.3	50.7	9.7
Mexico	$ 8,970	3.1	59.1	19.3
Brazil	$ 7,770	2.0	64.4	31.5
China	$ 4,510	4.7	50.0	10.7
Egypt	$ 3,810	8.6	43.6	5.1
India	$ 2,670	8.9	41.6	4.7
Nigeria	$ 860	4.4	55.7	12.8

Source: United Nations Development Programme (UNDP), *Human Development Report 2004. Cultural Liberty in Today's Diverse World:* Human Development Indicators, Tables 13 and 14, http://www.undp.org/.

Ultimately, however, a country's standard of living is determined not only by its per-capita income, but also by how that income is distributed. Columns 3 to 5 in Table 1.1 indicate how equitably or how unequally income is distributed in these countries. Column 3 reveals the percentage of a country's annual income that is earned by the poorest 20 percent of the population; column 4 indicates the income share going to the wealthiest 20 percent of the population; and, finally, the last column shows the ratio of incomes for those in the richest 20 percent of the population to those in the poorest 20 percent. It is often said that distribution of income is much more inequitable in developing countries than in economically advanced nations (that is, that there is a greater gap between the "haves" and "have nots"), and for the most part that is true. However, column 5 reveals that there is also considerable variation within both developing and developed nations. For example, while Japan has perhaps the most equitable income distribution in the world, the United States has one of the most unequal distributions among advanced industrial nations. Thus, Table 1.1 indicates that although Americans earn, on average, considerably more than the Japanese (column 2), the poor in the United States earn a far smaller *share* of the nation's wealth. Whereas the richest 20 percent of the Japanese population earns 3.4 times as much as the poorest 20 percent, in the United States the richest Americans earn 8.4 times as much as the poorest.

Among the Third World nations listed in Table 1.1, Brazil has by far the greatest income inequality, with the rich earning on average 31.5 times as much as the poor (one of the most inequitable distributions of income in the world). Income inequality was also relatively high in Mexico, Nigeria, China, and Hong Kong. At the same time, contrary to stereotype, income is actually substantially more equally distributed in India and Egypt than in the United States.[9] For the most part, Latin America is the region of the world with the highest income inequality, and Asia has the least of any Third World region, less in many cases than the United States. Africa has the greatest variation. For example, although income is relatively equally distributed in nations such as Ethiopia and Mozambique, in Sierra Leone the richest 20 percent of the population earns 57.6 times as much as the poorest, and in Namibia they earn 56.1 times as much (the two highest ratios in the world).[10]

Several factors seem to influence a country's or a region's income distribution pattern. First, as we just noted, is the *level of industrialization and economic development*. Countries moving into the middle- and upper-middle levels of development generally experience a growing economic gap between the middle to upper classes and the poor, as a new class of business people and professionals emerges with far higher incomes, such as Hong Kong's and Brazil's industrialists and financiers. But there are variations within this pattern. A second important factor is the historical *pattern of land ownership*. Regions or countries that were colonized by the Spanish or Portuguese, such as Latin America and the Philippines, saw land ownership concentrated in a relatively small number of hands (see Chapter 6). In contrast, most Asian countries have historically allowed less concentration of rural property. Third, *government policies* on land ownership, taxation, welfare programs, and the like can either reduce or intensify income inequality. Countries with large and open educational systems, agrarian reform programs, and progressive taxation can reduce income gaps. Generally speaking, communist and former communist countries, such as

Mongolia and the Slovak Republic (not shown in the table), have among the world's lowest levels of inequality, but they are closely trailed by some of East Asia's capitalist success stories, such as Japan, Taiwan, and South Korea (both former colonies of Japan).[11] In both models, welfare communism and egalitarian capitalism, government policies reduced income disparities. Conversely, since the 1980s, when China moved from a command (communist) economy to a predominantly free-market economy without adequate government protections, income inequality has widened considerably.

Social Underdevelopment

Poverty and poor public policy have often adversely affected social conditions in the Third World, narrowing opportunities for human development. Consequently, among the greatest challenges facing the LDCs has been improving their educational systems. Indeed, expanding education, particularly raising literacy rates, is a major prerequisite for economic and political modernization. An educated workforce—be it peasants who can read the instructions on insecticide containers or doctors and construction engineers—contributes to higher labor productivity. Increased education and literacy also expand mass political participation and increase government accountability to the governed. Thus, it is not surprising that a higher literacy rate has been found to be one of the most crucial prerequisites for democratic government throughout the world.[12]

Table 1.2 presents data for several important indicators of social development. It compares two developed nations (Canada and the United States); six middle to upper-middle income Third World countries (South Korea, Saudi Arabia, Argentina, Cuba, Mexico, and Brazil); three poorer countries (China,

TABLE 1.2   Indicators of Social Development (by Country)

Country	Human Development Index (rank)	Life Expectancy (Years)	Adult Literacy (percent)	Real Income Rank (PPP) minus HDI Rank
Canada	.943 (4)	79.3	99.0	+5
United States	.939 (8)	77.0	99.0	−4
South Korea	.888 (28)	75.4	97.9	+9
Argentina	.853 (34)	74.1	97.0	+14
Cuba	.809 (52)	76.7	96.9	+39
Mexico	.802 (53)	73.3	90.5	+5
Brazil	.775 (72)	68.0	86.4	−9
Saudi Arabia	.768 (77)	72.1	77.9	−33
China	.745 (94)	70.9	90.9	+5
Egypt	.653 (120)	68.6	55.6	−12
India	.595 (127)	63.7	61.3	−10
Nigeria	.466 (151)	51.6	66.8	+15
Ethiopia	.359 (170)	45.5	41.5	−1

Source: United Nations Development Programme (UNDP), *Human Development Report 2004. Cultural Liberty in Today's Diverse World:* Human Development Indicators, Table 1, http://www.undp.org/.

Egypt, and India); and two extremely poor nations (Nigeria and Ethiopia) drawn from the major regions of the Third Word. Column 2 lists each country's Human Development Index (HDI), a composite measurement of school enrollment, literacy, infant mortality, life expectancy, and income. More than per-capita income or any other single indicator, the HDI is considered to be one of the best measures of a nation's living standard. The highest possible HDI score a country may achieve is 1.000, and the lowest is .000. Column 2 contains each country's raw HDI score and, in parentheses, its worldwide HDI ranking. Thus, Canada has the world's fourth highest HDI (.943), while India ranks 127th. The figures indicate that some Third World countries (such as Argentina, Mexico, Cuba, and, especially, South Korea) have relatively high indices, placing them in the top one-third of all nations. Indeed, their scores are comparable to those of less developed European nations, such as Portugal, Hungary, and Latvia. On the other hand, many South Asian and African countries—such as Egypt, India, Nigeria, and Ethiopia—have very low HDI scores, reflecting a combination of intense poverty, low educational levels, and limited life expectancy.

Life expectancy (Column 3) and adult literacy (Column 4) are among the best individual (nonindexed) measures of mass living standards. The first statistic is greatly influenced by the availability of health care, adequate nutrition, and safe drinking water; the second statistic indicates the availability of education. Unlike per-capita income, statistical averages for life expectancy and education cannot be distorted by highly skewed distributions.[13] The table shows a substantial gap separating South Korean and Cuban life expectancy (both greater than 75 years, not far below the United States) from the levels in Nigeria and Ethiopia (both less than 52 years). Similarly, while adult literacy levels(Column 4) in South Korea, Argentina, and Cuba are very close to those in the United States and Canada, the rates in Egypt, India, Nigeria, and Ethiopia lag far behind.

Although economic development usually brings about improvement in social indicators, government social policy also helps determine the share of the country's economic resources that is invested in education, sanitation, and health care—that is, how much economic growth translates into social development. Column 5 compares a country's worldwide rank for per-capita income with its rank for HDI. If a hypothetical country ranked 45th in the world in per-capita income and 40th in the HDI, it would receive a score of 5 (Income rank minus HDI rank) in column 5. If a nation's HDI rank were lower than its GDP per-capita rank (for example, 52nd in per capita GDP and 63rd in HDI), it would receive a negative score in column 5 (−11 in this hypothetical case). Thus, a high positive score, such as Cuba's (+39) or Nigeria's (+15), indicates that the country's social indicators are higher than its per-capita income would lead us to expect, presumably because of a strong government commitment to health, education, and economic equity. Conversely, a negative score (such as Brazil's, Egypt's, India's, and, especially, Saudi Arabia's) indicates the government's failure to translate adequately its available economic resources into an improved quality of life. Cuba has by far the highest score in this area, while both wealthy Canada and impoverished Nigeria have positive scores as well. On the other hand, both the wealthy United States and poorer Brazil and India have negative scores. In other words, although Nigeria's HDI score is quite low (ranking 151st in the world), that rank is actually somewhat higher than we might expect in a country with that level of poverty. Many of the worst performers on this comparative measure, including Saudi Arabia (−33) and other oil-rich nations not shown in the table (United Arab Emirates and Oman), owe their low scores to their failure to educate adequately their female population because of religious or other cultural barriers (see Chapter 5).

Despite substantial economic declines in Africa and Latin America during the 1980s and early 1990s, and despite East Asia's economic crisis in the late 1990s, LDCs as a whole have made considerable progress in social development in the past 40 to 50 years. For example, adult illiteracy in developing countries has been more than cut in half since 1965, falling from 59 percent to 23 percent. Improved health care and sanitation have helped reduce infant mortality rates by 60 percent. Together with other advances in public health care, these changes have raised life expectancy from 53.4 years in 1960 to 64.6 years in 2003.[14] At the same time, the United Nations Development Program (UNDP) estimates that the rate of Third World poverty fell faster in the last 50 years of the twentieth century than in the previous 500 years. Still, an estimated 1 to 2 billion people continue to live in poverty today.[15] Meanwhile, AIDS has actually sharply reduced life expectancy in several African nations in the past decade or so. From 1990 to 2000 life expectancy declined from 53.6 to 36.3 in Lesotho, from 55.3 to 35.7 in Swaziland, and from 56.6 to 33.9 in Zimbabwe.[16] Taken together, these figures indicate both how much progress has been made in several critical areas and how much remains to be done.

Table 1.3 shows substantial differences in social and economic development among the various regions of the developing world. Latin America, despite relatively slow economic growth since the 1980s (about 2.4 percent annually) and several economic downturns, still has the developing world's highest per-capita income, HDI, and life expectancy, while trailing East Asia only slightly in adult literacy. East Asia, the world's fastest-growing regional economy since the 1980s (7.4 percent annual GDP growth), ranks close behind Latin America in HDI score and life expectancy and has the developing world's highest literacy rate. In recent decades, economic growth has accelerated dramatically in South Asia (5.4 percent annually since 1980), but the region still lags far behind Latin America and East Asia in the table's indicators. Meanwhile, Sub-Saharan Africa has achieved very modest economic growth (2.1 percent annually, often not enough to keep

TABLE 1.3   Indicators of Social and Economic Development (by Region)

Region	Human Development Index	Life Expectancy (years)	Adult Literacy (percent)	GDP per cap (PPP)
Third World	.663	64.6	76.7	$4,054
Arab Nations	.651	66.3	63.3	5,069
East Asia/Pacific	.746	69.8	90.3	4,768
Latin America and Caribbean	.777	70.5	88.6	7,223
South Asia	.584	63.2	53.6	2,658
Sub-Sahara Africa	.465	46.5	63.2	1,790

Source: United Nations Development Programme (UNDP), *Human Development Report 2004. Cultural Liberty in Today's Diverse World:* Human Development Indicators, Tables 1 and 13, http://www.undp.org/.

pace with population growth) after a period of decline but continues to trail well behind the rest of the world, most dramatically in life expectancy.[17]

While macroeconomic performance has varied considerably from region to region and decade to decade, many countries have made impressive progress in critical areas of public health and education. African countries such as Angola, Ethiopia, and Senegal—all of which had shockingly high infant mortality rates in the 1960s (ranging from 173 to 208 infant deaths for each 1,000 live births)—reduced those rates by 40 to 65 percent by the closing years of the twentieth century. Asia's two giants, China and India (with approximately 40 percent of the world's population between them), reduced their infant mortality rates by 76 percent and 55 percent, respectively, during that same period. Cuba, which started that era with one of the LDC's lowest infant mortality rates, reduced its rate by a further 79 percent, while Chile's rate fell by 89 percent.[18] During a comparable period of time (1970–1995), adult illiteracy declined impressively across much of the Third World. South Korea and Cuba, which started the period with relatively low illiteracy rates (12–13 percent), made dramatic further strides in cutting their rates to 2–4 percent. Meanwhile, Jordan and Kenya, which started with high illiteracy rates in 1960 (53 and 68 percent), also made very impressive progress, reducing their rates of illiteracy by 75 and 68 percent, respectively.[19]

Still, as an aggregate, less developed countries continue to lag considerably behind the developed world. Third World adult literacy rates, life expectancy, and calorie consumption still trail those of the industrialized nations by about 20 percent. As of the late 1990s, some 1.3 billion people (about one-third of the developing world's population) lived on incomes of less than $1 per day, and 800 million of them did not get a sufficient amount to eat. Furthermore, within the LDCs great gaps persist between urban centers—where, for example, at the close of the past century, 72 percent of the population had access to proper home sanitation—and rural areas, where that figure fell to 20 percent.[20]

Political Underdevelopment

When Western political scientists began to study the Third World systematically, they eventually recognized that evaluating political systems in cultural and socioeconomic settings very different from their own was particularly challenging. While many modernization theorists felt that Third World governments should model themselves after Western industrialized democracies, they were also mindful of important differences between the two regions that limited that option. Recognizing that most Western European countries did not become meaningfully democratic until they were well along the path to industrial development, scholars were often reluctant to criticize the authoritarian systems prevailing in the newly industrializing or unindustrialized nations of the Third World. A number of African social scientists added to the debate by arguing that their continent had extensive village- and tribal-based democracies that adequately substituted for competitive elections at the national level. Others feared that in the ethnically divided countries of Africa and Asia, multiparty systems would inevitably develop along ethnic lines, contributing to national disintegration.

Conscious of such land mines, some prominent political scientists despaired of defining political development in any meaningful way.[21] Others, however, offered a set of standards that they believed were relatively free of ideological and cultural biases. Political development, they suggested, involves the creation of specialized and differentiated government institutions that effectively carry out necessary functions, such as collecting tax revenues, defending national borders, maintaining political stability, stimulating economic development, improving the quality of human life, and communicating with the citizenry. In addition, they argued, developed governments must be responsive to a broad segment of society and respect the population's fundamental freedoms and civil rights. Presumably, any government satisfying these standards would enjoy a reasonable level of *legitimacy* (i.e., citizens would recognize and accept its right to govern), leading individuals and groups to pursue their political objectives peacefully through established political institutions rather than through violent or illegal channels.

But while analysts agreed that governments should be responsive, representative, and nonrepressive, they were not all convinced that developed political systems need necessarily be democratic, at least as that term has been defined in the West. That definition of democracy encompasses the following basic components: honest and competitive elections in which opposition parties have a realistic chance of winning; universal or nearly universal suffrage; widespread opportunities for political participation; free and open mass media; and government respect for human rights, including minority rights.[22] As we have seen, many political scientists initially felt that it was unrealistic and perhaps culturally biased to expect liberal democracy to flourish in developing countries. Others argued that many, if not most, developing nations were not ready for democracy. Concerned about the high levels of violence and instability in those political systems, they claimed that the LDCs' first priority had to be political stability, even if that might initially require military rule or other forms of authoritarian government.[23]

More recently, however, troubled by extensive government repression in the Third World and the obvious failures of most authoritarian regimes, political scientists have begun to insist that democracy and some degree of social equality must be understood as integral parts of political development.[24] Beyond its obvious moral attractions, democracy also has pragmatic appeal. For example, governments that are held accountable to their citizens by means of competitive elections are more likely to be efficient and honest (although the disappointing records of democratic governments in countries such as Brazil and the Philippines demonstrate that there are no guarantees). Similarly, free and independent forms of mass media help keep governments accountable. The collapse of the Soviet bloc and the fall of other types of dictatorship in the Third World since the early 1980s demonstrate that while authoritarian regimes may be stable in the short run, they are fragile in the long term. Thus, there is not necessarily a tradeoff between democracy and political stability, as many had imagined. In fact, democracies are generally immune to revolutionary insurrection and are less prone than dictatorships to other forms of mass violence.

Only a restricted (but growing) number of developing countries conform closely to all of the standards of political development listed above; these include the Bahamas, Uruguay, and Costa Rica (all small countries). Others—such as Brazil, India, South Korea, and Taiwan—currently satisfy most of the criteria. Even a cursory review of the developing world, however, soon reveals that most governments fall woefully short in terms of democratic practices. At one extreme, in several countries such as Somalia and Sierra Leone, warlords divided control over the country and so undermined the capacity of the national government to function that political scientists have referred to them as "countries without a state." Most Central American regimes respond disproportionately to the demands of the affluent minority. Many Middle Eastern and North African nations are ruled by self-perpetuating and self-serving elites, while some Sub-Saharan African governments serve the interests of the dominant ethnic groups. Political corruption, government inefficiency, and repression are endemic in much of the developing world.

In the recent past, class-based revolutionary movements have erupted in various Asian and Latin American nations, and a number of African countries have been torn apart by ethnic civil wars. Thus, until recently most Third World governments were neither democratic, nor stable, nor legitimate. In recent decades, however, democracy (and with it, government legitimacy) has advanced in much of the developing world, most notably in Latin America and East Asia (see Chapter 2). It is still uncertain, however, how enduring this positive trend will become.[25]

Some Relationships among the Components of Development

It would be logical to assume that political, economic, and social underdevelopment are interrelated. More economically advanced countries can better educate their populations and provide them with better health care. An educated citizenry, in turn, contributes to further economic growth and participates in politics more responsibly. Responsive and legitimate governments, constrained by competitive elections, are more likely to educate their people and to make informed economic decisions. Indeed, these logical intuitions are supported by empirical evidence. Wealthier countries tend to have greater life expectancy, higher literacy rates, and more stable and democratic governments.

But these correlations are not absolute. For example, a country's literacy and infant mortality rates depend not only on its economic resources but also on government policies in the areas of education, public health, and welfare. Thus, as we saw earlier, elitist government policies in some countries have contributed to social indicators (HDIs) that are far lower than those of other nations with comparable economic resources. This is most apparent in many petroleum-rich states (such as Saudi Arabia and the United Arab Emirates) but holds true in countries such as the Dominican Republic and Tunisia as well.[26] On the other hand, governments in Cuba, Uruguay, and Vietnam—with strong commitments to social welfare programs—have generated much higher life expectancy rates and educational levels than their economic resources alone would lead us to predict.

Both economic and social development also tend to correlate with political development. Wealthier, more educated countries such as Barbados, Botswana, Costa Rica, and Taiwan tend to have more politically stable, responsive, and democratic governments than poor nations such as Mozambique, Haiti, and Cambodia. Indeed, Third World countries are very unlikely to become democracies unless they have attained a minimal threshold of socioeconomic development.[27] That does not imply, however, that wealthier countries are assured of becoming democratic. An economic threshold is a somewhat necessary, but not sufficient, condition for democratization.

Moreover, there is not a linear relationship between economic and political development. In other words, as countries become more economically developed, there often is not a continuous movement toward greater stability, democracy, or other components of political development. In fact, Samuel Huntington has observed that while it is true that the richest countries in the world (such as Switzerland, Japan, and Canada) are politically very stable and that the poorest countries (Afghanistan, Congo, and Haiti) are generally very unstable, countries that are still in the process of moving from economic underdevelopment to greater development often actually become more unstable as they pass through the intermediate stages of economic growth.[28] Thus, for example, some of Latin America's most economically advanced countries (Argentina, Brazil, Chile, and Uruguay) experienced internal conflicts and political unrest in the 1960s and 1970s, resulting in the collapse of their democratic governments and the emergence of highly repressive military dictatorships. In 2001–2002, nearly two decades after the restoration of its democratic regime, Argentina experienced an economic crisis, urban rioting, and political instability that resulted in five presidents in the space of less than a month. Huntington explained such political instability in more developed Third World nations by suggesting that as countries modernize, the spread of urbanization, education, and mass media consumption produce an increasingly politically aware and mobilized society whose citizens make greater demands on the government. All too often, however, political institutions, particularly political parties, cannot be strengthened quickly enough to channel and respond to this rising tide of demands. As a result, he maintained, the system becomes overloaded and unstable.

Guillermo O'Donnell posited another theory explaining the rise of extremely repressive dictatorships in South America's most economically modern nations during the 1960s and 1970s. He suggested that as those countries reached a more advanced stage of industrial growth, they required extensive new investment that could only be secured by attracting foreign capital. That, in turn, required controlling the countries' militant labor unions and keeping down the wage levels of industrial workers. To achieve those goals, the nations' business leaders and technocrats turned to repressive military rule.[29]

In a similar vein, many analysts have noted that the Asian countries that had been enjoying the most spectacular economic growth from the 1970s to the mid-1990s—Indonesia, Malaysia, Thailand, Singapore, Taiwan, and South Korea—were all ruled by authoritarian governments during their economic takeoffs. Consequently, many observers concluded from this that an authoritarian government was necessary in the early to middle stages of industrialization in order to control labor and reduce workers' consumption levels so as to enable management to invest heavily in productive resources (see Chapter 10). Although these theories remain subject to debate, they suggest that the relationships among political, economic, and social development are complex. While the three often go hand in hand, they don't always progress at the same rate.

THE CAUSES OF UNDERDEVELOPMENT

Our initial discussion suggested that there is some debate concerning the very *definitions* of political and socioeconomic underdevelopment. Social scientists disagree even more intensely over the underlying *causes* of underdevelopment and the most desirable pathways to change. How, for example, do we account for constant military intervention in Pakistani politics, political turmoil in Somalia, government repression in Syria, or a financial crisis in Argentina? Do these problems originate from internal factors such as authoritarian cultural values, weak political parties, or misguided economic planning? Or are many of these political and economic problems caused by foreign domination stretching from the colonial era to the age of multinational corporations (MNCs) and the International Monetary Fund (IMF)?

Questions about the origins of underdevelopment or the pathways to development elicit very different responses from social scientists. Frequently, their evaluations reflect their personal cultural backgrounds or ideologies. Thus, for example, theories that blame Third World political unrest or economic backwardness on traditional cultural values generally have emanated from the United States. On the other hand, approaches such as dependency theory and world systems theory, which condemn Western exploitation as the root cause of Third World underdevelopment, are particularly popular among Latin American and African analysts. Similarly, liberal social scientists are drawn to different explanations than are either conservative or Marxist scholars.

For years, two competing paradigms have shaped scholarly analyses of Third World politics and economic change. The first, *modernization theory,* emerged in the early 1960s as American political science's mainstream interpretation of underdevelopment. The second, *dependency theory,* originated in Latin America and offered a more radical perspective on development, one more popular among Third World scholars. In time, dependency theory came to exert tremendous influence over political research on Latin America, Africa, and other parts of the developing world.[30]

Modernization Theory and the Importance of Cultural Values

During the 1950s and 1960s, as the demise of European colonialism produced a host of newly independent nations in Africa and Asia, Western social scientists began to study Third World politics and economics intensively. From that interest came a complex conceptual model of underdevelopment and development known as modernization theory. Its proponents included some of the most prominent figures in comparative politics: Gabriel Almond, James Coleman, Samuel Huntington, Lucian Pye, and David Apter, among others.[31] For perhaps a decade, modernization theory reigned supreme in the study of political development. Though later challenged, it has continued to influence our understanding of the Third World. While there has been variation and disagreement among modernization theorists, they generally share a number of underlying assumptions and perspectives.

Despite the tremendous array of problems facing the LDCs, modernization theory was initially relatively optimistic about prospects for development. After all, Western industrialized democracies had also started out as underdeveloped countries. Most Third World countries, the theory argued, could—and should— follow a path of political and economic modernization parallel to the one first traveled by the advanced Western nations. To accomplish this, modernization theorists insisted, developing nations had to acquire modern cultural values and create modern political and economic institutions.

Transforming traditional cultures was seen as the first step in the modernization process. Drawing on the theories of such eminent sociologists as Max Weber and Talcott Parsons, these analysts distinguished between "traditional" and "modern" values.[32] Modern men and women, they maintained, tend to judge others by universalistic standards (that is, to hire, vote for, or otherwise evaluate people based on their ability rather than family or ethnic origins); to believe in the possibility and desirability of change; to think about issues outside the sphere of one's family, neighborhood, or village; to believe that one can—and should—try to influence the political system.[33]

But how can a traditional society make the transition to modernity? How does a culture modernize its values? Education, urbanization, and the spread of mass media were identified as the central agents of change. As peasants move to cities, modernization theory argued, as more children attend schools that teach modern values, and as more citizens access the mass media, cultural modernization will progress. Another critical component, it was suggested, was the diffusion of modern ideas from highly developed nations (especially the West) to the developing world and from city to countryside within the LDCs. Foreign aid and institutions such as the Peace Corps could help to speed this process.

Gabriel Almond and G. Bingham Powell, depicting modernization as a rather inexorable force, contended that "the forces of technological change and cultural diffusion are driving political systems in certain directions, which seem discernible and susceptible to analysis in terms of increasing levels of development."[34] Others envisioned modernization as a process of getting developing nations to think and act "more like us" (i.e., the West). "As time goes on," Marion Levy predicted, "they and we will increasingly resemble one another … [The] more highly modernized societies become, the more they resemble one another."[35] Today, as the forces of modernization spread McDonald's, computer technology, Hollywood movies, American rock music, and democratic values around the world, that prophecy seems reasonably accurate.

At the same time, developing nations would have to create more specialized and complex political and economic institutions to complement those modern values. For example, whereas a tribal culture might have a council of elders that carries out legislative, executive, and judicial activities, a modern society needs separate, specialized institutions for those tasks. Modernizing societies also need trained bureaucracies in which advancement is based on merit rather than personal connections, and decisions are made according to uniform and consistent standards. Political parties have to channel popular demands and aspirations effectively to government policymakers. Eventually, it was argued, as these cultural and institutional changes progress, a modernizing society can lay the foundation for a more stable, effective, and responsive political system.

In time, however, many assumptions of early modernization theory had to be modified. To begin with, it had been too optimistic and simplistic in its initial view of change. Its proponents expected developing countries to achieve economic growth, greater equality, democracy, stability, and greater national autonomy simultaneously and smoothly. As Samuel Huntington noted, the theory erroneously assumed that "all good things go together."[36] In fact, economic growth proved to be no guarantee of democracy or other elements of political development. As we have seen, in nations such as Brazil, Mexico, South Korea, and Taiwan, industrialization and economic development originated and advanced for many years under the direction of authoritarian governments.

Analysts were particularly disturbed to find that the very process of social and economic modernization often ushered in political instability and violence.[37] For example, in some of Latin America's most economically developed nations (Argentina, Brazil, Chile, and Uruguay), industrial growth unleashed bitter class conflict, the collapse of democratic institutions, and the rise of repressive military dictatorships.[38] Elsewhere, in much of Africa, Asia, and the Middle East, the hopes once inspired by decolonization have given way to ethnic conflict, military coups, and political repression.

Thus, the process of development often turned out to be more complex and unpredictable than originally imagined. Modernization theory's initial optimism gave way to *conflict theory*. Developing nations, suggested the new perspective, would have to make hard choices between seemingly irreconcilable development goals. Concerned about the growing political turmoil in many developing nations, Samuel Huntington insisted that political stability was crucial, even if maintaining it might necessitate authoritarian rule for a period of time. That is to say, democracy might have to take a backseat to stability, at least temporarily. At the same time, many economists and political scientists argued that initial economic growth required wealth to be concentrated in a small number of hands so that incipient capitalists could acquire sufficient capital for investment.

More recently, the experiences of several countries in East Asia and Latin America have produced yet another new perspective. While certainly less naively optimistic than the earliest modernization theories, current analysis is also less pessimistic than conflict theory. The *reconciliation approach*, as put forth by contemporary modernization theorists, suggests that under the right circumstances developing nations can simultaneously achieve goals previously thought to be incompatible.[39] Taiwan and South Korea, for example, have shown that it is possible to achieve rapid economic development along with a highly equitable distribution of income. Barbados and Costa Rica have managed to achieve democracy and stability simultaneously. Consequently, current research tries to isolate factors such as state policy, historical traditions, and cultural values that may explain which factors contribute to successful development.

A different modification of modernization theory addresses its initial view of cultural change. First, the differences between traditional and modern culture, scholars now agree, are not always as stark or clear as originally thought. For example, even though the United States is a highly modern society, many Americans have retained traditional values such as judging others by the color of their skin. Second, contrary to early modernization theory, it now appears that some traditional values not only are worth keeping, but they also contribute to political and economic development. For example, students of contemporary Japanese culture and religion have argued that traditional religious values have contributed to that nation's work ethic. Even "magic and miracles," notes one expert on East Asian religions, "are entirely compatible with the 'rationality' of industrial society."[40]

Finally, while modern (Western) values have swept across the Third World, they have not been as universally welcomed as some analysts had expected. In Afghanistan, Iran, Saudi Arabia, and other parts of the Muslim world, for example, many people, including some with advanced education, have rejected Westernization in favor of both peaceful and violent forms of Islamic fundamentalism. The September 11, 2001 attacks on New York and Washington and the March 2004 train bombings in Madrid, perpetrated by the Al Qaeda terrorist network, were the most extreme reflections of the hatred that some Muslims feel toward Western values and lifestyles. Although extremists such as these represent only a very small fraction of the Muslim world, many other nonviolent Muslims also reject Western culture, which they view as immoral—sullied by pornography, extramarital sex, and the like.

Dependency Theory

During the 1960s and 1970s, social scientists in Latin America and the United States raised more fundamental objections to modernization theory, insisting that the various modifications of the theory had failed to correct its fundamental flaws. Under the banner of *dependency theory*, they challenged modernizationists' most fundamental assumptions.

To begin with, *dependencistas* (as dependency theorists are known) rejected the claim that Third World countries could follow the same path to development as Western nations had because the first industrialized nations changed the landscape for those that followed them. When Britain became the world's first industrial power, it faced no external economic competition. Today, however, newly industrializing countries must compete against such well-established industrial giants as the United States, Japan, and Germany. In addition, argued Brazil's Theotonio Dos Santos, Third World countries have to borrow financial capital and purchase advanced technology from the developed world, thereby making them dependent on external economic forces beyond their control and weakening their development.[41]

Indeed, whereas modernization theory views Western influence in the Third World as beneficial, because it spreads modern values and institutions, dependency theorists maintain that Western colonialism and economic imperialism themselves initially turned Africa, Asia, and Latin America into sources of cheap food and raw materials for the colonial powers. Moreover, long after Third World nations had achieved political independence, these critics charge, developed countries have continued to use their economic power to create an international division of labor between nations. That division meant that production and export of manufactured goods—the most profitable economic activities—were originally concentrated in the *core*, the industrialized West. Third World nations, in the *periphery*, were largely relegated to the production and export of food and raw materials and were forced to trade for industrial imports on unfavorable terms.[42]

Finally, *dependencistas* contend that this economic dependence has caused the LDCs' political dependency. Within the periphery, Third World political, military, and economic elites, backed by the economic and military power of the core nations (especially the United States), maintained a political system that benefited the powerful few at the expense of the many. These elites reaped substantial profits from their country's relations with the West and were backed by its military and economic might. Dependency theorists note, for example, France's frequent military intervention in French-speaking Africa to maintain allied, but unrepresentative and corrupt, governments in its former colonies.

As one might imagine, dependency theory was enthusiastically embraced by scholars in many parts of the Third World, for it suggested that underdevelopment was not the LDC's fault, but rather the result of foreign domination and exploitation. But even in the United States and Europe, dependency theory for a time challenged, and often displaced, modernization theory as the major scholarly paradigm explaining the nature and causes of underdevelopment.

However, just as early modernization theory had been overly optimistic about the prospects for simultaneous economic and political development, early dependency theory proved to be excessively pessimistic about the likelihood of economic and political development. Analysts such as Andre Gunder Frank had warned that Third World nations, consigned to producing nonindustrial goods and ruled by unrepresentative elites, were doomed to continued backwardness. Some *dependencistas* believed that radical revolutions were the only solution; others merely prescribed greater economic independence for developing nations; still others offered no solutions.

Yet, despite the bleak prognosis of early dependency theorists, it was clear by the mid-1960s that nations such as Brazil and Mexico were undergoing substantial industrialization. In a far more sophisticated version of dependency theory, Brazil's Fernando Henrique Cardoso rejected the contention that all Third World countries were condemned to underdevelopment and precluded from industrial growth.[43] Drawing heavily from the experiences of his own country, Cardoso noted that through the active intervention of the state and the linkage of domestic firms to multinational corporations, some developing countries could industrialize and enjoy considerable economic growth. He referred to this process as *associated dependent development.*

Cardoso radically altered dependency theory by insisting that countries such as Argentina, Brazil, Colombia, and Mexico could experience industrialization and economic growth while remaining dependent on foreign banks and MNCs for loans, investment, and technology. Brazilian industrialization, he noted, had been stimulated to a large extent by a sharp rise in investment from multinational corporations. But Cardoso and his colleagues viewed dependent development as tainted in several important ways. It still meant that key economic decisions were being made by MNCs outside of the LDCs' control. Furthermore, associated dependent development was centered in companies that were heavily mechanized and consequently did not hire substantial local labor. Those industries also produced more profitable and expensive consumer goods destined for the country's middle and upper classes. Thus, rather than reduce poverty, *dependencistas* argued, associated dependent development had widened the income gap separating the poor from the middle and upper classes. At the same time, Peter Evans and others maintained, an alliance of the MNCs with Latin American economic, political, and military elites helped maintain the power of nonrepresentative regimes such as Brazil's military dictatorship.

Modernization and Dependency Theory Compared

The dependency approach offered useful corrections to modernization theory. Moreover, it highlighted an important influence on Third World societies that modernization theory had largely neglected: international trade, finance, and investment patterns. Indeed, many political scientists argue that a principal characteristic defining Third World countries is their peripheral economic and cultural status relative to the major core nations. Thus, even wealthy nations such as Saudi Arabia or stable democracies such as Costa Rica are still considered part of the Third World because their economic and political systems are largely shaped by the developed world.[44]

Regardless of how they view dependency theory, contemporary analysts of underdevelopment have been forced to recognize that political and economic modernization requires more than adopting new values or changing domestic political structures. Dependency theory shifted the focus of research from exclusively internal factors to international economic and cultural relations, contributing to new fields of research, including international political economy. Dependency theorists also helped redefine the concept of economic development. Whereas early research on Third World economies focused on issues of economic growth, *dependencistas* emphasized the importance of economic distribution and social justice. When rapid economic growth is accompanied by an increased concentration of wealth and income in the hands of a minority, as has frequently happened, it offers little benefit to the impoverished majority, who may be left even worse off. Influenced by dependency theory and other leftist critiques, even such pillars of the establishment as the World Bank reoriented their focus toward "growth and redistribution."[45]

Despite its contributions, however, dependency theory suffered from some serious failings. Just as early modernization theorists overemphasized the *internal* causes of underdevelopment, *dependencistas* erroneously attributed virtually all of the Third World's problems to *external* economic factors. Furthermore LDCs were often portrayed as helpless pawns with no way out of their poverty. Indeed, what is striking about much of the dependency literature is its economic determinism and neglect of independent social or political influences. Its proponents frequently dismissed Third World governments as agents of the local economic elite who colluded with Western- or Japanese-based MNCs. Consequently, there is a disturbing sameness to some of the dependency-based political research on individual nations. The details of Mexican, Nigerian, or Peruvian politics may differ, but they all allegedly follow the same broad pattern.

Cardoso refined the theory by insisting that developing nations had options within the limits of dependency. Depending on the relationships among a nation's social classes and depending on government policies (both internal factors), various forms of associated dependent development were possible. Combining Cardoso's ideas with elements of modernization theory, Argentinean political scientist Guillermo O'Donnell offered a powerful explanation for the rise of authoritarian military governments in the more developed nations of South America.[46]

However, East Asia's "economic miracle" in recent decades—most notably in South Korea, Taiwan, Hong Kong, and Singapore—has confounded dependency theory. These countries have linked themselves very closely to the developed world through trade, credit, investments, and technology transfers. Contrary to what even the more sophisticated dependency scholars had predicted, however, they achieved spectacular economic growth coupled with comparatively equitable income distribution. Countries like Singapore and Taiwan now have standards of living approaching or even matching those of First World nations (Singapore's per-capita income, for example, exceeds Britain's and Italy's). Some *dependencistas* may object that East Asia's recent economic crisis (1997–2001) validated dependency theory, since it was caused, in part, by the region's dependence on foreign investment. When Thailand was forced to devalue its currency, foreign capital fled the region, sending East Asian stock markets and currencies on a downward spiral. Still, the region's recovery since 2002 suggests that the financial crisis was a temporary setback, though also a signal that the Asian growth model needed some modifications. Moreover, in a further blow to dependency theory, in recent years India, Asia's second largest nation, has become one of the world's fastest growing economies by opening its doors to foreign trade and investment. Even Fernando Henrique Cardoso—once dependency theory's most brilliant exponent in his role as a university scholar—later embraced foreign investment, trade, and technology for Brazil in his roles as that country's finance minister and later its president.

Contemporary Perspectives

Today, few analysts accept either modernization or dependency theory in its entirety, particularly not in their original formulations. Subsequent theories and approaches, such as *bureaucratic authoritarianism* (which attempted to explain the rise of military dictatorships in some of the Third World's most economically developed nations) or *neoliberal economics* (which offered a set of conservative prescriptions for the LDCs), have generally avoided global explanations of development and underdevelopment, focusing instead on more specific issues. Indeed, most contemporary analysts reject the very idea of a *single* theory of development.[47] For one thing, the Third World is too diverse and the processes of political and socioeconomic development too complex to be explained by a universal theory of change.

This does not mean, however, that the insights offered by dependency and modernization theories have not been useful. Our current understanding of development draws on the strengths of both approaches, while recognizing their limitations. Today, however, most political scientists limit themselves to more manageable and focused issues, such as the function of political parties, the role of government in the economy, or the prerequisites for consolidated democracy.

The chapters that follow turn from general development theory to specific issues facing less developed countries today. Chapter 2 discusses what is surely the most important development in world politics during the past thirty to forty years: the spread and legitimization of democratic government. The causes and effects of democratization will be an underlying theme of this text, and most of the succeeding chapters will include some discussion of the effects of democratic change. Chapters 3 through 7 discuss some of the broad social forces that impact contemporary politics in the developing world: the political impact of religion; the nature of ethnic politics and ethnic conflict; the role of women in Third World economic and political development; agrarian reform and rural change; and the political implications of rapid urbanization. Chapters 8 and 9 explore two important types of political regimes—revolutionary and military—that have been common to much of the Third World. They examine each one's approach to the problems of development and the reasons why both have become less prevalent in recent years. Finally, Chapter 10 examines economic development strategies currently being utilized in much of the Third World.

DISCUSSION QUESTIONS

1. To what extent is democracy an integral part of political development? Why were political scientists initially reluctant to include democracy in their definitions of political development?
2. To what degree do social and economic development contribute to or undermine political development?
3. What do you believe are the most important differences between modernization theory and dependency theory?
4. How have both early modernization theory and early dependency theory been modified? Why were those modifications needed?
5. What is the difference between economic and social underdevelopment?
6. What indicators or measurements would you suggest might be used to measure political development?

NOTES

1. For a discussion of the strengths and many weaknesses of the term, see Allen H. Merriam, "What Does 'Third World' Mean?" in *The Third World: States of Mind and Being*, eds. Jim Norwine and Alfonso Gonzalez (Boston: Unwin Hyman, 1988), 15–22.

2. The term *liberal democracy* indicates that the political system not only supports free and contested elections but also respects civil liberties such as free speech, freedom of the press, and religious freedom. For more on different aspects of democracy, see chap. 10. Strictly speaking, since the term *Second World* referred to the Communist bloc of nations led by the former Soviet Union, that grouping no longer exists. But, this book uses that label to refer to *former* communist countries in Europe, such as Poland, Hungary, or Romania. This usage is consistent with the original meaning of the term, which indicated that Second World members had been the second group of countries to industrialize (following the Western capitalist nations, the First World).

3. Scholars have disagreed on whether to include non-European communist nations such as China, Cuba, and Vietnam in the Third World. I include them in this category because they resemble other developing nations on many dimensions.

4. Merriam, "What Does 'Third World' Mean?" 20.

5. Christopher Clapham, *Third World Politics: An Introduction* (Madison: University of Wisconsin Press, 1985), 2.

6. Gross Domestic Product (GDP) is a measure similar to Gross National Product (GNP), the indicator often used in the United States, but excludes "net factor income from abroad." Economists and international agencies such as the U.N. generally use GDP, rather than GNP,

for comparing the living standards of different countries.

7. Like all statistics, these have their limitations. For example, depending on what statistical methods they use, various institutions (such as the World Bank, IMF, or the United Nations Development Programme) may publish somewhat differing figures for a particular country's GNP or GDP, or its ranking relative to other nations. Furthermore, national statistics fail to reveal what are sometimes considerable income variations *within* particular nations. Thus, China's coastal region is relatively developed, comparing well with South Korea or Mexico. Its interior, however, is generally quite impoverished, more analogous to rural Pakistan or Bangladesh.

8. While most nonspecialists speak of a country's "per-capita *income*" (the average income per person), economists and the sources of these data call the figures in Column 2 "Real Gross National Product (GNP) per capita converted to Parity Purchasing Power (PPP)." That is to say, it is a measure of average economic *production* per person (in a given year), which is then statistically controlled to remove the influences of varying price structures and exchange rates in different countries. Thus, PPP adjustments allow a more meaningful comparison of what per-capita incomes in different countries can actually purchase.

9. Of course, even though the gap between rich and poor is greater in the United States than in India, the poor in India are clearly far worse off since their *absolute* income level and standard of living are far lower than those of their counterparts in the United States.

10. Unless otherwise indicated, all data in this section come from the same sources as indicated in Tables 1.1 to 1.3.

11. Robert Wade, *Governing the Market* (Princeton, NJ: Princeton University Press, 1990).

12. Axel Hadenius, *Democracy and Development* (London: Cambridge University Press, 1992).

13. A simple example illustrates the problem with income averages. If one person in a generally poor village makes a million dollars a year, he or she will totally distort the town average, producing a figure that in no way reflects how the average villager really lives. But the same kind of distortions do not take place with social indicators such as life expectancy, infant mortality, and literacy.

14. That increase was achieved entirely between 1960 and 1990. Since 1990, the AIDS pandemic in Africa and parts of Asia has actually *reduced* Third World life expectancy slightly from 64.7 to 64.6 years. Currently, life expectancy in Sub-Saharan Africa is only 46.4 years, almost 20 years below the Third World average.

15. Twentieth-century data in this paragraph come from United Nations Development Programme (UNDP), *Human Development Report, 1997* (New York: Oxford University Press, 1997), 24–26.

16. UNDP Press Release (Bangkok: July 14, 2004).

17. Economic Growth data are from The World Bank Group, *WorldDevelopment Indicators 2004*. Table 4.1 Growth of Output www.worldbank. org/data/

18. Adapted from data in Chandrika Kaul and Valerie Tomaselli-Moschovitis, eds., *Statistical Handbook on Poverty in the Developing World* (Phoenix, AZ: Oryx Press, 1999), 327–334. Their data were drawn from the World Bank.

19. UNDP, *Human Development Report, 1997*, 4.

20. *Ibid.*, 24-26. Literacy and life expectancy comparisons between the First and Third Worlds are based on the UNDP's 2004 data.

21. Samuel P. Huntington, "The Goals of Development," in *Understanding Political Development*, eds. Myron Weiner and Samuel P. Huntington (Boston: Little, Brown, 1987), 3.

22. Hadenius, *Democracy and Development*; Robert A. Dahl, *Democracy and Its Critics* (New Haven, CT: Yale University Press, 1989); Scott Mainwaring, "Transitions to Democracy and Democratic Consolidation," in *Issues in Democratic Consolidation: The New South American Democracies in Comparative Perspective*, eds. Scott Mainwaring, Guillermo O'Donnell, and Samuel Valenzuela (Notre Dame, IN: University of Notre Dame Press, 1992); Samuel P. Huntington, *The*

Third Wave: Democratization in the Late Twentieth Century (Norman: University of Oklahoma Press, 1991).

23. Samuel P. Huntington, *Political Order in Changing Societies* (New Haven, CT: Yale University Press, 1968).

24. Guillermo O'Donnell and Philippe Schmitter, *Transitions from Authoritarian Rule: Tentative Conclusions about Uncertain Democracies* (Baltimore, MD: Johns Hopkins University Press, 1986); Abraham Lowenthal, ed., *Exporting Democracy* (Baltimore, MD: Johns Hopkins University Press, 1991); Dahl, *Democracy and Its Critics*.

25. Huntington, *The Third Wave*.

26. Eighty-six members of the United Nations have been ranked on both economic resources (per-capita GNPs) and socioeconomic indicators of living standards (HDIs). If we subtract each country's HDI rank from its GNP rank, a positive score indicates the country is performing better on social indicators than its economic ranking would predict, while a negative score suggests the opposite.

27. Huntington, *The Third Wave*; Mitchell A. Seligson, "Democratization in Latin America: The Current Cycle," in *Authoritarians and Democrats: Regime Transition in Latin America*, eds. James M. Malloy and Mitchell A. Seligson (Pittsburgh, PA: University of Pittsburgh Press, 1987); Hadenius, *Democracy and Development*.

28. Huntington, *Political Order*.

29. Guillermo O'Donnell, *Modernization and Bureaucratic-Authoritarianism: Studies in South American Politics* (Berkeley: University of California Press, 1973).

30. For a useful summary of major theories of development, see Alvin Y. So, *Social Change and Development* (Newbury Park, CA: Sage Publications, 1990); for ongoing contributions in these areas, see Weiner and Huntington, *Understanding Political Development*; Vicky Randall and Robin Theobald, *Political Change and Underdevelopment* (London: Macmillan, 1985).

31. The modernization literature is extensive. The most important works include Huntington, *Political Order*, widely considered the best work in this area; Gabriel Almond and James Coleman, eds., *The Politics of Developing Areas* (Princeton, NJ: Princeton University Press, 1960); Lucian Pye and Sidney Verba, *Political Culture and Political Development* (Princeton, NJ: Princeton University Press, 1965); and Cyril E. Black, ed., *Comparative Modernization: A Reader* (New York: Free Press, 1976). These works, as well as those mentioned below regarding dependency theory, are recommended for advanced undergraduates.

32. Max Weber, *The Protestant Ethic and the Spirit of Capitalism* (New York: Scribner, 1958); Talcott Parsons, *The Social System* (Glencoe, IL: Free Press, 1951).

33. For examples of such arguments, see Parsons, *Social System*; Gabriel Almond and Sidney Verba, *The Civic Culture* (Princeton, NJ: Princeton University Press, 1963); Pye and Verba, *Political Culture*; Alex Inkeles and David Horton Smith, *Becoming Modern: Individual Change in Six Developing Countries* (Cambridge, MA: Harvard University Press, 1974); Daniel Lerner, *The Passing of Traditional Society* (Glencoe, IL: Free Press, 1958); David McClelland, *The Achieving Society* (Princeton, NJ: Van Nostrand, 1961).

34. Gabriel A. Almond and G. Bingham Powell, *Comparative Politics: A Developmental Approach* (Boston: Little, Brown, 1966), 301.

35. Marion Levy, Jr., "Social Patterns (Structures) and Problems of Modernization," in *Readings on Social Change*, eds. Wilbert Moore and Robert Cooke (Upper Saddle River, NJ: Prentice Hall, 1967), 207.

36. Huntington, "The Goals of Development."

37. Huntington, *Political Order in Changing Societies*.

38. See Juan Linz and Alfred Stepan, eds., *The Breakdown of Democratic Regimes: Latin America* (Baltimore, MD: Johns Hopkins University Press, 1978); David Collier, ed., *The New Authoritarianism in Latin America* (Princeton, NJ: Princeton University Press, 1979).

39. Huntington, "The Goals of Development."

40. Winston Davis, "Religion and Development: Weber and the East Asian Experience," in Weiner and Huntington, eds., *Understanding Political Development*, 258; see also So, *Social Change and Development*, chap. 4.

41. Theotonio Dos Santos, "The Structure of Dependence," *American Economic Review* (May 1970).

42. Werner Baer, "The Economics of Prebisch and ECLA," in *Latin America: Problems in Economic Development*, ed. C. T. Nisbet (New York: Free Press, 1969). Major early dependency studies include Andre Gunder Frank, *Capitalism and Underdevelopment in Latin America* (New York: Monthly Review Press, 1967); and Paul Baran, *The Political Economy of Growth* (New York: Monthly Review Press, 1957).

43. The most influential work on this sophisticated version of dependency theory is Fernando Henrique Cardoso and Enzo Faletto, *Dependency and Development in Latin America* (Berkeley: University of California Press, 1979). A more readable work on the same topic is Peter Evans, *Dependent Development: The Alliance of Multinational, State and Local Capital* (Princeton, NJ: Princeton University Press, 1979).

44. Clapham, *Third World Politics*, 3.

45. Hollis Chenery et al., *Redistribution with Growth* (London: Oxford University Press with the World Bank and the University of Sussex, 1974).

46. O'Donnell, *Modernization and Bureaucratic-Authoritarianism*.

47. See, for example, two works that dismiss the search for a single paradigm of development: James Manor, ed., *Rethinking Third World Politics* (New York: Longman, 1991), especially the introduction by Manor and the chapter by Geoffrey Hawthorn; Paul Cammack, David Pool, and William Tordoff, *Third World Politics*, 2d ed. (Baltimore, MD: Johns Hopkins University Press, 1993).

chapter 2

Democratic Change and the Change to Democracy

The early years of the twenty-first century were particularly hard for former dictators and quasi-dictators. The former president of Yugoslavia, Slobodan Milosevic, arrested months earlier by Serbian authorities, was put on trial at the United Nations International War Crimes Tribunal in The Hague (Netherlands).[1] The father of Serbia's genocidal war against Bosnia and its attacks on the Serbian province of Kosovo, Milosevic became the only head of government since World War II to face charges of human rights violations before an international court. Augusto Pinochet, Chile's military dictator for 16 years (1973–1989), fought a possible human rights trial in Chilean courts after returning from a humiliating extended house arrest in England. Indonesia's long-term dictator, General Suharto, also faced possible arrest after having been forced from office by popular demonstrations. Like Pinochet, this once all-powerful leader now hid behind the humiliating court plea that he was too old and mentally incompetent to stand trial. Alberto Fujimori, who had subverted Peruvian democracy after having been fairly elected to that country's presidency, took refuge in Japan (the home of his parents) rather than face anticipated arrest charges in Peru. In Argentina, Carlos Menem, who like Fujimori had been democratically elected initially but then used his presidential powers to weaken democracy, was indicted for illegal arms sales and held for a time under house arrest. Morever, most recently, United States and allied troops ousted Iraqi dictator Saddam Hussein in 2003. He too now awaits trial.

These events capped three decades of transitions from authoritarian to democratic government throughout the world. Beginning with a 1974 military revolt that brought down Portugal's fascist dictatorship, authoritarian regimes throughout the world, and especially throughout the Third World, began to fall in the face of spreading democratic movements. The collapse of Soviet and Eastern European communism was the democratic wave's most renowned manifestation. But in the developing nations, equally dramatic events inspired our attention. In early 1990, Nelson Mandela, the world's most revered political prisoner, left his cell in Pollsmoor Prison and was transported triumphantly to South Africa's capital, Pretoria, ending 27 years of incarceration. There, he and other freed Black leaders of his recently legalized political party, the African National Congress, eventually negotiated an end to White minority rule. President Mandela's triumph accelerated Africa's *second independence* —a wave of political liberalization (easing of repression) that has sometimes culminated in electoral democracy.[2]

In Asia, Corazon Aquino succeeded her assassinated husband as leader of Filipino "people's power"—mass peaceful demonstrations for democracy staged by students, shopkeepers, professionals, businesspeople, and even nuns. Backed by the Catholic clergy, her supporters took to the streets day after day, peacefully challenging government troops. Ultimately, when then dictator, Ferdinand Marcos, tried to deny Ms. Aquino her apparent victory in a hastily called "snap presidential election" (1986), the commander of the armed forces, General Fidel Ramos, along with Defense Minister Juan Ponce Enrile, joined the opposition, forcing Marcos to step down. Soon after, student-led demonstrations against South Korea's military regime (inspired, in part, by events in the Philippines) accelerated that country's transition to democracy. In 1998, "people's power" demonstrations in Indonesia toppled the 30-year dictatorship of President Suharto. Most recently, mass demonstrations in the former Soviet, Central Asian republic of Kirghizia ousted that country's dictatorial government. Of course, not all Asian pro-democracy movements have been successful. In China, massive student demonstrations were crushed by army tanks in Tiananmen Square, while Myanmar's military squashed democratic protests by killing thousands of Burmese citizens. But these setbacks notwithstanding, much of Asia has made significant progress toward democracy in the past two decades.

The most sweeping democratic changes, however, took place in Latin America (1978–1990), affecting almost every country in the region. Whereas all but a handful of countries (Colombia, Costa Rica, and Venezuela) had some type of authoritarian or semi-authoritarian government in the mid-1970s, 20 years later only Cuba, Mexico, and Haiti had failed to establish electoral democracy. More recently, Mexico also has made the transition to democracy but Venezuela has regressed somewhat. Unlike Asia and Africa, Latin America's democratization generally lacked charismatic heroes in the mold of Mandela, Aquino, or Burmese opposition leader and Nobel Peace Prize winner Daw Aung San Suu Kyi. Nor was it typically precipitated by mass demonstrations. Instead, democratic transitions often followed extended negotiations between the outgoing authoritarian government and its opponents, with change coming in stages.

Yet Latin America enjoyed two important advantages over Africa and Asia. To begin with, prior to its wave of military takeovers in the 1960s and 1970s, the region had enjoyed the developing world's strongest democratic tradition, most notably in Chile, Costa Rica, Uruguay, and Venezuela. Furthermore, Latin American nations were among the first LDCs to achieve the levels of literacy and economic development that are usually needed for stable democratic government. Not surprisingly, then, the region's current transition or return to democracy has been more sweeping and more successful than elsewhere in the Third World, ultimately affecting virtually every country in the hemisphere.

In all, since the 1970s the upsurge of political freedom in the developing world, coupled with the collapse of Soviet and Eastern European communism, has produced history's greatest advance ever toward democracy. If these changes can be maintained, they promise to influence virtually every aspect of Third World politics discussed in this book.[3]

DEMOCRACY DEFINED

Discussions of democratic transformations have frequently been complicated by disagreements over the precise meaning of democracy. Currently, most political scientists define democracy procedurally. That is, democracy is explained in terms of essential procedures governing the election and behavior of government officials. The least demanding, minimalist definition focuses almost exclusively on elections. It simply defines democracy as a political system that holds relatively fair, contested elections, with near universal adult suffrage, on a regular basis.[4] We will call countries that meet that minimal standard *electoral democracies*. Although this bare-bones definition seems reasonable (after all, most Americans define democracy in terms of free elections), it allows a number of rather questionable governments to be included in the "democratic club." For example, the current governments in Colombia, Turkey, and Sri Lanka meet this standard, yet they massively violate human rights while battling armed insurgencies.[5] In all of those countries, government troops routinely massacre villagers and torture prisoners. Guatemala and Thailand also meet the standards of electoral democracy, yet their armed forces have regularly intervened in politics, often overriding decisions made by elected officials.

As the norm of open elections has become more universally accepted in recent decades, the number of electoral democracies worldwide tripled from 1974 to 2005. But many of these governments still manipulate the mass media and violate their citizens' civil liberties. In this chapter I use the term *semidemocracies* to refer to those electoral democracies whose governments repress civil liberties and otherwise breach the principles of a free society. Their elections may be relatively free, but their societies are not. Semidemocracies currently include Bolivia, Malaysia, Nigeria, and Singapore.

A more stringent definition of democracy, the one used here, demands more than just fair elections. Instead, it defines *full democracy* (sometimes called *liberal democracy*) as a political system in which most of the country's leading government officials are elected; there is nearly universal suffrage; elections are largely free of fraud and outside manipulation; opposition-party candidates have a real chance of being elected to important national offices; and minority rights as well as general civil liberties are respected, including free speech and a free press.[6] All of these conditions help guarantee that democratic governments are accountable to their citizens in a way that authoritarian regimes are not.[7] Thus, full democracies require not only freely contested elections but also respect for civil liberties, support for pluralism in civil society, respect for the rule of law, accountability of elected officials, and civilian control over the armed forces.[8] This definition suggests that competitive elections have limited value if unelected individuals or groups who are not accountable to the public (such as military officers, organized crime bosses, business elites, or foreign powers) control elected officials from behind the scenes. And free elections do not bring full democracy if elected officials violate their citizens' civil liberties or arbitrarily arrest opposition leaders.

Finally, some scholars offer an even higher standard for democracy. They argue that *any* purely procedural definition of democracy, no matter how exacting, is incomplete. Instead, they insist, real democracy requires not only fair elections and proper government *procedures* (as just outlined) but also fair and just government *policy outcomes* ("substantive democracy"). For example, true substantive democracy requires that citizens have equal access to public schooling and health care regardless of their social class or ethnicity. Consequently, they argue, any procedural democracy—such as India or Brazil—that tolerates gross economic inequalities, ethnic prejudices, or other major social injustices is not truly democratic.

These critics make an important point. Procedural democracy alone does not guarantee a just society; it is merely a step in the right direction. But it is a more important step than they acknowledge. Because governments in procedural democracies are accountable to the people, they are less vulnerable to revolution and other forms of civil unrest. They are also extremely unlikely to make war against other democracies (indeed, war between two liberal democracies is virtually unknown). Prodded by a free press and public opinion, they are more responsive to domestic crises such as famines (indeed, there has never been a prolonged famine in any procedural democracy), and the many previously cited exceptions notwithstanding, democracies are generally more respectful of civil liberties.[9]

Mindful of the fact that democratic societies never correct all social injustices (the United States, for example, has long tolerated poverty and racial discrimination), this book defines democracy strictly procedurally. Issues of substantive democracy (eradicating poverty, racism, sexism, and the like) are obviously important, but they are a separate matter.

DEMOCRATIC TRANSITION AND CONSOLIDATION

In the discussion that follows, the term *democratic transition* (or *transition to democracy*) means the process of moving from an authoritarian regime to a democratic one. The transition period begins when an authoritarian government shows the first significant signs of collapsing or of negotiating an exit from power. It ends when the first freely elected government takes office. Thus, for example, in South Africa the democratic transition began in 1990 when the White minority government of President Frederik de Klerk decided to free Nelson Mandela and open negotiations with the African National Congress Party. It concluded four years later when Mandela was inaugurated as the nation's freely elected president. Even after a transition is complete, however, new democracies often remain fragile, with the distinct possibility that they will falter.

Only when democratic institutions, practices, and values have become deeply entrenched in society can we say that a country has experienced *democratic consolidation*. Consolidation is a process through which democratic norms (democratic "rules of the game") become accepted by all powerful groups in society—including business, labor, rural landlords, the church, and the military—and no important political actor contemplates a return to dictatorship. Or as Juan Linz and Alfred Stepan put it, democracy is consolidated when it becomes "the only game in town," even in the face of severe economic or political adversity.[10] Consolidation may begin when the democratic transition ends, and it is only complete when democracy is securely entrenched.

Unfortunately, however, not all transitions to democracy are subsequently consolidated. Many countries revert to dictatorship or remain mired in political disorder. For example, between 1958 and 1975, 22 countries that had democratized during the postwar era (1943–1962) slipped back to authoritarianism. Similarly, some of the most recently installed democracies have already collapsed, while democratic values and practices in other countries—such as Guatemala,

Indonesia, Russia, and Mozambique—are anything but secure. It is worth noting, for example, that Russia's parliament has been dominated for years by antidemocratic parties (the Communists, Liberal Democrats, and, most recently, United Russia), and that President Vladimir Putin has concentrated enormous power in his own hands, frequently violating democratic norms in his treatment of parliament, media critics, business opponents, and the Chechen rebellion.

On the other hand, in successfully consolidated (or reconsolidated) democracies such as South Korea, Chile, and Uruguay, democratic values predominate. Even previously antidemocratic political parties and groups (such as Chile's Communist Party and Uruguay's former Tupamaru guerrillas) accept democracy as "the only game in town," and the once-dominant armed forces now seemingly accept civilian control. That does not mean that consolidated democracies can *never* collapse. "Never" is a long time, and in the past, seemingly consolidated Third World democracies such as the Philippines, Chile, and Uruguay were toppled by authoritarian forces. However, at the least, consolidated democracies are secure for the foreseeable future. And they will probably continue to endure unless some deep societal divide emerges to tear them apart.

AUTHORITARIAN BEGINNINGS

With the disintegration of Soviet bloc communism and the expansion of democracy in the developing world, a growing worldwide consensus has emerged in support of democracy as the best form of government. But that has not always been so. In the decades after World War II, as a legion of African, Asian, and Middle Eastern countries achieved independence, many Third World leaders and foreign observers believed that these emerging nations were not ready for democratic government, and perhaps that democracy was not even desirable at that stage of their socioeconomic development. To be sure, a number of newly independent countries—particularly former British colonies in the Caribbean, Asia, and Africa—established parliamentary government and other democratic political institutions modeled after their former colonial masters, just as Latin American countries more than a century earlier had patterned their political institutions after those of the United States. But only in a small number of cases (including India, Costa Rica, Jamaica, and a number of other small island nations in the Caribbean) did democracy take hold.

Since that time, Middle Eastern nations generally have been ruled by monarchs (Saudi Arabia, Kuwait, Morocco, and Jordan), all-powerful single parties (Egypt, Sudan), or personalistic dictators (Iraq, Syria). In Sub-Saharan Africa, single-party systems were established in many new nations (including Tanzania, Senegal, Guinea), often to be followed by military dictatorships (Nigeria, Liberia) or absolute, one-man rule (Uganda, Central African Republic). Democracy fared somewhat better in Asia but was frequently cut short by the military (Thailand, South Korea, Myanmar). Corrupt and inept postwar governments in China, Vietnam, Cambodia, and Laos were overthrown and replaced by communist revolutionary regimes. Latin America, benefiting from more than a century of self-rule and from greater socioeconomic development, had the most success in nurturing democracy. Indeed, during the 1950s relatively democratic governments pervaded in that region. But political intervention by the armed forces persisted, and in the 1960s and early 1970s a new wave of military takeovers swept the region. It was not until the 1980s that democracy once again became the norm.

JUSTIFYING AUTHORITARIAN RULE

In the midst of democracy's current worldwide advance, it seems hard to believe that not long ago, freely elected governments and flourishing civil societies were often considered unattainable or even undesirable in many LDCs. Moderniza-tion theorists frequently claimed the newly emerging states of Africa and Asia were not sufficiently developed, economically or socially, to sustain political democracy.[11] And dependency theorists declared that democracy was unlikely to emerge in the LDCs because powerful industrialized nations had allied with local political and economic elites to bolster unrepresentative governments.

Some scholars worried that levels of mass political participation were out-stripping many governments' capacities to accommodate society's political demands. Unless Third World political institutions could be strengthened, they warned, political unrest threatened to derail economic and political develop-ment.[12] Given the dangers of social disorder, some analysts and Third World leaders justified authoritarian rule as a necessary stopgap. Only after socioeco-nomic modernization, they argued, could LDCs produce citizens capable of effective political participation. Increased education and literacy were seen as necessary to expand society's political understanding and develop effective political participation. We now know that countries are unlikely to establish stable, democratic government unless they have risen above the bottom ranks of poverty (as expressed by per-capita income) and have reached a literacy rate of 50 percent or more.[13] In addition to raising literacy, modernization also enlarges the size of the middle class and the organized (unionized) working class, both of whom are essential for a more stable and inclusive democracy.[14]

But an obvious chicken-and-egg quandary presented itself. If socioeco-nomic modernization is necessary to establish democracy, how can a demo-cratic government be the agent of modernization? Some answered that it couldn't and that only a strong and stable authoritarian government—such as General Augusto Pinochet's dictatorship in Chile or South Korea's various military governments—could jump-start modernization. Only later, when the country was "ready," would dictatorships give way to democracy.[15] Other scholars noted yet another obstacle to democratic government in the deve-loping world. They argued that many LDCs, held back by authoritarian tradi-tional values and deep ethnic divisions (Chapters 3 and 4), lacked a democratic political culture and that democracy would have to be preceded by modern-ization of social values.[16]

Not long ago, many Third World leaders insisted that not only would it be difficult to establish democracy in their countries, but that it was not even desir-able at that stage of their development. In Africa, many first-generation, post-colonial leaders created single-party systems, banning or restricting opposition political parties. They often argued that ethnic tensions in their country made competitive elections too risky because they would prompt different political parties to represent contending tribes or clans, further polarizing the country (see Chapter 4). Other leaders of emerging nations were influenced by Marxist-Leninist ideology, more popular at that time than now. They maintained that poverty, tribalism, and dependency at home were so severe that an all-powerful state linked to a vanguard party (one that knows what is in the best interests of the people) was needed to lead the country forward. Later, as many of these governments failed miserably, military dictators took their place, claiming that civilian rulers were too corrupt or too weak to govern effectively (Chapter 9). In the Middle East, similar justifications were used for one-party or military rule. More recently, Islamic fundamentalist governments in Iran, Sudan, and Afghanistan have prohibited or restricted political opposition groups.

While many Latin American nations had democratic or semidemocratic governments in the 1950s and early 1960s, during the two following decades a series of military coups installed repressive governments in most of the region. These new authoritarian leaders often justified their rule by pointing to perceived leftist threats and the need to reinvigorate the economy. Meanwhile, in East Asian nations such as South Korea, Taiwan, and Singapore, authoritarian rulers clung to power long after their countries had surpassed the thresholds of economic and social modernization normally associated with democratic transitions. Their leaders insisted that their dictatorships were necessary to ward off external threats (from North Korea, China, or Indonesia) and that their own society's Confucian cultures rejected political opposition groups as disruptive to social harmony.

According to one expert count, in the mid-1970s only 39 of the world's nations were functioning democracies. Virtually all of them were industrialized, economically prosperous countries in North America, Europe, and Australia-New Zealand. Meanwhile, democracy seemed to be in retreat in the Third World, as countries such as Argentina, Chile, Nigeria, and the Philippines succumbed to dictatorships. Thus, Larry Diamond notes:

> The mid-to-late 1970s seemed a low-water mark for democracy ... and the empirical trends were reified by intellectual fashions dismissing democracy as an artifice, a cultural construct of the West, or a "luxury" that poor states could not afford.[17]

THE THIRD WAVE AND ITS EFFECT ON THE THIRD WORLD

Since that time, however, developing countries have played a significant role in the world's most sweeping transition from authoritarianism to democracy or semidemocracy. Writing shortly before the fall of the Soviet Union, Samuel Huntington counted 29 countries throughout the world that had democratized in the previous 15 years alone (1974–1989). Of these, 20 were LDCs.[18] While some of the countries on that list had questionable democratic credentials (Romania, Peru, and Pakistan, for example) and others slid back to authoritarian rule, there can be no denying that the worldwide trend toward democracy since the mid-1970s has been palpable.

Huntington noted that the current surge of democratic expansion is, in fact, the third such wave that the modern world has experienced since the early 1800s. In each case, democratic political forces and intellectual trends in key countries had a contagious impact on other nations. However, the first two waves were followed by periods of backsliding in which some countries reverted to authoritarian rule. As we have noted, that process has already begun in some third-wave nations.[19] The first democratic wave (1828–1926), by far the longest, began under the influence of the American and French Revolutions (as well as the Industrial Revolution) and ended not long after World War I. Change was largely confined to Europe and to former British colonies with populations of primarily European descent (the United States, Canada, New Zealand, and Australia). The second, much shorter wave (1943–1962) was precipitated by the struggle against fascism during World War II and the subsequent collapse of European colonialism in Africa and Asia. In this period, democracy was introduced to a number of LDCs, but in most cases the new governments at best only met the standards of electoral democracy (competitive elections).

It is the recent third wave (1974–) that most draws our attention here because of its pervasive and seemingly lasting reverberations in the Third World. Of course, third-wave transitions were most dramatic in the former Soviet Union and its Eastern European communist allies. Pictures of young Germans chopping at the Berlin Wall and of Boris Yeltsin facing down a military coup in the Soviet Union were among the most powerful political images of the late twentieth century. But in developing nations as diverse as South Africa, Mali, the Philippines, South Korea, Argentina, and Chile, years of authoritarian or semi-authoritarian rule were ending as well.

This wave of democratization continued into the start of the new century, with some notable setbacks in countries such as Pakistan and Sudan. According to Larry Diamond, between 1988 and 1994 the number of electoral democracies in Africa rose from only 3 to 18.[20] Using a less stringent definition, Michael Bratton and Nicolas van de Walle calculate that 5 of 47 Sub-Saharan states were electoral democracies in 1988 (with leaders chosen in "free and fair" elections) and that the number rose to 21 by 1994.[21] And by 2004, Freedom House rated 23 percent of Sub-Saharan African nations as "Free" and 42 percent as "Partly Free."[22] In recent years, student-led demonstrations in Indonesia, the world's fourth most populous nation, toppled Asia's most enduring military dictator and opened the way to the country's first democratic elections since independence. At the close of the twentieth century, Nigeria, Africa's most populous nation, also restored democracy. And at the start of the current century, Vicente Fox was elected president of Mexico, ending the 71-year reign of the PRI, the world's longest-ruling political party.[23]

As of 1974, only 27.5 percent of the world's countries allowed free and fair national elections (electoral democracy). By 1996, however, that proportion had risen to 63 percent.[24] Each year Freedom House, the most widely cited source of worldwide data on democracy, rates the level of *political rights* (electoral competition) and *civil liberties* in 192 countries. Based on their average rating for those two dimensions of democracy, each country is then placed into one of three broad categories—*Free, Partly Free,* and *Not Free.*[25] In 2004 the organization rated 46 percent of the world's countries as Free (liberal democracies), 29 percent as Partly Free, and only 25 percent as Not Free—a vast improvement over the situation three decades earlier and the highest level of Free nations since the survey began in 1972.[26] Latin America currently has the highest proportion of liberal democracies and the Middle East has the lowest.

INTERNATIONAL CAUSES AND CONSEQUENCES
OF THE THIRD WAVE

Obviously, worldwide political changes of this magnitude are inspired and influenced by broad currents that transcend national boundaries. A number of factors contributed to the most recent democratic revolutions. For one thing, the economic crisis that devastated so many Third World countries in the 1980s revealed that authoritarian governments were no more effective and no less corrupt (and, in fact, were often less efficient and more corrupt) than the elected governments that they had earlier so contemptuously swept aside. Furthermore, because dictatorships lack the legitimacy that free elections bestow on democratic governments, their support depends much more heavily on satisfactory job performance. So when authoritarian governments in countries such as Argentina, Nigeria, and Peru dragged their country into war, corruption, or economic decay, their support rapidly eroded. In Africa, the gross mismanagement and corruption of both military and single-party regimes caused their economies to implode, as the continent's per-capita GNP declined by some 2 percent annually in the 1980s. In Latin America, military rulers performed relatively well economically in Chile, and for a period of time in Brazil, but fared poorly elsewhere. In time, almost all of the region's authoritarian regimes were undermined by the 1980s' debt crisis.

By contrast, many East Asian dictatorships (most notably in South Korea, Taiwan, Indonesia, and Singapore) enjoyed spectacular economic success (interrupted from 1997 to 2001 by the region's financial crisis). Ironically, however, rather than generate wider support for those governments, rapid economic growth and modernization often generated a burgeoning middle class possessed of democratic aspirations and the political skills to pursue them. As in Africa and Latin America, the growing body of informed citizens was often incensed by the lack of opportunities for meaningful political participation, the scope of government repression, and the extent of state corruption.

Throughout the world, no sooner had democratic upheavals occurred in one nation than they then spread quickly to neighboring countries. In Eastern Europe, Poland's Solidarity movement inspired democratic efforts in Hungary, East Germany, and what was then Czechoslovakia. They, in turn, prompted protests in Bulgaria, Albania, and Romania. Students in South Korea watched evening news stories covering anti-government demonstrations in the Philippines and took the lessons of "people's power" to heart.

As the democratic tidal wave swept forward, some authoritarian leaders began to get the message. Generals in Ecuador and Paraguay watched neighboring military dictatorships fall and decided to abdicate while the going was still good. After more than 40 years of political domination by the ethnic Chinese minority and authoritarian rule by the Guomindang Party, Taiwan's government opened up the political system to authentic electoral competition and political freedom. In Africa, a number of single-party states liberalized their political systems, allowing more freedom and greater political space for opposition groups, while a smaller, but growing, number became liberal democracies (including Ghana, Cape Verde, Mali, and São Tomé and Príncipe).

As we noted earlier, the demise of Soviet and Eastern European communism exposed more clearly the deficiencies of Marxism-Leninism. As communism was discredited, even among many of its once-fervent adherents, democracy assumed greater worldwide legitimacy. The end of the Cold War also permitted the United States to be more consistent in its defense of democracy. That is to say, the United States now had no reason to coddle friendly Third World dictators whose friendship it had previously cultivated in the struggle against Soviet communism. For example, the United States had supported corrupt and repressive dictators in Zaire, Somalia, and the Philippines, because they were considered necessary allies in the Cold War. With the collapse of the Soviet bloc, there no longer was reason to stand by such rulers.

To be sure, the United States and Western Europe had already begun more actively championing Third World democratic reform in the years preceding the fall of Soviet communism. The Reagan administration, for example, reversed its initial support for Chile's military dictatorship and allowed its reform-minded ambassador to that country to work closely with the democratic opposition. But the end of the Cold War allowed Washington to pursue its democratic agenda more aggressively. In the Caribbean—where the United States once supported such notorious dictators as Fulgencio Batista (Cuba), Rafael Trujillo (Dominican Republic), and "Papa Doc" Duvalier (Haiti)—President Bill Clinton threatened U.S. military intervention in Haiti unless its generals allowed the country's ousted elected president, Jean Bertrand Aristide, to return to office.[27]

THE PREREQUISITES OF DEMOCRACY IN INDIVIDUAL COUNTRIES

Although these international trends served as catalysts, providing developing countries with incentives and opportunities to democratize, they fail to explain important variations in how different Third World nations reacted to those external factors. At the start of the twenty-first century (25 years after the start of the third wave), some LDCs—such as North Korea, Myanmar, and Saudi Arabia—remain mired in dictatorship, with little or no opening in the political system to date. Others—such as El Salvador, Mozambique, and Thailand—are in some stage of democratic transition. Finally, some fortunate countries (including Chile, Costa Rica, Botswana, South Africa, South Korea, and Taiwan) seem to have consolidated their democracies.[28]

What accounts for these differences? What determines whether a specific country embarks on the road toward democracy, whether it completes that voyage successfully, and whether it eventually consolidates democratic values, practices, and institutions? For example, how do we know if democracy will take root and survive in Brazil, Indonesia,, or Madagascar? Why is it that democratization has advanced further in Latin America than in Africa or the Middle East?

As with most fundamental questions about politics, there are no simple answers. Scholars have debated these issues for decades and have identified a number of historical, structural, and cultural variables that help account for democracy's presence in, say, India and Uruguay, and its absence in countries such as Syria or Laos. But these analysts still disagree about the relative importance of specific variables and about the minimum levels a country must surpass in order to achieve democracy. In the discussion that follows, we examine a number of factors that have been widely identified as prerequisites for democracy.

Social and Economic Modernization

Over 40 years ago, Seymour Martin Lipset observed that democracy was far more prevalent in industrialized countries such as the United States and Sweden than in poorer nations—a finding congruent with modernization theory (Chapter 1).[29] Subsequent research by a wide range of political scientists has supported that claim. The reasoning behind this relationship was that

> industrialization leads to increases in wealth, education, communication and equality; these developments are associated with a more moderate lower and upper class and a larger middle class, which is by nature moderate; and this in turn increases the probability of stable democratic forms of politics.[30]

Over the years, statistical analysis has identified more precisely the particular aspects of modernization that promote democracy. Philips Cutright determined that when other factors are held constant, there is a strong correlation between the extent of a country's mass communications and its degree of democracy, stronger even than the correlation between economic development and democracy.[31] A free and active mass media and opportunities for citizens to exchange ideas, he reasoned, promote a free society. Years later, Axel Hadenius, examining the influence of dozens of independent variables, found that democracy correlates most strongly with higher levels of literacy and education.[32] An educated population, it appears, is more likely to follow politics and to participate. It is also more capable of defending its own interests. One hopeful sign for the future of democracy in the Third World is the substantial growth of literacy in recent decades. For example, since 1965 adult illiteracy in developing countries has fallen by more than half, with Third World literacy currently at 77 percent.[33] As we have noted, countries whose populations are over half literate are more likely to sustain democracy than those that fall below that mark. Similarly, Mitchell Seligson has found an income threshold for sustaining democracy. Although that dollar amount has risen over the years (because of inflation), the per-capita income at which democracy becomes likely is currently about $2,500.[34]

That does not mean that countries inevitably become more democratic as their economies develop. In fact, there is evidence that middle-income countries are frequently *less* stable and more prone to dictatorship.[35] For example, in the 1960s and 1970s, although South America's most industrialized countries (Argentina, Brazil, Chile, Uruguay) were ranked as upper-middle-income nations by the World Bank, their democratic governments were toppled by military dictatorships. These exceptions are quite important, but the long-term global evidence still shows a correlation between economic development and democracy. While poor countries may be as likely to make the transition to democracy as richer ones, they are less likely to sustain democratic government. In recent decades, for example, East Asia's rapid economic growth, higher literacy, and expanding middle classes promoted democratic transitions in South Korea, Thailand, and Taiwan. In Latin America, where levels of modernization are relatively high by Third World standards, democracy has been growing since the close of the 1970s. Conversely, Africa, which is home to most of the world's poorest nations, has had less democratic success.

However, as the third wave of democracy has spread to further reaches of the Third World, the correlation between economic development and democracy has weakened somewhat. In fact , a growing number of very poor countries has overcome the odds and established some level of liberal democracy. As of 2004, there were 38 countries with per-capita incomes of $3,500 or less that Freedom House rated as "free" (liberal democracies), 15 of which had incomes of $1,500 or less.[36]

Class Structure

Some scholars maintain that it is not economic growth per se that induces and sustains democracy but rather the way in which that growth affects a country's social structure. Specifically, they reason, economic development supports stable democracy only if it induces appropriate changes in the country's class structure.

Since the time of Aristotle, political theorists have linked democracy and political stability to the presence of a large and vibrant middle class. The middle class, they suggest, tends to be politically moderate and serves as a bridge between the upper and lower classes. Its members also have the political and organizational skills necessary to create political parties and other important democratic institutions. So, in those countries where economic growth fails to create a politically independent and influential middle class, modernization does not necessarily buttress democracy and may even weaken it. In fact, the independence and power of the emerging middle class have varied greatly in different regions of the world that industrialized in disparate historical eras. For example, industrialization and urbanization produced a larger, more powerful, and more independent middle class in Northern Europe than it did one century later in Latin America, where wealth and income were far more concentrated and the middle class correspondingly weaker and more dependent. Predictably, democracy did not take hold as readily in Latin America as it had in Northern Europe.

Barrington Moore Jr. in his widely acclaimed study of economic and political change, *The Social Origins of Dictatorship and Democracy*, identified three discrete paths to modernization, each shaped by the relative power of the state (the national government apparatus) and the strength of significant social classes. In one path, typified by nineteenth- and early-twentieth-century Germany, modernization was led by a strong state allied with powerful and antidemocratic agricultural land owners and a bourgeoisie (business class) that was dependent on the state. In Germany and subsequently in Third World countries with a similar political configuration, that combination ultimately resulted in the rise of fascism (or other ultra-rightist, authoritarian regimes). A second path to modernization, found in countries such as China, featured a highly centralized state, a repressive land-owning class, a weak bourgeoisie, and a large and eventually rebellious peasantry. The end result of that alignment was a communist revolution fought by the peasantry.

Finally, Moore's third path, identified most closely with Britain, was distinguished by an internally divided state and a strong bourgeoisie that was at odds with the rural land-owning elite. Only that alignment of forces, distinguished by the urban business class's (the bourgeoisie's) powerful and independent political role, has led to liberal democracy. "No [strong and independent] bourgeoisie," Moore noted, "no democracy."[37] Similarly, in developing nations today, a vibrant middle class, including an influential bourgeoisie, is a necessary ingredient for establishing and consolidating democracy. It should come as no surprise, then, that in countries as diverse as Chile, Indonesia, the Philippines, and South Korea, middle-class citizens, including university students (often the children of the bourgeoisie), have been on the front lines in recent struggles for democracy. During the 1992 pro-democracy street demonstrations that brought down Thailand's military government, student leaders could be seen using their cell phones to coordinate their protests—a far cry from Southeast Asia's peasant revolutions decades earlier.

Very poor countries, such as Afghanistan, Haiti, Kenya, or Nepal, whose middle classes are small and dependent on the state or on rural landlords, are far less likely to attain or maintain democracy. But it is also important to remember that even though a strong middle class and bourgeoisie are *necessary* for democracy, those groups are not *always* democratically oriented. For example, in pre-Nazi (Weimar) Germany and in Argentina and Chile during the 1970s, as the middle class felt threatened by social unrest from below, it threw its support to fascist or other right-wing extremist dictatorships.

More recently, Rueschemeyer, Huber Stephens, and Stephens have focused attention on the importance of organized labor in building democracy. They argue that while the bourgeoisie and the middle class generally fostered democracy in Western Europe, Latin America, and the Caribbean, those groups usually favored a restricted form of democracy that enhanced their own political strength (vis-à-vis the upper class and the state) but also limited the political influence of the lower class. Consequently, countries have only achieved comprehensive democracy when, in addition to a large bourgeoisie, they also had a politically potent working class organized into strong labor unions that pushed for broader political representation and increased social justice.[38]

In summary, democracy tends to flourish best where economic modernization produces a politically influential and independent bourgeoisie/middle class and where labor unions effectively defend the interests of the working class. When any of those classes are small, weak, or politically dependent on authoritarian elements in society such as large rural land owners, democratic development is less likely.

Political Culture

In the final analysis, however, neither a country's level of socioeconomic development nor its class structure can fully explain successful or failed democratization. For example, during the early decades of the twentieth century, Argentina was one of the most affluent nations on earth (far wealthier than Italy or Japan), with substantial middle and working classes. Yet rather than develop into a liberal democracy, by the 1930s that country had embarked on a half century of recurring coups and military dictatorships. More recently, Singapore, South Korea, and Taiwan retained authoritarian governments for many years after those countries had attained considerable socioeconomic development.[39] Also, Middle Eastern petroleum states such as Kuwait and Saudi Arabia have made little progress toward democracy despite their considerable economic wealth. On the other hand, India has sustained democracy for most of its 50 years of independence despite its extensive poverty and low literacy rate. As we noted earlier, a growing number of very poor countries have developed liberal democratic regimes.

Along with its level of economic development and its class structure, a nation's democratic potential is also influenced by its *political culture*—that is, its cultural norms and values relating to politics. A country's constitution may require contested elections, a free press, and the separation of powers, but unless the people, especially elites and political activists, value these objectives, constitutional protections are unlikely to hold up. Some of the most important values needed to sustain democracy include the conviction that voting and other forms of individual political participation are important and potentially productive; tolerance of dissenting political opinions and beliefs, even when those views are very unpopular; accepting the outcome of fair elections as definitive, regardless of who wins; viewing politics as a process that requires compromise; and commitment to democracy as the best form of government, regardless of how well or poorly a particular democratic administration performs.

The recent wave of successful and failed democratic transitions has renewed interest in how a country's political culture affects its potential for consolidating democracy. Survey research allows us to measure more precisely the nature of a nation's political beliefs. For example, surveys conducted after the collapse of the Soviet Union revealed that Russia had yet to develop a broadly based democratic political culture. Only one in eight Russians expressed confidence in the new postcommunist administration. A substantial minority, distressed by Russia's economic decline, yearned for the security and stability of the communist era, and many respondents cared little for protecting civil liberties and minority rights. For example, almost one in three favored the death penalty for homosexuals and for prostitutes. A smaller, but still significant, number actually supported the execution of physically disabled people.[40] Ordinary Russians have also been highly intolerant of ethnic minorities (such as central Asians) in their midst. And the country's political elite has manifested little spirit of compromise. One cause for optimism, however, is that younger Russians are more likely to endorse democratic values than older citizens are.

Robert Dahl, a renowned democratic theorist, observes that all political systems eventually confront a serious crisis such the Maoist insurgency in Nepal or ethnic violence in Nigeria. At those times, political leaders in unconsolidated democracies are often tempted to seek authoritarian solutions such as limiting civil liberties or imposing martial law.[41] But if a broad segment of the population, including political elites, shares democratic values—that is, if a democratic political culture has begun to take root in society—democracy can survive the crisis intact. Dahl stresses two particularly important democratic values: first, the armed forces and police must willingly submit to the control of democratically elected civilian authorities; second, government and society must tolerate and legally protect dissident political beliefs.

The first value (civilian control of the military) is taken for granted in industrialized democracies, but not in countries such as Guatemala, Nigeria, and Turkey, where the armed forces have long exercised veto power over the policy decisions of elected officials. Even in a relatively consolidated democracy such as contemporary Chile, the military still insists on substantial autonomy. Dahl's second cultural standard (tolerance of dissent) also presents a challenge to many developing countries where even freely elected governments sometimes silence critics and muzzle opposition leaders. The crucial question, then, says Dahl, is: "How can robust democratic cultures be created in countries where they previously have been largely absent?"[42] He responds that there is no easy answer; developing a democratic culture is a gradual process in which socioeconomic modernization and political development need to mutually reinforce each other.

Sometimes external factors may promote or even impose a democratic political culture on another country, as U.S. occupation forces did in Japan after World War II. Many African and Asian countries were first introduced to modern politics by the colonial powers that controlled them. Statistical analysis of developing countries reveals that one of the factors most closely associated with democratic government is having once been a British colony.[43] Of course, not all former British colonies are democracies; in fact, most of those in Africa are not. However, in general, countries that experienced British colonial rule were far more likely to maintain democracy after independence than were those nations previously colonized by France, Belgium, Netherlands, Spain, or Portugal. This pattern suggests that Britain more successfully inculcated its colonies with democratic values than did other European powers. However, external interventions have had a mixed record. Indeed, many analysts question whether the current U.S. intercession in Afghanistan and Iraq will contribute to the emergence of a democratic political culture in those two nations.

It seems obvious that a country's political culture influences its political system in some manner. For example, communities with high levels of mutual tolerance and citizens who actively follow politics are more hospitable to democracy than are less tolerant or less knowledgeable societies. But how fixed in a nation's psyche are such values? Is there something inherently more democratic or more authoritarian about Norwegian, French, or Chinese cultures? Are some religions, such as Christianity, more conducive to democracy than, say, Hinduism? Here we find scholars disagreeing strongly. Cultural stereotypes are inherently controversial and often prejudiced. But is it not possible that objective analysis might show that countries with certain religions or cultural traditions are more likely to support democratic values, while others are more prone to authoritarianism? In fact, we do find that predominantly Christian nations, particularly Protestant ones, are more likely to be democratic than are countries with other dominant religions, even when other possible causal factors (such as economic development or literacy) are held constant. "Protestantism is said to foster individual responsibility and is … thereby also more skeptical and less fundamentalist in character."[44]

More recently, observers have noted democracy's poor track record in Islamic countries, especially in the Middle East. Some maintain that Islamic beliefs do not readily support democratic institutions because they fail to separate religion and politics (i.e., church and state). Similarly, when impressive economic growth and increased educational levels during the 1970s and early 1980s failed to bring democracy, at least initially, to China, Singapore, South Korea, and Taiwan, some experts concluded that cultural constraints must be overriding the positive influences of economic modernization. They argued that Confucian culture promotes rigidly hierarchical societies and encourages excessive obedience to authority, both of which are antithetical to democracy.[45]

Not surprisingly, cultural explanations such as these are highly controversial. They are very difficult to prove and often smack of prejudice and ethnocentrism. Thus, Catholics may feel uneasy with theories that contrast the traditional strength of democracy in the United States, Canada, and the English-speaking Caribbean with Latin America's authoritarian tradition and suggest that Catholic values are more authoritarian than Protestant norms.[46] Similarly, most Muslims and Confucianists reject theories that depict their religions as authoritarian. But do the facts support these hypotheses, however unpleasant some people may find them?

Although Protestant nations are more likely to be democratic than are countries with other religions, and democracy certainly has not fared well in most Islamic nations, it is difficult to ascertain how much these disparities reflect different religious values rather than myriad other historical, economic, and cultural factors that are not easily controlled for. We know that Islamic nations—such as Turkey, Lebanon, Malaysia, and, most recently, Indonesia—*have* achieved at least partial democracy. Alfred Stepan and Graeme Robertson have demonstrated that non-Arab, Muslim nations have a record of democratic achievement at least as strong as a matched sample of non-Muslim countries with comparable levels of economic and social development.[47] Finally, if there were inherently less democratic values in Islamic or Catholic culture, one would expect that American Catholics or Bosnian Muslims would be less democratically inclined than their Protestant or Christian compatriots. There is no evidence to support that assumption, however.

Furthermore, even if it were true that certain religions tend to predispose their adherents toward democracy or authoritarianism, there is so much variation *within* most world religions (for example, Unitarian and Southern Baptist branches of Christianity, or Shi'ia, Sunni, and Sufi sectors of Islam), each with its own political culture, that it is misleading to suggest that Protestant, Muslim, or Buddhist political cultures are homogeneous.

Finally, religious and national political cultures are capable of change and do not permanently mire a country or region in a particular value system. For example, during World War II, the Japanese and German political cultures were inherently bellicose and authoritarian. Today, however, these countries are highly consolidated democracies whose citizens are far less inclined to support armed interventions (such as in Iraq) than Americans are. Similarly, not long ago, many analysts viewed Confucian values as obstacles to East Asian democratization. However, despite such pessimism, Confucianism has apparently not impeded South Korea's and Taiwan's democratic transitions. The fact that Catholic societies were less hospitable to democracy in the past did not mean that they remained so in the closing decades of the twentieth century. Indeed, from Portugal and Spain to Chile, Brazil, and Uruguay, democracy has recently taken root in Catholic nations that not long ago were depicted as culturally authoritarian. Moreover, in recent decades the Church hierarchy itself has been a pivotal voice for democratic change in Catholic countries such as Poland, the Philippines, Chile, and Brazil.[48]

In short, political cultures appear to be more malleable than previously recognized. As Larry Diamond notes, often "democratic culture is as much the product as the cause of effectively functioning democracy."[49] Just as democratic political culture supports democratic consolidation, sustained democratic behavior helps inculcate democratic values. So, while some new democracies may initially lack a healthy democratic political culture, the longer they continue democratic practices, the better are their chances of absorbing democratic values. Indeed, if countries can sustain democracy for two decades, they are unlikely to ever see it fail. Thus, Robert Dahl's examination of 52 countries in which democracy had collapsed identified only two (Chile and Uruguay) that had enjoyed democracy for more than 20 years prior to that collapse.[50] And even those two exceptions have since more successfully reinstituted democracy than have neighboring countries such as Bolivia and Peru, which lack comparable democratic traditions. The Czech Republic has enjoyed a similar advantage over its Eastern European neighbors.

HOW DO DEMOCRACIES PERFORM?
PUBLIC POLICY COMPARED

While the benefits of democracy are obvious as they relate to human freedom and state power restricted by the consent of the governed, over the years scholars have debated whether democratic governments also better provide for the welfare of their citizens. Just as some analysts once argued that well-organized and technically skilled authoritarian governments—such as South Korea or Chile—could generate more rapid economic growth than democracies could, others have argued that authoritarian governments in China, Cuba, and Singapore have provided better health care and greater educational opportunities, especially for the poor, than their democratic counterparts in countries such as India or Jamaica.

It is difficult to make comparisons of this sort since there are so many other factors that may explain why two groups of countries have contrasting records of accomplishment. For example, each country begins at a different starting point, has different economic resources, and faces different international economic environments. Consequently, rather than compare the policy outcomes of the two regime types, I will compare the *commitment* of selected democratic and authoritarian regimes in Asia and Latin America to the health and educational welfare of their citizens by examining their budgetary expenditures in those two areas. Table 2.1 presents data on government expenditures for public education during the late 1980s and 1990s (expressed as a percentage of GNP and as a percentage of total government expenditures) and on health services in the late 1990s (expressed as a percentage of GDP), along with data on private health expenditures in eight Asian, Latin American, and Caribbean nations: two long-standing liberal democracies (Barbados and Costa Rica), two countries that have relatively recently made the transition from authoritarian to democratic government (Chile and South Korea), two Marxist-Leninist regimes (China and Cuba), and two capitalist, semi-democracies (Malaysia and Singapore).[51]

The data in column 2 suggest that liberal democracies, particularly long-standing democracies, generally spend somewhat more for their citizens' education than do authoritarian regimes. It is true that Cuba allocated the highest percentage of its GNP to education (6.75 percent), but that was just slightly ahead of democratic Barbados (6.7 percent). At the same time, communist China ranked last in public educational expenditure by a substantial margin. To be sure, no clear pattern emerged for this particular indicator. The two long-standing liberal democracies—Barbados and Costa Rica—allocated the highest average percentage of their respective GNPs to public education (5.83 percent). The capitalist semi-democracies—Malaysia and Singapore—were next with 4.68 percent, followed by communist China and Cuba (averaging 4.53 percent)

TABLE 2.1   Social Expenditures: Democratic and Authoritarian
Regimes Compared

| Country | Public Education Expenditures[a] | | Total Health Expenditures[b] | |
	As % of GNP	As % of total government expenditures	Public (as % of GDP)	Private (as % of GDP)
Barbados	6.7	18.1	4.5	2.2
Costa Rica	4.95	22.2	5.2	1.5
Chile	3.6[a]	24.8[c]	2.7	3.1
South Korea	3.7[a]	17.5[c]	2.4	3.0
China	2.3	11.65	2.1	3.0
Cuba	6.75	15.5	NA	NA
Singapore	3.45	17.4	1.1	2.1
Malaysia	5.9	17.1	1.4	1.0

NA, Data not available.

[a]Public Education Expenditures are averages for 1985-87 and 1995-97.

[b]Total Health Expenditures are for 1998.

[c]Education Expenditures for Chile and South Korea reflect only the years 1995-97 when these countries had established democratic governments.

Source: UNDP, *Human Development Report* 2002 (Oxford and New York: Oxford University Press, 2002), 166-169, 178-181.

and, lastly, the two recently consolidated liberal democracies—Chile and South Korea (3.65 percent). In all, public education expenditures for the four democratic governments averaged 4.74 percent of the GNP, only very slightly higher than the 4.60 percent spent by their authoritarian counterparts.

Shifting our focus to public educational expenditures as a percentage of total government outlays (column 3)—a more direct measure of government spending priorities—we find that all four democracies had higher expenditure rates than each of their authoritarian counterparts. Education accounted for an average of 20.65 percent of total government expenditures in the four democracies, substantially more than the 15.41 percent spent by the nondemocracies. Interestingly, the two newly established democracies—Chile and South Korea—ranked highest in educational expenditures (21.15 percent of total government outlays), though their lead over the two established democracies—Barbados and Costa Rica—(at 20.15 percent) was relatively small. The two capitalist semi-democracies ranked next with average public educational allocations of 17.25 percent of the total budget and, surprisingly, the two Marxist nations—China and Cuba—ranked last with 12.58 percent, well behind the others. However, it should be remembered that since communist governments involve themselves in a far wider range of economic activities—and consequently have more noneducational expenses—than do their capitalist counterparts, the percentage of the Cuban and Chinese budget allocated to education might be expected to be somewhat lower.

Finally, Table 2.1 presents both public and private sector health care expenditures (columns 4 and 5) for all of the countries with available information (all but Cuba). Here we encounter an even sharper contrast, with all four democracies expending more on public health (as a percentage of GDP) than the three authoritarian governments. Finally, if we calculate *total* (private and public) health expenditures (columns 4 and 5 combined) in the original seven countries (all except Cuba), we find again that all four liberal democracies outspent each of their three authoritarian counterparts. Barbados and Costa Rica, the long-standing liberal democracies, spent the most (6.7 percent); the newly instituted or restored democracies—South Korea and Chile—followed (5.6 percent); and the three authoritarian or semi-democratic nations lagged well behind (2.45 percent) at levels less than half those of the democracies.

CONCLUSION: DEMOCRATIC CONSOLIDATION

What makes democracy endure? Now that a substantial number of developing countries have democratized, which ones have the qualities needed to maintain and consolidate democracy? To answer that question, Adam Przeworski and his associates analyzed statistics covering a 40-year period (1950–1990) from 135 different countries.[52] Democracy, they found, is most fragile in poor countries (with per-capita incomes of less than $1,000) and becomes more stable as national income rises. "Above $6,000 [per-capita income], democracies are impregnable and can be expected to live forever; no democratic system has ever fallen in a country where per-capita income exceeds $6,055 (Argentina's level in 1976)."[53] Several factors explain why richer democracies are more likely to endure. For one thing, they usually have one crucial foundation for democratic government—higher educational levels.[54] For another, class conflicts over the distribution of economic rewards are typically less intense in more affluent societies.

Contrary to what many political scientists have believed, Przeworski et al. also found the faster a nation's economy grows, the more likely it is to sustain democracy. Conversely, democracy is less likely to survive in countries suffering economic decline, high inflation rates, or other forms of economic crisis. However, important as domestic economic factors are, the authors discovered that international political conditions exert a more powerful influence on a country's chances for democratic survival. Specifically, the more prevalent and fashionable democratic government becomes worldwide, the more likely any particular Third World country is to sustain democracy, regardless of its per-capita income, literacy rate, or economic growth rate. In other words, as many scholars had suspected, democracy is contagious.

Other analysts have noted that developing and maintaining effective political institutions—including representative and responsible political parties, a broad array of interest groups, a representative and influential legislature, a strong but controlled executive branch, an honest and independent judicial system—are absolutely critical for maintaining stable and effective democracy. Too often Third World judicial systems are insufficiently independent of the executive branch, have inadequate legal training, and are excessively corrupt. Consolidating democracies must strengthen their judiciary systems so that they can stand up to a power-hungry president or prime minister and so that court decisions are respected by the electorate.

A related problem in many new and reestablished democracies is executive-branch dominance over the national legislature. In Latin America, Russia, and elsewhere, democratically elected presidents have sometimes interpreted their electoral victories to mean that the voters had, in effect, delegated absolute authority to them. For example, although elected democratically, Presidents Carlos Menem (Argentina) and Alberto Fujimori (Peru) ran roughshod over their nation's congress and court system upon assuming office. That is perhaps one reason that Juan Linz and Arturo Valenzuela have found that democracy is more likely to collapse in presidential systems than in countries with parliamentary forms of government.[55]

Finally, emerging democracies need to address serious social and economic injustices that threaten democratic consolidation. In 2004 the United Nations Development Program conducted a survey of 18,643 citizens in 18 Latin American countries. While Latin America has made the most far-reaching progress among all Third World regions in achieving democratic government, the survey showed widening disillusionment in the region regarding the value of democratic rule in the face of widespread poverty and economic stagnation. In the region as a whole, 55 percent of all respondents said that they would favor a dictator over a democratically elected leader if that improved their economic conditions.[56] Voter turnout has been declining in recent Latin American elections and elected presidents in several countries—including Bolivia, Ecuador, and Haiti—have been toppled by mass protest demonstrations in recent years.

Without improved social conditions, democratic governments may be unable to continue commanding the support of the country's poor. In Latin America, where income inequality is higher than in any world region, the gap between "haves" and "have nots" has generally widened since the region's recent transition to democracy, with the notable exception of Uruguay. Similarly, the gap between rich and poor has widened greatly in the newly democratizing countries of Eastern Europe and the former Soviet Union. From the Philippines to Pakistan, from Colombia to Peru, the urban and rural poor suffer from highly unequal land and income distribution, pervasive poverty and crime, deficient public health systems, and corrupt and repressive local police and judicial systems. Until such injustices are addressed, democracy will remain incomplete and precarious.

DISCUSSION QUESTIONS

1. Discuss the differences between electoral democracy, liberal democracy, and substantive democracy. Which definition seems most useful to you?
2. What is the third wave of democracy, and what accounts for its emergence?
3. Which social classes have historically been most supportive of democracy, and which have been most antagonistic? What kind of class structure is most likely to support democratic consolidation?
4. What is the evidence that some religions are more supportive of democracy than others? What are the strengths and weaknesses of the argument that there is a link between a country's religion and its potential for democracy?
5. What is the relationship between social and economic development, on the one hand, and democracy, on the other?
6. What arguments would suggest that the third wave of democratization is coming to an end in the Third World, and what might suggest that more developing nations will become democratic? In either case, why is there reason to believe that, even if there are more transitions to democracy, the *rate* of democratization is almost certain to decrease?
7. Compare the performances and policy commitments of democratic versus authoritarian governments as they relate to economic growth, education, and health care.

NOTES

1. Serbia is a part of the Yugoslav federation, which once included the republics of Croatia, Slovenia, and Bosnia, among others. When those states left Yugoslavia the country was reduced to two republics. In 2002 those two agreed to change the name of the country from Yugoslavia to the Federation of Serbia and Montenegro.

2. Richard Joseph, "Africa: The Rebirth of Political Freedom," in *The Global Resurgence of Democracy*, eds. Larry Diamond and Marc F. Plattner (Baltimore, MD: Johns Hopkins University Press, 1993), 307–320. In retrospect, Joseph's chapter was overly optimistic about Africa's progress toward democracy.

3. By definition, consolidation of democracy reduces military rule. It also lowers the likelihood of revolutionary movements. Greater democracy also should eventually contribute to better conditions for women, the urban poor, and peasants, though those effects are not necessarily apparent immediately.

4. For example, Samuel P. Huntington, *The Third Wave: Democratization in the Late Twentieth Century* (Norman: University of Oklahoma Press, 1991).

5. Colombia is one of Latin America's more enduring electoral democracies, but its government is perhaps the region's worst human rights violator. See *New York Times* (April 26, 1994). Sri Lanka's civil war seemed to be nearing an end but more recently the picture there has become more clouded.

6. Of course, in all democracies some major officials are appointed, such as the justices of the U.S. Supreme Court and members of the U.S. national cabinet. But these people are appointed by a popularly elected official (the president) and are subject to confirmation by the Congress. If this standard is rigorously applied, the United States could not be considered a full democracy prior to the 1960s because large numbers of southern Blacks were barred from voting. In the nineteenth and early twentieth centuries, of course, women could not vote.

7. There has been a long, ongoing debate over what conditions, and how many of those conditions, a country must meet in order to be called a democracy. The definition offered here represents the current consensus and is drawn from the following sources: Philippe C. Schmitter and Terry Lynn Karl, "What Democracy Is … and Is Not," *Journal of Democracy* 2, no. 2 (Summer 1991): 75–88; Scott Mainwaring, "Transitions to Democracy and Democratic Consolidation," in *Issues in Democratic Consolidation: The New South American Democracies in Comparative Perspective*,

eds. Scott Mainwaring, Guillermo O'Donnell, and Samuel Valenzuela (Notre Dame, IN: University of Notre Dame Press, 1992), 297–298; Robert A. Dahl, *Polyarchy: Participation and Opposition* (New Haven, CT: Yale University Press, 1971); Robert A. Dahl, *Democracy and Its Critics* (New Haven, CT: Yale University Press, 1989); Huntington, *The Third Wave*.

8. Civil society is essentially the array of societal organizations—churches, unions, business groups, farmers' organizations, women's groups, and the like—that influence the political system but operate *independently* (i.e., free of government control). Typically, authoritarian governments attempt to weaken civil society by trying to place these groups under government command. So rebuilding and strengthening civil society becomes an essential task for establishing and consolidating democratic government.

9. Huntington, *The Third Wave*, 28–30.

10. Juan Linz and Alfred Stepan, "Toward Consolidated Democracies," in *Consolidating the Third Wave Democracies*, eds. Larry Diamond, Marc F. Plattner, Yun-han Chu, and Hung-mao Tien (Baltimore, MD: Johns Hopkins University Press, 1997), 15.

11. Seymour Martin Lipset, *Political Man: The Social Basis of Politics*, expanded and updated ed. (Baltimore, MD: Johns Hopkins University Press, 1980). For a review of such research see Dietrich Rueschemeyer, Evelyne Huber Stephens, and John D. Stephens, *Capitalist Development and Democracy* (Chicago: University of Chicago Press, 1992), chap. 2.

12. Samuel P. Huntington, *Political Order in Changing Societies* (New Haven, CT: Yale University Press, 1968).

13. Mitchell A. Seligson, "Democratization in Latin America: The Current Cycle" in *Authoritarians and Democrats: Regime Transition in Latin America*, eds. James M. Malloy and Mitchell A. Seligson (Pittsburgh, PA: University of Pittsburgh Press, 1987), 7–9. Since the time that Seligson did his research, the mid-1980s, literacy rates have risen sharply and few countries now have literacy rates below 50 percent. Perhaps a more useful threshold today might be about 65 percent literacy.

14. It is generally agreed that the emergence of the middle class and business class (bourgeoisie) in Western Europe was associated with the growth of modern democracy. See, for example, Barrington Moore Jr., *The Social Origins of Dictatorship and Democracy* (Boston: Beacon Press, 1966). More recently, political scientists such as Rueschemeyer, Huber Stephens, and

Stephens, *Capitalist Development*, have emphasized the contributions of organized labor.

15. Of course, even defenders of authoritarian governments had to concede that most dictatorships are not efficient modernizers. Far from it. The developing world has had more than its share of corrupt dictators (Mobutu in Zaire, Somoza in Nicaragua, Marcos in the Philippines) who have stolen millions, run their country's economy into the ground, and wrecked the nation's infrastructure and educational system. What these scholars did claim, however, was that *efficient* dictatorships such as Taiwan or Singapore offered the best hope for modernization. Communists, of course, saw revolutionary dictatorships such as Cuba or China as necessary for greater social equality, improved literacy, better health care systems, and related indicators of modernization.

16. For example, Glen Caudill Dealy, *The Latin Americans, Spirit and Ethos* (Boulder, CO: Westview Press, 1992). The ground-breaking study of political culture was Gabriel A. Almond and Sidney Verba, *The Civic Culture: Political Attitudes and Democracy in Five Nations* (Boston: Little, Brown and Company, 1965), which examined political culture in the United States, Britain, Germany, Italy, and Mexico.

17. Larry Diamond, "Introduction: In Search of Consolidation," in *Consolidating the Third Wave Democracies*, xv. While Diamond suggests there were 39 democracies, Samuel Huntington counted only 30 at that time. Huntington's lower total partially reflects the fact that he did not consider countries with a population under 1 million.

18. Huntington, *The Third Wave*, 271. That figure includes Turkey, which I have characterized as a less-developed country.

19. Huntington, *The Third Wave*.

20. Larry Diamond, *Prospects for Democratic Development in Africa* (Stanford, CA: Hoover Institution Press, 1997), Appendix; Adrian Karatnycky, "The 1999 Freedom House Survey: A Century of Progress," *Journal of Democracy* 11 (January 2000): 187–200.

21. Michael Bratton and Nicolas van de Walle, *Democratic Experiments in Africa: Regime Transitions in Comparative Perspective* (New York: Cambridge University Press, 1997), 120.

22. Adrian Karatnycky, "National Income and Liberty", *Journal of Democracy* 15 (January 2001): 82–93. See note 25 for an explanation of the Freedom House scoring.

23. I have not included the 2003 ouster of Iraqi dictator Saddam Hussein because it was an aberration in that he was removed by foreign intervention rather than by indigenous forces.

Moreover, prospects for democracy in that country remain highly uncertain.

24. Diamond, *Consolidating the Third Wave Democracies*, xvi.

25. Freedom House asks a panel of experts to rate each country's level of political rights and civil liberties on a scale of 1 (most free) to 7 (least free). Countries which had an average score of 1.0-2.5 were categorized as "Free." Those with average ratings of 3.0-5.0 were ranked as "Partly Free." And those countries with ratings of 5.5-7.0 were labeled "Not Free."

26. The 2004 Freedom House Survey is summarized in Karatnycky, "National Income and Liberty."

27. For a broader discussion on international influences favoring democratization, see Laurence Whitehead, ed., *The International Dimensions of Democratization: Europe and the Americas* (New York: Oxford University Press, 1996); Abraham F. Lowenthal, ed., *Exporting Democracy: The United States and Latin America* (Baltimore, MD: Johns Hopkins University Press, 1991). Ironically, years later, following an urprising against Aristide, the Bush administration helped force him from power.

28. Determining whether democracy has been consolidated (i.e., has become "the only game in town") in any particular country is a judgment call over which experts may disagree. Only the test of time ultimately reveals whether a democratic government endures.

29. Seymour Martin Lipset, *Political Man*, 1st ed. (Garden City, NY: Anchor Books, 1960).

30. Rueschemeyer, Huber Stephens, and Stephens, *Capitalist Development and Democracy*, 14.

31. Philips Cutright, "National Political Development: Measurement and Analysis," *American Sociological Review* 28 (April 1963).

32. Axel Hadenius, *Democracy and Development* (New York: Cambridge University Press, 1992).

33. United Nations Development Programme, *Human Development Report, 2004* Table 1: Human Development Indicators <http://hdr.undp.org//reports/global/2004>

34. Seligson, "Democratization in Latin America: The Current Cycle."

35. Huntington, *Political Order in Changing Societies*. On the rise of repressive authoritarian regimes in Latin America's most industrialized nations, see Guillermo O'Donnell, *Modernization and Bureaucratic Authoritarianism* (Berkeley, CA: Institute of International Studies, 1973).

36. Adrian Karatnycky, "National Income and Liberty." As litercy rates have climbed sharply in poorer Third World nations, the gap in litaracy between LDCs that are relatively more affluent

and those that are most poor has narrowed. Thus, even poorer countries now most exceed Seligson's threshold of 50 percent literacy.

37. Barrington Moore, *The Social Origins*, 418.

38. Rueschemeyer, Huber Stephens, and Stephens, *Capitalist Development and Democracy*.

39. South Korea and Taiwan have subsequently democratized, but Singapore still has not.

40. Stephen White, "Russia's Experiment with Democracy," *Current History* 91 (October 1992): 313.

41. Even in a deeply consolidated democracy such as the United States, many critics charge that the Homeland Security Act, which followed the 9/11 terrorist attacks, contains troubling infringements on this country's civil liberties.

42. Robert Dahl, "Development and Democratic Culture," in *Consolidating the Third Wave Democracies*, 34.

43. Kenneth A. Bollen and Robert Jackman, "Economic and Non-economic Determinants of Political Democracy in the 1960s," in *Research in Political Sociology*, ed. R. G. Braungart (Greenwich, CT: Jai Press, 1985).

44. Hadenius, *Democracy and Development*, 118–119.

45. Samuel P. Huntington, "Will More Countries Be Democratic?" *Political Science Quarterly* 99 (1984): 193–218; Huntington, *The Clash of Civilizations and the Remaking of World Order* (New York: Simon & Schuster, 1996).

46. For an argument along those lines, see Dealy, *The Latin Americans*.

47. Alfred Stepan with Graeme B. Robertson, "An 'Arab' More than 'Muslim' Electoral Gap," *Journal of Democracy* 14, no. 3 (July 2003): 30-44.

48. Daniel Philpott, "The Catholic Wave," *Journal of Democracy* 15, no. 2 (April 2004): 32-

49. Larry Diamond, "Three Paradoxes of Democracy," in *The Global Resurgence of Democracy*, 104.

50. Robert A. Dahl, "The Newer Democracies: From the Time of Triumph to the Time of Troubles," in ed. Daniel N. Nelson, *After Authoritarianism: Democracy or Disorder?* (Westport, CT: Greenwood Press, 1995), 7.

51. These countries are categorized according to rankings found in Larry Diamond, *Developing Democracy: Toward Consolidation* (Baltimore: Johns Hopkins University Press, 1999), 279-281, which, in turn, are based on ratings by Freedom House.

52. Adam Przeworski et al., "What Makes Democracies Endure?" in *Consolidating Third Wave Democracies*, ed. Larry Diamond et al., 295–311.

53. Ibid., 297. All dollar figures are in constant dollars, meaning that they are adjusted for inflation so that a per-capita income of $1,000 in 1960 and 1990 is actually equivalent.

54. In other words, countries that are more economically advanced have higher literacy and education rates, and countries with higher literacy rates are more likely to be democratic. There are several petroleum-producing countries in the Middle East (such as Saudi Arabia and the United Arab Emirates) which, though wealthy, don't have exceptionally high literacy rates. None of those are democracies.

55. Juan Linz and Arturo Valenzuela, eds., *The Failure of Presidential Democracy* (Baltimore, MD: Johns Hopkins University Press, 1994).

56. *The New York Times* (April 22, 2004 and June 24, 2004).

chapter 3

Religion and Politics

A death knell for traditional religion was sounded in the 1960s, not by an opponent of religion, but by one of America's preeminent Protestant theologians, Harvey Cox. He was not predicting the demise of religion per se, but rather of its traditional form, including its historic role in politics and other forms of public life. Cox's influential book *The Secular City* coincided with the observations and predictions of social scientists at that time. And while religion obviously remained a pervasive force in the Third World, secularization of society seemed inevitable there as well.

In Latin America the Catholic Church no longer exercised nearly as much control over education as it once did. Following independence, the government of India tried to ameliorate the injustices of the caste system, a cornerstone of Hindu religious practice. And in the Middle East, modernizing regimes in Egypt, Iraq, and Syria created more secular political systems. Accordingly, one leading authority, Donald Eugene Smith, observed, "Political development includes, as one of its basic processes, the secularization of politics, the progressive exclusion of religion from the political system."[1]

Generally speaking, early modernization theorists viewed religion as an impediment to political and economic development, while dependency theorists deemed it so unimportant as to warrant only an occasional footnote in their writings (see Chapter 1). Since the time Cox and Smith chronicled its decline, however, religion has been an unexpectedly resilient political force, withstanding the onslaughts of modernization, and even, at times, being stimulated by it. As David Little observed, "Modernization was supposed to mean the gradual decline and eventual disappearance of religion from public life, but, as we know, that hasn't happened. Religion is very much alive as a part of politics."[2] In fact, since the 1970s much of the Third World, and the developed world too, for that matter, has experienced a religious resurgence intensifying the role of religion in the political arena.[3] In the Middle East, "ironically, the technological tools of modernization have often served to reinforce traditional belief and practice as religious leaders who initially opposed modernization now use radio, television, audio- and videotapes to preach and disseminate."[4]

Nowhere is the change more apparent than in the Middle East and parts of Asia, where a resurgence of Islamic fundamentalism (or *Islamism*, the term preferred by many analysts) has had a dramatic political impact on Afghanistan, Iran, Lebanon, Algeria, Egypt, Saudi Arabia, and Pakistan. Since 1979 the seizure of American hostages in Iran and Lebanon, the assassination of Egyptian President Anwar Sadat, the bombings of a U.S. military housing installation in Saudi Arabia and of two U.S. embassies in East Africa, the March 2004 (3/11) bombing of four packed commuter trains in Madrid, the recurring suicide bombings in Iraq, and, especially, the 9/11 attacks on the World Trade Center and the Pentagon have all focused Western attention on "religion and politics." In fact, with the collapse of Soviet communism and the end of the Cold War, many politicians and journalists labeled radical (militant) Islamic fundamentalism as the greatest threat to Western security. Even before the 1991 Gulf War, a Gallup Poll survey revealed that 37 percent of British respondents expected a war in the 1990s between Muslims and Christians.[5] The U.S. overthrow of Afghanistan's Taliban government, the Iraqi quagmire, and ongoing Al Qaeda-linked terrorism have revived such sentiments. While these perceptions are often based on prejudice and misunderstanding, the discussion of Islamic and Hindu fundamentalism later in this chapter indicates some reason for concern.

THE MEETING OF CHURCH AND STATE

Many of our preconceptions about religion and politics are based on serious misunderstandings, both of our own government and of political systems elsewhere. Americans generally accept a constitutional separation between church and state as natural. Such formal barriers, however, do not exist in many industrialized democracies or LDCs. Moreover, even in the United States, religious organizations and beliefs continue to influence political behavior. Black Baptist churches, for example, have been in the forefront of the American civil rights movement and the Republican party is influenced by "the Christian right." Recently, conflicts over issues such as school prayer and abortion have led one expert to observe that "far from rendering religion largely irrelevant to politics the structure of [American] government may actually encourage a high degree of interaction."[6] Most Western European nations, though more secular than the United States in most aspects of everyday life, have not built walls between religion and politics. In Britain, for example, the Anglican Church (or Church of England) is the official state religion. The Catholic Church was closely linked to the Italian Christian Democratic Party, once that nation's leading party.[7]

Religion is more firmly embedded in most Third World cultures, and its impact on politics is correspondingly more pronounced than is ours. Indeed, religion is so central to traditional values that we often identify national or regional cultures by the predominant religion: Buddhist culture in Thailand, Confucian culture in China and Korea, Hindu culture in much of India and Nepal, and Islamic culture in North Africa and the Middle East.[8]

The blending of religion and politics is most apparent in theocratic states such as Iran where, since that nation's 1979 Islamic revolution, public policy has been shaped by the Shi'a clergy. But it is also significant in Islamic fundamentalist states like Sudan, and American allies such as Pakistan and Saudi Arabia. Afghanistan's Taliban government made politics totally subservient to religion. In Brazil and Nicaragua, the theology of liberation, espoused by progressive members of the Catholic Church, motivated priests and nuns to organize the poor against economic and political injustices. And in India, the Bharatiya Janata Party (BJP), recently the country's largest political party and head of its governing coalition, carries the torch of Hindu fundamentalism.

GREAT RELIGIONS OF THE THIRD WORLD

Four of the world's "great religions" are predominant in the Third World. *Catholicism*, the only major religion to have penetrated extensively into both industrialized democracies and the developing world, is preeminent throughout the Philippines and Latin America, while also representing important portions of the population in countries such as Lebanon and parts of Sub-Saharan Africa. *Hinduism* is confined primarily to India, along with neighboring Nepal and parts of Indonesia and Sri Lanka. *Buddhism* is a major influence in East Asia and Southeast Asia, along with parts of South Asia. Finally, *Islam*, the world's second largest religion, predominates across a broad span of Asia, the Middle East, and Africa, stretching from Indonesia in the east through Pakistan and Bangladesh in the Indian subcontinent, the former Soviet republics of Central Asia, the Middle East, and North Africa. It also represents about half the population of Malaysia and Nigeria, as well as substantial minorities in countries as far-flung as the Philippines, Tanzania, and Trinidad.[9]

To be sure, not everyone in the developing world subscribes to one of these major religions. Protestantism is the leading religion in the English-speaking islands of the Caribbean and represents important minorities in a number of other LDCs. Confucianism still influences Chinese society, even after its revolution. Christian Orthodox minorities are significant in Lebanon and Egypt, and a large portion of Black Africa's population believes in local traditional religions. The impact of these religions on politics, however, is more limited. Consequently, this chapter limits its analysis to the four global religions described earlier, with particular emphasis on Islam and Catholicism.

None of the Third World's major religions is monolithic, though the Catholic Church, with its doctrine of papal infallibility and its hierarchical structure, comes closest. Buddhism has two major schools, each basing its doctrines on different ancient texts. Theravada ("Way of Elders") Buddhism, practiced in Myanmar (Burma), Sri Lanka (Ceylon), Thailand, Laos, and Cambodia, is believed to be closer to the original teachings of the Buddha. Mahayana ("Great Vehicle") Buddhism emerged in China, Japan, Korea, Vietnam, and Tibet.[10]

Perhaps the most important division within Islam is between its Sunni and Shi'a branches (Sufism, a third branch, is much smaller). The split between them, dating to the period following the death of the Prophet Muhammad, centered on the issues of "who should succeed him and the nature of the successor's role" spiritually and politically.[11] Ninety percent of the Muslim population is Sunni, while Shi'ism, which has drawn great attention in the West because of its periodic nationalistic and militant manifestations, accounts for only about 8 percent. Shi'ism is the dominant faith only in Iran, where it is centered. But it also represents some 60 percent of Iraq's population, a plurality in Lebanon, and significant minorities in Afghanistan, Pakistan, Syria, Kuwait, and other Gulf states. In countries such as Iraq, having both significant Sunni and Shi'a populations, there are commonly sharp political and cultural tensions between the two.[12]

Even religions that have no formal divisions experience important political differences. Latin American Catholics span the ideological spectrum from right-wing followers of *Opus Dei* to leftist adherents of liberation theology. In the name of God and anticommunism, some Latin American Catholics have supported fascist movements, rightist death squads, and repressive military regimes. Conversely, in the name of God and social justice, other Catholic priests and nuns have supported the Sandinista revolution in Nicaragua, fought with Marxist guerrillas in Colombia, and politically organized the poor in the slums of Brazil and Peru.

RELIGION, MODERNITY, AND SECULARIZATION

We have already observed that modernization does not necessarily produce a decline in religious observance, at least not in the short run. What about the other side of the relationship? That is, what is the impact of religion on modernity? Here again, early theorists felt they were incompatible. "It is widely, and correctly, assumed," said Donald Smith, "that religion is in general an obstacle to modernization."[13] In the realm of politics, this interpretation suggested that the intrusion of religious institutions into government impedes the development of a modern state. Others associated traditional Catholic, Islamic, and Hindu beliefs with authoritarian values.

Subsequently, political scientists have developed a more nuanced understanding. Religious institutions may inhibit development in some respects, while encouraging it in others. For example, all of the great religions have legitimized the state's authority at some point in history. As nations modernize their political systems, religious authorities or groups may oppose important aspects of change (Hindu and Islamic fundamentalists, for example), or they may offer explicit or tacit support (Islamic leaders in Indonesia and Catholic clergy in Chile). No longer facilely dismissing religion's possible contribution to development, many scholars have now credited Confucianism with facilitating East Asia's rapid modernization in recent decades.[14] Specifically, they have noted that religion's work ethic and spirit of cooperation.

Depending on their theology and structure, individual religions may either bolster or impede government development initiatives. Different religions emphasize distinctive values; thus, states wishing to create welfare programs based on communal responsibility (i.e., programs tied to ethnic communities) often receive strong support from Islamic leaders or the Catholic Church. At the same time, modernizing political leaders who emphasize individual rights and responsibilities find those values warmly received by Buddhist monks. Ultimately, then, organized religions can strengthen the modern nation-state by bestowing legitimacy and by disseminating the government's political message. Should religious leaders oppose the state, however, they can often delegitimize the political system.[15]

The argument that political modernization requires secularization has two components, one empirical and the other normative. The *empirical* component notes that as Western societies modernized (i.e., became more literate, urban, institutionally organized, and industrial), their political systems invariably became more secular. In effect, there has been a specialization of functions. Increasingly, the state has controlled politics, while the church has overseen religion, and each has refrained from interfering in the other's realm. Political scientists anticipated that as the Third World modernized, it would experience the same division of responsibilities. The related *normative* assumption holds that secularization is not only a common trend, but it is also *desirable* since it increases religious freedom, reduces the likelihood of state persecution of religious minorities, and permits the state to make more rational decisions free of religious bias.

We have already indicated the weakness of the first assumption. To be sure, modernization has induced political secularization in many developing countries, such as Turkey and Mexico. But elsewhere it has not altered church-state relations; indeed, it has precipitated a religious backlash when pursued too rapidly. Saudi Arabia, India, and Iran illustrate three possible governmental approaches to managing the forces of modernization. In the most cautious approach, the Saudi royal family has introduced far-reaching socioeconomic changes but has carefully controlled the style of modernization in order to preserve a very traditionalist Islamic culture and maintain the close links between Islam and the state. India represents an intermediate case, where the modernization of politics and constitutional secularization was generally accepted (at least until recently). Religious factors in India do affect government in some respects; thus, Hindus and Muslims are governed by distinct legal norms in areas such as family law. And while the prime minister's post has always been held by a Hindu (the religious majority), the largely ceremonial presidency has been reserved for a Muslim. Iran represents one of the most marked examples of religious backlash against modernization and a relinking of church and state. As we will see, the Shah (emperor) imposed rapid Western-style socioeconomic development (including "unveiling" women), which destabilized society and helped precipitate a radical Islamic revival.

At an individual level, many people in Africa, Asia, and the Middle East have defied the notion that more educated and professionally trained citizens will be less religiously orthodox. For example, Hindu and Islamic fundamentalist activists in India, Afghanistan, and Egypt are frequently professionals, not poor uneducated peasants.[16] Most of the terrorists who attacked the Pentagon and World Trade Center in 2001 were relatively well educated and middle class. Nor are traditional religious values and modern technology necessarily incompatible. In Iran, opponents of the Shah undermined his authority by distributing audiotapes of Ayatollah Ruhollah Khomeini's political message throughout the country. Once in power, the theocratic government made extensive use of television and other modern technologies to maintain its influence.

Normative evaluations of the church-state relationship need to be more complex than early development theory had assumed. Clearly, some religious influences contradict accepted norms of modernity, as when they induce political leaders to violate the rights of religious minorities (or majorities). Iran's Islamic government, for example, has persecuted members of the Baha'i faith.[17] In Guatemala, the government of General Efraín Rios Montt, a right-wing Evangelical, converted Catholic peasants to Protestantism at virtual gunpoint. Similarly, religiously inspired restrictions on racial minorities or women (the latter a common feature of Islamic fundamentalist societies) are clearly antithetical to modernization.

Can one infer from such cases, however, that there need always be a strict wall between politics and religion or between clerics and politicians? The same people who lamented the political activities of Catholic priests in Nicaragua and Brazil, the protest marches by Buddhist monks in Sri Lanka, or the fundamentalist government in Afghanistan, may have cheered political involvement by Dr. Martin Luther King Jr. or the Reverend Jerry Falwell in the United States.

Ultimately, most people's normative evaluations of religion's role in politics are influenced by whether that religious activity furthers the goals and policies they believe in. Perhaps this is as it should be. The recent histories of Iran and Tibet illustrate this point well. Iran has been a theocracy (a religiously driven political system) since its 1979 revolution, just as Tibet had been prior to its absorption by China in the 1950s. Each has had a political system "in which the political structures are clearly subordinate to the ecclesiastical establishment."[18] Yet the world has judged them quite differently.

Under the leadership of its Islamic mullahs (clerics), Iran became an international outcast because of its repression of civil liberties, persecution of religious minorities, support for international terrorism, and its nuclear program. Until the late 1950s, Tibetan politics was also dominated by clerics.[19] Viewed as divine by his people, the Dalai Lama had been the country's secular and spiritual leader. Buddhist monks held key posts in the government bureaucracy. Because of Tibetan Buddhism's record of pacifism and tolerance, however, theocratic rule aroused no foreign indignation. Indeed, the world was appalled when China occupied Tibet and secularized the state. Since that time the Dalai Lama's long struggle to free his people has won him worldwide admiration and the Nobel Peace Prize. All of this suggests that the issue of separation of church and state may be less important than the way in which "the church" uses its political influence when it holds power.

STRUCTURAL AND THEOLOGICAL BASES
OF CHURCH-STATE RELATIONS

The extent to which religions influence political attitudes and behavior and the degree of political involvement by organized religions vary considerably from place to place. Just as the separation of church and state in Western Europe has historically been more clearly defined in predominantly Protestant nations (for example, Denmark and Britain) than in Catholic ones (for example, Italy and Spain), the political impact of the Third World's four major religions also differs. Two factors are particularly relevant: the particular religion's theological view on the relationship between temporal and spiritual matters, and the degree of hierarchical structure within the religion. The second factor refers to how well organized and centrally controlled a religion is.

Donald Smith distinguishes two different types of religio-political systems: the organic and the church. In the first case, the *organic* system, the clergy is insufficiently organized to challenge the country's political leaders who are, consequently, less restricted by religious institutions. Examples of organic systems include the Hindu and most Sunni Islamic cultures. *Church* religio-political systems, on the other hand, have a well-organized ecclesiastical structure that exercises considerable authority over politics. Such churches include Catholicism, Shi'a Islam, and sometimes Buddhism (in countries such as Tibet and Myanmar). All have more formalized relations between church and state, with greater potential for religious challenges to the political order or political domination of the church than in organic systems. In some church systems, the state dominates the religious order; in others, the church dominates; and yet in others, there is an equal partnership.[20]

Islam

From its inception in seventh-century Arabia, Islam has been a "religio-political movement in which religion was integral to state and society."[21] Perhaps more than any other great religion, traditional Islam usually recognized no borderline between religion and politics. On the one hand, the Islamic faith and its clergy legitimized the state. At the same time, however, the political leadership recognized the supremacy of Islamic law, called the *Shariah* (path of God). Thus, prior to the intrusion of colonialism, many Muslims assumed that they lived in an Islamic state. Since religious Muslims believe that God wants them to live in a community governed in accordance with the Quran (or Koran, divinely revealed law, much of it temporal), the very concept of separating church and state is alien to their culture. This does not mean that traditional Islamic culture and theology were inhospitable to other religions. Perhaps because it accepted Jewish and Christian scriptures and drew from both of those religions since its inception, Islam was often highly tolerant of other faiths. During the Middle Ages, for example, the large Jewish community in Muslim-controlled Spain enjoyed perhaps its greatest period of freedom and influence anywhere in Europe.[22] But even then, ultimate political authority remained Muslim.

The bond between Islam and politics remains strong in most Muslim societies today, though there is considerable variation. John Esposito distinguishes three types of Islamic regimes: the secular state, the Islamic state, and the Muslim state.[23] Turkey is perhaps the most noted *secular state* in the Islamic world. Starting in the 1920s, Mustafa Kemal Ataturk (the father of modern Turkey) ousted the sultan of the Ottoman empire, abolished the basis of the sultan's religious authority, emancipated women, closed seminaries, and westernized Turkish society in many ways. Today, Turkey is not fully secularized because its constitution still endorses belief in God, but the political system offers Islam no special status and, in fact, prohibits certain traditional Islamic practices.[24]

During the 1980s and 1990s, however, an Islamic political party, the Refah (Welfare) Party, steadily gained strength, particularly among residents of Turkey's urban slums, who had migrated from the countryside to large cities and had found modern, secular culture difficult, corrupt, and oppressive. As its name indicates, the Welfare Party gained considerable support among the poor by offering them social services that the government had failed to provide. In the 1995 parliamentary elections, Refah won the largest number of seats, setting off a frantic effort by Turkey's other major parties to exclude it from power. When those parties were unable to put together a stable governing coalition, Refah formed the new government. Despite its sometimes radical and inflammatory rhetoric, the Welfare Party's policies in office were relatively moderate when compared to those of many other Islamic parties in the region. Still, its program of religious reforms—including a proposed amendment eliminating the constitutional ban on religious dress so as to allow female students to cover their hair with scarves at school—was unacceptable to the powerful Turkish military, which views itself as the guardian of the country's secular tradition. In 1998, the military forced parliament to remove the Welfare Party from office and dissolve it as a legal political party.[25]

At the other end of the spectrum, *Islamic states* base their governing philosophies on the Quran and other Islamic law. Afghanistan (under the Taliban), Iran, and Saudi Arabia are among the best-known examples, but Sudan, Pakistan, and Libya also fall in this category. These regimes can be quite distinct from each other. Whereas Iran subscribes to Shi'a Islam, the other countries are primarily Sunni. Islamic regimes in Afghanistan (before U.S. intervention), Libya, Iran, and Sudan have pursued militantly anti-Western foreign policies and have supported terrorism, while Saudi Arabia is quite conservative and closely allied to the West (though, for strategic reasons, it has often tried to appease Al Qaeda and other radical Islamist groups). Thus, the term *Islamic state* (like the concept of fundamentalism) must be used carefully to avoid creating artificial categories that hide more than they reveal.

Finally, *Muslim states*, such as Egypt and Morocco, occupy an intermediate position on church-state relations and the role of religion. Unlike secular states, they identify Islam as the official religion and require the head of state to be Muslim. However, the impact of religion on politics is far more limited than in Islamic states. For example, unlike Taliban Afghanistan and contemporary Iran, political leaders are not clerics, and some are even non-Muslims. In Iraq and Egypt, Christians have served as foreign ministers and deputy foreign ministers (most notably, Egypt's Boutros Boutros-Ghali, who later served as secretary general of the United Nations), and many of the founders of Syria's ruling Baath party were Christians. Christians also occupy high posts in the Palestinian Authority.

Catholicism

More than any other major religion, Catholicism has a well-defined and hierarchical ecclesiastical structure that enables it to have a great impact on the political order. At the Church's apex is the Pope, whose authority is unchallenged and whose pronouncements on matters of faith and morals are believed to be infallible. Consequently, papal declarations can carry considerable political weight. For example, many of the twentieth-century, Catholic-based reform movements in Latin America can be traced to Pope Leo XIII's 1891 encyclical, *Rerum Novarum*, which included an indictment of early capitalism's exploitation of the working class. Within each country, the Church hierarchy is headed by bishops, who often have tremendous political influence in Latin America and in Catholic countries such as the Philippines.

Like Islam in the Middle East, Catholicism used to be the state religion in most Latin American countries. For example, in Colombia as recently as 1953, government treaties with the Vatican gave the Church special authority in areas such as education.[26] Over the years, however, most Latin American nations either ceased having an official state religion or have rendered that link unimportant. Still, Church doctrine has generally supported the established political regime and helped legitimize it. "The ruling powers," said one encyclical, "are invested with a sacredness more than human. ... Obedience is not the servitude of man to man, but submission to the will of God."[27]

That does not mean, however, that the Church has always supported the government. Over the years, there have been periodic clashes between the two, most notably when the state challenged Church authority in areas such as education. In the Philippines, Church support of Corazón Aquino's political reform movement helped topple the dictatorship of Ferdinand Marcos. Similarly,

Catholic authorities opposed conservative military dictatorships in Brazil and Chile during the 1970s and 1980s. Church relationships with Marxist regimes in Cuba and Nicaragua were often tense, though relations with Castro's government improved substantially since the Pope's visit to Cuba.[28] And in El Salvador, Archbishop Romero spoke out forcefully against the regime's severe human-rights violations in the 1980s. Shortly after one of his most powerful pronouncements, Romero was assassinated by the military. In other countries, however, the local hierarchy has been far more cautious about criticizing the government.

Hinduism and Buddhism

Asia's organic religions, Hinduism and Buddhism, generally have been less directly involved in politics than have Catholicism and Islam. (India's powerful BJP, a Hindu party, is not a part of the Hindu religious order.) Of course, Hinduism's cultural and philosophical values, most notably the caste system, have affected Indian and Nepalese politics profoundly. For example, the king of Nepal is worshiped as the incarnation of the god Vishnu.[29] But the religion is so diverse, composed of local religious groups, cults, and sects loosely tied together by a common set of beliefs, that there is no centralized political influence. Moreover, although there are gurus, holy men, temple priests, and even a priestly caste (Brahmans, though most of them no longer choose to be priests), there is no ecclesiastical organization.

Buddhism grew out of the Hindu religion in the sixth century B.C.E., emerging from the teachings of a Nepalese prince, Siddhartha Gautama, who later came to be known as the Buddha (Enlightened One). Though greatly influenced by Hinduism, Buddhism rejects one of its basic tenets, the caste system. Indeed, as Buddhism spread through Asia, one of its great appeals was its egalitarian outlook. Today, many of India's untouchables continue to leave Hinduism for Buddhism, a religion far more hospitable to them.[30] Buddhism differs from Hinduism in having an organized ecclesiastical organization, namely the *sangha* (the monastic orders). In some countries, such as Myanmar, each sangha has its own leader, providing a hierarchical structure. Still, when compared to the Roman Catholic Church or the mullahs of Shi'a Islam, Buddhism's religious structure is less centralized and, thus, less able to impact the political system.

To be sure, Buddhist and Hindu groups sometimes have strongly influenced their nation's politics. During the early 1960s, Burma was declared a Buddhist state, though that was terminated after a few years. Protests led by Buddhist monks during that decade also helped topple three successive South Vietnamese leaders in a short period of time.[31] Monks have led major protests against government human-rights violations in Tibet, Myanmar, and Thailand as well. The modern liberator of India, Mahatma Gandhi, drew upon reformist Hindu theology when demanding greater equality for untouchables and the lower castes.

In addition to having less-hierarchically organized ecclesiastical orders, Eastern religions are less theologically oriented toward political involvement than are Catholicism and Islam. Their otherworldly philosophy places less emphasis on such temporal matters as politics; hence, the remainder of this chapter focuses more heavily on the political impact of Islam and Catholicism in the Third World.

RELIGIOUS FUNDAMENTALISM: ISLAM AND HINDUISM

No manifestation of religious influence on Third World politics has attracted more attention or inspired more fear and loathing than Islamic fundamentalism. In the 1980s and early 1990s, highly influential Washington columnists such as *U.S. News and World Report*'s Morton Zuckerman and the *New Republic*'s Charles Krauthammer have warned of "religious Stalinism" and a fanatical international movement orchestrated from Iran.[32] Nor are such concerns limited to Westerners. They are frequently expressed by the leaders of moderate Muslim nations who find themselves under siege from militant fundamentalists. Thus, for example, Tunisia's President, Zine el-Abidine Ben Ali, cautioned about a "fundamentalist international" financed by Iran and Sudan.[33]

The horrific September 11, 2001, plane hijackings and attacks on the World Trade Center and the Pentagon confirmed the world's worst nightmares about Islamic fundamentalist terrorism. However, most experts on Islam maintain that it is unfair to blame a major world religion that has hundreds of millions of adherents for the actions of a small minority. President George W. Bush and other leading U.S. government officials went out of their way to make that very point in the days after the attack. Some people have noted that blaming the Islamic religion for Osama bin Laden's actions would suggest that we should hold Christianity responsible for violent actions taken in the name of that religion. Recall that David Koresh and the Branch Davidians in Waco, Texas, claimed to be acting in the name of Christianity, as did "pro-life" extremists who assassinated doctors or bombed abortion clinics, killing workers inside.

Others scholars further argue that not all Islamic fundamentalists support violence. Indeed, many scholars reject the very term *fundamentalism* to describe current militant revivals. The word, they charge, may falsely imply the existence of a unified threat to the West and, in the case of Islam, it lumps together groups and regimes that have little in common, such as conservative Saudi Arabia and radical Libya. Instead, these analysts prefer such terms as *revivalism* or *militancy* or *Islamist movements* rather than Islamic fundamentalism.[34] Still, a number of leading authorities accept and even use the label *fundamentalism* in their writings.[35] Fred Halliday notes that "there are some problems with applying the term fundamentalist to Muslim movements, but with the necessary caveats it can legitimately be so used."[36] In this chapter I use *fundamentalism* because of its common usage in contemporary political discourse. On occasion, however, I employ the term *revivalism* interchangeably (referring to the desire to revive the true faith) or use *Islamism* to refer to Islamic fundamentalism.

Semantic questions aside, experts such as John Esposito and Fred Halliday warn that whatever labels they use, Western writers too often distort and exaggerate the nature of the "Islamic threat."[37] Many of these critics also seem unaware of a long tradition of liberal theology within Islam that has advocated religious tolerance, progress for women, and democratic values.[38]

> At the very core of this supposed challenge or conflict lie confusions: the mere fact of peoples being "Islamic" ... [has been confused] with that of their adhering to beliefs and policies that are ... "Islamist" or "fundamentalist." It has been assumed ... that most Muslims seek to impose a political program supposedly derived from their religion. The fact that most Muslims are not supporters of Islamist movements is obscured.[39]

Clearly, the recent upsurge in Islamist terrorism in Israel, the United States, and other parts of the world (including the September 11 attacks) indicates that though it is wrong, as Esposito and Halliday insist, to speak of an "Islamic threat," it is reasonable to speak of an "Islamic *fundamentalist* threat." Hopefully, this chapter's discussion of Islamic (as well as Hindu) fundamentalism conveys that distinction. When I discuss Islamic and Hindu revivalism at some length, two caveats should be kept in mind: most Muslims and Hindus are not fundamentalists, and not all fundamentalists are repressive at home or violent abroad.

Defining and Explaining Fundamentalism

> Fundamentalism is the ... effort to define the fundamentals of a religious system and adhere to them. One of the cardinal tenets of Islamic fundamentalism is to protect the purity of Islamic precepts from the adulteration of speculative exercises. Related to [Islamic] fundamentalism is ... revival or resurgence, a renewed interest in Islam. Behind all this is a drive to purify Islam in order to release all its vital force.[40]

The precise meaning of fundamentalism varies somewhat from religion to religion.[41] But revivalists do share certain points of view across religions. To begin with, they all wish to preserve their religion's traditional worldview and resist the efforts of religious liberals to reform it. They also desire to revive the role of religion in private and public life, including politics, lifestyle, and dress.

In the developing world, fundamentalism often appeals particularly to people who are disgusted by the inequalities and injustices in their country's political-economic system. This disgust reflects popular revulsion against local political and economic elites, against pervasive corruption and repression. In Lebanon the radical Hizbullah grew out of Shi'a resentment against the economically powerful Christian community, as well as anger against Israel and the West. In India, the BJP attracted much of its support from voters (including some non-Hindus) embittered by government corruption. And in Algeria, Egypt, and the Sudan, militant fundamentalists expanded their support as a result of the government repression directed against them.[42]

Radical, Islamic fundamentalists also tend to be nationalist or chauvinistic, rejecting "outside" influences they feel challenge or pollute their culture and their true faith. Western culture is perceived as particularly deleterious, with its immodest dress, films, and music that allegedly promote promiscuous sex, drugs, and the like. But Western values are rejected for another reason. For years government leaders such as the Shah of Iran and Egypt's President Anwar Sadat promoted Western-style modernization as the route to national development. After decades of failed development in the Middle East, North Africa, and other parts of the Third World, however, many of those regions' citizens feel that they were deceived and must look elsewhere for answers to their problems.

Fundamentalists: Radical and Conservative

Finally, a distinction must be made between radical and conservative fundamentalists. Radicals, inspired by a "sacred rage," feel that they are conducting a "holy war" against forces that threaten to corrupt their fundamental religious values.[43] As a Hizbullah manifesto declared, "We have risen to liberate our country, to drive the imperialists and the invaders out of it and to take our fate in our own hands."[44] Holy war was first waged by Islamic mujahideen in Afghanistan against the country's Soviet occupiers as well as the Afghan Marxist government, which Soviet troops defended.[45] Iran's Ayatollah Khomeini and Osama bin Laden both declared *jihads* (holy wars) against the United States ("the great Satan"). Elsewhere, the battle has been waged against internal enemies as well. Having been denied an almost certain electoral victory in 1992 (the military canceled the elections after the first round), Algeria's fundamentalist Islamic Salvation Front (FIS) attacked the nation's armed forces, police, and secular politicians, as well as foreigners.[46] More violent militants, most notably the Armed Islamic Group (GIA), also launched massive terrorist attacks on civilians, often mixing banditry with religious warfare. From 1992 through early 2001, more than 100,000 people were killed either by armed Islamic groups or by the Algerian military and its allied civilian militias, which reacted with equal savagery. In India, Hindu fundamentalists have periodically directed their rage against the country's Muslim minority. (For a more detailed discussion of the massive communal violence between Hindus and Muslims in the post-independence period, see Chapter 4.) Because these are perceived to be holy wars against a grave threat, religious militants feel justified in attacking their Muslim neighbors in India, or killing 3,000 people in New York City, or bombing civilians in Iraq.

Such radical militancy contrasts with the views and behavior of conservative fundamentalists, including Hasidic Jews and Saudi Arabian princes, who do not envision themselves in such a battle. They too wish to shield their flocks from unwanted outside influences, but they do not view adherents of other religions or nonfundamentalist members of their own faith as enemies.[47]

In recent years, radical Islamic fundamentalists have become a major political force in Middle Eastern and North African countries such as Algeria, Lebanon, and Sudan. Afghanistan's Taliban government was perhaps the world's most rigidly fundamentalist; for example, prohibiting girls and women from attending school or being employed, and banning television, sports, and dancing. They also sheltered Osama bin Laden and his Al Qaeda terrorist group. Until the 1990s and the emergence of Al Qaeda's onto the world scene, however, nowhere did radical Islamic fundamentalism have a greater international impact than in Iranian revolution, which served as a beacon for other revivalist movements in various parts of the Muslim world.

"Sacred Rage and the Iranian Revolution": Radical Fundamentalism as a Reaction to Western-Style Modernization

The origins of the Iranian revolution can be traced to the early decades of the twentieth century, in the Muslim clergy's continuing resistance to secular modernization imposed by the royal family.[48] Military, political, and economic intervention by a series of foreign powers—Czarist Russia, Britain, and finally, the United States—turned the country into "a virtual protectorate" and made the ruling Shahs (emperors) appear to be tools of the great powers.[49] Thus, resentment against foreign domination was later to become an important component of the Islamic revolution.

During the 1920s and 1930s, Shah Reza Khan antagonized the Muslim mullahs (clergy) with a series of reforms.[50] Influenced both by the West and the secularization of Turkey, he prohibited the veiling of women, opened all public places to women, required Western dress for both sexes, limited the mullahs' economic resources, and established state control over schools, courts, and taxes that previously had been controlled by the clergy. This secularization of society and its accompanying diminution of Islamic power inspired the quiet opposition of a popular young mullah, Ruhollah Khomeini.

In the decades after he assumed the royal throne in 1941, Shah Mohammad Reza Pahlavi accelerated his father's policies, funneling the country's massive oil wealth into one of the Third World's most ambitious modernization programs. In 1963, prodded by the United States, he launched a "White Revolution" involving land reform, expanded literacy, voting rights for women, and other socioeconomic reforms. In the United States, the Shah was hailed as a progressive modernizer. Indeed, only two years before the Islamic revolution ousted the Shah, then-President Jimmy Carter visited Iran and praised the monarch for establishing "an island of stability in one of the more troubled areas of the world."[51]

To be sure, the land reform had benefited some three million peasants, education had expanded greatly, and oil wealth had doubled the size of the middle class.[52] And by 1976, Iran had the highest GNP per capita in the developing world. At the same time, however, the gap between rich and poor had widened, and the government was widely resented for its corruption and brutality. Even many Iranians who had gained economically felt psychologically wounded by the pace of Westernization. The Shah was widely viewed as a tool of American neocolonialism. The mullahs, supported by other religious Muslims, objected to the erosion of their political influence, the progressive secularization of society, and the decline of traditional values. Together with many urban merchants, middle-class nationalists, and students, they resented the political influence of the American government and Western petroleum companies. Like Afghanistan's Taliban government and Al Qaeda, which followed them, the Iranian mullahs despised globalization, the spread of Western political and economic power, and, perhaps most of all, Western cultural values.

In the early 1960s, as tension between the government and the clergy intensified, Ruhollah Khomeini became one of the Shah's most acerbic critics. When he was briefly imprisoned in 1964, riots broke out in a number of cities, culminating in the massacre of up to 10,000 demonstrators by the Shah's army.[53] Khomeini was sent into exile for nearly 15 years. The effect was to turn him into a martyr in a culture that especially admires martyrdom, thereby greatly enhancing his influence over the masses. By 1978 a substantial segment of Iran's urban population was involved in strikes and demonstrations against the regime. Finally, in January 1979, the Shah went into exile amid growing mass unrest. Khomeini returned home to a frenzied welcome shortly thereafter. By then he had achieved the rank of Grand Ayatollah, the most exalted level of religious interpreters in the Shi'a clergy.[54]

Like many new revolutionary regimes, Iran's turned increasingly radical in its early stage.[55] Over the years, three interrelated developments set the tone for the Islamic revolution. First was the merger of the country's religious and political leadership. The new "Islamic republic," declared the Grand Ayatollah, was "the government of God."[56] While nonclerical figures have held a significant number of government posts since then, including most members of parliament, ultimate power resides in the hands of the Revolutionary Council (a body of hard -line Islamist clerics), which often overrules both the parliament and the president.[57]

The second important development has been the revival of traditional Islamic observances. Women must be veiled in public and are strongly encouraged to wear the *chador*, the shapeless shroud that conceals all parts of the body. Highly intrusive Revolutionary Guards penetrated all aspects of Iranian life, policing possible violations of Islamic behavior (as defined by the mullahs). In the first years of the Revolution (into the early 1990s) the Guards joined with neighborhood vigilante committees to arrest or harass Iranians who violated the clerics' highly conservative Islamic standards. During the 1980s, in the Shi'a tradition of martyrdom, thousands of young volunteers died in a holy war against Saddam Hussein's Iraq. Assuring their families that it is a privilege to die for the faith, the Ayatollah Khomeini proclaimed, "We should sacrifice all our loved ones for the sake of Islam. If we are killed, we have performed our duty."[58]

Finally, Iran's radical revivalism embraced an aggressive foreign policy that encompassed support for kindred radical groups abroad, such as Lebanon's Hizbullah, and a burning hostility toward foreign powers that are perceived as enemies of Islam—especially, Israel and the Western powers. Prior to the revolution, Khomeini had declared, "America is worse than Britain! Britain is worse than America! The Soviet Union is worse than both of them! They are all worse and more unclean than each other!"[59] The regime's hostility toward the outside world was best illustrated by two events. On November 4, 1979, revolutionary students seized the U.S. embassy in Tehran, taking diplomats and embassy staff hostage in an extraordinary breach of diplomatic protocol.[60] While the Iranian regime claimed that the students had acted independently, no one doubted that the government was capable of releasing the hostages any time it chose. It was not until 444 days later that the last of the 52 hostages was released. That event, as well as Iran's subsequent support for terrorist groups in the Middle East, and its clandestine nuclear weapons program, has made it an international pariah.

For the Iranian people, however, a second manifestation of their country's radical foreign policy—a prolonged war against Iraq (1980–1988)—was far more tragic. The war had multiple origins, most of them unrelated to religion. The most proximate cause was a long-standing border dispute. Also at play, however, was Iran's support for Iraq's repressed Shi'a population, as well as each government's desire to lead the Gulf region. Once the conflict began, "both sides ... portrayed the war as a noble crusade: Iraq (governed by Saddam Hussein) as a historic defense of Arab sovereignty ... against the marauding Persians; Iran as a holy war against the [Iraqi] infidels."[61] Ironically, during the early years of the war, the United States supported Saddam against its common Iranian enemy. Before the war finally ground to a halt in 1988 with no victor, it had inflicted grave damage on the Iranian economy and cost the country several hundred thousand lives. Even then, Khomeini, who had vowed to pursue the battle until Saddam was toppled, only reluctantly agreed to the truce, which he called "more deadly than taking poison."[62]

Since Khomeini's death at the end of the 1980s, the Islamic revolution has moderated somewhat. The Revolutionary Guard has relaxed its grip on daily life; fewer women now wear the chador; students openly violate Muslim orthodoxy; in the secrecy of their homes, middle-class Iranians dance to Western music at social gatherings and women shed their veils; and the country has retreated from its aggressive foreign policy.[63] In recent years, the Iranian people have twice elected a reformist president, Mohammad Khatami, who is bent on moderating the revolution and increasing individual liberties. Reformers for a period also had a majority in parliament. Until now, however, both the president and parliament have been stymied by the hard -line Revolutionary Council and the military. Still, many observers feel that, in time, an increasingly assertive population will force the Islamist *mullahs* to moderate their rule.

While Iran's official brand of Islam has struck Westerners as extreme, it has not been nearly as fanatical as the Taliban's later interpretation in neighboring Afghanistan. For example, while the Taliban regime prohibited girls and women from schools and the workplace, the Iranian Islamist regime (even in its most militant stage) has sharply raised female literacy and has generally allowed women to pursue their careers. Interestingly, both Islamist hard-liners and aspiring reformers in the Iranian government strongly opposed the Taliban government in neighboring Afghanistan, as Iran armed and supported anti-Taliban guerrillas. While the reasons for that hostility are related to Taliban persecution of Shi'a Muslims in Afghanistan (and not doctrinal differences), the split demonstrates that there is no united front, even among militant Islamic fundamentalists.

Al Qaeda and Militant Islamic Fundamentalism

As Iran has somewhat moderated its hostility toward the West, international attention on Islamic fundamentalism has focused on the Al Qaeda terrorist network. Although government intelligence agencies, the media, and scholars have revealed a great deal about that organization (and its leader, Osama bin Laden), many aspects of its objectives, religious beliefs, organization, and activity remain unclear. Because of Al Qaeda's secretive nature and its links to a religious tradition little understood in the West, a number of analysts have waged heated debates about its nature.[64] Much of the controversy—particularly as it relates to the war on terrorism—lies outside the scope of this chapter. What we focus on, instead, is the origin of this terrorist network, its relationship with Islamic religious beliefs, and its level of support among the world's Muslims.

Defeating the Soviet Infidels in Afghanistan (1979–1989) Although founded in 1988, Al Qaeda's roots can be traced back to 1979, with the Islamic Revolution in Iran and the Soviet invasion of Afghanistan. The victory of the Iranian mullahs heartened Islamic fundamentalists anxious to challenge Western-style modernization and to oust Muslim national leaders whom they perceived as corrupt and not sufficiently pious. At the same time, despite their common enemy, the tensions and distrust between Iran's Shi'a government and the jihadist Sunnis directing Al Qaeda limited relations between the two. As we have seen, for example, Iran opposed Al Qaeda's Taliban protectors in Afghanistan.

A more powerful event spurring bin Laden and his associates was the Soviet Union's occupation of Afghanistan, aimed at shoring up that country's unpopular communist regime.[65] As religiously motivated Afghan *mujahideen* (a name literally meaning "strugglers" but referring specifically to guerrilla holy warriors in Afghanistan and other countries) began their resistance to the

Soviet occupation, they were joined by a growing number of foreign volunteers drawn largely from the Middle East. Among the earliest arrivals was Osama bin Laden, the Saudi-born son of a self-made, construction tycoon. Under the influence of his mentor at that time, Dr. Abdullah Azzam, a Palestinian, Islamist leader bin Laden used his enormous wealth, international contacts, and magnetic personality to recruit large numbers of foreign volunteers. Ironically, the mujahideen, particularly their Afghan core, also received support and encouragement from their future enemies, the Saudi and U.S. governments.

In 1984, Azzam and bin Laden established the Afghan Service Bureau (MAK)–later to form the base of Al Qaeda—which

> played a decisive role in the anti-Soviet resistance. ... In addition to recruiting, indoctrinating and training thousands of Arab and [other] Muslim youths from countries ranging from the US to the Philippines, MAK distributed $200 million of [the] Middle Eastern and Western, mainly American and British, aid destined for the Afghan *jihad.* Osama also channeled substantial resources of his own to the cause, a gesture that resonated with his fighters, raising his own credibility.[66]

Ultimately, foreign mujahideen (primarily Saudis, Egyptians, Yeminis, and Algerians) came to number between 25,000 and 50,000 fighters who helped their 200,000 or more Afghan counterparts in forcing the Soviet military withdrawal from Afghanistan in 1989.[67] Only a year earlier, Abdullah Azzam, bin Laden, and Ayman Muhammad al-Zawahiri (an Egyptian physician who led one of that country's most infamous terrorist groups) created Al Qaeda, built largely out of MAK and two Egyptian, Islamist terrorist organizations. Soon thereafter, Azzam and his two sons were killed in a bomb explosion in Pakistan, Al Qaeda's base at the time. Bin Laden assumed undisputed leadership of the organization, with al-Zawahiri as his chief ideologist.[68]

Fighting Another Super Power The United States with the Soviets vanquished and many of the "Arab Afghans" (as the Middle-Eastern volunteers were called) returning home, bin Laden and al-Zawahiri looked for new worlds to conquer. So, they embraced a struggle that far exceeded their first objective of defending an Islamic nation against conquest by infidels (those who do not believe in Islam). In their expanded jihad, they vowed to topple religiously derelict Islamic regimes in countries such as Egypt and Indonesia, and to support the struggles of Muslims against non-Islamic governments in countries or regions such as the Philippines, Chechnya (Russia), and Kashmir (India). Finally, the mujahideens' unanticipated victory over the Soviets in Afghanistan convinced Al Qaeda's leaders that they were also capable of defeating the world's only remaining superpower, the United States.

A number of factors spurred Al Qaeda's hostility toward the United States. First was American support for Israel, a nation reviled in the Arab world for its control of Jerusalem (holy to the Muslim world) and for its occupation of the Palestinian homeland. Second, they blamed the United States for propping up corrupt and despotic Muslim regimes in Egypt, the Gulf states, and elsewhere—regimes that many Islamists considered to be heretics. Finally, like most Islamic fundamentalists, bin Laden and Al Qaeda despised the West's secular values and its perceived moral decay.

Iraq's invasion of Kuwait and the ensuing Gulf War brought a major turning point for Al Qaeda. Following the Iraqi invasion, bin Laden offered Al Qaeda's troops to Saudi Arabia's King Fahd—a close friend of bin Laden's father and a major supporter of the mujahideen in Afghanistan—to protect the kingdom and its sacred Muslim cities against Saddam Hussein's military (Saddam was a secular leader whom bin Laden despised). When the king refused the offer and turned, instead, to the United States and the West for protection, bin Laden was outraged. His rage intensified after the Gulf War when U.S. troops remained in Saudi Arabia in close proximity to the Moslem holy places of Mecca and Medina. "The presence of infidels on Arabian sacred soil was too much for ... bin Laden to bear."[69] By 1994, his relationship with his former supporter, the Saudi government, had deteriorated to the point where the Saudis revoked his citizenship.[70]

From 1989 to 1991, as Al Qaeda's relations with the Pakistani government also deteriorated, bin Laden took over 1,000 of his most radical and battle-trained supporters to Sudan, an African nation bordering on the Muslim regions in the Horn of Africa as well as Egypt. Now they were much closer to the Middle East, the primary interest of most mujahideen. Sudan's fundamentalist regime welcomed them and the financial resources that bin Laden brought. The dispatch of 25,000 American troops into strife-torn Somalia ("Operation Restore Hope"), to establish order and undertake famine relief (1992–1993), reinforced bin Laden's determination to protect Muslim nations such as this against Western intervention.[71] Three years later, as U.S. pressure forced Sudan to expel Al Qaeda, bin Laden moved his forces back to Afghanistan. There they were protected by their allies, the Taliban government, until the United States ousted that regime in 2001, following the 9/11 attack.

Western intelligence agencies were slow to understand that an international terror network, Al Qaeda, existed. And even today experts differ sharply over questions such as the extent of its involvement in a several high-profile terrorist strikes and how much top-down control bin Laden and his lieutenants exert over many of its tactical operations. There is general agreement, however, that bin Laden and Al Qaeda were directly or indirectly responsible for the following: the 1993 truck-bombing of the World Trade Center in New York; the attack on the American military barracks (Kobar Towers) in Saudi Arabia (1996); the nearly simultaneous bombing of the U.S. embassies in Tanzania and Kenya, which killed 258 people and wounded more than 5,000 (1998); the attack on the naval ship, USS *Cole* in the port of Aden (2000); the 9/11 assault on the World Trade Center and the Pentagon, which killed some 3,000 people, and, most likely, an intended attack on the White House or the Capitol by a fourth hijacked plane that crashed in Pennsylvania (2001); the bombing of a nightclub in Bali (Indonesia), (2002); the bombing of commuter trains in Madrid, (2004); subway and bus bombings in London (2005); and many of the suicide bombings in Iraq.

Still, many experts view it, not as a centrally controlled, tight-knit unit whose every move is controlled by bin Laden and al-Zawahiri, but as a loosely linked network of organizations, many of which operate independently as "terrorist entrepreneurs" who come to Al Qaeda (the name means "the base"or "base of operation") for financial or logistical support. In the words of one analyst:

> Although bin Laden and his partners ... create[d] a structure ... that attracted new recruits and forged links among preexisting Islamic militant groups, they never

created a coherent terrorist network. ... Instead, Al Qaeda functioned like a venture capital firm—providing funding, contacts, and expert advice to many different militant groups and individuals from all over the Islamic world.[72]

The destruction of Al Qaeda's home in Afghanistan and the death or capture of many of its leaders since 2001 have furthered decentralization. "Some analysts have suggested that the word *Al Qaeda* is now used to refer to a variety of groups connected by little more than shared aims, ideals and methods." In the eyes of many experts, such as Britain's International Institute of Strategic Studies, this has made it even more elusive. "more insidious [than] and just as dangerous" as it was at the time of 9/11.[73]

Support for bin Laden Al Qaeda's Ideology and Islamic Theology in the aftermath of the 9/11 tragedy, it may be shocking to learn that Osama bin Laden still enjoys considerable support in the Muslim world. For example, media reports have described the popularity of Osama T-shirts in countries such as Jordan and Indonesia and noted frequent instances of newborns named after him in Pakistan and other Islamic nations. To be sure, a Gallup opinion poll of Muslim countries conducted one year after 9/11 found that a majority of respondents in eight of the nine surveyed nations condemned the attack.[74] Yet, results of a 2004 survey conducted by the respected Pew Research Center for the People and the Press revealed that almost two-thirds of Pakistanis (65%) and approximately half the populations of Jordan (55%) and Morocco (45%) viewed bin Laden favorably.[75]

Many respondents could reconcile these seemingly contradictory attitudes since in five of the nine Islamic countries a majority didn't believe that Al Qaeda or any Arab group was really behind the September 11 events. Instead, many claimed that the American or Israeli governments had staged the attack in order to pin the blame on Al Qaeda and the Taliban government. For that or other reasons, most Muslims—89 percent of Indonesians, 80 percent of Pakistanis, and 69 percent of Kuwaitis—believed that the U.S. invasion of Afghanistan in the wake of 9/11 was "morally unjustifiable."[76] At the same time, however, the Pew survey found that 86 percent of all Jordanians, 74 percent of Moroccans, and 47 percent of Pakistanis felt that suicide attacks on Israelis (including those that kill civilians) *are* justifiable.[77]

Those attitudes persist even though many leading Islamic clerics and scholars maintain that the killing of innocent civilians is not moral or compatible with Islamic values. How well, then, do bin Laden's words and deeds correspond to traditional Islamic beliefs? Sohai H. Hashmi, a scholar of Islamic thought, suggests that there are two relevant questions to be asked: first, "under what circumstances or for what ends is war justified?"—a question also much debated in the Western, Christo-Judaic tradition of "just war." Second, "once war has begun, how may fighting be properly conducted?"[78] That is, what *means* are acceptable to achieve legitimate jihadist goals?

In two major Al Qaeda policy statements (issued in 1996 and 1998), bin Laden and his associates declared a holy war against "the Zionist-Crusader alliance and their collaborators"—i.e., Israel, the Jews, Christians, and Muslim states such as Saudi Arabia, Egypt, Morocco, and Jordan who have ties to the United States. The use of the term *Crusaders* to refer to the West was meant to evoke historical Islamic resentment against the Christian Crusades and contemporary opposition to the presence of American troops in Saudi Arabia, Islamic sacred soil. The 1996 declaration also expressed bitterness over Israel's occupation of Jerusalem. Hashmi argues, the stated *goal* of Al Qaeda's attacks on the West—protecting the Muslim world against the threat of U.S. and Israeli imperialism—is consistent with the long-established Islamic tradition of "defensive jihad" and, therefore, resonates with many mainstream Muslims and clerics. "By declaring that it is willing to take on the world's greatest power in order to redress widely felt injustices [in Saudi Arabia, Israel, and elsewhere], Al Qaeda garners the support of many ordinary Muslims."[79] Other analysts agree that in mainstream Islamic doctrine, "Muslims are enjoined to take up arms against their oppressors, be they local despots or foreign occupiers. Jihad is one of the fundamental duties of a Muslim."[80]

But, Hashimi and others argue, where bin Laden and Al Qaeda clearly fail to adhere to Islamic standards of morality is in the *means* it has adopted to achieve that goal—a willingness to kill innocent civilians including women, children, and elderly men. Bin Laden has justified the killing of civilians by claiming that it is merely reciprocity for what the West has done to the Muslims. Thus, in an October 21, 2001 interview with the Arabic television network, al-Jazeera, he stated, "We will do as they do. If they kill our women and our innocent people, we will kill their women and their innocent people until they stop." But Hashmi draws on Koranic verse, the Prophet Muhammad, and "the vast majority of 'ulama [orthodox Islamic scholars] who have condemned his terrorism" to insist that "the jihad tradition relaxes restrictions on the weapons or methods of warfare in the face of military necessity, but never the principle that civilians are not to be directly targeted." These scholars "cite well-known sayings of Prophet Mohammad that forbid killing the enemy's women and children or burning down their vegetation - what are today known as scorched earth tactics."[81]

Still, despite mainstream Islamic theological objections to its use, terrorism will continue to attract considerable support within the Muslim world as long as its practitioners are a leading voice, perhaps *the* leading voice, against corrupt and repressive Middle-Eastern regimes, against American and Israeli military power, and against the perceived "sinful" aspects of Western culture.

Radical Hindu Fundamentalism

Compared to its Muslim counterpart, Hindu fundamentalism has received scant attention in the West. This is probably because Hinduism is largely confined to one country (India); its leading political voice (the BJP) has only emerged from political obscurity to national leadership in the past 15 years or so; and the party has not pursued an expansionist or anti-Western foreign policy.[82] The BJP itself is divided into factions. Hard -liners take a militant stance and often use inflammatory language against the nation's Muslim minority. Indeed, leaders of India's center and left opposition parties, and many of India's 120 million Muslims, blame that faction for the destruction of a major Muslim mosque in 1992 and for anti-Muslim riots that killed 3,000 people in 1995. On the other hand, BJP moderates and pragmatists who headed the national government recently recognized that the party has nowhere near a parliamentary majority and must cooperate with secular parties and act responsibly if it is to govern. Hence these leaders have preached a form of

Hindu nationalism that stresses broad Indian cultural themes and even opens its arms to Muslims, a small portion of whom vote for the BJP.

But the roots of Hindu revivalism lie in India's communal politics, that is, the tensions between the Hindu majority (more than 80 percent of the country), the Muslim minority (12 percent of the population), and the smaller Sikh population (about 2 percent) (see Chapter 4). During the 1980s, militant Hinduism grew rapidly, partly as a response to the surge of Islamic revivalism in Pakistan and the Middle East. Indeed, Muslim, Sikh, and Hindu fundamentalists all feed on their common hostility toward each other. The rise of fundamentalism of all kinds was indirectly encouraged by politicians from the ruling Congress Party, most notably Prime Minister Indira Gandhi, who played the dangerous game of using communal politics for their own advantage. Another factor that has troubled many Hindus and increased their militancy is the conversion of large numbers of untouchables to Buddhism or Islam. In the eyes of many middle- and higher-caste Hindus, these conversions threaten the caste system, a linchpin of Hinduism. The BJP and other Hindu nationalist groups also gained considerable support among voters disgusted with corruption within the secular parties, such as the powerful Congress Party (though once in office the BJP had its own corruption scandals). BJP strength is rooted in northern India's Hindi-speaking heartland but extends throughout the country, particularly within the urban middle class.

Because Hinduism is a less well-organized religion than Islam and lacks a formal church structure, its fundamentalist beliefs are less clearly spelled out. Nationalism is certainly an important element, specifically the movement's demand that India cease giving legal support to multiculturalism and, instead, define itself as a Hindu nation. Sometimes fundamentalist spokespersons endorse traditional religious practices shunned or prohibited by modern Indian society. For example, some party leaders have defended *sati*, the brutal traditional Hindu practice in which a widow throws herself on her husband's funeral pyre and dies in flames. However, the BJP has several female members of parliament and a number of active women's organizations.

In the absence of an organized Hindu church or clergy, revivalist leadership has been divided between various interest groups and parties, not all of which share the same positions. Furthermore, some groups (including the BJP itself) have changed their positions sharply over time. Two of the most militant groups, the Vishwa Hindu Parishad (VHP) and Shiv Sena, have openly encouraged attacks on Muslim mosques and neighborhoods, most notably in the Hindu strongholds of Uttar Pradesh, Madhya Pradesh, and Bihar states. The political consequences of Hindu-Muslim conflicts can be significant. For example, in 1990 Prime Minister V. P. Singh's government fell when he sent troops to prevent a Hindu mob from tearing down a revered Muslim mosque. The mosque, built on the site where the Hindu god Ram is believed to have been born, is bitterly resented by Hindu militants. Bloody communal riots regarding the site in 1989, 1992, and 2002 left thousands dead.

The majority of India's Hindus rejected the fundamentalist position for many years. The BJP and its predecessor party, the Bharatiya Jana Sangh (BJS), were shunned by the country's secular parties and excluded from national and state coalition governments. Since the mid-1980s, however, the party's electoral support has soared as voters have become increasingly disenchanted with the mainstream secular parties, particularly the once-dominant Congress Party. A 1992 BJP rally in New Delhi calling for limits on Islamic rights attracted one million demonstrators. In its platform, the BJP called for Indian production of nuclear weapons (India has since tested such weapons), limits on foreign investment, greater economic self-sufficiency, and reduced imports. Party leaders also opposed birth control programs and expressed the belief that it is not necessary for peasants and other poor Indians to be literate.[83] After moderating its rhetoric, however, the BJP emerged as the largest party in parliament following the 1996 national elections and headed a new government coalition. Faced with the need to maintain the support of their secular coalition partners, the party's pragmatic leadership generally avoided anti-Muslim positions or other forms of extremism. A BJP-dominated parliamentary coalition ruled much of the time from 1996–2004.

Under BJP leader, Prime Minister Atal Behari Vajpayee, India—like Pakistan, its longtime Muslim neighbor and antagonist—developed nuclear weapons, a fulfillment of the party's program. At times their decades-old conflict over Kashmir (a region populated primarily by Muslims but ruled by India) seemed to bring these two nuclear antagonists perilously close to the brink of war. When a December 2001 suicide attack on India's parliament (only three months after 9/11) by Islamic Kashmiri militants, allegedly based in neighboring Pakistan, killed twelve people, relations between the two nations took a particularly hostile turn However, in 2003 Pakistani President Pervez Musharraf, under pressure from the United States in the war on terrorism and threatened by Islamic extremists in his own country, pledged to contain Kashmiri guerrilla attacks on India. Soon, in a startling turn of events, Musharraf and Prime Minister Vajpayee began a dramatic series of confidence-building diplomatic moves and public relations gestures (including a cricket match between the two nations). With surprisingly strong public support in both their countries, both leaders moved toward an historic rapprochement. That peace offensive continued after the BJP was voted out of office in 2004 because of discontent over its economic policies. Thus, just as U.S. President Richard Nixon, previously known for his hard -line anticommunist views, opened up the door for relations with Communist China, Vajpayee's Hindu nationalist party may have opened the door for peace with Pakistan. Still, differences between the two countries regarding Kashmir remain unresolved and fundamentalist groups in both countries (Muslim and Hindu) continue to oppose any compromise settlement.

THE PROGRESSIVE CATHOLIC CHURCH

At roughly the same time that many Muslims and Hindus were turning in a reactionary direction (starting in the 1970s), important sectors of Latin America's Catholic Church were embarking on a progressive path. From the time of Spanish colonialism through the first half of the twentieth century, the Church had supported the political and economic status quo, thereby legitimizing Latin America's elite-based governments. In a region marked by a high concentration of income and wealth, the Church was often a majorland owner. Alienated by the anticlerical sentiments of European and Latin American liberals, it usually allied with conservative political factions.

In the decades after World War II, however, that pattern began to change dramatically among important portions of the clergy, particularly at the parish level. The process of change accelerated greatly in the 1960s, when Pope John XXIII moved the "Church universal" in a far more liberal direction, placing greater emphasis on social concerns. "The Second Vatican Council [convened by Pope John between 1962 and 1965] moved international Catholicism from a generally conservative and even authoritarian position to one that supported democracy, human rights and social justice."[84] Catholics were encouraged to address social issues and to enter into a political dialogue with liberals and even leftists.

In 1968, the Latin American Bishops Conference (CELAM) met in Medellín, Colombia, to apply the lessons of Vatican II to their own region. Boldly challenging the status quo, their ideas reflected the influences of the reformist and radical theologians who represented the "progressive church."[85] The themes of dependency and liberation of Latin America's oppressed poor echoed through many of CELAM's pronouncements. The clergy, said the bishops, must heed the "deafening cry ... from the throats of millions asking their pastors for a liberation that reaches them from nowhere else." To do so, the Church must "effectively give preference to the poorest and the most needy sectors." In short, an institution historically allied with the region's power elite was now to be the Church of the poor.[86]

The Medellín conference must be understood in the broader context of political change that was shaking Latin America at the time. In 1959, the triumph of Cuba's revolutionaries spotlighted the poverty and oppression afflicting so much of Latin America. The far-reaching educational, health, and land reforms being carried out in Cuba impressed and radicalized many Catholics. In Colombia, Father Camilo Torres had left the priesthood to join a guerrilla movement three years before the conference. He was soon killed by counterinsurgency forces, thereby becoming a hero to leftists throughout Latin America.[87] Elsewhere in Latin America, few priests or nuns became involved in an armed struggle. Many, however, organized and politicized the poor and accepted important elements of Marxist political and economic analysis.

Though always a minority within the Church, leftist clergy had an important influence in Central America during the 1970s and 1980s, most notably in Nicaragua, El Salvador, and Guatemala.[88] Many Nicaraguan priests and nuns actively supported the Sandinista revolution in the 1970s. When the Sandinistas came to power, Father Miguel D'Escoto was named foreign minister, Jesuit priest Xavier Gorostiaga was appointed head of national planning, Father Ernesto Cardenal served as minister of culture, and his brother, Father Fernando Cardenal, became director of the national adult literacy campaign and was subsequently named minister of education. No government in Latin America has had nearly the number of priests in its cabinet as did Nicaragua's Marxist revolutionary government.

For most of Latin America, however, the 1960s and 1970s were not years of revolution. Instead, much of the region was governed by right-wing military dictatorships. Reacting to a perceived radical threat, repressive military regimes replaced civilian democracies in Brazil, Argentina, Chile, and Uruguay. At the same time, armed-forces rule continued in much of Central America and the central Andes, where democratic traditions had never been strong.

Ironically, right-wing repression spurred the growth of the progressive Church more than the Cuban or Nicaraguan revolutions had.

Not surprisingly, radical clergy and laity were outspoken in their criticism of the military regimes and, consequently, suffered severe reprisals. Dozens of priests and nuns were murdered and many more persecuted in Brazil, El Salvador, and Guatemala. In El Salvador, for example, a far-right death squad called the White Warriors distributed handbills reading, "Be a Patriot, Kill a Priest."[89] But such repression only brought more moderate Catholic figures into the opposition. "When committed Catholics were imprisoned, tortured, and even killed, bishops in a significant number of cases then denounced the state, setting off a spiral of greater repression against the Church, followed by new Church denunciations of authoritarianism."[90]

In Chile, Brazil, El Salvador, and Peru, the Church became a leading critic of government human-rights violations.[91] The most celebrated example was El Salvador's Archbishop Oscar Romero, the nation's highest-ranking cleric, who, ironically, had begun his tenure as a conservative.[92] Increasingly appalled by his government's massive human-rights violations, he gradually moved to the left. In 1980, Romero wrote President Carter asking him to terminate U.S. military aid to the ruling junta until human-rights violations had ended. Subsequently, he broadcast a sermon calling on Salvadorian soldiers to disobey orders to kill innocent civilians. "No soldier is obliged to obey an order against God's law," he declared. "In the name of God and in the name of this suffering people, I implore you, I beg you, I order you—stop the repression."[93] The following day Archbishop Romero was murdered by a right-wing hit squad as he said a requiem mass.

Like Romero, Latin America's progressive clergy are far more likely to be reformers than radicals. At times their political rhetoric and analysis may find some common ground with the Left. Thus, they share the Marxists' indignation over the plight of the poor, and many of them identify dependency and U.S. domination as root causes of Latin American underdevelopment. But they reject revolutionary violence and the Leninist state as solutions. Reform, not revolution, was also the proscription of CELAM's bishops when they suggested progressive Catholic theology as an alternative to both capitalism and Marxism.

A number of the bishops' pronouncements at Medellín originated with a radical Peruvian priest, Gustavo Gutiérrez, the father of liberation theology. In the succeeding decades, writings by Gutiérrez and other liberation theologians greatly influenced the progressive Church in Latin America and other parts of the world. Liberation theology calls on Catholic laity and clergy to become politically active and to direct that activity toward the emancipation of the poor. Drawing on Marxist analysis, Gutiérrez accepts the notion of class struggle, but his form of struggle is nonviolent. The poor, liberation theologians argue, should organize themselves into Christian (or Ecclesial) Base Communities (CEBs) where they can raise their social and political consciousness. In that way, they can recognize the need to transform society through their own mobilization.[94] CEBs spread through much of Latin America, most notably to Brazil, Chile, Peru, and Central America. While the number of communities and even their precise definition are subject to debate, a CEB is essentially "any group that meets on a regular basis to deepen its members' knowledge of the gospel, stimulate reflection and action on community needs, ... and evangelize."[95] In part, the

Church created CEBs as a response to the serious shortage of priests in Latin America, particularly among the poor.

Typically composed of 10 to 40 people, Ecclesial Base Communities are primarily found in poor urban neighborhoods and, to a lesser degree, in rural villages (though there are also some middle-class CEBs). Estimates of how many exist in Latin America vary widely, but one estimate placed the number at their peak in the 1980s at perhaps 200,000, with a total membership of several million people. Perhaps 40 percent of all communities were in Brazil, home of the world's largest Catholic population.[96] The majority of CEB members is probably not politically active and joins for strictly religious purposes.[97] Still, many communities were the foundations for popular protests against oppression, most notably in Central America but also in Brazil, Chile, and Peru.[98] In other cases, CEBs helped raise political awareness and sharpen political skills among the poor.

Since the early 1980s, the influence of Latin America's progressive Church has diminished considerably.[99] One cause, ironically, has been the transition from military dictatorships to democracy in much of the region. Absent massive human-rights violations and open assaults on the poor, the clergy has had less motivation to enter the political arena. Furthermore, without a common foe, moderate and radical priests no longer have a common cause. Finally, many political activists who had used the Church as a protective "umbrella" during the military dictatorships (it was, after all, respectable to be an active Catholic) are now able to participate in politics through other, newly legal political organizations.[100]

Since the 1980s, the Vatican, has been unsympathetic to any type of political activism among priests and nuns, particularly when related to the CEBs and liberation theology. "Rome has called liberation theologians such as Leonardo Boff and Gustavo Gutiérrez to account, if not to recant."[101] As progressive bishops and archbishops such as Brazil's Don Helder Camara have died or retired, they have been replaced by more conservative clerics.[102] The Vatican's conservatism and hostility to Liberation Theology and its outgrowths will undoubtedly continue under Pope Benedict XVI. Though liberation theology and the progressive Church have lost much of their momentum, they still made an important contribution to the political mobilization of Latin America's poor.

RELIGION AND POLITICS IN THE DEVELOPING WORLD: LOOKING TO THE FUTURE

The hold of religion on the human heart and its consequent impact on the political process have been frequently misunderstood by Western scholars. As we have seen, the initial error of both modernization and dependency theorists was to underestimate its significance. Several factors account for the unanticipated resurgence of fundamentalism and other forms of religiously based politics in recent decades. In many countries, rapid modernization has left people psychologically adrift, searching for their cultural identity. The breakdown of traditional village life and long-accepted customs often creates a void not filled by the material rewards of modern life. In the Middle East, the indignities of colonialism and then neocolonialism, resentment against Israel and the West, and feelings of failed development have all contributed to that region's religious revival.[103] However, contrary to many Western stereotypes, the appeal of Islamic fundamentalism is not at all limited to poor and uneducated Muslims only somewhat familiar with modern Western ideas and lifestyles. After all, most of the 9/11 terrorists had university educations and had lived outside the Muslim world. A recent biographical study of 173 jailed, Islamist terrorists—from nearly a dozen countries—found that the majority were middle or upper class, most had received secular educations in primary and secondary school, nearly two-third had at least some college or university education, and more than 40 percent were professionals (including physicians, architects, teachers, and preachers).[104] Other research, with similar findings, suggests that many Al Qaeda jihadists involved in major terrorist operations outside the Middle East have been young men who have lived in the West (primarily Europe) where they had felt like outcasts, isolated from their own culture.

In Latin America, the progressive Church offered a shield against political repression and a voice for the poor. As different as they are, Islamic revivalism and the progressive Catholic Church both received much of their impetus from government repression and corruption. In short, the resurgence of Third World religion was, in part, a reaction to the deficiencies of social and economic modernization and the corruption and incompetence of the new political-economic order.

Contemporary analysts also risk miscalculating the impact of religion on Third World politics by overstating its importance. To begin with, the political weight of the movements that have attracted the most attention—Islamic and Hindu radical fundamentalism and progressive Catholicism—must be put into perspective. Influential as they have been, they are not representative of the religions from which they have sprung. This point requires particular emphasis in relation to Islam, since a militant minority has left many Westerners with an extremely negative image of the entire Muslim religion. Islam is seen as backward and intolerant when, in fact, like all religions, it encompasses a range of outlooks, some very progressive.[105] For example, the media may suggest that Muslim women are all repressed and confined, yet there are many Islamic feminists and professional women in countries such as Egypt, Lebanon, and Malaysia. It is worth remembering that four Muslim nations—Bangladesh, Indonesia, Pakistan, and Turkey—have had female prime ministers or presidents in recent years, something the United States has yet to accomplish. Similarly, contrary to stereotype, some Muslim countries, including fundamentalist Saudi Arabia, are on very good terms with the West. Finally, in at least some cases, such as Turkey and India, when fundamentalist parties finally led national governments, their behavior in office was moderated by their need to attract coalition partners in parliament and to appeal to a wider range of voters in future elections.

When considering the broader scope of the current religious revival, again, its importance should be recognized but not exaggerated. History reveals that "religious resurgence is a cyclical phenomenon."[106] Thus, Jeff Haynes argues, "There is no reason to doubt that the current wave of religion-oriented political ideas and movements will in time give way ... to [a] partial resurrection of secular ideologies."[107] For the foreseeable future, however, religion will continue to be an important force in the politics of many developing nations. Nowhere is this more dramatically evidenced than in fundamentalist terrorist groups such as Al Qaeda.

CONCLUSION: RELIGION AND DEMOCRACY

Two important questions come to mind when discussing the relationship between religion and democracy. First, does liberal democracy require the separation of church and a secular political system? Second, are the cultural values of some religions more supportive than others of democracy?

In his classic work, *Democracy in America*, the French author Alexis de Tocqueville suggested that a linchpin of democracy in the United States was the separation of church and state.

> I learned with surprise that [the clergy] filled no public appointments ... [and] I found that most of its members seemed to retire from their own accord from the exercise of power, and that they made it the pride of their profession to abstain from politics. ... They saw that they must renounce their religious influence if they were to strive for political power.[108]

Today, many analysts still believe that maintaining the pluralist values and the tolerance that underlie democracy requires limiting the influence of religion on politics. But other contemporary analysts reject the notion that democracy requires a strict separation of church and state. In their recent publication, *Religion and Democracy*, David Marquand and Ronald Nettler insist:

> Even in the absence of a ... bargain keeping church and state apart, religion and democracy can coexist. Communities of faith do not necessarily imperil the foundations of pluralist democracy by seeking to pursue essentially religious agendas through political action.[109]

But, they add, there is a restriction that is necessary if this intermingling of religious political action and democracy is to work. "A degree of mutual tolerance, or at least of mutual self-restraint, is indispensable. Religious groups have to accept the right of other religious groups—and ... the right of the non-religious—to abide by their own values."[110] Often that tolerance is present, but in many fundamentalist religions—Islamic or otherwise—it frequently is not.

Our second question—whether certain religious cultures are more supportive than others of democratic values—has been the subject of intense debate. Various empirical studies have shown that Protestant countries are significantly more likely to be democratic than are Catholic or Muslim nations.[111] By contrast, Islamic nations have had a rather poor track record for maintaining democracy, leading some analysts to conclude that Islam and a number of other religions have authoritarian underpinnings. For example, in the mid-1990s, Turkish sociologist Serif Mardin suggested that the values of democracy may be tied to broader Western cultural values, values the Islamic world does not accept.[112]

The problem with such arguments is that, while they may have an element of truth, they fail to take into account differences within religions or important value changes over time. Not all religious Catholics or priests, for example, have the same political values. Militant Islamic fundamentalist cultures that have flourished in Afghanistan and Sudan are indeed unacceptable environments for democracy. Yet many scholars feel that Islamic values can be quite compatible with democracy in a more moderate Muslim setting such as Malaysia and Indonesia.[113] Consider, for example, Abdurrahman Wahid, Indonesia's first democratically elected president (in 1999). Wahid is a Muslim cleric who supported the values of tolerance so essential to democracy. He spoke out against grass-roots violence directed against Indonesia's Christian minority and insisted that Christians were equal to Muslims in the eyes of God. In a rather dramatic departure from most Islamic heads of state, he publicly and enthusiastically supported Zionism and made one of his first state visits as president to Israel.[114] Similarly, while it is true that historically the Catholic Church had been associated with authoritarian political forces in Europe and Latin America, since the 1970s it also has been in the forefront of the fight against right- and left-wing dictatorships in those regions.

Like most institutions and value systems, religions change over time. Once it was widely understood that Protestant countries were more hospitable to both economic growth and democracy, while Catholic and Confucian nations were less so. Today both parts of that argument are far less tenable. Confucian East Asia and Catholic Southern Europe both enjoyed rapid economic growth in the second half of the twentieth century, faster growth than in many Protestant countries. And more recently, as democracy has spread to a variety of Catholic and Confucian nations (including Spain, Portugal, Poland, Brazil, Mexico, Taiwan, and South Korea), the suggested linkage between religions and democratic norms has become more questionable. That doesn't mean that some religions are not more tolerant or less authoritarian than others. Rather, it does mean that we need to avoid sweeping generalizations and consider differences *within* religions and changes over time.

DISCUSSION QUESTIONS

1. Discuss the various types of relationships that exist between church and state as they exist under the world's major religions—Catholicism, Protestantism, Islam, and Hinduism.
2. What factors caused the growth of the progressive Church in Latin America, and what is distinct about its followers' beliefs? Why has the progressive Church lost much of its influence in recent years?
3. Discuss why the Buddhist and Hindu religions have usually been less actively involved in national politics than Islam or Catholicism. How has that changed in India in recent years?
4. What factors have led to the resurgence of Islamic fundamentalism (or revivalism) in Afghanistan, Iran, and other parts of the Muslim world? Why do you think so many people in that part of the world admire Osama bin Laden?
5. Discuss the debate over *jihad* (holy war) in the Muslim religion and how Al Qaeda's vision of *jihad* differs from that of mainstream Muslim clerics.

NOTES

1. Donald Eugene Smith, ed., *Religion and Modernization* (New Haven, CT: Yale University Press, 1974), 4.

2. Quoted in Timothy D. Sisk, *Islam and Democracy* (Washington, DC: United States Institute of Peace, 1992), 3.

3. Emile Sahliyeh, ed., *Religious Resurgence and Politics in the Contemporary World* (Albany, NY: SUNY Press), 1–16.

4. John L. Esposito, *Islam and Politics*, 4th ed. (Syracuse, NY: Syracuse University Press, 1998), 311.

5. Jeff Haynes, *Religion in Third World Politics* (Boulder, CO: Lynne Rienner Publishers, 1994), 3.

6. Kenneth D. Wald, "Social Change and Political Response: The Silent Religious Cleavage in North America," in *Politics and Religion in the Modern*

World, ed. George Moyser (New York: Routledge and Kegan Paul, 1991), 240.

7. The Christian Democratic Party was the dominant party in Italian politics for decades but was devastated in the early 1990s by scandal. It has since changed its name to the Italian Popular Party.

8. One of the most influential and controversial books using the framework of clashing, religiously based cultures is Samuel P. Huntington, *The Clash of Civilizations and the Remaking of World Order* (New York: Simon & Schuster, 1996); see also Bernard Lewis, "The Roots of Muslim Rage," *Atlantic Monthly* 226, no. 3 (September 1990). Leonard Binder, a leading specialist on the Middle East, is critical of such terminology, arguing, for example, that Islam is only one part of Middle Eastern culture; see *Islamic Liberalism* (Chicago: University of Chicago Press, 1988), 80–81.

9. For data on the size and percentage of the Islamic populations in the nations of the world, see John L. Esposito, ed., *Islam in Asia* (New York: Oxford University Press, 1987), 262–263. While the absolute size of Muslim populations has obviously changed since Esposito's book was published, his data are still relevant for comparative measurements.

10. Donald Eugene Smith, *Religion and Political Development* (Boston: Little, Brown, 1970), 40.

11. Latif Abul-Husn, *The Lebanese Conflict: Looking Inward* (Boulder, CO: Lynne Rienner Publishers, 1998), 35; see also Robin Wright, *Sacred Rage: The Crusade of Modern Islam* (London: Andre Deutsch, 1986), 63; William Montgomery Watt, *Islamic Fundamentalism and Modernity* (London: Routledge and Kegan Paul, 1988), 125–131; Dilip Hiro, *Holy Wars: The Rise of Islamic Fundamentalism* (New York: Routledge and Kegan Paul, 1989), 5–26.

12. Akbar S. Ahmed, *Discovering Islam* (New York: Routledge and Kegan Paul, 1988), 55–61; Saleem Qureshi, "The Politics of the Shia Minority in Pakistan," in *Religious and Ethnic Minority Politics in South Asia*, eds. Dhirendra Vajpey and Yogendra K. Malik (New Delhi, India: Monhar, 1989), 109.

13. Smith, *Religion and Political Development*, xi.

14. For a discussion of the strengths and weaknesses of such arguments, see Winston Davis, "Religion and Development: Weber and the East Asian Experience," in *Understanding Political Development*, eds. Myron Weiner and Samuel Huntington (Boston: Little, Brown, 1987), 221–280.

15. Terrance G. Carroll, "Secularization and States of Modernity," *World Politics* 36, no. 3 (April 1984): 362–382.

16. John L. Esposito, *Islamic Revivalism* (Washington, DC: American Institute of Islamic Affairs, American University, 1985), 5–6; Eden Naby, "The Changing Role of Islam as a Unifying Force in Afghanistan," in *The State, Religion, and Ethnic Politics*, eds. Ali Banuazizi and Myron Weiner (Syracuse, NY: Syracuse University Press, 1986), 137; Yogendra K. Malik and V. B. Singh, *Hindu Nationalism in India* (Boulder, CO: Westview Press, 1994), 53, 206.

17. John L. Esposito, *Islam and Politics*, 2d ed. (Syracuse, NY: Syracuse University Press, 1987), 231.

18. Smith, *Religion and Political Development*, 70.

19. H. E. Richardson, *Tibet and Its History* (London: Oxford University Press, 1962).

20. Smith, *Religion and Political Development*, 57–84.

21. Esposito, *Islam and Politics*, 2d ed., 1.

22. Contemporary hostilities between Jews and Muslims in the Middle East, as well as Islamic fundamentalist hostility toward the West, are relatively recent phenomena that are not rooted in Islam's core beliefs.

23. John L. Esposito, *The Islamic Threat: Myth or Reality?* (New York: Oxford University Press, 1992), 78–79.

24. Anthony H. Johns, "Indonesia: Islam and Cultural Pluralism," in *Islam in Asia*, 203.

25. In 2001 the Welfare Party reorganized as the Justice and Development Party, which now governs Turkey. It maintains close and cordial ties with the west and seeks to lead Turkey into the European Union.

26. Donald Eugene Smith, *Religion, Politics and Social Change in the Third World* (New York: Free Press, 1971), 12–22.

27. Smith, *Religion and Political Development*, 54.

28. At the same time, however, many parish priests and nuns supported the revolution in Nicaragua, and several priests served in the first Sandinista cabinet.

29. Ibid., 34–39, 57; Haynes, *Religion in Third World Politics*, 146.

30. Janet A. Contursi, "Militant Hindus and Buddhist Dalits: Hegemony and Resistance in an Indian Slum," *American Ethnologist* 16, no. 3 (August 1989): 441–457.

31. Donald Eugene Smith, "The Limits of Religious Resurgence," in *Religious Resurgence and Politics*, 36–39.

32. Morton Zuckerman, "Beware of Religious Stalinists," *U.S. News and World Report* (March 22, 1993), 80; Charles Krauthammer, "Iran: Orchestrator of Disorder," *Washington Post* (January 1, 1993), A19. Both articles are also cited in the 1993

preface to the paperback edition of Esposito, *The Islamic Threat.*

33. Esposito, *The Islamic Threat*, vii.

34. Contursi, "Militant Hindus"; Esposito, *The Islamic Threat*, 7–24; Shireen T. Hunter, ed., *The Politics of Islamic Revivalism* (Bloomington: Indiana University Press, 1988); Esposito, *Islamic Revivalism*; Sisk, *Islam and Democracy*, 2–7, 73, fn. 1, 2.

35. Among the many examples are Watt, *Islamic Fundamentalism and Modernity* and Hiro, *Holy Wars.*

36. Fred Halliday, *Islam and the Myth of Confrontation: Religion and Politics in the Middle East* (London: I. B. Tauris Publishers, 1996), 233, fn. 1.

37. Esposito, *The Islamic Threat*; Akbar S. Ahmed, *Discovering Islam* (New York: Routledge and Kegan Paul, 1988); Esposito, *Political Islam: Revolution, Radicalism or Reform* (Boulder, CO: Lynne Rienner Publishers, 1997); Halliday, *Islam and the Myth of Confrontation.*

38. Charles Kurzman, ed., *Liberal Islam: A Source Book* (New York: Oxford University Press, 1998).

39. Halliday, *Islam and the Myth*, 107.

40. Hiro, *Holy Wars*, 1–2.

41. Watt, *Islamic Fundamentalism and Modernity*, 2.

42. Peter Woodward, "Sudan: Islamic Radicals in Power," in *Political Islam* (Boulder, CO: Lynne Rienner Publishers, 1997).

43. Wright, *Sacred Rage.*

44. Robin Wright, "Lebanon," in *The Politics of Islamic Revivalism*, 66.

45. Naby, "The Changing Role of Islam," 124–154; Paul Overby, *Holy Blood: An Inside View of the Afghan War* (Westport, CT: Praeger, 1993).

46. For a discussion of the origins of the FIS and the nature of Algeria's violence since 1992, see Claire Spencer, "The Roots and Future of Islamism in Algeria," in *Islamic Fundamentalism*, eds. Abdel Salam Sidahmed and Anoushiravan Ehteshami (Boulder, CO: Westview Press, 1996), 93–109; also Esposito, *Islam and Politics*, 4th ed., 302–307.

47. To be sure, some Israeli "ultra-orthodox" Jews are radical fundamentalists who have carried out violent attacks against Muslims and secular Jews. The most notorious examples were the attack by an ultra-orthodox Jewish gunman against worshipers in a Hebron mosque and the assassination of Israeli Prime Minister Izhak Rabin by a Jewish fundamentalist who objected to Rabin's efforts to achieve peace with the Palestinian Liberation Organization (PLO). But they are exceptional.

48. Useful sources on the background of the revolution include Robin Wright,*In the Name of God: The Khomeini Decade* (New York: Simon & Schuster, 1989); Hiro, *Holy Wars*, chap. 6.

49. Hiro, *Holy Wars*, 151.

50. Ibid., 151–153; See also Shireen T. Hunter, *Iran after Khomeini* (New York: Praeger, 1992), 11–12. Hunter argues that the shahs also antagonized Iranian Muslims, by emphasizing the country's (pre-Islamic) Persian heritage at the expense of its Islamic (Arabic) heritage.

51. Hiro, *Holy Wars*, 57.

52. Cheryl Bernard and Zalmay Khalilzad, *The Government of God: Iran's Islamic Republic* (New York: Columbia University Press, 1984), 12–13.

53. Hiro, *Holy Wars*, 160.

54. M. M. Salehi, *Insurgency through Culture and Religion: The Islamic Revolution of Iran* (New York: Praeger, 1988), 54.

55. The classic study of the natural cycle of revolutions is Crane Brinton, *The Anatomy of Revolution* (New York: Vintage, 1965).

56. Wright, *In the Name of God*, 65.

57. A few parliamentary seats were even reserved for religious minorities, including Jews, Christians, and Zoroastrians (though not the persecuted Baha'i minority); Wright, *In the Name of God*, 180–181.

58. Ibid., 87.

59. Quoted in Bernard and Khalilzad, *The Government of God*, 151–152.

60. Wright's *In the Name of God* offers one of the better accounts, but there are many others.

61. Gary Sick, "Trial by Error: Reflections on the Iran-Iraq War," in *Iran's Revolution*, ed. R. K. Ramazani (Bloomington: Indiana University Press, 1990), 105.

62. Ibid., 104.

63. Wright, *In the Name of God*, 191; Hunter, *Iran after Khomeini*, 32–41. Hunter gives a more cautious view of the move toward moderation.

64. Several recent articles and books on the subject feature attacks on alleged myths about the organization. See, for example: Jason Burke, "Think Again: Al Qaeda," *Foreign Policy* (May/June 2004) reprinted in wysiwyg://2http://www.foreignpolicy.com/story, and Rohan Gunaratna, *Inside Al Qaeda: Global Network of Terror* (New York: Columbia University Press, 2002). Many authors on both sides of the debates voice their positions with absolute certainty.

65. On the Soviet war in Afghanistan, see Steve Coll, *Ghost Wars: The Secret History of the CIA, Afghanistan, and bin Laden, from the Soviet Invasion to September 10, 2001* (New York : Penguin Press, 2004); Artem Borovik, *The Hidden War: A Russian Journalist's Account of the Soviet War in Afghanistan* (New York: Atlantic Monthly Press, 1990); Henry S. Bradsher, *Afghanistan and the Soviet Union* (Durham, N.C. : Duke University Press, 1983).

66. Gunaratna, *Inside Al Qaeda*, 18–19.

67. Peter L. Bergen, *Inside the Secret World of Osama bin Laden* (London: Weidenfeld & Sicolson, 2001), 59–60.

68. Since he and bin Laden had come into conflict over the use of terrorism as a tactic, particularly against Muslim governments such as Egypt,—Azzam opposed it but bin Laden, after initially opposing that strategy, embraced it—many analysts believe that Osama either ordered the assassination of his former mentor or, at least, condoned it. Bin Laden, for his part, never acknowledged their falling out.

69. Marc Sageman, *Understanding Terror Networks* (Philadelphia: University of Pennsylvania Press, 2004), 38.

70. *Ibid.*, 35. There is evidence, however, that the Saudi regime continued to accommodate Al Qaeda until 2004. A lawsuit filed by relatives of 9/11 victims charged that members of the Saudi royal family paid the network $300 million in "protection money" during the 1990s (see London's *Sunday Times*, August 25, 2002) and others have alleged that some members of the royal family funneled additional money to bin Laden through fictitious charities.

71. In December 1992, during the final weeks of his administration, President George H.W. Bush ordered U.S. troops into Somalia as civil war and lawlessness was destroying that nation and spreading famine. Despite their success in restoring humanitarian food relief, the troops were repeatedly engaged by armed Somali militias and were increasingly resented by many civilians. After an American helicopter was shot down in October 1993, 18 soldiers were killed and several of their bodies were dragged through the streets of Mogadishu, the Somali capital. President Clinton then withdrew U.S. forces from that country. These events were popularized in a 2001 Hollywood film entitled *Blackhawk Down*. Al Qaeda allegedly provided training for some of the Somalis who attacked the American troops.

72. Jason Burke, "Think Again: Al Qaeda."

73. Both quotes are from a May 16, 2003 BBC report; see http://newsvote.bbc.co.uk/mpapps; in a March 21, 2004 interview with Australian television, Dr. Rohan Gunaratna, head of terrorism research at Singapore's Institute of Defense and Strategic Studies and a leading authority on Al Qaeda, also voiced the opinion that despite the capture or demise of many of its top leaders, the organization "has grown significantly in the past two years. ... [by infecting] local groups with its ideology. ... " See http://seven.com.au/sundayssunrise/politics_040321_gunaratna.

74. http://www.publicagenda.org/specials/terrorism cited in Jeff Haynes, "Al-Qaeda:

Ideology and Action" (Uppsala, Sweden: Paper prepared for the EPCR Joint Sections of Workshops, April 2004), 2.

75. The Pew Research Center for the People and the Press, "A Year After the Iraq War: Mistrust of America in Europe Even Higher, Muslims Anger Persists" (March 16, 2004), 1. http://people-press.org/reports

76. Haynes, "Al-Qaeda," 2.

77. Pew Research Center, "A Year After," 1.

78. Sohail H. Hashmi, "9/11 and the Jihad Tradition," in *Terror, Culture, Politics: 9/11 Reconsidered*, eds. Daniel J. Sherman and Terry Nardin (Bloomington: Indiana University Press, forthcoming 2005).

79. *Ibid.*

80. "Analysis: Interpreting Islam," *BBC* (Friday, 9 July, 2004) at http://news.bbc.co.uk/1/h/world/middle_east/3880151.stm

81. *Ibid.*

82. This section draws heavily on Gail Omvelt, "Hinduism, Social Inequality and the State," in *Religion and Political Conflict in South Asia*, ed. Douglas Allen (Westport, CT: Greenwood Press, 1992), 17–36. See also Ian Talbot, "Politics and Religion in Contemporary India," in *Politics and Religion in the Modern World*, 135–161; and Malik and Singh, *Hindu Nationalism in India*.

83. *New York Times*, February 26, 1993.

84. Paul Sigmund, *Liberation Theology at the Crossroads* (New York: Oxford University Press, 1990), 19; David Lehmann, *Democracy and Development in Latin America* (Cambridge, England: Polity Press, 1990), 108–110.

85. Scott Mainwaring and Alexander Wilde, eds., *The Progressive Church in Latin America* (Notre Dame, IN: University of Notre Dame Press, 1989).

86. Sigmund, *Liberation Theology at the Crossroads*, 29–30.

87. Father Camilo Torres, *Revolutionary Writings* (New York: Harper & Row, 1962).

88. Philip Berryman, *Stillborn Hope: Religion, Politics and Revolution in Central America* (Maryknoll, NY: Orbis Books, 1991); Margaret E. Crahan, "Religion and Politics in Revolutionary Nicaragua," in *The Progressive Church*.

89. Jennifer Pearce, "Politics and Religion in Central America: A Case Study of El Salvador," in *Politics and Religion*, 234.

90. Mainwaring and Wilde, *Progressive Church*, 13.

91. Scott Mainwaring, *The Catholic Church and Politics in Brazil* (Stanford, CA: Stanford University Press, 1986); Brian H. Smith, *The Church and Politics in Chile* (Princeton, NJ: Princeton University Press, 1982).

92. Philip Berryman, "El Salvador: From Evangelization to Insurrection," in *Religion and Political Conflict in Latin America*, ed. Daniel H. Levine (Chapel Hill: University of North Carolina Press, 1986), 58–78.

93. Ibid., 114.

94. Sigmund, *Liberation Theology at the Crossroads*, 28–39.

95. W. E. Hewitt, *Base Christian Communities and Social Change in Brazil* (Lincoln: University of Nebraska Press, 1991), 6.

96. Hewitt, *Base Christian Communities*; Thomas C. Bruneau, "Brazil: The Catholic Church and Basic Christian Communities," in *Religion and Political Conflict in Latin America*, 106–123.

97. John Burdick, "The Progressive Catholic Church in Latin America," in *Latin American Research Review* 24, no. 1 (1994): 184–198; Hewitt, *Base Christian Communities*.

98. Daniel H. Levine and Scott Mainwaring, "Religion and Popular Protest in Latin America," in *Power and Popular Protest: Latin American Social Movements*, ed. Susan Eckstein (Berkeley: University of California Press, 1988).

99. Burdick, "The Progressive Catholic Church."

100. Thomas C. Bruneau, "The Role and Response of the Catholic Church in the Redemocratization of Brazil," in *The Politics of Religion and Social Change*, eds. Anson Shupe and Jeffrey K. Hadden (New York: Paragon House, 1986), 95–98.

101. Mainwaring and Wilde, *Progressive Church*, 30.

102. Lehmann, *Democracy and Development*, 144–145.

103. Mark Tessler and Jamal Sanad, "Women and Religion in Modern Islamic Society: The Case of Kuwait," in *Religious Resurgence*, 209.

104. Sageman, *Understanding Terror Networks*, 74–78.

105. For a collection of writings by progressive Islamic scholars and political figures, see Kurzman, ed., *Liberal Islam*.

106. Smith, "The Limits of Religious Resurgence," 34.

107. Haynes, *Religion in Third World Politics*, 155.

108. Alexis de Tocqueville, *Democracy in America*, ed. Alan Ryan (London: Everyman's Library, 1994), 309–312.

109. David Marquand and Ronald L. Nettler, "Forward," in *Religion and Democracy*, eds. David Marquand and Ronald L. Nettler (Oxford, England: Blackwell Publishers, 2000), 2–3.

110. Ibid., 3.

111. Axel Hadenius, *Democracy and Development* (New York: Cambridge University Press, 1992).

112. Serif Mardin, "Civil Society and Islam," in *Civil Society: Theory, History, Comparison*, ed. John A. Hall (Cambridge, England: Polity Press, 1995); for a similar perspective, see Chris Hann, "Introduction: Political Society and Civil Anthropology," in *Civil Society: Challenging Western Models*, eds. Chris Hann and Elizabeth Dunn (London: Routledge, 1996), 1–26.

113. Robert W. Hefner, *Civil Islam: Muslims and Democratization in Indonesia* (Princeton, NJ: Princeton University Press, 2000).

114. In 2001, parliament removed Wahid from office based on his incompetence as president and possible corruption. I am not arguing that Wahid was a perfect democrat. When faced with impeachment, he acted questionably on a number of occasions. Nor am I suggesting that all Indonesian Muslim leaders were as tolerant as he was. I am merely noting that Wahid, despite his obvious faults as president, represented a brand of Islam that is quite compatible with democracy. Despite the enormous economic and ethnic problems facing Indonesia's new government, democracy stands a good chance of surviving.

chapter 4

The Politics of Cultural Pluralism and Ethnic Conflict

The start of the twenty-first century, much like the early decades of the century that preceded it, periodically featured brutality and carnage inflicted by Third World ethnic, racial, and religious groups on rival cultural groupings. In early 2004, following nearly two years of negotiations, the Sudanese government reached a preliminary peace accord with the Sudan People's Liberation Movement/Army (SPLM/A)—a secessionist movement representing Christian and animist Blacks in the country's south. If successful, the agreement will end 21 years of civil war that resulted in the deaths of an estimated two million people, mostly southerners killed or starved by the government.

At the same time, however, possible peace in the south seems to have intensified ethnic cleansing in the western Sudanese region of Darfur, where government-supported militias killed thousands of Muslim Blacks from the Fur, Masalit, and Saghawa tribes, "raped women and destroyed villages, food stocks, and other [essential] supplies," and drove some one million people into refugee camps in Darfur or the neighboring nation of Chad.[1]

Nearly a century before (1915 to 1916), in the midst of World War I, Turkey's government massacred some 1.5 million Armenians within that country's borders.[2] Some 30 years after that, as Britain relinquished power over India, it divided that "jewel in the [imperial] crown," into two nations, largely Hindu India and Muslim Pakistan. The religious communities in each country then turned on each other savagely, with a resulting death toll of perhaps one million. More recently, Hutu villagers in the African nation of Rwanda massacred over a half-million of their Tutsi countrymen, while in the former country of Yugoslavia, Serbian militias initiated "ethnic cleansing" of their Muslim and Croat neighbors, killing and raping untold thousands more. During the twentieth century, violent confrontations, civil wars, and genocidal activity were frequently motivated by religious conflict (India, Northern Ireland, Lebanon), tribal animosities (Nigeria, Rwanda), racial prejudice (South Africa), and other forms of ethnic animosities. Continuing ethnic tensions in the early years of the twenty-first century seem to confirm Mahabun ul Haq's prediction—that wars between "peoples" (an ethnic, religious, or cultural group) will continue to far outnumber wars between nation-states.

Classic accounts of modernization, particularly [but not exclusively] those influenced by Marx, predicted that the old basis for divisions, such as tribe and religion, would be swept aside. As hundreds of millions of people poured from rural to urban areas worldwide, during the nineteenth and twentieth centuries, it was expected that new alliances would be formed, based on social class in particular.[3]

But, significant as class conflict has been, no cleavage has more sharply, and oftentimes violently, polarized nations in modern times than ethnicity. "Cultural pluralism [i.e., ethnic diversity]," argues Crawford Young, "is a quintessentially modern phenomenon." It has been closely linked to the growth of the middle class and the emergence of politicians who articulated nationalist or other ethnic aspirations while mobilizing workers and peasants behind that ideal.[4]

To be sure, ethnic minorities have been victimized by violence for hundreds of years. One needs only look to the nineteenth-century frontier wars between White settlers and Native Americans in the United States and Chile to identify just two examples. Furthermore, contrary to common perception, the level of ethnic protests and rebellions within states has actually diminished somewhat since the start of the 1990s, after rising steadily for the previous 50 years.[5] Alarmist warnings notwithstanding, the world has not been crumbling into a maze of small ethnically based states.[6]

Still, as we begin a new century, the level of ethnically based *internal* conflict is still far higher than in the decades prior to the 1990s, in marked contrast to the dramatic decline in wars *between* nations during that period. Indeed, over the past 50 years, the most frequent arenas for violent conflict have not been wars between sovereign states, but rather internal strife tied to cultural, tribal, religious, or other ethnic animosities.[7] According to one recent estimate, "nearly two-thirds of all [the world's] armed conflicts [at that time] included an ethnic component. [Indeed], ethnic conflicts are four times more likely than interstate wars."[8] Another study claimed that 80 percent of "major conflicts" in the 1990s had an ethnic element.[9] Any listing of the world's most brutal wars in the past few decades would include ethnically based internal confrontations in Bosnia, Kosovo (Serbia), Rwanda, Congo (formerly Zaire), Ethiopia, Sudan, Lebanon, and Indonesia (East Timor).[10] Perhaps 20 million people have died in ethnic violence since World War II.[11] Most recently, the collapse of Soviet and Eastern European communism has released a torrent of pent-up ethnic hatreds in Azerbaijan, Armenia, Chechnya, Georgia, the former Yugoslavia, and other parts of Central and Eastern Europe. Particularly since the end of the Cold War, the world's attention has focused increasingly on ethnic clashes.

Warfare among Serbs, Croats, Bosnian Muslims, and Kosovars in the former Yugoslavia, separatist movements among French-speaking Québécois, racially based riots in Los Angeles, Basque terrorism in Spain, and Protestant-Catholic clashes in Northern Ireland all clearly demonstrate that interethnic friction and violence can also erupt in Western democracies or in former communist countries. But ethnic conflict has been particularly widespread and cruel in Africa, Asia, and other parts of the Third World—in part because countries in those regions tend to have more ethnically diverse populations, and in part because their political systems are generally less capable of peacefully resolving tensions. One widely cited recent study determined that there are some 275 "minorities at risk" throughout the world (ethnic groups facing actual or potential repression), with a total population of slightly more than one billion (about one-sixth of the world's populations) scattered in 116 countries. Approximately

85 percent of those at risk live in the LDCs. Although Asia has the highest *absolute* population of ethnic minorities, Sub-Saharan Africa has the highest *proportion* of its population at risk (some 36 percent), followed by North Africa and the Middle East (26 percent).[12]

The intensification of ethnic, racial, and cultural hostilities for much of the twentieth century undercut basic assumptions of modernization theory; it also contradicted an influential social psychology theory known as the "contact hypothesis." That hypothesis predicted that as people of different races, religions, and ethnicities came into greater contact with each other, they would better understand both sides' common human qualities, causing group prejudice to decline.[13] Although there is evidence to support the contact hypothesis at the individual level (i.e., as individuals of different races or religions come to know each other better, their prejudices often, though certainly not always, diminish), increased interaction between ethnic or racial groups, occasioned by factors such as urban migration, frequently intensifies hostilities. This is particularly true when the political and economic system is biased in favor of one ethnic or cultural group or if ethnic leaders play on group prejudices to advance their own political agendas.

This chapter focuses on the most protracted and extreme conflicts between ethnic groups in the developing world. In doing so, it runs the risk of presenting readers with the mistaken notion that all LDCs are aflame with violent ethnic clashes. In truth, most ethnic tensions do not lead to systematic violence. Ethnic warfare is more pronounced in the Indian subcontinent, the Middle East, Southeast Asia, and portions of Africa, and is less common in Latin America and the Far East. Some developing countries—Uruguay and Nepal, for example—either lack substantial ethnic minorities, thereby eliminating the possibility of internal conflict, or have arrived at a relatively stable, if not always just, relationship between ethnicities—Venezuela, Ghana, and Taiwan. Thus, although this chapter focuses on the most unstable cases in order to illustrate the obstacles that ethnic conflicts frequently present to political and economic development, it should not give the reader the false impression that *all* LDCs are riddled with ethnic tensions or violence.

DEFINING ETHNICITY

Although it is difficult to define ethnicity precisely, certain common qualities set ethnic groups apart. Most analysts agree that ethnic identity is a *social construction*—a way that certain groups have come to view themselves as distinct from others over time—rather than an inherent or primordial characteristic. Each ethnicity "share[s] a distinctive and enduring collective identity based on a belief in a common descent and on shared experiences and cultural traits."[14] While usually having a basis in fact, these identities and histories frequently are partly created, or at least embellished, by entrepreneurial politicians, intellectuals, or journalists who gain some advantage by "playing the ethnic card." The real or imagined common history, traditions, and values not only unite the group's members but distinguish them from other cultures with whom they come in contact, and at times they encourage group conflict.[15] Thus, J. E. Brown's cynical definition of a "nation" can be applied to many other ethnic identities as well: "A group of people united by a common error about their ancestry and a common dislike of their neighbors."[16] In times of great change and uncertainty (including national independence or subsequent rapid economic modernization), ethnic intellectuals and politicians are likely to create historical myths that give their ethnic group a sense of security in the face of perceived challenges from other groups. In the words of Vesna Pesic, a Serbian intellectual and peace activist, ethnic conflict is caused by the "fear of the future, lived through the past."[17]

Pakistanis in Uganda, Chinese in Malaysia, Kurds in Iraq, Hmong in Laos, or highland Quechua speakers in Peru may join political organizations, business groups, social clubs, and mutual-benefit societies. This does not necessarily mean that these ethnic groups are socially homogeneous or politically united. In fact, they are often divided by factors such as class, ideology, or religion. For example, Sri Lanka's Tamil minority is divided between those who have lived in the country for centuries and those brought from India in the nineteenth century to work the coffee and tea plantations. These subgroups are, in turn, split by caste. Indian Muslims and Nigerian Ibos are divided by class. And African Americans may be Protestant, Catholic, Muslim, or even Jewish. Still, the factors that bind an ethnic group together are more powerful than those that separate it. Ibo peasants generally identify more closely with businesspeople from their own tribe than they do with fellow peasants from the Hausa or Yoruba tribes. Cynthia Enloe has noted, "Of all the groups that men [or women] attach themselves to, ethnic groups seem the most encompassing and enduring."[18]

Sometimes ethnic classifications were artificially imposed initially by outsiders. In the Belgian Congo, for example, White colonial administrators, missionaries, explorers, and anthropologists erroneously lumped together people of the upper Congo region into a nonexistent tribe (or ethnicity) called the Bangala. After a number of decades, the "myth of the Bangala" took on a life of its own, as migrants from the upper Congo settling in the city of Kinshasa joined together politically under the ethnic banner that had been externally imposed on them.[19] Similarly, the classification of "Colored" once used to denote racially mixed South Africans was an artificial construct established by the White regime. And although few Mexicans feel much in common with Cubans, Ecuadorians, or Nicaraguans when they live in their home countries, all of them become a new ethnic group called "Latinos" or "Hispanics" after they immigrate to the United States and are viewed as a homogeneous mass by their "Anglo" neighbors. Once individuals begin to accept the group label imposed on them, however, even those externally created ethnic classifications become politically relevant.[20]

Ethnic groups may have their own social clubs, soccer teams, schools, or cemeteries. For an insecure Peruvian Indian recently arrived in Lima from her rural village, or the Hausa seeking a job in Lagos, ethnically based social clubs are invaluable for finding employment, housing, and friendships in an otherwise cold and inhospitable city. In the threatening environment associated with modernization and social change, "fear, anxiety and insecurity at the individual level can be reduced within the womb of the ethnic collectivity."[21] At the same time, however, ethnic consciousness usually creates barriers between groups. Interreligious or interracial marriages, for example, may be frowned upon. In countries such as Canada, Malaysia, and Trinidad, ethnic divisions are managed relatively amicably and peacefully. More frequently, however, they are not. In multiethnic countries such as the United States, India, Liberia, and Congo, common consciousness and culture bind together certain religious, caste, tribal, or racial groups while creating barriers to other ethnicities.

ETHNIC AND STATE BOUNDARIES

If the world were composed of relatively homogenous countries such as Uruguay, South Korea, or Iceland, ethnically based wars might continue between states, but there would be no internal strife based on communal antagonisms.[22] In other words, the underlying cause of most internal ethnic conflict is that boundaries for *nations* (distinct cultural-linguistic groups such as Serbs, Russians, or Kurds) and other ethnicities frequently fail to coincide with boundaries for *states* (self-governing countries).[23] If large numbers of Albanians had not lived in Serbia's Kosovo province and in Macedonia, there would not have been such carnage in those regions in the past decade. The absence of an independent state to house the Kurdish nation has spurred conflict in Iraq, Iran, and Turkey. Sikh militants in the Indian state of Punjab have demanded the creation of an independent state. In all of these cases, ethno-national and political boundaries do not correspond. When minority (or, on occasion, majority) groups feel they have been denied their fair share of political and economic power, they will frequently turn to protest and confrontation.

A look at the world's population map reveals how many independent nation-states include multiple ethnic groups that are frequently uncomfortable with each other or even hostile, particularly in less developed countries. A recent examination of 191 independent countries throughout the world revealed that 82 percent contain two or more ethnic groups.[24] Furthermore, an earlier study indicated that in 30 percent of the world's countries, no single ethnic group accounts for even half of the total population.[25] This pattern is most striking in Sub-Saharan Africa, where virtually every country is composed of several ethnic (tribal) groups.[26] For example, it is estimated that Nigeria, the most populous Black African state, has more than 200 linguistic groups.[27]

Many Africans attribute their continent's legacy of tribal conflict to the European colonizers who divided the region into administrative units little connected with ethnic identities. In some areas, antagonistic groups were thrown together in a single colonial unit, while elsewhere individual tribes were split between two future countries. In Africa, Asia, and the Middle East, many colonial powers exacerbated ethnic tensions by favoring some groups over others, and by using "divide and conquer" strategies to control the local population. Yet colonialism must be seen as but one of many factors contributing to ethnic discord. Given the enormous number of tribal groups in Africa, even if the European powers had shown greater ethnic sensibility, some combination of multiethnic nations inevitably would have developed. The only alternative would have been the creation of hundreds of small states that would not have been economically viable.

Ironically, the breakdown of European colonialism in the Third World has also led to some singularly unhappy ethnic marriages. In Southeast Asia, when the Portuguese withdrew from the colony of East Timor in 1975, neighboring Indonesia annexed it against the local population's will. In its efforts to crush the indigenous organized opposition, the Indonesian military caused some

150,000 deaths (about 25 percent of the area's population), either directly through military action or, more commonly, indirectly through policies leading to mass starvation and disease. After the local population was finally allowed to vote for independence in 1999, Timorese militias tied to the Indonesian military slaughtered thousands more.[28] Elsewhere, following years of Italian colonial rule and a brief British occupation, the East African colony of Eritrea was forcibly merged with Ethiopia in the 1940s. The Eritrean people (who were generally more Westernized and modernized than the Ethiopians) were barely consulted and subsequently began a long struggle for independence.[29] The result was three decades of civil war that resulted in the deaths of hundreds of thousands. Ultimately, the Ethiopian army fell to rebel forces from the provinces of Eritrea and Tigray.[30] The associated collapse of the Ethiopian revolutionary government allowed both provinces to achieve independence, though bloody warfare resumed between Ethiopia and Eritrea in the late 1990s.

TYPES OF ETHNIC-CULTURAL DIVISIONS

In order to better grasp the variety of ethnic tensions that currently pervade much of the developing world, I will first classify all ethnicities into a set of somewhat overlapping categories: nationality, tribe, race, and religion.[31]

Nationality

In ethnic analysis the term *nation* takes on a specialized meaning distinct from its more common usage designating a sovereign country (as in the United *Nations*). It refers, instead, to a population with its own language, cultural traditions, historical aspirations, and, often, its own geographical home. Frequently, nationhood is associated with the belief that "the interests and values of this nation take priority over all other interests and values."[32] As opposed to other types of ethnicity, many nationalities claim sovereignty over a specific geographic area. However, as we have seen, frequently these proposed *national* boundaries do not coincide with those of sovereign states. For example, Russia, India, Spain, and Sri Lanka are all *sovereign states* (independent countries) that encompass several distinct *nationalities* (cultural identities). In each case, members of at least one of those nationalities—Chechyns (Russia), Muslim Kashmiris (India), Basques (Spain), and Tamils (Sri Lanka)—have been fighting for independence. On the other hand, the Chinese are a nationality that, through migration, has spilled over to several East Asian states and to other parts of the world. The Kurds also reside in several countries, including Turkey, Iraq, Iran, and Syria. Unlike the Chinese, however, they are a nation without a state of their own.

As with many types of ethnicity, the political significance of national identity is grounded in highly subjective factors. That is to say, nationality becomes politically important only when members believe themselves to have a common history and destiny that both unites them and *distinguishes them from other ethnicities* in their country. Perhaps the most important factor is the extent to which a group maintains a distinct spoken language. Because French Canadians, Turkish Kurds, and Malaysian Chinese have maintained their "mother tongues," their national identities remain politically salient.[33] Chicano nationalists in Texas,

California, and New Mexico have sought to protect Mexican American rights and cultural integrity. Some have run for local government office under the banner of *la raza unida* ("the united race") but have no interest in separating from the United States. Chinese speakers in Southeast Asia have maintained their own cultural and political organizations while feeling strong emotional, and sometimes financial, ties to China. In countries such as Indonesia and Vietnam, the Chinese have periodically been persecuted by their non-Chinese neighbors. Quebec's government, often headed by the separatist Parti Québécois, has supported autonomy or independence for the province. On the other hand, whenever migrants to countries such as the United States or Australia fully assimilate into the national language and culture, gradually dropping their original language, their previous national identity diminishes in significance.

The appeal of militant ethnic nationalism may vary over time as a result of changing political and economic conditions. Despite its distinct language and culture, Spain's Basque population began to assimilate into Spanish society in the nineteenth century. However, during the 1970s two factors caused an upsurge in Basque-nationalist extremism aimed at self-rule (marked by bombings and assassinations). The first was the democratization of Spain's political system following the death of long-time dictator Francisco Franco, which raised Basque hopes for greater autonomy and allowed nationalist parties to campaign openly. The other was an economic downturn in the region's industrial economy.[34]

In their most limited manifestations, nationalist movements may simply seek to preserve their group's cultural identity and promote their collective economic and political interests. For example, Lebanese in Brazil, Irish in Liverpool, or East Indians in Guyana and Trinidad have not entertained visions of self-governance. On the other hand, nationalist aspirations become far more volatile when they seek to create an independent ethnic state. Such separatist movements are most likely to arise when an ethnic minority is concentrated in a particular area of the country and represents a majority of the population in that region. Those conditions exist in Sri Lanka (formerly Ceylon), off the coast of India, where the Tamil-speaking population is most heavily concentrated in the country's northern and eastern provinces, particularly the Jaffna region in the far north.[35] Even before the intrusion of Dutch, Portugese, and British colonizers, the Tamils kept themselves apart from other ethnicities inhabiting Ceylon. The British conquest and colonization of the entire island (from 1815 onwards) produced a nationalist reaction linked to Buddhist chauvinism within the Sinhalese majority and provoked friction between them and the Tamil minority.

Since independence in 1948, political power has been concentrated in the hands of the Sinhalese (about three-fourths of the country's population). As in most domestic controversies between nationalities, language issues intensified the conflict. In 1956, Sinhalese replaced English as the country's official language, giving the Sinhalese population a significant advantage in securing government jobs. As one Tamil political leader put it, "Not until 1956 did we really believe that we were second-class citizens. Until then all we were engaged in were preventive measures, which we thought would hold."[36] From that point forward, however, the battle for Tamil self-rule intensified. Conversely, when Tamil was given legal status in 1978, many Sinhalese, particularly those aspiring to government jobs, felt victimized. Religious differences between the largely Hindu Tamils and the predominantly Buddhist Sinhalese augment their language and cultural divisions.

As early as 1949, Tamil leaders (representing some 18 percent of the country's population) demanded a federal system that would grant Tamil regions substantial autonomy.[37] Sinhalese nationalists, in turn, tried to impose their language on the entire nation. Even though they were far more numerous than the Tamils, the Sinhalese population suffered from a "minority complex," feeling threatened by the 50 million Tamils living on the nearby Indian mainland. In 1958, Sinhalese mobs attacked Tamils in various parts of the country, and in 1964, the Sri Lankan government signed an agreement with India calling for the eventual return to India of 525,000 Tamils whose families had once migrated from India.[38] Faced with such threats, Tamil nationalism became increasingly strident and violent. Early calls for separatism or autonomy (a degree of self-rule within the Sri Lankan state) were superseded by demands for full secession and the creation of a sovereign Tamil state. By the early 1980s, the most powerful force in the country's predominantly Tamil areas was the Liberation Tigers of Tamil Eelam (better known as the Tamil Tigers, or LTTE), a secessionist force engaged in guerrilla warfare and terrorism.[39]

In 1987, following a major national government offensive against the LTTE, India (with its own Tamil minority) intervened militarily in Sri Lanka. The resulting Indo-Lanka Peace Accord called for a multiethnic, multilingual Sri Lankan state with greater regional autonomy for Tamil areas. Though signed by the Indian and Sri Lankan governments and supported by much of the Tamil population, the accord was rejected by many Sinhalese, particularly the ultra-nationalist National Liberation Front (JVP). From 1987 to 1989, the JVP launched their own campaign of strikes, boycotts, and terrorism, resulting in thousands of deaths. A brutal government campaign eventually crushed the JVP, but the war against the Tamil Tigers continued. Although many Tamils welcomed the Indo-Lanka accord, the Tigers viewed it as inadequate. Instead, they expanded their bloody guerrilla war, first against the 60,000—man Indian army of occupation, and then, after the withdrawal of Indian troops in 1990, against the Sri Lankan government and moderate Tamils.[40]

The LTTE allegedly raises more than $60 million annually by smuggling illegal immigrants and drugs into Europe and the United States and receives millions more in donations from Tamil supporters living abroad. It is believed to be responsible for the 1993 assassination of Sri Lankan President Ranasinghe Premadasa and the June 2000 bombing that killed a cabinet member and 22 others. Human rights groups have condemned the Tigers for using young girls to conduct suicide bombings because they are more likely to get past police and army checkpoints with bombs strapped to their bodies. As of mid-2000, an estimated 62,000 people in a relatively small nation had been killed in the civil war. A cease-fire signed in 2002 has restored some level of peace to that devastated country. But efforts by Norway since that time to broker a peace treaty have so far stalled, impeded by divisions with Tamil factions and by distrust on both sides. A significant possibility remains of a breakdown in the peace process and a resumption of fighting.[41]

Tribe

The very use of the term *tribe*, especially as applied to African cultures, is fairly controversial. Many anthropologists and political scientists find it arbitrary and unhelpful. They note that cultural anthropologists who first worked in Africa, parts of South Asia, and Australia-New Zealand frequently assumed that the social characteristics of the small groups of people they were studying could automatically be extended to larger units they called a *tribe*.[42] (In this regard, I wrote previously about the upper Congo's "myth of the Bangala.") Critics also point out that the term is sometimes used to describe groups in Africa as large as Nigeria's 15 million Yorubas, a population that elsewhere in the world would be called a *nationality*. Hence, many scholars prefer the term *ethnicity* to *tribe*. This section, however, still refers to tribal groups for the simple reason that the term is familiar to most readers and has long been used by many scholars of ethnic politics and by numerous political leaders in Africa and Asia. For example, in describing the problems of his own country, former Ugandan President Milton Obote lamented "the pull of the tribal force."[43] In this chapter I use *tribe* to describe *sub*national groups, particularly in Africa, that share a collective identity and language and believe themselves to hold a common lineage. In India, Vietnam, Burma, and other parts of Asia, tribe refers to nonliterate hill peoples, such as the Laotian Hmong, living very traditional lifestyles in relative isolation from modern society. The term has also been used, of course, in regard to North American Indians as well as the lowland (Amazonian) Indians of South America. In none of these regions do we use the term pejoratively.

Intertribal conflict has frequently sparked violence in Sub-Saharan Africa, affecting more than half the countries on that continent at one time or another. Nigeria, Ethiopia, Rwanda, Burundi, Uganda, Sudan, Congo, and Ivory Coast, among others, have been torn apart by civil wars that were largely, or at least partially, ethnically based. In Liberia, Angola, and Mozambique, civil conflicts initially fought over other issues were aggravated by overlapping ethnic divisions. From the time of its independence, Nigeria experienced antagonism between the Muslims in the North and the peoples of the South and East. With 50 percent of the country's population, the Hausa-Fulani and other northern tribes were a dominant political force, resented by southerners such as the Ibo, who considered them backward.[44] Northerners, in turn, feared the influence of the more modern and commercially successful Ibo people who prevailed in the East. Each of the three major ethnic groups (Hausa-Fulani, Ibo, and Yoruba) prevailed in one region of the country, casting a shadow over smaller tribes in their area. Each major tribe, in turn, feared being dominated by the other.[45]

Two military coups in 1966 intensified friction between officers of differing ethnic backgrounds and sparked violence against the many Ibos who had migrated to the North. In fear of their lives, more than a million Ibos (perhaps as many as two million) fled to their homeland. In May 1967, Colonel Chukwuemeka Ojukwu, an Ibo military leader, declared that Eastern Nigeria was withdrawing from the country to become the independent nation of Biafra. Backed by the Organization of African Unity (OAU), the Nigerian national government was determined not to let Biafra secede.[46] Despite its initial military success, Biafra eventually suffered from the antipathy that many smaller eastern tribes felt toward the Ibos. A number of those tribes sided with the federal army. Ultimately, the armed forces surrounded Biafra and tightened their grip. Thousands of Ibos starved to death in a pattern of war and famine that subsequently became tragically familiar in other parts of Africa. When Biafra finally did surrender in early 1970, however, the Nigerian military government was quite disciplined, refraining from acts of vengeance. Since that time, the Ibos have been relatively successfully reintegrated into Nigerian society, but inter-tribal tensions and periodic religious violence persist.[47]

Unfortunately, the Nigerian conflict was merely one of the earliest African civil wars that transpired over the years between antagonistic tribal and cultural groups. One of the most tragic was the long and bitter fight by the Eritrean and Tigrayan minorities to secede from Ethiopia. Elsewhere, Burundi's ruling Tutsi minority crushed a series of uprisings by the majority Hutus (some 85 percent of the population) over the last three decades, massacring perhaps 100,000 people in 1972 alone.[48] In 1993, when a Tutsi soldier assassinated Melchior Ndadaye, a Hutu who was the country's first elected president, new intertribal bloodshed erupted. One year later, in the neighboring country of Rwanda, the Hutu president's death in a plane crash set off an orgy of violence. A government-directed massacre led by Hutu extremists was directed at the minority Tutsis and, to a lesser extent, moderate Hutus. Within weeks, approximately 500,000 Tutsis were beaten or hacked to death by local Hutu militia and villagers.[49] Eventually, a disciplined Tutsi revolutionary army, supported by neighboring Uganda, gained control of the country and jailed thousands of Hutus. Hundreds of thousands more fled to nearby Congo, where many of them were massacred or starved to death by the anti-Hutu regime of then-President Laurent Kabila.

In other conflicts, such as the Angolan and Mozambican civil wars (which had both ideological and ethnic bases), external intervention intensified the war and added to the carnage. Cold War superpowers often armed opposing sides or interceded through surrogates. For example, acting in consort with the Soviet Union, Cuba provided military assistance to the leftist national governments of Ethiopia, Angola, and Mozambique. The United States armed UNITA, the Angolan rebel force, while the South African military supported Mozambique's bloody RENAMO guerrillas. Belgium and France armed the Rwandan regime prior to its genocidal attacks on its Tutsi population. In each of those countries, hundreds of thousands perished from warfare or starvation. Although the end of the Cold War has reduced external intervention in Africa's tribal conflicts, the recent brutal wars in Congo, Liberia, Sierra Leone, and Ivory Coast suggest that African interethnic violence will almost certainly persist for the foreseeable future. During the late 1990s, Rwanda, Uganda, Zimbabwe, and Angola all intervened in the ethnically related civil war in Congo. Several million people probably died there, either directly from the warfare or, more commonly, from resulting famines. Most recently a civil war set the Ivory Coast's mostly Christian south against its Muslim north. In other cases, corrupt dictators launched campaigns against tribal minorities in order to curry favor among powerful ethnic groups and thereby deflect protest against their own governments. Thus, in recent years Kenyan President Daniel Arap Moi brutalized the Kikuyu, and Congolese President Laurent Kabila massacred the Hutu minority in his country for precisely that purpose.

Race

Race is normally the most visible ethnic division within society. That is to say, although it may be difficult to pinpoint a person's religion or tribe from his or her appearance, physical differences between Blacks, Whites, and East Asians are usually rather apparent. In some instances, however, even racial distinctions are more subtle and elusive. The Aymara-speaking woman in La Paz, Bolivia, who wears a bowler hat and a distinctive native skirt, is obviously an Indian yet her Spanish-speaking son, wearing a suit and teaching at a nearby high school, is considered a Mestizo (a person of mixed Indian and White heritage). African Americans or South African "Coloreds" of mixed racial origin are sometimes physically indistinguishable from Whites. Unlike other ethnic divisions, racial divisions are not necessarily linked to language or cultural differences.

We have noted that cultural identity involves a common set of values and customs and a shared sense of history and destiny. Of course, people of the same race living in a particular country may not experience that sense of community. Serbs, Croats, Bosnian Muslims, and Albanian Kosovars in the former Yugoslavia are all Whites; Lebanese Shi'as (Muslims) and Christians are both Arabs; and Ethiopia's Amharic majority as well as the Eritreans and Tigrayans who seceded from the country are all Blacks. Yet despite their common racial backgrounds, these groups most assuredly do not share a common cultural bond. Since there were no other races in each country, race could not be an ethnic marker. Only when people live in *multiracial* settings do individual racial groups define themselves and set themselves apart from "others" on the basis of race. Indeed, "there was no common sense of being 'African', 'European,' or [American] 'Indian,'" notes Crawford Young, "prior to the creation of multiracial communities by the population movements of the imperial age."[50] Slavery and other manifestations of Western imperialism in the Third World produced a wide range of negative racial stereotypes about Asians, Africans, and (North and South) American Indians. The subsequent migration of Asians to the plantations of East Africa and the Caribbean created further racial cleavages.

South Africa presented the most notorious and intractable example of racially based political conflict. From its colonization by the British until its 1994 transition to majority rule, the country was ruled by a White minority constituting only 15 percent of the population. In the years following World War II, political power shifted from English-speaking Whites to the more conservative Afrikaners, descendants of Dutch and French Protestant settlers.[51] Meanwhile, Blacks (constituting about 70 percent of the nation's population) were denied fundamental legal and economic rights, including the right to vote or hold political office.

Until renounced by President F. W. de Klerk's administration (the last White minority government), the legal centerpiece of South African racial policy was *apartheid* (separateness). That system rigidly segregated employment, public facilities, and housing, envisioning a day when most Blacks lived in eight allegedly self-ruling "homelands." In fact, these homelands, consisting of desolate rural regions, could not possibly support the country's Black population. Moreover, since important sectors of the South African economy, most notably its mines, are dependent on Black labor, the geographical segregation envisioned by apartheid was implausible even from the perspective of the White business community. But the millions of Blacks who still lived outside the homelands were denied the right to own land or to enjoy fundamental civil liberties.

Apartheid was based on a fourfold racial classification that defied international ethical standards and often fell victim to its own logical contradictions. *Blacks* were the largest group and were subjected to the greatest level of legal discrimination. *Coloreds* (constituting less than 10 percent of the country's population) and *Asians* (about 3 percent) had greater legal rights than Blacks but still ranked considerably below Whites. Finally, *Whites*, of course, maintained virtually all political and economic power. Although the Constitutional Act of 1983 established a three-house Parliament—representing Whites, Coloreds, and Asians, but not the Black majority—the powers of the Colored and Asian houses were minimal.

By the 1980s, however, cracks began to develop in South Africa's segregation policies, as many middle-class Coloreds and Asians moved into "Whites only" neighborhoods by subletting from Whites. Hoping to isolate Colored professionals and businesspeople from the Black population, the government often turned a blind eye to such violations, while simultaneously brutally repressing Black civil rights demonstrations in the townships.

At the same time, South Africa came under intense domestic and international pressure to end apartheid and White domination. The country had become an international pariah, subject to diplomatic and cultural isolation, including a United Nations boycott restricting trade, travel, and investment. South African athletes could not compete in the Olympics or other international sporting events. Though slow to take effect, economic sanctions, particularly restrictions on investment, eventually began to limit the country's economic growth. Growing protest and unrest in the Black townships, coupled with international isolation and a worldwide trend toward democracy, compounded the pressures for change.[52] Finally, a growing number of powerful voices within the White economic, legal, and intellectual elites (including Afrikaners) were pressuring the government for racial reform.

By the start of the 1990s, then, the de Klerk government, recognizing that apartheid was no longer viable, began to rescind a variety of segregation laws. It also legalized the African National Congress (ANC), the leading Black opposition group, along with two more radical organizations, after decades of banishment. The Congress's legendary leader, Nelson Mandela, perhaps the world's most renowned political prisoner, was released from jail together with hundreds of other political prisoners. These changes, coupled with the ANC's suspension of their armed struggle, opened the door to a new constitution enfranchising the Black majority and ending White minority rule.

In December 1991, the Convention for a Democratic South Africa (CODESA) brought together the government, the ANC, the Zulu-based Inkatha Freedom Party, and 16 smaller groups for discussion of the new political order. Public opinion among Whites was mixed but generally supportive of the process. Thus, Nelson Mandela expressed amazement at the hundreds of Whites who lined the road to cheer him when he was released from prison. In a 1992 national referendum called by de Klerk, nearly 70 percent of all White voters endorsed negotiations with the ANC and other Black groups. The following year the government and the ANC agreed to the election of a constitutional assembly that would create a new political system with equal rights for all South Africans. Universal suffrage ensured a Black majority in the assembly, but Whites were guaranteed special minority protection until 1999. In May 1994 the ANC parliamentary majority elected Nelson Mandela president of the new South Africa.

A decade later, the road to multiracial democracy remains difficult. Blacks have discovered that although majority rule has engendered greater social justice and human dignity, it has not improved living standards for many of them. To be sure, government housing programs have benefited many urban slum dwellers. However, with most farm land still owned by Whites and limited funds available for schools and clinics in the countryside, the Black rural population remains impoverished. Due to high unemployment, soaring crimes rates, and one of the world's highest incidences of AIDS, the urban poor continue to struggle. The governments of President Mandela and his successor, Thabo Mbeki, have pursued moderate economic policies to reassure the White business community. And the ANC continues to dominate national elections. Over time, however, if Black living conditions do not improve and if there is not a substantial redistribution of economic resources, the ANC's Black constituency may demand more radical policies. The country's soaring crime rate, a reflection of widespread poverty and pervasive inequality, could also turn into wider political violence.

Religion

Because it involves deeply felt values, religion has frequently been the source of bitter communal strife. In Chapter 3, we examined the influence of religious *beliefs* on political attitudes and behavior, particularly those of fundamentalists and others favoring close links between church and state. We saw that people's religious orientation shapes their views of their political rights and obligations, the nature of their constitution and legal system, and other fundamental political issues. In some countries with multiple religions, the state must create inheritance and family laws that are acceptable to religious communities with dissimilar views on these issues. In Israel, for example, different codes of family law apply to Jews, Muslims, and Christians. The same is true in India for Hindus, Muslims, and Sikhs.[53]

In this chapter, we look at a related but distinct aspect of religion, namely the degree to which coreligionists identify strongly with each other and seek political or economic dominance over other religious groups. In other words, we are concerned here, not with the constitutional and legal ramifications of religion (considered in Chapter 3), but with the relations and disagreements *between* religious groups (defined here as ethnic communities) living in the same country. The likelihood of conflict between these religious groups is influenced by at least two important factors: first, the extent to which one community feels dominated by another; and, second, the degree to which any religion in a given country believes that it is the one true faith and that alternate theologies are unacceptable. Thus, Catholics and Protestants coexist rather harmoniously in the United States and Germany because neither of these conditions applies. On the other hand, in Northern Ireland, where Catholics resent the Protestants' political and economic power and Protestants fear that the Catholic majority may prevail over them, even the widely hailed peace accord has not fully ended more than three decades of conflict.

In 1992, Hindu fundamentalists destroyed a sixteenth-century Muslim mosque in the north Indian town of Ayodhya. Like many such clashes, the incident grew out of centuries-old beliefs and hostilities.[54] The Ayodhya mosque had been built by the Mogul emperor Babur on the spot where many Hindus believe their god Ram had been born some 5,000 years earlier. To the Bharatiya Janata Party (BJP), the leading Hindu political party, and to the militant World

Hindu Council, the mosque was a symbol of Islamic foreign domination during the hundreds of years of Mogul rule prior to the British colonial era. Indeed, only two years before the attack, Indian Prime Minister Vishwanath Pratap Singh's National Front government had been forced to resign because of its refusal to raze the mosque and replace it with a Hindu temple. Within days of the assault, rioting in northern and central India left about 2,000 dead. Ten years later (2002), Hindu mobs in the village of Ahmedabad, India (Mohandas Gandhi's adopted hometown), murdered over 1,000 Muslims, raping women and burning them alive, cutting fetuses out of pregnant women.[55]

Ironically, some of the worst Hindu-Muslim bloodshed in 1992 took place in Bombay, India's financial and cultural center and one of the country's most modern and least sectarian cities. An extremist Hindu group, Shiv Sena, with some 30,000 armed members in that city, was responsible for much of the violence. Since that time, not only have city authorities failed to prosecute Shiv Sena's leader, but he has been protected by the Bombay police. In neighboring Islamic countries, Pakistani crowds attacked Hindu temples while Bangladeshis assaulted Hindu-owned shops and burned Air India offices.

To be sure, India and Pakistan were born of communal violence, and neither has been free of it since. Although both countries had been part of a single British colony, when negotiations for independence advanced in the late 1940s, the Muslim League insisted on the creation of a separate Muslim state. Using language that classically defines an ethnic group, League leader Mohammed Ali Jinnah declared: "We are a nation with our own distinctive culture and civilization, language and literature ... customs ... history and tradition."[56] In 1946, as independence approached, political conflict between the Muslim League and the leading voice of Indian independence, the Congress Party (a nonreligious party led largely by secular Hindus), touched off Hindu-Muslim communal violence that left thousands dead. Finally, the British reluctantly divided their most important colony into two countries: India, with roughly 300 million Hindus and 40 million Muslims; and Pakistan, with approximately 60 million Muslims and 20 million Hindus. No sooner had independence been declared (August 15, 1947), when horrendous religious massacres began in both countries. Whole villages were destroyed, 12 million refugees of both faiths fled across the border, more than 75,000 women were abducted and raped, and up to one million people were killed in one of the twentieth century's worst ethnic conflagrations.[57] Two decades later, Pakistan split in two as language and cultural differences divided the Muslim population. With support from India, the country's Bengali-speaking eastern region broke away from the primarily Urdu-speaking West to form the country of Bangladesh.

Today, Muslim separatists in the Indian state of Kashmir are waging guerrilla warfare aimed at either Kashmiri independence or unification with Pakistan. In 2001 Muslim fundamentalists attacked the Indian parliament, once again bringing India and Pakistan (both nuclear powers) to the brink of war. Since early 2004, India and Pakistan have engaged in a series of peace talks and confidence-building measures, as both countries have made an impressive effort to move back from the brink of conflict. But basic differences over Kashmir keep that region potentially volatile.

Other religious conflicts also continue to extract a heavy toll from India's political system. In the economically dynamic state of Punjab (where members of the Sikh religion constitute 55 to 60 percent of the population), Sikh militants demand the creation of their own nation, called Khalistan.[58] Ironically, it is believed that former Indian Prime Minister Indira Gandhi bears some responsibility for the spread of Sikh extremism. Allegedly, her government secretly financed and encouraged the most militant Sikh organization, the outlawed Dal Khalsa, thereby hoping that its violent behavior would discredit the more limited cause of Sikh autonomy favored by moderate Sikh parties.[59] If so, the tactic proved to be a serious miscalculation. Sikh terrorism, including random murders of Hindu civilians, and police-military brutality against Sikhs created an ever-rising cycle of violence. In 1984, government troops attacked the holy Golden Temple of Amritsar where the militant Sikh leader Sant Jarnail Singh Bhindranwale and many of his followers were holed up. In a three-day battle on the temple grounds, more than 1,000 people, including Bhindranwale, were killed. Thousands of Sikh troops in the Indian armed forces then mutinied, some of them battling loyal army units. Finally, on October 31, months after the attack on the Golden Temple, two Sikh members of Prime Minister Gandhi's personal bodyguard assassinated her, as she became the victim of her own earlier strategy. Lashing out after the assassination, roaming Hindu mobs killed thousands of innocent Sikh civilians. Despite attempts at reconciliation by Indira's successor, her son Rajiv Gandhi, government repression and Sikh terrorism continued unabated. By the mid-1990s, following some 20,000 deaths on both sides, the Indian military seemed to have contained the separatist movement, but the Punjab could easily erupt again at any time.

During the 1970s and 1980s, Lebanon was also a battlefield for warring religious factions. Among the 17 religious communities that shared political power after independence, the most important were Maronite Catholics, Shi'a Muslims, Sunni Muslims, and Druse (a Muslim sect).[60] Ironically, despite such religious heterogeneity, for the next 30 years the country was considered "the Switzerland of the Middle East"—a bastion of peace and economic prosperity in the midst of a troubled region. During that time the dominant Maronite and Sunni communities coexisted under the terms of a political power-sharing arrangement dating back to the 1920s (during limited home rule) and reinforced by a national pact two decades later (1943) as the country neared independence.

But power-sharing and the peace it had brought broke down in the 1970s as the Muslim population, particularly the Shi'a community, perceived that the terms of the old agreement no longer reflected the population sizes of the various religious groups. Muslims, with between 55 and 70 percent of the population (depending on which side's estimate one believed), had long been allocated only 50 percent of the nation's bureaucratic and political posts. Religious, economic, and political differences also caused conflict between Shi'a and Sunni Muslims. Shi'as had less political power and a lower standard of living than the Sunnis, and their illiteracy rate was three times higher than the Christians. Moreover, although the Shi'as were the country's largest religious community, they were allocated less than 20 percent of the seats in the parliament. At the same time, Lebanon's two most important political offices—president and prime minister—were reserved, respectively, for a Maronite Christian and a Sunni.[61]

Tensions were further exacerbated by external interventions. The influx of many Palestinian refugees (mostly fleeing Jordan), including armed PLO militia, radicalized the country's political debate. Many impoverished Shi'as were drawn to the Palestinians' revolutionary rhetoric. On the other hand, Christian leaders became concerned that PLO attacks against Israel were provoking retaliatory Israeli raids into Lebanon. Soon, Israel allied itself with Christian militias who feared both Shi'a militias and the Palestinian guerrilla fighters and were determined to maintain their community's privileged economic and political position. Syria, wishing to expand its power in the Middle East and create a buffer between its territory and Israel, occupied much of Lebanon and manipulated various factions.[62] By 1975 Lebanon's national government had become a hollow shell as power shifted to a range of communal warlords, each defending his own turf and using his militias for both political and criminal purposes. Confrontations between the army and civilian protestors, along with clashes between Palestinian guerrillas and Christian militias, engulfed Lebanon in a civil war that lasted more than 15 years and took more than 150,000 lives. The country's religious conflict had elements of a class struggle as well, pitting the more prosperous Christian community against Shi'as, who saw themselves as the oppressed poor. Foreign forces in the form of Palestinian national aspirations, Israeli occupation of parts of southern Lebanon, and Syrian military domination of much of the rest of the country all added to the bloodshed. Over time, alliances sometimes shifted, with Shi'as and Syrians, for example, supporting the Palestinians at some points and fighting them at others. Finally, as key Lebanese cities lay in ruins and Palestinian, Israeli, and Syrian forces threatened to destroy the nation's sovereignty, the Arab League (representing the Arab countries of North Africa and the Middle East) helped negotiate a treaty between the warring Lebanese factions. The Taif Accord, signed in late 1989, raised the percentage of Muslim government officials relative to the Christians and established the basis for a "national pact" between the warring factions.[63] Although the peace has held for over a decade and Lebanon has rebuilt much of its shattered economy and infrastructure, external interventions by the Palestinian Liberation Organization (PLO), the Syrians, or the Israelis could destabilize the country once again. In 2005, however, popular protests caused Syria to withdraw its troops.

Currently, tensions and violence continue between Muslims and Christians in Ivory Coast and Nigeria, between Sunni and Shi'a Muslims in Iraq, and along various religious divides in other Third World nations.

INDEPENDENCE, MODERNIZATION, AND ETHNIC CONFLICT

Western scholars and other analysts once assumed that improved education and communications in the Third World would break down ethnic conflicts. Because of their own history as a "melting pot" for so many immigrant groups, Americans in particular have supposed that socioeconomic modernization enhances ethnic integration and harmony.[64] Yet in Africa and Asia, political development (in the form of national independence) and socioeconomic modernization have quite frequently politicized and intensified ethnic antagonisms. Indeed, Crawford Young notes that "cultural pluralism [and ethnic strife] as a political phenomenon" was not significant in traditional societies but, rather, emerged "from such social processes as urbanization, the revolution in communications and spread of modern education."[65] Early modernization theorists, who were quite optimistic regarding the positive effects of literacy, urbanization, and modern values, clearly underestimated the extent to which these factors might mobilize differing ethnic groups and set them against each other. Dependency theorists, on the other hand, provided a rather superficial analysis of ethnic issues, tending to blame conflicts on colonialism or neocolonialism (economic domination of the developing world by developed capitalist nations even after the LDCs had achieved independence).

During the era of European colonialism, ethnic divisions in Africa and Asia were kept somewhat in check by independence movements, which sought a common front against the Europeans. "The transcendent obligation of resistance to the colonizer ... largely obscure[d] the vitality of ethnicity as a basis of social solidarity."[66] After independence, however, previously submerged ethnic rivalries frequently rose to the surface.[67] In the new political order, religious, racial, tribal, and nationality groups compete with each other for such state resources as roads, schools, medical clinics, irrigation projects, and civil service jobs. Subsequently, rural-to-urban migration brought many ethnic groups into close proximity for the first time. At the same time, urbanization, rising educational levels, and the spread of mass communications politicized previously unmobilized sectors of the population. Because so many of them identify primarily with their own caste, religion, nationality, or tribe, their newly acquired political awareness often brings them into conflict with others. Furthermore, the spread of higher education, rather than generating greater harmony, often produces a class of ethnically chauvinistic intellectuals who became the ideologists of ethnic hostilities. For all of these reasons, then, ethnic conflict has remained a potent and often growing phenomenon in the developing world.

LEVELS OF INTERETHNIC CONFLICT

Although most countries are ethnically heterogeneous, there are wide variations in how the various ethnicities relate to each other. In some cases, different races or religions interact fairly amicably; in others, deep resentments inspire the most horrifying barbarities. Having examined the various *categories* of ethnic communities, we will now consider the *nature* and *intensity* of relations *between* them. To gauge these relationships, we may employ such measures as the frequency of interethnic friendships and marriages, the presence or absence of political parties, trade unions and other civic organizations that represent specific ethnic groups, and the correlation between ethnic affiliation and social class. In any particular country, relations between ethnic communities may range from relative harmony (Brazil) to systematic violence (the former Yugoslavia).

Relative Harmony

Modernization, as we have seen, often intensifies ethnic antagonisms in the short run, but it usually ameliorates them in the long term. Consequently, affluent democracies are more likely than LDCs to boast of amicable ethnic relations. In Switzerland, for example, German-, French-, and Italian-speaking citizens have lived together peacefully for centuries. That record is particularly impressive because linguistic barriers within a country are generally the most difficult ethnic divisions to overcome.[68] The United States and Canada also enjoy relative ethnic harmony, having successfully assimilated a large assortment of immigrant groups. In North Dakota or Saskatchewan, for example, few are concerned when a person of Ukrainian-Orthodox or German-Catholic origin marries a Lutheran of Norwegian ancestry. Despite considerable progress in recent decades, race relations in the United States constitute the one glaring exception to the pattern of ethnic harmony.

Instances of *relative ethnic harmony* in developing countries are less plentiful. However, in Brazil and the island nations of the Caribbean, relations between Blacks and Whites are generally more harmonious than in the United States. Interracial dating and marriages, for example, are quite common, particularly among lower-income groups. Still, that harmony is relative, since even those countries have maintained a clear social hierarchy between races. Although there are many middle-class Black Dominicans, Brazilians, and Panamanians, most Blacks remain mired in the lower class, and virtually none make it to the highest ranks of the political and economic order.

In short, even the countries classified as harmonious are only categorized that way relative to other, more conflict-ridden societies. Glaring examples of ethnic antagonisms and discrimination persist. In Cuba, for example, despite a long history of interracial marriage and more recent government efforts to promote equality, Blacks have yet to attain their share of political leadership positions. Racial slurs remain common in personal conversations.[69] And Canada, in many ways a more successful melting pot than the United States, has not resolved the vexing problem of French separatism in Quebec. But such tensions are the exception, and conflict is rarely or never violent, except in cases such as the African American urban riots of the 1960s and more recently in Los Angeles.

Uneasy Balance

In developing nations such as Trinidad-Tobago and Malaysia, divisions between the principal ethnic groups are somewhat sharper than in the previous category of relative harmony. Although still generally peaceful, interethnic relations are at times strained; for example in Malaysia, the Muslim Malay majority has largely controlled the political system, including parliament and the government bureaucracy, while the Chinese minority has dominated the private sector. Race riots in 1969 led the Malaysian government to introduce a "New Economic Policy" designed, in part, to redistribute more of the country's wealth to the Malays. Fearful of Chinese domination, the Malays have also benefited from a system of ethnic preferences in education and the civil service.[70] Today the two communities continue to maintain a social distance, and some analysts see signs of slowly growing communal antagonisms. Still, despite the stress created by the economic crisis at the end of the 1990s, ethnic relations have remained peaceful.

The Caribbean nation of Trinidad-Tobago offers another interesting example of uneasy balance. During the second half of the nineteenth century, British colonial authorities encouraged the migration of indentured plantation workers from India who joined the Black majority and the small White elite. Contrary to the usual Caribbean practice of extensive racial mixing, there was little interracial marriage or childbearing between Blacks and East Indians.[71] Although there was little overt hostility, each group developed negative stereotypes about the other.[72] Following Trinidadian independence in 1962, ethnic frictions increased as Blacks and Indians began to compete for state resources. Most of the important political, civil service, military, and police positions since that time have been held by Blacks, who predominate in the country's urban middle class and working class. The upper ranks of the business community continue to be filled by the small White minority. For many years the East Indian population generally belonged to one of two groups: middle- and upper-middle-class urban businesspeople (especially merchants) with considerable collective economic power; and a large, impoverished rural population of farm workers and small farmers.

Trinidadian politics do not feature the same overt ethnic appeals that characterize many LDCs, but most of its political parties and unions largely represent one race. For 24 years (1962 to 1986) the national government was headed by the People's National Movement (PNM), a political party primarily headed and supported by Blacks. During that time the opposition was led by various Indian-dominated parties, including the Democratic Labour Party (DLP) and the United Labour Front (ULF). Major labor unions tended to be either primarily Black or largely East Indian.[73] Only in 1986 did the newly formed National Alliance for Reconstruction (NAR) finally dislodge the PNM from power by forging an electoral alliance between Indian voters and the Black middle- and upper-middle classes.[74] Although Black and Indian political and labor leaders have cooperated periodically over the years in efforts such as this, the two communities continue to maintain their social, political, and economic distance. In the 1990s, a radical Black Power movement, the Jamaat al Muslimeen, managed to briefly capture the parliament building and hold the prime minister and members of parliament hostage for five days while rioting shook the nation's capital. But violent behavior of this sort is an aberration. Eventually the Jammat militants were granted amnesty. In 1995, Basdeo Panday became Trinidad-Tobago's first prime minister of Indian ancestry despite the country's predominantly Black population.

Enforced Hierarchy (Ethnic Dominance)

As we have seen, one important factor permitting ethnic balance in countries such as Malaysia and Trinidad-Tobago has been the division of political and economic power between the different ethnicities. In *enforced hierarchies*, however, both forms of power are concentrated in the hands of the ruling ethnic group. South African apartheid represented the most blatant example of such a relationship. Through the 1980s, Whites dominated both the private sector and the state, including the courts, police, and armed forces. Blacks were denied the most basic rights of citizenship. Until the dismemberment of apartheid legislation, the legal system even restricted or prohibited interracial marriage, sexual relations, and housing.

Latin American nations with large Indian populations—including Guatemala, Bolivia, Ecuador, and Peru—have a less overt, but still significant, form of hierarchy. Historically, being an Indian in those countries was virtually synonymous with being a poor peasant at the bottom of the social and political ladder. Even today, despite important recent gains in Indian rights, most positions of political and economic influence are still held by Whites and Mestizos. At the same time, however, racial classifications in Latin America are more culturally and less biologically defined than in the United States, thereby allowing for some upward mobility. In other words, if a young Indian villager moves to the city, adopts Western dress, and speaks Spanish, he or she is considered a Mestizo. And in the rural highlands of Ecuador and Peru, many peasant communities that spoke Quechua a generation ago have switched to Spanish in a process of *mestizaje* (becoming Mestizo). Consequently, over the years the percentage of the population viewed as Mestizos (a more prestigious category than Indian) has increased, while the proportion speaking indigenous (Indian) languages has diminished. Although defining race culturally has created a somewhat more open society, unfortunately until fairly recently it also meant that Indians could only enjoy upward mobility by abandoning their own culture.[75]

Since the 1980s, however, Indians in these countries have begun to assert their cultural rights and political influence. In Bolivia, the head of an Indian-based political party was elected vice president of the country and, more recently, Indian-led protests toppled an elected president. In Ecuador, a national Indian federation seized Congress and joined the military in a coup that ousted that nation's president and briefly installed a three-person ruling junta (including the president of the federation). Recently, an Indian-dominated political party named Pachakutik (the Quichua word for "reawakening") held five of Ecuador's 22 provincial governorships.[76] And in Mexico, the 1994 Zapatista rebellion (in rural Chiapas) in behalf of Indian rights received a remarkable amount of national support from Mexicans of all ethnicities and social classes.

In all of these cases of enforced hierarchy, racial and class distinctions are closely intertwined. Those higher up the social ladder tend to be lighter skinned; those at the lower ranks of society are generally darker. One study of more than 80 members of the Ecuadorian industrial and commercial elite revealed only a single business leader who admitted having any amount of Indian ancestry, though some others likely had some small proportion.[77] And in Brazil, being Black is largely synonymous with being poor. Indeed, people of color who rise to the middle or upper-middle class frequently are no longer considered Black by their peers. But although upward mobility through the class-race hierarchy is possible, it remains difficult. Racial prejudice shapes social relationships and creates subtle, or not so subtle, barriers to equality.

Unlike South African apartheid, Latin America's racial hierarchy is informal—not written into the legal system. And unlike South Africa, it generally hasn't been enforced by police and military repression. But during nearly 40 years of revolutionary upheaval and intense government repression, the Guatemalan armed forces considered rural Indian communities to be breeding grounds for leftist guerrillas. Consequently, successive military regimes massacred tens of thousands of Indian peasants in a policy bordering on genocide. Fortunately, since the 1990s a peace treaty with the guerrillas has curtailed such violence.[78] Indian villagers in Peru also suffered greatly from the military's recent war against the Maoist Shining Path and from the revolutionaries' brutal tactics. Although Shining Path organizers focused on class struggle rather than racial divisions, much of their support came from Indian peasants resentful of the White-Mestizo power structure.[79]

Systematic Violence

In the worst-case scenario, deep ethnic resentments have sometimes burst into open violence or even civil war. As we have seen, in a number of Third World countries as well as in some European nations, *systematic violence* has resulted in thousands or hundreds of thousands of deaths and huge numbers of displaced refugees, rape victims, and the like. This category includes Bosnia, Chechnya, Lebanon, India, Bangladesh, Ethiopia, Nigeria, Rwanda, and Sudan, among others. Often, just as with enforced hierarchies, violence develops when ethnic divisions are reinforced by class antagonisms. In Northern Ireland, for example, Catholics have resented the Ulster Protestants' dominance over the region's economic and political structures. The 1998 Good Friday peace settlement, even if it can be kept on track, changed the political relationship but not the economic imbalance. Antipathy between Lebanon's Christian and Muslim communities was fueled by the former's economic superiority. Similarly, in Nigeria many Islamic northerners have taken exception to the economic success of the Christian Ibos. Ethnic bloodshed may follow when a shift in political power from one ethnicity to another provokes retribution against the former ruling group. Thus, when General Idi Amin seized power in Uganda, he ordered the slaughter of Langi and Acholi soldiers who were identified with the regime of ousted President Milton Obote. Following the overthrow of the communist government in 1992 in Afghanistan, the country began to disintegrate as Tajiks, Hazars, and Uzbeks challenged the long-standing political dominance of the Pashtun (Pathan) population. Today, President Hamid Karzai struggles to keep peace between antagonistic ethnic factions.

OUTCOMES AND RESOLUTIONS

When ethnic antagonisms arise from competition for government resources, from resentments over the division of political power or economic resources, or from an ethnic community's demands for greater autonomy, a number of results are possible. Although some outcomes are entirely peaceful, many others spawn intense violence. And while some resolutions are successful, others do not endure. Potential solutions are always constrained by the broader political culture and by the intensity of ethnic cleavages. Inevitably, potential outcomes and the options available to political leaders are limited, both by historical ethnic animosities and past patterns of cooperation. Within these constraints, however, the ethnic and government leaders' political creativity and statecraft can contribute to successful solutions. Political elites may seek reasonable, negotiated solutions, or they may choose to play on ethnic tensions for their own advantage. For example, the surprisingly peaceful final dismantling of South Africa's White minority rule was made possible by the leadership and spirit of compromise demonstrated by ANC leader Nelson Mandela and national President F. W. de Klerk.

All too often, however, self-serving, chauvinistic political leaders make a bad situation worse.[80] For example, although Bosnian Serbs and Muslims had enjoyed relatively amicable relationships for many years, extremist leaders such as former Serb President Slobodan Milosevic arouse ethnic hatred and promote atrocities in order to build their own political power base. In the end, Milosevic (on trial before an international tribunal for crimes against humanity) brought both Bosnia and his own country to ruin.[81] Similarly, the appalling 1994 massacres in Rwanda were substantially directed from above. Government officials induced Hutu villagers to attack their Tutsi neighbors with whom they had been living peacefully and whom they had often married over the years.

When elites are willing to resolve intense ethnic conflicts through negotiations, they arrive at several types of resolutions. In the next section, we examine those possible outcomes and also look at several options that have been attempted when negotiations failed. Although the alternatives presented here are not exhaustive, they cover a wide range of Third World experiences.

Power Sharing: Federalism and Consociationalism

Power-sharing arrangements are designed to create stability by constitutionally dividing political power among major ethnic groups. These settlements generally follow protracted negotiations and constitutional debate. If power sharing is introduced into the constitution at the time of independence, it may head off ethnic conflict before it gets started. Unfortunately, however, such arrangements often break down.

Federalism the primary form of power sharing, is "a system of government [that] emanates from the desire of people to form a union without necessarily losing their various identities."[82] It may involve the creation of autonomous or semi-autonomous regions, each of which is governed by a particular ethnicity.[83] For example, prior to its collapse, Yugoslavia consisted of six autonomous republics mostly governed by individual nationalities, including Serbs, Croats, and Slovenes. The constitution mandated power sharing between the various republics at the national level. However, that compromise began to unravel in the 1970s following the death of Marshal Joseph Broz Tito, the country's long-term strong man. It collapsed completely in the early 1990s when the Communist Party lost its grip on several republics. The Soviet Union represented another federalist effort that lasted for nearly 70 years but also disintegrated with the demise of Communist Party rule. It should be noted, however, that, unlike Yugoslavia, Soviet federalism was largely a fraud, since Moscow exercised firm control over the ethnically based republics, and Russians (constituting slightly over half the Soviet population) dominated the union entirely.

Industrialized democracies have had greater success with ethnically based federalism. Each of Switzerland's 22 cantons is dominated by one of the country's three major language groups, as German, French, and Italian cantons coexist rather harmoniously. Canada's federalism, though not based on ethnic divisions, has allowed the primarily French-speaking province of Quebec a substantial amount of autonomy on language and other cultural matters. Although the country's constitutional arrangement has not satisfied Québécois nationalists, it has accommodated many of their demands and, at least until now, has induced the province's voters to reject independence. Whether such harmony can be maintained in the future remains to be seen, particularly because the French-nationalist party, which has usually governed Quebec since 1994, continues to advocate independence. On two occasions Québécois voters rejected that option in provincial referenda. But the margin of difference narrowed the second time, and a third plebiscite could yield a different result (though a Liberal Party win over the separatist Parti Quebecois in the 2003 provincial elections seemed to signal a shift in public opinion away from separatism).

In the developing world, power sharing has been less successful. Following independence, Nigeria tried to accommodate its ethnic divisions through federalism. As previously noted, the country's northern region was dominated by the Hausa and Fulani, the east by the Ibos, and the west, to a lesser extent, by the Yoruba. Although the Biafran war took a terrible toll, a new federal solution has subsequently taken hold. On the other hand, Pakistani federalism failed to overcome the antipathy between the country's more powerful western region (populated largely by Urdu speakers) and the Bengali-speaking east. In 1971, relations between the two regions broke down completely, resulting in the massacre of some 500,000 Bengalis by western Pakistani troops.[84] When India went to war with Pakistan, the eastern region was able to secede and form the new nation of Bangladesh. Federalist arrangements also failed to prevent the breakup of Ethiopia because the central government did not adequately respect them.[85]

Consociationalism offers another potential solution to ethnic conflict. Like federalism, however, it has had a mixed record at best. Consociational democracy in plural (multiethnic) societies entails a careful division of political power designed to protect the rights of all participants.[86] It involves the following components:

1. The leaders of all important ethnic groups form a ruling coalition at the national level.
2. Each group's leader has veto power over government policy, or at least over policies that affect his or her constituents.
3. Government funds and public positions, such as the civil service, are divided between ethnicities on a roughly proportional basis.
4. Each ethnic group is afforded a high degree of autonomy over its own affairs and over the region it populates.[87]

Thus, consociational democracy consciously rejects pure majority rule. Instead, it seeks to create a framework for stability and peace by guaranteeing minorities a share of political power—even, if need be, veto power—to protect them against the majority. Not surprisingly, negotiators for South Africa's outgoing White-ruled government demanded consociational features in the country's new constitution that would provide protective guarantees for the White minority under the new Blackled regime. The irony of those demands could hardly be lost on South African Blacks, who had enjoyed no such protection under White rule.

Consociational democracy has been tried in several developing nations, including Cyprus (where it failed) and Malaysia (where it has generally succeeded). Perhaps the most widely known effort has been in Lebanon. From independence in 1943 until civil war erupted in 1975, Lebanon's government positions and political authority were divided proportionally between the nation's various Muslim and Christian communities. As we saw, the system ultimately broke down, in part because formulas for the proportional division of government posts were not adjusted to reflect the higher rate of population growth among Shi'as and other Muslims over time. After 15 years of fighting that left that once-admired Middle Eastern country shattered, Lebanon's civil war came to an end in 1990. The settlement restored consociational rule with a division of government positions that more accurately reflected the Islamic share of the population.

Arend Lijphart argues that the very success of consociational systems in reducing ethnic conflict often causes them to wither away. For example, after World War II, the Netherlands, Austria, Belgium, and Switzerland all crafted consociational democracies to manage internal ethnic divisions. Beginning in the late 1950s, however, they moved away from these arrangements as ethnic divisions diminished, largely as the result of consociationalism. Such success requires a high level of elite consensus across ethnic lines. Indeed, a degree of mutual trust and cooperation between the leaders of contending ethnic groups is the key to effective consociational arrangements. Trust is not easy to establish, however, and becomes ever more problematic when interethnic hostilities erupt in bloodshed.

Lijphart notes that power-sharing arrangements are most likely to succeed under two circumstances: first, when no single ethnic group constitutes a majority of the country's population; and, second, when the socioeconomic gap between the ethnic groups is not large.[88] But there are no certain formulas for success or, for that matter, for failure. Malaysia meets neither of these two standards (its Malay population constitutes a majority, and its Chinese minority is far more affluent), yet it has succeeded reasonably well with power sharing. Other countries with more auspicious circumstances have failed.

Secession

When power sharing or other forms of compromise fail, disgruntled ethnic minorities may attempt to withdraw (secede) from the country in order to form their own nation or join their ethnic brothers and sisters in a neighboring state. As one author put it, "Secession, like divorce, is an ultimate act of alienation."[89] It offers a potential way out of the "failed marriage" of ethnic groups within a nation-state. Unfortunately, however, like divorce, secessionist movements frequently provoke bitterness and hostility.[90]

Ralph Premdas indicates that these movements have several characteristics:

1. An ethnic group—defined by factors such as language, religion, culture, or race—claims the right of self-determination. That is to say, secession involves not just greater autonomy from the central government, but rather full independence. It should be noted, however, that disenchanted ethnic groups often begin by seeking only autonomy. If their more modest objectives are denied, however, they often escalate to a demand for full independence.
2. The ethnic community has a defined territorial base that it claims as its homeland.
3. There is virtually always some organized struggle.[91]

Given the large number of ethnically divided LDCs, we should not be surprised to find many secessionist movements. Central governments faced with such breakaway efforts virtually always try to repress them because they are unwilling to part with some of their country's territory or resources, just as President Abraham Lincoln was unwilling to part with the Confederate states in America's Civil War. This chapter previously examined secessionist movements by Tamils in Sri Lanka, Ibos in Nigeria, Eritreans in Ethiopia, and Sikhs in northern India.

To that list we might add Blacks in southern Sudan, Karens in Myanmar, Moros in the Philippines, Muslims in Kashmir (India), and many others.

Following the 1991 Gulf War, the world briefly focused its attention on Saddam Hussein's persecution of Iraq's Kurdish population. A decade later, Kurdish militia supported United States—led coalition forces in the conquest of northern Iraq (a Kurdish stronghold). But the Kurdish secessionist movement preceded Saddam's government and transcended Iraq's borders. Separatist efforts date to the collapse of the Ottoman empire at the close of World War I. Residing in a mountainous region that they call Kurdistan, more than 20 to 25 million Kurds live in neighboring regions of Turkey, Iraq, and Iran, with smaller communities in Syria.[92] Over the year, the Kurds periodically have been severely persecuted in all of those countries, and today they still have little prospect of attaining the independent Kurdistan that so many of them desire.[93]

Although many aggrieved Third World nationalities would like to secede, few have succeeded (though there have been several secessions in Eastern Europe since the fall of communism in that region). The Bangladeshi withdrawal from Pakistan is one of the few "successful" Third World cases, but it was achieved at a great cost in human lives. Moreover, it couldn't have happened without India's military intervention. Eritrea also achieved independence from Ethiopia in 1993 after decades of struggle. More often than not, however, the most that secessionist movements can hope to achieve is greater autonomy and some government recognition of their group's rights.

Noting the spread of secessionist conflicts in the 1970s and 1980s and the disintegration of the Soviet Union, Yugoslavia, and Czechoslovakia, many analysts have predicted that Eastern Europe and parts of the developing world would experience the disintegration of an ever-growing number of nation-states. Many voiced alarm about the violence and disorder that this prospect suggested. For example, a widely cited book by former U.S. senator and scholar Patrick Moynahan predicted that the number of independent states in the world would increase from about 200 to some 300 by the middle of the twenty-first century.[94] Contrary to that expectation, however, the number of secessionist wars has actually declined significantly since the start of the 1990s. From 1991 to 1999, 16 such wars were settled and 11 others were limited by cease-fires or continuing negotiations. Particularly in Africa, successful peace negotiations in one country have seemingly encouraged parallel efforts in other nations. Thus, as this century began, only 18 secessionist wars continued worldwide, fewer than at any time since 1970.[95]

Outside Intervention

"If the Bosnian Muslims had been needle-nosed dolphins," Edward Luttwak asked, "would the world have allowed the Croats and Serbs to slaughter them by the tens of thousands?"[96] His blunt words raise important ethical and pragmatic questions about the world's obligations and limitations in such situations. Considerable evidence indicates that the United States and Western Europe sidestepped many opportunities to save Jews from the Nazi holocaust, feeling that voters at home wouldn't want to get involved. More recently, the world community has stood by and allowed, or even indirectly abetted, ethnic bloodbaths in Bosnia, Indonesia, Rwanda, the Congo, and Sudan, despite immediate and graphic evidence (often presented by the mass media) documenting the carnage. Indeed, Belgium and France had armed and trained the Rwandan (Hutu-dominated) military right up to the time of the 1994 mass slaughter, despite being warned by experts that it was likely that those weapons would be turned on Tutsi civilians. Furthermore, government documents confirm that Washington ignored reports of the Hutu slaughter being sent daily from the American embassy in Rwanda.[97] Rather than promote international intervention to save the Tutsis, the United States supported the withdrawal of the small United Nations contingent already in the country. Although the rapid pace of mass murder there—about 500,000 to 800,000 people killed in three weeks—exceeded even the Nazi holocaust, the U.S. State Department refused to call the events "genocide" for fear that the international antigenocide treaty passed after World War II might obligate the United States and other Western powers to intervene.

What motivated such a seemingly callous position? Only a year earlier, the American public had been horrified when 18 U.S. Rangers had been killed while participating in a U.N. peacekeeping operation in Somalia, and television news had shown a mob dragging several of the bodies through the streets. When Rwandan events began to unfold, policy makers in Washington assumed that U.S. public opinion, still shaken by the images from Somalia, would preclude any new American intervention. Even a decade later, the "Somali Effect" made Washington policy makers reluctant to come to the defense of Bosnia's Muslims. Also, in 2004, a million people fled "ethnic cleansing" in Darfur and faced the threat of starvation, while the United Nations and the United States only pressured the Sudanese government diplomatically, failing to take stronger action.

Unless outside forces are invited in by a country's own government (as when Sri Lanka asked India's armed forces to quell its civil war), external intervention raises important questions of national sovereignty. However, such invitations are rare, particularly since it is often the government itself that has perpetrated, encouraged, or at least condoned the ethnic violence. In most cases, then, external interference raises a number of difficult questions: At what point, if any, do outside nations or international organizations (such as the United Nations and NATO) have the right to violate a country's sovereignty in order to save innocent lives? For example, should the United Nations or the West have sent troops into Bosnia at a much earlier point, with or without the permission of the Yugoslav government, in order to stop the "ethnic cleansing" there? Does the community of nations have any legal and moral obligations to protect the people of Darfur from genocide, even if it violates Sudanese sovereignty? If so, should the U.N. have been authorized to send troops into Birmingham, Alabama, or rural Mississippi during the 1960s to protect the lives of Blacks who were being terrorized by the Ku Klux Klan and the local police? Who is to decide whether outside intervention is legitimate or not? Under what circumstances does outside intervention (including military intervention) prevent ethnic persecution and impose a durable solution, and when will such efforts be futile, or will any success be short-lived? Will countries such as the United States, France, India, and Nigeria be willing to commit their soldiers and economic resources on a sustained basis to support future peacekeeping operations? How many casualties among their own personnel are peacekeeping nations prepared to accept?[98] Ultimately, governments contemplating a humanitarian intervention will have to weigh their own national interests and the costs of intervention against any commitments to sustain human rights abroad.

Most nations are reluctant to risk their soldiers' lives for humanitarian purposes. As we have just noted, after losing a relatively small number of peacekeepers in Somalia, Washington refused to intervene in Rwanda and was very slow to respond to atrocities in Bosnia. Only after thousands of refugees had died and many more faced starvation did the African Union send a tiny military force to Darfur, with the acquiescence of the Sudanese government. For the most part, peacekeeping forces are sent only to enforce or monitor set-tlements that the warring factions have already negotiated (as with recent U.N. peacekeeping missions in Liberia, Sierra Leone, and Ivory Coast), and only after prolonged conflict has already cost thousands of lives. At other times, when world opinion has forced the host government to accept external inter-vention, such as U.N. intervention in East Timor (Indonesia), troops are usually sent in *after* the worst outrages have already been committed.

To be sure, some seemingly intractable ethnic conflicts have had resolu-tions imposed on them by outside forces. In such cases, the intervening power is often a neighboring state that either has ties to one of the warring ethnic groups or has a strategic interest in the country it invades. Such was the case with India's intercession on behalf of the Bengalis in East Pakistan. Without that intervention, the nation of Bangladesh could not have been born. The Turkish invasion of Cyprus imposed an ethnic settlement there by partitioning the island's Greek and Turkish communities. Recent examples of intervention by *non*-neighboring nations include the U.S. and British protection of the Kurdish enclave in northern Iraq during the 1990s. In Central Europe, NATO bombing of Serbia in 1999 forced that government to cease its attacks on Kosovo's Albanian minority and allow in foreign troops. But NATO interven-tion was in great part a reaction to the West's earlier, embarrassing refusal to halt the ethnic cleansing in Bosnia that had left hundreds of thousands dead. Even in Kosovo, the West only carried out bombing missions (not ground action), which posed minimal risk to American and other NATO pilots.

At the same time, it must be recognized that externally imposed solutions have often ended badly. Many Iraqi Kurds retain bitter memories of earlier American assistance. In 1974, the United States and Iran supported a Kurdish rebellion against the government dominated by then Vice President Saddam Hussein. However, for Washington, Kurdish interests were secondary to its own policy objective—supporting the interests of Iran's royal government, America's ally and Iraq's enemy. Consequently, when the Shah of Iran tem-porarily resolved his differences with Iraq in 1975 and withdrew his support for the Kurdish insurrection, the CIA did the same. In the aftermath, thousands of Iraqi Kurds were killed or driven from their homes.[99] Other external interven-tions have also produced unhappy results. More recently, Uganda and Rwanda have supported tribal armies in neighboring countries in order to advance their own geopolitical interests.

As we have seen, India's attempt to settle the Tamil-Sinhalese conflict in Sri Lanka ended disastrously. Not only did it fail to resolve the civil war, but it led subsequently to the assassination of India's former Prime Minister Rajiv Gandhi by a Tamil Tiger suicide bomber. Although a 2002 cease-fire halted hostilities in the civil war, negotiations over a peace treaty have stalled and a mid-2004 Tiger suicide bombing in the country's capital further endangered the truce. Foreign intervention did halt ethnic violence in the former Yugoslavia (Bosnia and Kosovo), but the future remains uncertain as outside peacekeeping troops face an indefinite stay.

Thus, Glynne Evans notes:

> A half-hearted [outside] military response [to ethnic conflict] without any underlying political action is a poor option. ... Conflicts with a high degree of ethnic mobilization last for generations rather than years, and are intense in their impact. ... as neighbors turn on neighbors. An intervention for humanitarian purposes in such cases becomes a major military commitment, and one of long duration.[100]

Events in Rwanda, Sudan, and elsewhere suggest that this is a commitment that outside powers are rarely prepared to make. The world's only superpower, the United States, has been among the most reluctant to risk its soldiers in such situations. In the major exception—U.S. intervention in Iraq—Kurdish and Shi'a interests (ethnic groups that had been persecuted under Saddam Hussein) were quite incidental to the U.S. decision to topple the Iraqi dictatorship.

Outside Intervention in Iraq: The Effect of the U.S. Occupation on Ethnic Relations

Like many Middle-Eastern nations, Iraq has suffered the strains of ethnic tensions and conflict. Two major divisions have been particularly important: first, the divide within the Arab community between the majority Shi'a population and the Sunni minority, which had dominated the political system under Saddam Hussein. Second, the Kurds' long-standing desire for self-rule and associated government persecution, discussed in the following.

About half the world's Kurds reside in Turkey, but Iraq is home to some 5 million of them (the precise figure is in dispute). With about 3.7 million Kurds living in an area the size of Austria, they constitute the majority population in three of Iraq's 18 provinces.[101] Under the Ottoman empire, which governed most of the Middle East from the seventeenth to the early twentieth centuries, ethnic minorities were treated quite fairly. Hence, aside from occasional, relatively small rebellions, Kurdish nationalism did not blossom until Ottoman rule collapsed after World War I. At that time, several victorious nations—Britain, France, and Italy— signed the short-lived Treaty of Severe (1920), which promised the creation of an autonomous or independent Kurdistan.[102] However, just three years later, the Treaty of Lausanne terminated that commitment. As the Turkish and Iraqi states that succeeded the Ottoman empire periodically persecuted the Kurds, their dream of autonomy or independence remained unfulfilled.

When Iraq's monarchy was overthrown in 1958, the new government briefly allowed Kurdish culture to flourish. By 1960, however, the republican regime began a 15-year campaign designed to "Arabize" Kurdish regions. It featured forced removal of Kurds from their homelands to other parts of the country, destruction of Kurdish villages, and moving Arabs into Kurdish regions. When Iran, Israel, and the CIA encouraged an Iraqi Kurdish rebellion in 1974-75 and then withdrew assistance, many thousands of additional Kurds were killed or ousted from their villages. In 1980, only a year after an Islamic revolution had overthrown Iran's Shah, Iraq and Iran started a brutal, decade-long war. Because Iraq's Kurds largely supported Iran, Saddam Hussein undertook a genocidal campaign against them (called "al-*Anfal*") at the close of the 1980s. Tens of thousands of Kurds, perhaps as many as 182,000, were killed and many more were driven from their villages. In that process, the Iraqi military carried out "the first documented instances of a government employing chemical weapons against its own civilian population."[103]

After U.S.-led coalition forces drove the Iraqi army out of Kuwait in the Gulf War, Kurdish rebels in Iraq's north and Shi'a Arabs in the south rose up against Saddam Hussein's government. Quickly, however, the military recaptured the towns that had fallen to the rebels, forcing over one million Kurds to flee toward the borders with Turkey and Iran. As Turkey refused to allow them in and numerous refugees died of exposure, the European Community proposed, and the United States endorsed, the creation of a U.N.-protected, Kurdish enclave within Iraq. Under "Operation Provide Comfort," several Western nations placed troops on the ground as the allied air forces established a "no-fly zone" prohibiting Iraqi planes from flying north of the 36th parallel, thereby effectively creating the autonomous region that the Kurds had so long yearned for. The United States and its allies soon withdrew their ground troops to bases across the border with Turkey, but continued to provide aid while maintaining the no-fly zone. Many thousands of Kurdish families returned to the region and established democratic political institutions, including the election of a Kurdish National Assembly in 1992. Although fierce feuding between the two major Kurdish political parties caused the autonomous zone to break in two (1994), both regions continued to be ruled relatively democratically.

During the 2003 invasion of Iraq, U.S. forces received valuable military and intelligence support from Kurdish militias. The ouster of Saddam Hussein's regime raised the question of Kurdish participation in postwar Iraq. In deference to U.S. pressure and Turkish opposition, the Kurdish political and military leadership provisionally foreswore ambitions for an independent Kurdistan but demanded substantial autonomy in the new political order. After much debate, the U.S.-appointed Iraqi Governing Council not only provided considerable Kurdish autonomy under the 2004 interim constitution, but also granted the Kurds the power to block passage of a permanent constitution to be crafted in 2005 by the partially sovereign provisional government. Under the terms of that agreement, the proposed permanent constitution would be submitted to nation-wide referendum and would be rejected if two-thirds of the voters in any three of Iraq's provinces opposed it. Since the Kurds are the dominant majority in three provinces, this gives them virtual veto protection over the provisions of the permanent constitution.

Currently the future of the Iraqi Kurdish community remains uncertain. With the fall of Saddam's regime, some previously repressed ethnic groups, once united in their opposition to the dictator's Sunni (Arab)-dominated government, have turned against each other. Iraq's Shi'as (constituting about 60 percent of the country's population) and Kurds (mostly Sunnis) both rose up against Saddam following the Gulf War and both suffered greatly when their revolts failed. A decade later, however, Kurdish insistence on veto power over the permanent constitution has clashed with the Shi'a desire for comprehensive majority rule. Consequently, Ayatollah Ali Sistani, Iraq's most influential Shi'a cleric, briefly blocked Governing Council approval of the 2004 interim constitution when he convinced five Shi'a council members to reject the clause giving any three provinces the power to block the 2005 permanent constitution. Although Sistani relented and the provisional constitution was approved, various Shi'a political leaders subsequently have suggested that they will not be bound by those referendum rules. In response, Kurdish leaders have warned that if they are denied such protections of Kurdish autonomy, they will again consider "Kurdistan's" secession from the country.[104]

At the same time, in the northern city of Kirkuk, deep tensions have emerged between the city's Kurdish and Shi'a Turkmen populations. Under Saddam, many Kurds and Turkmen (an ethnic group distinct from either the Arabs or the Kurds) had been expelled from Kirkuk and replaced by Arabs relocated from the south. Located within one of the country's largest oil fields (with 10 billion barrels of proven oil reserves), Kirkuk has become a flashpoint for Kurdish-Shi'a tensions as both sides jockey for political and economic influence in the emerging Iraqi regime.[105] In short, although foreign intervention—the 1991 Gulf War and the war toppling Saddam—have greatly benefited both the Kurdish and Shi'a populations, it remains to be seen whether these formerly allied ethnic groups can coexist peacefully in the new political order.

Settlement through Exhaustion

Ultimately, many ethnic conflicts are resolved less through statecraft, constitutional arrangements, or external intervention than through the exhaustion of the warring parties. Although the Arab League helped negotiate an end to Lebanon's lengthy civil war, it was the weariness of the Lebanese, after the virtual destruction of Beirut, that permitted a settlement. Although the Ugandan government continues to clash periodically with the Acholi and Langi tribes, conflict has been kept in check as no Ugandans want to return to the ethnically based bloodshed of the Amin and Obote governments. In Mozambique, Angola, Liberia, and Sierra Leone, exhaustion helped drive the warring factions toward U.N.-brokered peace treaties that halted their long and bitter civil wars. And in Sudan, a similar process seems to be ending the 21-year war between the Arab north and the Black population of the south.

Toward a Peaceful Resolution of Conflict

If developing nations are to avoid the horrors of civil war, secession, and foreign intervention, they must arrive at legal, political, and social solutions that can constrain ethnic tensions. A conference of U.S. foreign assistance officials and scholars proposed the following measures:

- Writing a new constitution [that] offers the possibility of creating new institutional arrangements, such as federalism, for power sharing between ... ethnic groups.
- Establishing protection for ethnic minority rights, not only through constitutional and legal guarantees but also through civic education.
- Creating electoral systems with incentives for cooperation and accommodation among groups.[106]

Such institutional goals, though clearly reasonable, are more easily set out than achieved. More difficult still is the task of repairing the damage to multiethnic societies that have been torn apart by bloody conflict (e.g., Rwanda, Kashmir, and Lebanon) or by decades of prejudice and segregation (South Africa, the United States). Not long after South Africa's new, multiracial regime was installed in 1994, the government of Nelson Mandela created a Truth and Reconciliation Commission, before which perpetrators of racially based violence and injustices were invited to confess their crimes in return for amnesty.[107] The goal of the Commission was to further unearth the crimes of apartheid and, more importantly, to allow the nation's races to live to together more harmoniously. However, as one observer of the Commission's hearings has suggested, in countries that have experienced systematic repression or extensive ethnic violence (as in Rwanda, Sudan, and Bosnia), reconciliation—the establishment of harmony between formerly hostile parties—may be too much to hope for.[108] A more realistic goal may be to create the basis for *coexistence* between these groups. Toward this end, governments or international agencies trying to assist countries previously devastated by ethnic violence need to create trauma centers for the survivors of atrocities, multicultural educational programs, contact programs that bring together erstwhile perpetrators and victims of ethnic violence to establish dialogue, and cross-ethnic economic development programs, all designed to help former antagonists coexist. Not surprisingly, such efforts have had mixed records of success.[109]

CONCLUSION: ETHNIC PLURALISM AND DEMOCRACY

As modernization theory suggests, in the *long* term socioeconomic development is likely to reduce ethnic antagonisms by increasing education, establishing a more homogenous society, and creating greater economic resources and government assistance for all ethnic groups. Thus, highly developed countries like Belgium or Canada are less likely than LDCs to experience violent ethnic conflicts. At the same time, however, the major forces of change in the Third World—urbanization, education, increased literacy, and greater media exposure—have frequently fanned the flames of ethnic violence during the earlier stages of modernization. Dependency theory also fails to fully explain Third World ethnic tensions. Its proponents blame divide-and-rule tactics by colonial powers and the intensification of economic inequalities among ethnic groups during the spread of world capitalism. But ethnic tensions plague some Third World countries that were never colonized, and foreign intervention can hardly be the root cause of all ethnic violence in Africa, Asia, and the Middle East.

Crafting peaceful solutions for multicultural societies will remain one of the greatest challenges facing Third World leaders in this century. The frequency and intensity of ethnic conflicts peaked during the late 1980s and early 1990s and have decreased modestly since that time. Although Africa remained home to some of the world's most brutal conflicts during the last 10 to 15 years (Sierra Leone, Sudan, Congo), it also enjoyed the most progress of late in bringing ethno-warfare to a halt. Realizing that their countries and the powers of the state were being destroyed by ethnic hostilities and decades of economic decay, many of Africa's political leaders (government and rebel) have become more accommodating. Because the number of new ethnic conflicts has diminished in the past decade, most of the ethnic wars still being waged in the early years of the twenty-first century are unresolved conflicts dating back to the mid-1990s or earlier.

During the 1970s and 1980s, increased ethnic violence in the developing world and the former communist states of Eastern Europe often coincided chronologically with the spread of democratic government in those areas. This has raised two questions about the relationship between democracy and ethnic politics: first, are multiethnic countries less likely to maintain democracy than are culturally homogenous societies? Second, does the growth of citizen participation and the creation of democratic government intensify conflict between ethnic communities?

The first question is answered relatively easily. Democracy *is* clearly harder, though far from impossible, to establish or maintain in multiethnic countries. We have seen, for example, how Lebanon's political system, long admired as one of the most democratic in the Middle East, was devastated by civil war. Looking at democracy's failure to take root in most of Africa and Asia during the 1960s and 1970s, Alvin Rabushka and Kenneth Shepsle concluded that ethnic antagonisms were an important obstacle. Democracy, they argue, "is simply not viable in an environment of intense ethnic preference."[110] Here they refer to societies in which favored ethnic groups receive special privileges while others suffer discrimination.

An examination of both economically developed nations and LDCs reveals that democracy has fared best in countries that have been relatively ethnically homogeneous (such as Finland, Denmark, and Japan) or in countries of "new settlement" (including the United States, Canada, and Australia) populated primarily by immigrants who have created a new common culture.[111] In Africa, Asia, and the Middle East, where many countries labor under strong ethnic divisions, the growth of democracy and mass political participation may unleash communal hostilities, often intensified by cynical politicians who make use of such tensions to acquire a political following.

Ethnic pluralism poses a particular obstacle to democracy in poorer countries where each group must contend for limited government resources (schools, roads, civil service jobs, and the like) in a "politics of scarcity." But although democracy is more difficult to achieve in plural societies, it is not impossible. Despite its history of religiously based violence, India, one of the world's most ethnically diverse countries, has maintained democratic government for most of its half-century of independence. Trinidad-Tobago, a country divided by religion and race, has been among the Third World's most democratic countries.

To be sure, the initial transition to democracy frequently intensifies existing ethnic animosities. Newly formed political parties often base their support in competing ethnic communities. Opportunistic politicians, even those opposed to violence, are tempted to use ethnic appeals as a means of gaining public support. As public resources (such as roads, schools, clinics, and irrigation projects) are distributed through more open legislative decisions, ethnically based interest groups and political parties will likely fight for their fair share. Some analysts warn that "the opening of democratic space throws up many groups pulling in different directions, that it causes demand overload, systematic breakdown and even violent conflict," a danger particularly relevant in societies with deep ethnic tensions prior to their democratic transitions.[112] That danger is greatest in strict majoritarian democracies in which a single ethnic group or allied ethnicities can dominate parliamentary or presidential elections without affording constitutional or other institutional protections for minority groups. Thus, the Carnegie Commision on Preventing Deadly Conflict concluded that:

> In societies with deep ethnic divisions and little experience with democratic government and the rule of law [a common phenomenon in Africa, Asia and the Middle East], strict majoritarian democracy can be self-defeating. Where ethnic identities are strong and national identity weak, populations may vote largely on ethnic lines. Domination by one ethnic group can lead to a tyranny of the majority.[113]

But this merely indicates the importance on limiting majoritarian rule in democratic, multiethnic societies. It doesn't suggest that authoritarian government is preferable in such situations. Indeed, in the long run the only way ethnicities can resolve their differences is through open discussion and bargaining in a relatively democratic political arena, so long as majority rule is tempered by constitutional human rights guarantees, consociational arrangements, or other institutional protections for minorities such as those previously discussed.[114]

Although dictatorships in Yugoslavia and the Soviet Union were able to repress ethnic conflicts for many years, they actually intensified these grievances in the long run by denying their existence, silencing them, and failing to deal with them. After the fall of communism, long-repressed antagonisms in Croatia, Bosnia, Kosovo, and Chechnya burst to the surface, producing civil war or lesser forms of violence. Elsewhere, dictators such as Laurent Kabila (Congo), Suharto (Indonesia), and Saddam Hussein (Iraq) presided over ethnic massacres that would have been unthinkable in a democracy monitored by public opinion and a free press.

Conversely, democratic politicians are open to interest group pressure from ethnic minorities and, hence, are more likely to settle disputes peacefully before they degenerate into violence. Indeed, a recent exhaustive study of "minorities at risk" throughout the world revealed that democratic regimes are more likely than dictatorships to negotiate peaceful settlements of ethnic warfare. And during the 1990s, political discrimination and, to a lesser degree, economic discrimination against ethnic minorities were more likely to decline in democracies than under authoritarian governments.[115] In short, to accommodate ethnic pluralism and resolve tensions, what is needed is democratic, mature, and enlightened political leadership, a spirit of compromise, and the implementation of politically negotiated solutions such as federalism and consociational democracy.

DISCUSSION QUESTIONS

1. What do we mean by *ethnicity*, and what are some of the most important types of ethnic identification?
2. Discuss the effect that modernization has had on ethnic identification and ethnic conflict.
3. What are some factors that may cause interethnic relations to become violent?
4. How might outside intervention reduce or increase ethnic tension? Cite some specific successful examples of such intervention and some failures.

5. Discuss the ethnic identity of Middle Eastern Kurds and how their aspirations have created political divisions in Turkey, Iran, and Iraq during the past decades. How has American military intervention affected the status of the Kurds in Iraq?
6. Discuss how a country's transition to democracy might increase ethnic tensions in some cases and decrease it in others?
7. What are some reasons that might explain why major civil strife related to ethnicity has declined in the last 10 to 15 years?

NOTES

1. Human Rights Watch, *Darfur Destroyed Ethnic Cleansing by Government and Militia Forces in Western Sudan* 16, no. 6 (A) (May 2004): 1; on the earlier civil war in the south, see Douglas Hamilton Johnson, *The Root Causes of Sudan's Civil Wars* (Bloomington: Indiana University Press, 2003).

2. Eric Hobsbawm, *The Age of Extremes* (New York: Vintage Books, 1996), 50.

3. Yueh-Ting Lee, Fathali Moghaddam, Clark McCauley, and Stephen Worchel, "The Global Challenge of Ethnic and Cultural Conflict," in *The Psychology of Ethnic and Cultural Conflict*, eds. Y. Lee, C. McCauley, F. Moghaddam, and S. Worchel (Westport: Praeger, 2004), 3.

4. Crawford Young, *The Politics of Cultural Pluralism* (Madison: University of Wisconsin Press, 1976), 23–26. The quotation appears on p. 23.

5. Ted Robert Gurr, "Preface" and "Long War, Short Peace: The Rise and Decline of Ethnopolitical Conflict at the End of the Cold War," in *Peoples versus States: Minorities at Risk in the New Century*, ed. T. Gurr (Washington, DC: United States Institute of Peace Press, 2000), xiii and 27–56; David Carment and Frank Harvey, *Using Force to Prevent Ethnic Violence* (Westport: Praeger, 2001), 5.

6. For a hard-hitting attack on such gloom and doom prophecies, see Yahya Sadowski, *The Myth of Global Chaos* (Washington, DC: The Brookings Institution, 1998), esp. chap. 10.

7. Analysis of the years 1958 to 1966, for example, shows that of 164 conflicts with significant violence, only 15 involved clashes between two or more states. Most involved ethnic conflict within countries. See Abdul A. Said and Luiz R. Simmons, "The Ethnic Factor in World Politics," in *Ethnicity in an International Context*, eds. Said and Simmons (New Brunswick, NJ: Transaction Books, 1976), 16.

8. Monica Duffy Toft, *The Geography of Ethnic Violence: Identity, Interests, and the Indivisibility of Territory* (Princeton, NJ: Princeton University Press, 2003), 3; see also, Peter Wallensteen and

Margareta Sollenberg, "Armed Conflicts, Conflict Termination, and Peace Agreements, 1989-1996," *Journal of Peace Research* 34, no. 3 (1997): 339–358.

9. David Bloomfield and Ben Reilly (eds.), *Democracy and Deep-rooted Conflict: Options for Negotiations* (Stockholm: International Institute for Democracy and Electoral Assistance, 1998): 4.

10. During this period, only two or three international conflicts—the Iran-Iraq War, the Soviet war in Afghanistan, and perhaps the Gulf War—had comparable death tolls. Ironically, the last two were followed by internal ethnic violence. Of course, some brutal civil wars, such as those in El Salvador and Nicaragua, have not been ethnically related.

11. One study estimated some 10 million deaths as of the early 1970s. Harold Isaacs, *Idols of the Tribe: Group Identity and Political Change* (New York: Harper & Row, 1975), 3. Millions more have died since that time in the former Yugoslavia, Chechnya, Sudan, Mozambique, Angola, Congo, Rwanda, Burundi, Ethiopia, India, Iraq, Guatemala, Afghanistan, and elsewhere.

12. Gurr, *Peoples versus States*, 10–11.

13. First popularized by renowned social psychologist, G.W. Allport some 50 years ago—see Allport, *The Nature of Prejudice* (Cambridge, MA: Addison-Wesley Press, 1954), the hypothesis has quite recently been referred to as "one of the most long-lived and succesful ideas in the history of social psychology." See M. B. Brewer and R. J. Brown, "Intergroup Relations," in *Handbook of Social Psychology* (Vol. 2), eds. S. T. Fiske and G. Lindzey (Boston: McGraw-Hill, 1998).

14. Gurr, *Peoples versus States*, 5.

15. Donald Rothchild and Victor A. Olorunsola, "Managing Competing State and Ethnic Claims," in *State versus Ethnic Claims: African Policy Dilemmas*, eds. Rothchild and Olorunsola (Boulder, CO: Westview Press, 1983), 20.

16. Quoted in Francine Friedman, *The Bosnian Muslims: Denial of a Nation* (Boulder, CO: Westview Press, 1996), 1.

17. Quoted in David A. Lake and Donald Rothchild, "Spreading Fear: The Genesis of Transnational Ethnic Conflict," in *The International Spread of Ethnic Conflict*, eds. Lake and Rothchild (Princeton, NJ: Princeton University Press, 1998), 7.

18. Cynthia Enloe, *Ethnic Conflict and Political Development* (Boston: Little, Brown, 1973), 15.

19. Charles W. Anderson, Fred R. von der Mehden, and Crawford Young, *Issues of Political Development*, 2d ed. (Upper Saddle River, NJ: Prentice Hall, 1974), 31–33; Crawford Young, *Politics in the Congo* (Princeton, NJ: Princeton University Press, 1965), chap. 11.

20. Donald Horowitz, *A Democratic South Africa? Constitutional Engineering in a Divided Society* (Berkeley: University of California Press, 1991), 44–48.

21. Young, *Cultural Pluralism*, 20.

22. "Communal" conflicts or relations refer to conflicts or relations between ethnic communities of any kind.

23. Uri Ra'anan, "Nation and State: Order Out of Chaos," in *State and Nation in Multi-ethnic Societies*, ed. Ra'anan et al. (Manchester, England, and New York: Manchester University Press, 1991), 4–7.

24. Toft, *The Geography of Ethnic Violence*, 17, 149–152.

25. Said and Simmons, *Ethnicity in an International Context*, 10. With the spread of migration across state borders, even countries like Norway and Sweden (each having experienced an upsurge of Third World and Eastern European immigrants) are no longer fully homogeneous.

26. Scholars specializing in African culture and politics generally reject the use of the term *tribe* to describe the region's various cultural-linguistic groups; they prefer the term *ethnicity*. *Tribe* is used here because it is a term more familiar to readers and one still used in much of the ethnic literature. It also avoids confusion with the more broadly used meaning of the word *ethnicity*. More will be said of this later in the chapter.

27. Omo Omoruyi, "State Creation and Ethnicity in a Federal (Plural) System: Nigeria's Search for Parity," in *Ethnicity, Politics, and Development*, eds. Dennis L. Thompson and Dov Ronen (Boulder, CO: Lynne Rienner Publishers, 1986), 120. Since social scientists do not always agree on what constitutes a distinct ethnic group, other calculations would be far different.

28. Jaques Bertrand, *Nationalism and Ethnic Conflict in Indonesia* (Cambridge, England and New York: Cambridge University Press, 2004), 135–144.

29. Crawford Young, "Comparative Claims to Political Sovereignty: Biafra, Katanga, Eritrea," in *State versus Ethnic Claims*, 211–219.

30. On Ethiopia and the secessionist wars, see Christopher Clapham, *Transformation and Continuity in Revolutionary Ethiopia* (Cambridge, England: Cambridge University Press, 1988), and J. Markakis, *National and Class Conflict in the Horn of Africa* (Cambridge, England: Cambridge University Press, 1987). Subsequent events have superseded the material in both books.

31. Scholars such as Crawford Young maintain that "caste, race and religion belong to a larger genus ... called cultural pluralism." I will not discuss caste as an ethnic category because it exists only in India and a handful of other countries.

32. John Breuilly, *Nationalism and the State* (Manchester, England: Manchester University Press, 1982), 3.

33. Many Kurdish and non-Kurdish scholars dispute the Kurdish nationalists' assertion that there is a single Kurdish language with multiple dialects. They argue that the variations in various Kurdish languages are too great to call them part of a single language. Even so, the various Kurdish languages are closely related to each other and are distinct from the Turkish, Arabic, and Persian languages that predominate in the Kurds' home countries (though Kurdish is somewhat related to Persian). See Nader Entessan, "Ethnicity and Ethnic Challenges in the Middle East," in *Ethnicity and Governance in the Third World*, eds. John Mukum Mbaku, Pita Ogaba Agbese, and Mwangi S. Kimenyi (Hants, England: Ashgate Publishing, 2001) , 159.

34. David Brown, *Contemporary Nationalism: Civic, Ethnocultural and Multicultural Politics* (London and New York: Routledge, 2000), 70–88.

35. For a helpful recent analysis of Tamil-Sinhalese conflict in Sri Lanka, see A. Jeyaratnam Wilson, *Sri Lankan Tamil Nationalism* (Vancouver: University of British Columbia Press, 2000).

36. Appapillai Amirdhalingam, quoted in Eller, *From Culture to Ethnicity to Conflict*, 123.

37. S. W. R. de A. Samarasinghe, "The Dynamics of Separatism: The Case of Sri Lanka," and K. M. de Silva, "Separatism in Sri Lanka: The Traditional Homelands of the Tamils," in *Secessionist Movements in Comparative Perspective*, eds. Ralph R. Premdas, S. W. R. de A. Samarasinghe, and Alan B. Anderson (London: Pinter Publishers, 1990), 32–67; also, K. M. de Silva, *Managing Ethnic Tensions in Multi-Ethnic Societies: Sri Lanka 1880–1985* (Lanham, MD: University Press of America, 1986).

38. Eller, *From Culture to Ethnicity to Conflict,* 130–132.

39. *Eelam* is the Tamil word for Sri Lanka.

40. For a blistering criticism of the Indian intervention, see Chris Smith, "South Asia's Enduring War," in *Creating Peace in Sri Lanka: Civil War and Reconciliation,* ed. Robert I. Rothberg (Washington, D.C.: Brookings Institution Press, 1999), 19–25.

41. Anjana Pasricha, "Sri Lanka Peace Talks Deadlocked Over Renegade Tamil Leader," *Voice of America* Broadcast (July 1, 2004). See http://www.voanews.com

42. Aidan Southall, "The Illusion of Tribe," in *The Passing of Tribal Man in Africa, Journal of African and Asian Studies* 5 (special issue), nos. 1–2 (January–April 1970): 28–50. Cited by Young, *Politics of Cultural Pluralism,* 19.

43. Milton Obote, *Proposals for New Methods of Election of Representatives of the People to Parliament* (Kampala, Uganda: Milton Obote Foundation, 1970), 6. Quoted in Donald Rothchild, "Hegemonial Exchange: An Alternative Model for Managing Conflict in Middle Africa," in *Ethnicity, Politics and Development,* 77. The term *tribe* is used by various scholars in that volume as well as in Enloe, *Ethnic Conflict.*

44. Dov Ronen, *The Quest for Self Determination* (New Haven, CT: Yale University Press, 1976), 79–86.

45. Young, "Comparative Claims to Political Sovereignty," 204–211; Enloe, *Ethnic Conflict,* 89–92.

46. Frederick Forsyth, *The Biafran Story* (Baltimore, MD: Penguin Books, 1969).

47. See Toyin Falola, *Violence in Nigeria: The Crisis of Religious Politics and Secular Ideology* (Rochester, NY: University of Rochester Press, 1998), 193–226.

48. Basil Davidson, *The Black Man's Burden* (New York: Times Books, 1992), 250.

49. Gérard Prunier, *The Rwanda Crisis, 1959–1994* (London: Hurst & Company, 1995).

50. Anderson, von der Mehden, and Young, *Issues of Political Development,* 21.

51. Horowitz, *A Democratic South Africa,* 47.

52. Khehla Shubane, "South Africa: A New Government in the Making?" *Current History* 91 (May 1992): 202–207; Pauline H. Baker, "South Africa on the Move," *Current History* 89 (May 1990): 197–200, 232–233.

53. Jacob T. Levey, *The Multiculturalism of Fear* (Oxford and New York: Oxford University Press, 2000), 179.

54. *New York Times* (December 8, 1992).

55. *New York Times* (July 27, 2002).

56. Cited in T. Walker Wallbank, *A Short History of India and Pakistan* (New York: Mentor, 1958), 196.

57. Bernard E. Brown, "The Government of India," in *Introduction to Comparative Government,* 2d ed., eds. Michael Curtis et al. (New York: HarperCollins, 1990), 479–480; Robert L. Hardgrave, Jr., *India: Government and Politics in a Developing Nation,* 3d ed. (New York: Harcourt Brace Jovanovich, 1980), 40–42. Hardgrave offers an estimate of half a million dead. For personal accounts of the violence that followed partition, especially the recollections of women, see Urvashi Butalia, *The Other Side of Silence: Voices from the Partition of India* (Durham, NC: The Duke University Press, 2000).

58. Originating in the fifteenth century, the Sikh religion is related to both the Hindu religion and Islam.

59. Mohammed Ayoob, "Dateline India: The Deepening Crisis," *Foreign Policy* 85 (Winter 1991–1992): 173; Surendra Chopra, "Ethnic Identity in a Plural Society: A Case Study of System Breakdown in the Punjab," in *Ethnicity, Politics, and Development,* 196–197.

60. Latif Abul-Husn, *The Lebanese Conflict: Looking Inward* (Boulder, CO: Lynne Rienner Publishers, 1998), 29–44.

61. Elizabeth Picard, "Political Identities and Communal Identities: Shifting Mobilization Among the Lebanese Shi'a Through Ten Years of War, 1975–1985," in *Ethnicity, Politics, and Development,* 159–175. In the absence of dependable census information, estimates of Lebanon's religious composition varied widely.

62. Ronald D. McLaurin, "Lebanon: Into or Out of Oblivion?" *Current History* 91 (January 1992): 29–30.

63. Latif Abul-Husn, *The Lebanese Conflict;* Carole H. Dagher, *Bringing Down the Walls: Lebanon's Postwar Challenge* (New York: St. Martin's Press, 2000).

64. Of course, the American image as a successful melting pot has often been exaggerated. For example, substantial racial tensions continue to divide society. In recent decades, many Hispanic immigrants have found it difficult to integrate into the mainstream of American life, and various forms of prejudice abound against African Americans, Asian Americans, Hispanics, and other minority groups.

65. Young, *Cultural Pluralism,* 65.

66. Anderson, von der Mehden, and Young, *Issues,* 29.

67. A similar process is currently taking place in Eastern Europe, where the collapse of the Soviet multinational empire and the removal of repressive political systems have unleashed

ethnic conflict in Bosnia, the former Soviet Union, and elsewhere.

68. Karl W. Deutsch, *Nationalism and Social Communication* (Boston: MIT Press and John Wiley and Sons, 1953).

69. The Cuban government has been much more explicit in its campaigns against sexism than it has against racism. It tends to insist that pre-Revolutionary racial divisions were merely surrogates for class divisions. Consequently, the government erroneously maintains that the social and economic gains the Revolution brought to the lower classes have, by themselves, ended racism.

70. Gordon Means, "Ethnic Preference Policies in Malaysia," in *Ethnic Preference and Public Policy in Developing States*, eds. Neil Nevitte and Charles H. Kennedy (Boulder, CO: Lynne Rienner Publishers, 1986), 95–115; Young, *Cultural Pluralism*, 121–124.

71. The designation *East Indian* is used in Trinidad, Guyana, and other Caribbean nations to distinguish them from indigenous American Indians in the hemisphere.

72. Bridget Brereton, "The Foundations of Prejudice: Indians and Africans in 19th Century Trinidad," *Caribbean Issues* 1, no. 1 (1974): 15–28; John Gaffar LaGuerre, "Race Relations in Trinidad and Tobago," in *Trinidad and Tobago: The Independence Experience, 1962–1987*, ed. Selwyn Ryan (St. Augustine, Trinidad: University of the West Indies, 1988), 195.

73. Selwyn D. Ryan, *Race and Nationalism in Trinidad and Tobago* (Toronto: University of Toronto Press, 1972).

74. Kevin Yelvington, "Trinidad and Tobago, 1988–89," in *Latin American and Caribbean Contemporary Record*, eds. James Malloy and Eduardo Gamarra (New York: Holmes and Meier, 1991).

75. In recent years, however, a surge in Indian cultural pride and political influence has reversed that trend. For the first time, some government bureaucrats in Bolivia, Ecuador, and Peru can be seen wearing indigenous dress and speaking Aymara or Quechua, though much of their work is still conducted in Spanish. And bilingual education has spread in many indigenous areas.

76. For a discussion of rising Indian political mobilization and influence in Bolivia, Ecuador, and Peru, see "A Political Awakening," *The Economist* (February 19, 2004) reprinted on http://www.economist.com/world.

77. Howard Handelman, "The Origins of the Ecuadorian Bourgeoisie: A Generational Transformation," paper presented at the XVII International Congress of the Latin American Studies Association, Los Angeles, 1992.

78. Susanne Jonas, *The Battle for Guatemala* (Boulder, CO: Westview Press, 1991).

79. D. Scott Palmer, *The Shining Path of Peru* (New York: St. Martin's Press, 1992).

80. For an analysis of elite manipulation as a cause of ethnic conflict, see Paul Brass, *Ethnicity and Nationalism: Theory and Comparison* (New Delhi, India: Sage Publications, 1991).

81. V. P. Gagnon Jr., "Ethnic Nationalism and International Conflict: The Case of Serbia," *International Security* 19, no. 3 (Winter 1994/95): 130–166.

82. J. Isawa Elaigwu and Victor A. Olorunsola, "Federalism and the Politics of Compromise," in *State versus Ethnic Claims*, 282.

83. Enloe, *Ethnic Conflict*, 89–134.

84. Ibid., 111.

85. Young, "Comparative Claims to Political Sovereignty."

86. Consociationalism can exist between conflicting groups other than ethnicities, but we confine our discussion of it to that area.

87. Arend Lijphart, *Democracy in Plural Societies* (New Haven, CT: Yale University Press, 1977), 25–40.

88. Arend Lijphart, "The Power-Sharing Approach," in *Conflict and Peacemaking in Multiethnic Societies*, ed. Joseph V. Montville (Lexington, MA: Lexington Books, 1990), 497.

89. Ralph R. Premdas, "Secessionist Movements in Comparative Perspective," in *Secessionist Movements*, 12.

90. The only amicable secession that comes to mind took place in Central Europe where, not long after the collapse of Czechoslovakia's communist regime, the Czech Republic acceded to the Slovakian demand that the country be split in two.

91. Ibid., 14–16.

92. Some Kurds also reside in parts of the former Soviet Union. Kurdish leaders have claimed that their people number 35 million, but this is considered an exaggeration. On the other hand, national governments cite figures that are generally too low. Laura Donnandieu Aguado, "The National Liberation Movement of the Kurds in the Middle East," in *Secessionist Movements*; Nader Entessar, *Kurdish Ethnonationalism* (Boulder, CO: Lynne Rienner Publishers, 1992), 1–10; D. McDowall, *A Modern History of the Kurds*, revised edit. (London: I. B. Tauris, 2000), 3–18.

93. As of mid-2004, some powerful Shi'ite leaders have questioned the Kurds' considerable continuing autonomy granted by the provisional

constitution now in place. Should those provisions be striken from the new constitution to be issued in 2005, Kurdish leaders have threatened to secede. The chances of a successful secession, however, are somewhat remote.

94. Daniel Patrick Moynihan, *Pandemonium: Ethnicity in International Politics* (Oxford and New York: Oxford University Press, 1993).

95. Gurr, *People versus States*, 276.

96. Edward Luttwak, "If Bosnians Were Dolphins … ," *Commentary* 96 (October 1993), 27.

97. Samantha Power, "Bystander to Genocide," *The Atlantic Monthly* 288, no. 2 (September 2001); see also the *Frontline* documentary on PBS entitled "The Triumph of Evil," www.pbs.org/wgbh/pages/shows/evil.

98. Carment and Harvey, *Using Force to Prevent Ethnic Violence*.

99. Entessar, *Kurdish Ethnonationalism*, 119–127. The Pike Commission of the U.S. House of Representatives revealed details of U.S. involvement with the abortive Kurdish revolt.

100. Glynne Evans, *Responding to Crises in the African Great Lakes* (New York: Oxford University Press, Adelphia Paper 33, 1997), 75.

101. Carole O'Leary, "The Kurds of Iraq: Recent History, Future Prospects," *The Middle East Review of International Affairs* 6, no. 4 (December 2002).

102. G. Fuller, "Turkey's Restive Kurds: The Challenge of Multiethnicity," in *Ethnic Conflict and International Politics in the Middle East*, ed. Leonard Binder (Gainesville: University of Florida Press, 1999), 225.

103. Human Rights Watch, *1993 Report on the Anfal*, http://hrw.org/reports/1993/iraqanfal/ANFAL1.htm, chap. 1, p. 3; J. Ciment, *The Kurds: State and Minority in Turkey, Iraq and Iran* (New York: Facts on File, 1996), 62–63. Although chemical weapons were banned in international warfare by the Geneva Protocol of 1925, they were used by both sides in the Iraq-Iran war. When Saddam went before a war crimes' tribunal in 2004, he claimed, as he had before, that the gas attacks were the work of Iran. And there is some evidence that Iranian chemical shells may have killed Iraqi civilians at other times.

However, human rights groups and other observers agree that, on 16 March 1988, Iraqi aircraft shelled the Kurdish city of Halabja with chemical weapons, leaving 5,000 dead and 7,000 injured or with long-term illnesses.

104. *New York Times* (June 9, 2004): 1, and (June 10, 2004): 1.

105. Nicholas Blanford, "Iraq's Ethnic Tensions at Bursting Point," *Christian Science Monitor* (March 8, 2004).

106. Project on Democratization, *Democratization and Ethnic Conflict* (Washington, DC: National Academy Press, 1992), 16.

107. J. Edelstein, *Truth and Lies: Stories from the Truth and Reconciliation Commission in South Africa* (New York: New Press, 2001).

108. Michael Ignatieff, "Afterword: Reflections on Coexistence," in *Imagine Coexistence: Restoring Humanity After Violent Ethnic Conflict*, eds. Antonia Chayes and Martha Minnow (San Francisco: Jossey-Bass, 2003), 325–333.

109. Chayes and Minnow, *Imagine Coexistence*.

110. From *Politics in Plural Societies*, quoted in Larry Diamond and Marc F. Plattner, eds., *Nationalism, Ethnic Conflict, and Democracy* (Baltimore, MD: Johns Hopkins University Press, 1994), xix.

111. Francis Fukuyama, "Comments on Nationalism and Democracy," in *Nationalism, Ethnic Conflict and Democracy*, 23–28.

112. The quote summarizing this pessimistic analysis comes from Claude Ake, "Why Humanitarian Emergencies Occur: Insights from the Interface of State, Democracy and Civil Society," *Research for Action* 31 (1997), 8.

113. Quoted in Robin Luckham, Anne Marie Goetz and Mary Kaldor, "Democratic Instituions and Democratic Politics," in *Can Democracy Be Designed: The Politics of Institutional Choice in Conflict-torn Societies*, eds. Sunil Bastian and Robin Luckham (London and New York: Zed Books, 2003), 43.

114. That argument is presented in a number of essays in Bastain and Luckham (ed.), *Can Democracy be Designed?*

115. Gurr, *People versus States*, 152–163, 169, 204.

chapter 5

Women and Development

A Chinese saying observes that "Women Hold Up Half the Sky." Yet for many years, scholars, Third World governments, and Western development agencies appeared strangely oblivious to women's role in the modernization process. Most early studies of political and economic change in the LDCs said little or nothing about women's issues. In the past few decades, however, three factors have contributed to a new understanding of women in developing nations: the emergence of feminist or gender-related social science research; policy planners who heightened awareness of how women play a distinct and important role in national development; and the growing political empowerment of women in many parts of the developing world. Like examinations of ethnicity and class, gender analysis provides a greater understanding of underdevelopment. Economic planners, for example, have found that women in less-developed countries are concentrated in certain occupations and face barriers to entering others. Poorer women work primarily in agriculture or the semi-legal, underground urban economy known as the "informal sector" (discussed below).[1] Those who work in industry are disproportionately employed in labor-intensive and lower-wage industries such as apparel and electronics in the Far East and Southeast Asia and assembly plants in Mexico and the Caribbean. Like their counterparts in developed nations, female professionals are overrepresented in such nurturing professions as nursing and teaching. In a sample of Asian and Latin American countries—including China, Indonesia, Thailand, Argentina, Brazil, Chile, and Peru—women make up roughly half of the professional and technical workers, but less than 20 percent of the administrative and managerial employees.[2] These divisions between "women's work" and "men's work" have obvious economic and political implications, with women's jobs usually earning lower wages or salaries and wielding less power. At the same time, women are also very underrepresented in the political arena. Not only do they hold far fewer government posts than do men, but their share also diminishes as one moves up the pyramid of power.

Although evidence of gender inequality and exploitation exists in most societies, the problem is more severe in many parts of the developing world. In its most horrifying form, the list of injustices includes forced and painful female genital circumcision in parts of Africa; the sale of child brides for dowries in India; wife beatings in Zambia and the Andes; the murders of some 5,000 Indian women annually committed by husbands who were dissatisfied with the size of their dowries; courts that condone "honor killings" of women suspected of extramarital relations; and economic deprivation that forces large numbers of Third World women into prostitution.[3] Not long ago, a village tribal council in rural Pakistan found an 11-year-old boy guilty of having a sexual relationship with a higher-class woman (a relationship which government investigators later concluded had never happened). As punishment for the alleged acts, the council ordered four men to gang-rape the boy's adult sister. Villagers did nothing to stop it.[4] Less chilling, but no less significant, examples of gender inequality include divorce laws that greatly favor husbands; barriers to women seeking commercial credit for small businesses; the "double day" that working women typically face (coming home after a day's work and having to do most of the housework and child care); and restricted opportunities for women in government, the professions, and better-paid, blue-collar jobs.

But the study of women in the developing world is by no means confined to issues of inequality and victimization. After years of neglect, many international agencies and government planners have begun to recognize women's special status and particular needs in development projects. Nor have women necessarily been passive subjects who are "acted upon." Their political activity has ranged from the quiet subversion common to many oppressed groups to a more vigorous assertion of their political, economic, and social rights. A growing body of scholarly literature now focuses on women's *empowerment*. Throughout Latin America, for example, women have played a decisive role in the independent, grass-roots political organizations known as "new social movements (NSMs)" that have burst upon the scene since the 1970s. Focusing on gender issues, human rights, poverty, and a range of other concerns, NSMs have provided an important alternative to parties, unions, and other mainstream political organizations.[5] Elsewhere, such revolutionary movements in countries as El Salvador, Nicaragua, and China have opened up opportunities for female activism and leadership that had not existed previously. In nations as diverse as India, Bangladesh, the Philippines, Panama, and Nicaragua, women have headed the national government. And during the past 15 years a growing number of developing countries has reserved seats for women in national, state, or local legislatures, while other nations have intoduced gender quotas for those offices. Such measures have increased the number of female political leaders dramatically in many LDCs. All of these aspects of female economic and political activity deserve our attention.

THE POLITICAL AND SOCIOECONOMIC STATUS OF THIRD WORLD WOMEN

One of the notable problems in much of the developing world is that women have far fewer educational opportunities and lower literacy rates than men. In the most extreme, and obviously atypical, case, Afghanistan's recently toppled Taliban government banned all girls and women from going to school.[6] Since education and literacy substantially influence income, health practices, and political participation, these gender gaps impact many important facets of political and economic life. We know, for example, that as average educational levels for women rise in LDCs, birth rates and family size tend to decline.

Table 5.1 presents the relative literacy rate of adult men and women (all people 15 years of age or older) and that of young men and women (ages 15 to 24 only) in the Third World's major regions. It is important to keep in mind that *the percentages in that table do not represent the actual percentage of men or women who are literate*. Rather, they reflect a *comparison* between female and male literacy

TABLE 5.1   Women's Literacy Rates Compared to Men's

Region	Women's Literacy as a Percentage of Men's (15 years and older)	Young Women's Literacy as a Percentage of Men's (15–24 years old only)
Latin America and the Caribbean	98%	101%
East Asia	91	99
South Asia	67	70
Sub-Saharan Africa	79	90
Arab Nations*	70	87

*Arab nations include countries from the Middle East and North Africa.

Source: United Nations Development Programme (UNDP), *Human Development Report 2004. Cultural Liberty in Today's Diverse World:* Human Development Indicators, Table 26, http://www.undp.org/.

rates within each region. The lower the score in this table, the greater the *gender gap*. Thus, a country or region could have a high literacy rate for both men *and* women but have a greater gender gap than an area in which both men and women have low, but similar, rates of literacy. For example, if in some imaginary region males have a literacy rate of 90 percent and women have a rate of 60 percent, the *comparative* figure for that region would be 67 percent (i.e., the women's literacy is two-thirds, or 67 percent, as high as men's). On the other hand, if both men and women in another region were far less educated, with each gender only 30 percent literate, that region would have a comparative score of 100 percent, since there is no gender gap at all (i.e., male and female literacy levels are equally low).

If we examine the figures in Table 5.1, we find that South Asia (including India, Pakistan, and Bangladesh) and the Arab world have the greatest gender gaps in literacy. Thus, for example, in South Asia women are only 67 percent as likely as men to read and write. Among young adults (aged 15 to 24) in that region, the gender gap is slightly narrower, with women's literacy rates reaching 70 percent of the men's. On the other hand, Latin America and the Caribbean (including English-speaking islands such as Jamaica) have totally eliminated the gender gap in literacy, and young women actually enjoy a slightly higher literacy rate than their male counterparts. East Asia ranks next best, with Sub-Saharan Africa in the middle. One encouraging finding is that the gender gap for all regions is smaller among young adults than it is among adults generally. This suggests a trend toward reducing the gender literacy gap. Also, as we have noted, in Latin America and the Caribbean the gap has already been eliminated.

Table 5.2 turns from literacy to measures of women's influence in society. Column 2 presents the Gender Empowerment Measure (GEM) for each of the countries listed, a composite *index* that indicates the degree to which women hold significant positions in that country's politics and private sector. The highest GEM possible (that is, the highest level of female political and economic empowerment) is 1.0, and the lowest possible is 0. Next to each country's GEM in Column 2 (in parentheses) is that country's GEM rank compared to other nations. Thus, with a GEM of .908, Norway had the highest GEM ranking in the

TABLE 5.2   Measures of Gender Empowerment

Country	Gender Empowerment Measure (Rank)[a]	Percentage of Women as National Parliament Members[a]	Percentage of Women as Cabinet Ministers[b]
Norway	.908 (1)	36.4%	42.1%
United States	.769 (14)	14.0	31.8
Singapore	.648 (20)	16.0	5.7
Mexico	.563 (34)	21.2	11.1
Philippines	.542 (37)	17.2	33.3
Japan	.531 (38)	9.9	5.7
Malaysia	.519 (44)	16.3	—
Chile	.460 (58)	10.1	25.6
Egypt	.266 (75)	3.6	6.1

[a]Data is for 2004.
[b]Data is for 2001 except for the Philippines, which is for 2004.

Source: United Nations Development Programme (UNDP), *Human Development Report 2004. Cultural Liberty in Today's Diverse World:* Human Development Indicators, Table 25 and Table 29, http://www.undp.org/; data on Women in the cabinet in the Philippines is from 2004 Global Summit of Women Report: Women in Leaders Worldwide http://www.globewomen.com/summit/2004/GSW2004Report.htm.

world, while the United States ranked 14th. Egypt's score of .266 placed it 75th among countries that have data on GEMs. It should be added that GEM scores are available for only 78 of the nearly 180 countries in the world, with no data for most of the poorest LDCs.

Modernization theory suggests that the most economically developed nations in Table 5.2—Norway, the United States, Japan, and perhaps Singapore—should have the highest GEMs. That is, we would expect that as a country modernizes, its gender gap narrows. For the most part, the data in Table 5.2 (and data covering other nations) support that hypothesis. As expected, most of the countries on the list had GEM rankings that were fairly similar to their rankings on the Human Development Index (HDI, see Chapter 1). In other words, the higher a country's literacy and educational levels, the longer its life expectancy, and the higher its average income, the higher it tends to rank on GEM. But there are some notable exceptions to that pattern. Japan, one of the world's most economically advanced and educated countries, has a slightly lower GEM score than either Mexico or the Philippines, nations that are far less modern. Chile's HDI score is higher than Mexico's, Malaysia's, and especially the Philippines and is generally considered the most modern of those nations, yet it lags well behind in GEM. Similarly, the Philippines has an unexpectedly high GEM ranking. This suggests that other factors, including a nation's cultural values, beyond economic development and educational level influence the position of women in society.

Columns 3 and 4 in Table 5.2 speak to the influence and representation of women in national politics. They show what portion of the seats in the national parliament (or congress) and percentage of the nation's cabinet ministers were held by women in the early years of the twenty-first century. Norway's parliament (column 3), with more than 36 percent women, far surpasses the United States and Japan, as do the other Nordic countries (Denmark, Finland, Iceland, and Sweden) not shown in the table. Surprisingly, Mexico's national legislature also has a substantially higher percentage of women (21.2 percent) than the United States or Japan. Women are also slightly more represented in the parliaments of Singapore, Malaysia, and the Philippines (16.0 to 17.3 percent) than in the U.S. (14 percent) and far more represented than in Japan (9.9 percent).

The data on cabinet members (column 4) are particularly interesting because these positions are generally among the most powerful in the government. However, since cabinets tend to be relatively small (normally about 10 to 30 ministers) and since their members can be replaced at any time by the president or prime minister, the percentage of women ministers may vary significantly from year to year. Hence the data in the last column should be treated with caution. Once again Norway leads the field in our table (with a cabinet that was 42.1 percent female) while Japan and Egypt trail far behind. At the same time in both the United States and Chile, women were far more heavily represented in the cabinet (as of 2001) than they were in their national congress. The figure for the Philippines in this column is not fully comparable to the others. For all of the other countries in the table, cabinet data were drawn from U.N. statistics covering 2001. Since those figures did not include the Philippines, however, I have cited the Filipino cabinet figure for 2004 (taken from another source). The extremely high number of female Filipino ministers at that time (33 percent, or one-third, of the cabinet) was appointed by a woman president. Earlier World Bank data on all nations indicated that among major Third World regions, Latin America had the highest percentage of female ministers, and the Arab bloc had by far the fewest.[7]

Westernization, Modernization, and the Economic Status of Women

How was the status of women altered when developing areas were colonized or otherwise brought into the orbit of Western economic and military power? How have women been affected subsequently by the transition from traditional to modern society? Westerners often associate traditional social and economic systems with rigid religious and cultural values that relegate women to an inferior rank. That notion may lead us to assume that European colonization of Africa and Asia and the subsequent spread of Western-style modernization offered women greater opportunities and improved social status. But while modernization theory would have us believe that urbanization, industrialization, and the diffusion of Western values have an emancipating effect, "feminist scholars [often oriented toward dependency theory] have produced a wealth of literature that maintains that political and economic modernization have had many negative effects on women," at least initially.[8]

Although the status of women in precolonial Africa varied from place to place, oftentimes European colonialism undermined their social position. To begin with, colonial rule was introduced at a time (the nineteenth century) when Victorian England and other European societies had rather restricted views of women's roles.[9] Consequently, many colonial administrations in Africa and Asia treated women less equitably than traditional institutions had. In West African cultures, for example, women sometimes served as chiefs or in other important political positions. However, as the influence of such traditional leadership posts declined, first under colonialism and then after independence, these women lost their authority to male-dominated colonial or national governments. Among the Nigerian Ibos, for example, women had exercised significant political power prior to the British conquest. Colonial administrators, however, viewed politics as "a man's concern" and, consequently, downgraded female political influence.[10]

The commercialization of agriculture reduced women's *economic* power as well. In Asia and Africa, commercialization often led colonial governments to grant peasants legal titles to their farm land. In some regions that process trans-ferred plots that had been unofficially controlled by women to male owner-ship.[11] In addition, as families moved from subsistence agriculture (for family consumption) to commercial agriculture, and as commercial plantations were developed by foreigners, men were more likely than women to be hired as plantation workers. Commercialization also made farmers more dependent on the state for credit and for technical training. In both the colonial era and in the early decades of independence, women were usually frozen out of such aid. In Uganda, for example, even though female farmers frequently had begun the first commercial cotton cultivation, in 1923 the British administrator in charge of agriculture declared that "cotton growing [can] not be left to the women and old people."[12] Thus, as new agricultural technologies were introduced, they were taught mostly to men, ultimately driving women off the land. After inde-pendence, most African and Asian governments continued that pattern, as extension agents offered modern technologies, credits, and other assistance pri-marily to men. Most foreign aid programs were no less sexist. For example, when a Taiwanese foreign aid team went to Senegal to improve rice cultivation, they trained only men, even though women had been doing most of the rice cultivation. The result was that the women were not taught, the men ignored the instructors, and the new techniques never took hold.[13]

Just as modernization theorists and radical feminists hold different views of colonialism, they also disagree on how subsequent modernization has affected the lives of Third World women. Modernization theory contrasts the egalitarian values of modern culture with the allegedly sexist perspectives of traditional societies. Radical feminists, many of whom subscribe to depend-ency theory, counter that industrialization, urbanization, and the spread of world capitalism frequently have disadvantaged women. How might we rec-oncile these opposing viewpoints? The evidence suggests that modernization positively affects women's status over the long run, but is often deleterious in the short-to-medium term. Unquestionably, gender gaps in education, employ-ment, and political influence are much narrower in most developed nations than in the LDCs (see Tables 5.1 and 5.2). Economic growth eventually creates new opportunities for women. And expanded educational systems offer them additional opportunities while creating more egalitarian values and gender roles. For example, in East Asia, the region of the world that has enjoyed the greatest economic growth in the past 50 years, women's share of the labor force has grown in seven of the eight highest-growth countries (all but Thailand), ris-ing substantially in four of them (Singapore, South Korea, Malaysia, and Indonesia). Elsewhere in the Third World, high-growth nations have narrowed their gender gaps in education and literacy.

But, as we have seen, the initial transition to modernity often imposes particular hardships on women in its initial stages. The discussion that follows focuses on the negative short-term effects of economic growth, neoliberal economic reforms, and other elements of modernization. Policy makers and planners need to address these problems. However, they should not obscure the fact that, in the long run, modernization offers women the best hope for equality. The task, then, is to reduce the short-term pain and increase the likelihood of long-term gain.

Women in the Countryside

Women are critical players in Third World agriculture. A recent publication by the Food and Agriculture Organization (FAO) of the United Nations estimates that "women ... produce between 60 and 80 percent of the food in most developing countries."[14] Earlier research suggested that women dominate farming, particularly subsistence farming, in Africa, somewhat less so in Asia, and least in Latin America.[15] Moreover, particularly in Africa, the percentage of female farmers has grown substantially in recent decades. In its article on "The Feminization of Agriculture," the FAO points out that "war, sickness and death from HIV/AIDS have reduced rural male populations" as has male migration from the countryside to urban centers at home and abroad.[16]

But despite the predominance of female farming in the LDCs, Nici Nelson noted years ago that "too little attention has been given by researchers and administrators or planners to women and the roles they play in rural society."[17] Even though male "heads of household" are increasingly employed off the family farm, leaving its cultivation to their wives, government planners have generally clung to "the myth of the ever-present male head" while neglecting female farmers.[18]

In the years since the United Nations' Decade for Women (1975 to 1985), international agencies and Third World governments have become more aware of women's role in rural development. Significantly, the 1985 conference concluding the Decade for Women was the second largest U.N. conference ever held. Similarly, the World Bank, the United States' Agency for International Development (USAID), and many nongovernmental organizations (NGOs), such as rural development programs that had previously focused narrowly on agricultural production, have often given way to integrated rural development programs (IRDPs) designed to promote agricultural production, education, sanitation, and health care simultaneously. Over time, many of these programs have recognized the need to address the role of rural women. For example, USAID established an office for Women in Development to better address women's needs in U.S. foreign aid projects. More recently the United Nations issued "FAO's Plan of Action for Women in Development (1996–2001)." Still, even today, the FAO laments that "gender bias and gender blindness persist: farmers are still generally perceived as 'male' by policy makers, development planners and agricultural service deliverers. For this reason, women find it more difficult than men to gain access to valuable resources such as land, credit and agricultural inputs, technology, extension, training and services that would enhance their production capacity."[19]

Furthermore, the results of even the most well-intentioned programs have been mixed. Some projects have been very successful while others have fallen victim to poor planning or a misunderstanding of the cultural milieu. Thus, for example, one study of an IRDP project in India argued that it was undermined by the absence of female administrators and by inadequate early educational opportunities for women participants.[20] Cornelia Butler Flora's survey of projects designed to generate income for rural women in Latin America found that such programs tended to produce low-paying jobs with limited economic benefits. However, argues Butler Flora, despite their weak economic records, these projects are potentially valuable since the women's organizations they create may later mobilize their members for social and political action.[21]

Moreover, the importance of training rural women and raising their educational levels far transcends the need to raise food production. For example, many agencies involved in population control now recognize that merely making family planning services available will not get the job done. Rather, fertility rates fall most significantly when women have received access to greater educational and occupational opportunities. Indeed, that was a core conclusion of the 1994 United Nations Conference on Population and Development. Ultimately, as Butler Flora suggests, the only way rural women are likely to make government more responsive to their demands will be through political mobilization and pressure.

Urbanization and the Status of Women

The early harmful effects of modernization on women extend beyond the countryside. In her study of Ghana's Ga tribe, Claire Robertson found that women's status declined when their families moved to the capital city and entered a more modern, urbanized environment. Although married couples had previously cooperated rather closely on economic matters in their fishing and farming villages, such cooperation declined among urban migrants. After their arrival in the cities, husbands had greater access than wives to education and higher-paying jobs, giving men a level of economic security that they had not heretofore enjoyed. Women, in turn, became more dependent on their husbands and tended to own a smaller share of family property than they had in their villages.[22]

In much of Latin America, the majority of migrants to urban centers has been women. Once arrived, many are only able to secure low-end jobs. Indeed, the most common type of employment among female migrants is domestic service, for which they are generally paid the legal minimum wage or lower. At one time 25 percent of all women in the Mexican urban work force were either maids in private homes or cleaning women in commercial establishments and hotels.[23] Another important source of employment is the so-called "informal sector"—including street vending and employment in "sweat shop" industries that defy government regulation.[24] While some informal-sector workers earn higher incomes than blue-collar laborers in the mainstream economy, many others fall below the poverty line. Finally, in newly industrializing countries, women are frequently employed in low-wage manufacturing. Over time, however, as many factories become more technologically sophisticated and as wages rise, the percentage of female employees in those firms tends to decline.[25]

In East Asia, the industrial boom since the 1980s has created many new jobs for women, particularly in labor-intensive industries such as apparel and electronics. For several reasons, those firms often prefer to hire young unmarried women: many of the jobs require manual dexterity, a skill that employers associate with women; because they are not the principal breadwinners in their families, young women are usually willing to work for lower wages; and, finally, women are less likely to join unions or participate in strikes. During the late 1990s, the region's economic crisis caused numerous plant closings and layoffs. Women were often the first fired since most employers believed that men needed their jobs in order to support their families. The crisis also forced many poor and middle-class families to withdraw their daughters from school in order to save the costs of school uniforms, educational fees, and tuition. Indeed, Indonesian girls are six times more likely than boys to drop out of school before the fourth grade.[26]

As we have seen (Table 5.1), in most developing regions women tend to have fewer educational opportunities than men, a deficit that later limits their occupational opportunities. All too often, poverty and a lack of vocational skills force desperate women into prostitution. Despite Thailand's economic boom since the mid-1960s, continuing rural poverty has driven many young female migrants into Bangkok's thriving "sex tourism" industry. One study of Manila (the Philippines) and Bangkok (Thailand) revealed that 7 to 9 percent of female employment in those two cities was "prostitution related."[27] Since that study was conducted prior to the region's financial crisis in the late 1990s, those percentages are surely higher today. Some desperately poor families in that region have sold young daughters to brothels or given them as collateral for loans. A study of Southeast Asia by the U.N.'s International Labour Organization (ILO) estimated the number of sex workers shortly before the crisis to be 140,000 to 230,000 in Indonesia, 43,000 to 142,000 in Malaysia, and 200,000 to 300,000 in Thailand. In the economically depressed Philippines, the situation was even worse as "the estimated 400,000 to 500,000 prostitutes in the country *approximated the number of its manufacturing workers* (italics added)." The situation worsened considerably during the Asian financial crisis when many employed in other areas needed to supplement their income: "the number of Southeast Asians earning a living directly or indirectly from prostitution—including waitresses, security guards, escort services, tour agencies—could easily [have] reached 'several millions.'"[28] While many sex workers enter the trade voluntarily, many others (including underage girls) do not. A 2001 State Department report on the status of women notes that a survey by a human rights NGO in Cambodia "found that 40 percent of women and girls who work as prostitutes do so voluntarily, while 60 percent have been forced to work as prostitutes or have been deceived into prostitution."[29] In the squatter settlements of Kenya's capital, Nairobi, impoverished women are rarely equipped to gain employment in the economy's modern sector. Consequently, illegal brewing of beer and prostitution have been the two major sources of female employment.[30]

While these studies all show the severe problems that often accompany modernization in the LDCs, it is also true that, at the same time, economic growth, most notably in many parts of Asia, has also provided millions of underprivileged women improved incomes in the modern sector of the economy. This is particularly true in those countries where educational opportunities rise as well. For example, research on the South Asian labor market shows that increased education has given poor urban women a vehicle for improving their jobs and incomes.[31]

For Third World, middle- and upper-middle-class women, educational and occupational opportunities are more comparable to those of men with the same social status. There are, however, interesting differences between countries and regions. In her pioneering research, Ester Boserup presented data on the proportion of people between the ages of 15 and 24 who were still in school (essentially high school and university). Not surprisingly, the overall (combined male and female) rate of school attendance in individual countries was linked to the nation's level of economic development. In other words, more economically developed countries like Costa Rica, Singapore, and South Korea had higher *overall* rates of high school and university attendance than did poorer nations.

However, cultural rather than economic factors seemed to determine what proportion of these students were women. In Latin American nations, about half of the student population was female, regardless of whether the country was more developed (Venezuela, Panama) or comparatively poor (Honduras, El Salvador). In Asia, women also made up nearly half of the 15-to-24-year-old students in the Philippines and Hong Kong, but constituted less than one-third in India, Malaysia, and Indonesia. The percentages of females among students attending high school or college in Africa and the Middle East were generally quite low, frequently less than 25 percent. As a consequence of these educational patterns, women in Latin America constitute a far higher percentage of all professionals than they do in other parts of the developing world.[32]

As Table 5.1 indicates, since that time the gender gap in education has narrowed considerably. In countries such as Brazil, the number of women attending university has grown far more quickly than has the ranks of men. And in many LDCs today—including, surprisingly, Kuwait—the number of female university students outpaces the males. For the most part, however, the regional differences remain similar to those found by Boserup many years ago.

WOMEN AND POLITICS

Many of the same traditions and prejudices that have undermined women's socioeconomic positions in the Third World have also disadvantaged them politically. In Latin America, for example, women won the right to vote substantially later than they did in industrialized democracies. Whereas the United States and most European democracies legalized female suffrage in the first two decades of the twentieth century, only 7 of 20 Latin American countries allowed women to vote before the close of World War II.[33] Ecuador was the first nation in that region to extend the franchise (1929) and Paraguay the last (1961).[34] In Africa and Asia the situation was different. Since most of the countries in those regions achieved independence in the decades after World War II when female suffrage was a universally accepted principle, women were usually enfranchised from the onset. However, Arab Gulf States such as Bahrain only enfranchised women in 2001, while, to date, Kuwait did the same in 2005. However, given the low number of democratically elected governments in Asia and Africa until recently, the franchise was often of no great value to women (or to men). Today, women generally continue to vote at a lower rate than men, but that gender gap is narrowing.[35]

In many parts of Africa, Asia, and the Middle East, traditional cultural values have limited women's political participation and activism.[36] One study of transitional Hindu families in India (partly traditional and partly modernized) revealed an important generational difference between women who had completed a university education at the time of national independence and their more traditional mothers. The women analyzed in this study were the daughters of Westernized fathers who had worked for the colonial civil service and who had been quite politically involved. At the same time, however, their mothers generally spoke no English, believed in female submissiveness, and were quite apolitical.[37] In contrast, the university-educated daughters were far more politically involved than their mothers. In the absence of such educational opportunities, political participation levels remain low for the vast majority of women in South Asia, the Middle East, and much of Africa, who lack the resources available to those born to affluence.

Indeed, social class correlates particularly strongly with female political participation in the LDCs. Among highly educated, Westernized women born to elite families, office-holding often equals or even excels the levels of their cohorts in the Western world. It is worth noting, for example, that all the countries of the Indian subcontinent—India, Pakistan, and Bangladesh—as well as neighboring Sri Lanka have had female prime ministers, a record not nearly equaled by North America or Western Europe. The first woman president of the United Nations General Assembly and the first female chair of the Security Council were both from Africa, not the advanced, industrial nations.[38] And today in 16 Latin American and Caribbean countries, women hold a higher percentage of the seats in parliament or congress than in the United States.

Middle-class women have also benefited in many ways from elements of a Western lifestyle. For example, the greater availability of birth control devices "has ruptured [women's] previously existing physiological fatalism," enabling them to work outside the home and involve themselves in political movements.[39]

But modernization has sometimes been unkind to the mass of Third World women, the underprivileged who may face diminished opportunities for political participation. Indeed, in Africa, while traditional cultures often included women's organizations and production techniques that bound women together, increased modernity (including urbanization and the decline of the extended family) frequently deprived them of the organizational foundations they had previously enjoyed. In Nigeria, Africa's most populous Sub-Saharan nation, women in the urban informal sector have been less prone to demonstrate politically since independence than they were under colonial rule.[40] Throughout the developing world, the mechanization and commercialization of agriculture and the accompanying decline of traditional labor relations have frequently deprived rural women of their specialized labor functions. In doing so, these changes may, at least temporarily, reduce women's political influence.

In short, because the developing world encompasses so wide a variety of cultural traditions, and because social change has impinged so differently on the various social classes and sectors within individual nations, there can be no simple generalizations about the way in which modernization has influenced women's political status. Modernization theory would lead us to expect that more socioeconomically developed countries would be quicker to grant political rights to women than their poorer counterparts. If we look at Latin America, however, we find that there is only a mild correlation between a country's literacy rate or its GNP per-capita and the year in which it enfranchised women.[41] Thus, the spread of education alone does not seem to guarantee women greater political equality. However, in countries such as Rwanda, Mozambique, South Africa, Argentina, Costa Rica, and Cuba, mass educational programs, conscious efforts to change traditional values, and, most recently, reserved seats and quotas for women in parliament have given women greater political opportunities and have advanced gender equity.[42]

Women's Political Activism at the Grass Roots

Perhaps women exert the greatest influence on Third World politics when acting through grass-roots organizations in their own neighborhoods and communities. Community-based groups afford them opportunities for participation and leadership normally absent at the national or regional level. For one thing, they typically focus on issues of immediate importance to underprivileged women such as housing, health care, potable drinking water, and education. Furthermore, neighborhood and village organizations are more accessible to poor women, who have no day care for their young children or cannot travel far from home. Hence, many women who have been excluded from mainstream political parties, interest groups, or government institutions are attracted to these groups because of their accessibility and relevance to their own lives.

In recent decades a range of grass-roots organizations representing poor and middle-class women has emerged throughout the developing world. Some represent women exclusively, while others include members of both sexes but are led by women or contain women's wings.[43] Jana Everett examined several Indian community groups in urban and rural settings, finding important similarities and differences. Both types were initially led by politically experienced, middle-class women committed to organizing the poor. And in both locations, as low-income women became more involved in neighborhood activities, their political awareness, confidence, and assertiveness grew, stimulating, in turn, greater participation in the broader political system.

However, urban and rural groups usually had different tactics and goals. The Self-Employed Women's Association (SEWA) of Madras and the Annapurna Mahila Mandal of Bombay (named after the Goddess of Food) represented urban women involved in home-based production, street vending of food, and other informal-sector activities. Serving extremely poor women who were unable to secure government services, the groups' tactics were moderate and peaceful. Their objectives were also fairly conventional, such as better government enforcement of minimum-wage laws for female workers or securing loans for women with very small businesses and no lines of credit.

In contrast, the organizations representing poor, rural women often escalated to more militant tactics. For example, at an early training session for women in a Bhil tribal organization, members complained about alcoholism and wife beatings by men in their villages. Emboldened by their own discussions, the women spontaneously marched to an illegal liquor still and smashed it. They then briefly held the local police inspector captive to protest his earlier failure to shut down illegal liquor production.[44]

In general, Everett found that the rural, grass-roots groups were more likely than urban organizations to stage demonstrations or other protests and were more prone to demand redistributive economic remedies such as land reform. Armita Basu's study of female rural protests in the Indian state of Maharashtra also noted their militancy. In one case, when a woman villager complained that she had been unable to get help from the local police against a landlord who had beaten her severely, a crowd of 300 women and 150 men "smeared [the landlord's] face with cow dung ... and paraded him through the surrounding villages."[45] The rural women's greater aggressiveness likely resulted from the more hostile political atmosphere in which they operated. Since village political and economic elites are usually less willing than urban elites to redress poor villagers' grievances through normal political channels, these women were forced to use more radical tactics.

Social movements often develop as a response to a specific crisis or danger. For example, the 1985 earthquake that destroyed large sections of Mexico City had a particularly devastating effect on seamstresses in the city's apparel industry. The quake hit early in the morning when most people had not yet left home for work. But since seamstresses work longer hours, many of them were already at work and were trapped under rubble at their places of employment. To their horror, some found that their employers were more interested in saving their sewing machines than in bringing out trapped employees. The clothing workers subsequently formed their own labor union led by women from their ranks, independent of the government-affiliated federation to which most Mexican unions belong. With more honest leadership than is typically found in the Mexican labor movement, the new union not only has bargained with employers and the government for better working conditions but has also provided day care and related services for its members.

In Latin America, a major catalyst for grass-roots political activity during the 1970s and 1980s was opposition to the authoritarian military governments that governed much of the region at that time. In Argentina, Brazil, Chile, and Uruguay, bureaucratic-authoritarian (BA) regimes halted the electoral process, banned political parties and unions (particularly on the Left), and arrested, tortured, and killed large numbers of suspected "subversives" (see Chapter 9). At the same time, a major debt crisis in the 1980s, coupled with harsh government economic remedies, produced the region's worst recession since the 1930s and a precipitous decline in popular living standards (Chapter 10). Women played an important role in antiauthoritarian social movements that helped pave the way for the restoration of democracy in the 1980s and 1990s.

The women's movement incorporated three types of political organizations, all largely urban based. First were feminist groups, led primarily by women from middle- and upper-middle-class families. They included many professional women who previously had been active in leftist political parties but had become disillusioned by the Left's disinterest in women's issues. A second type, neighborhood organizations, represented women from the urban slums. In the face of the region's severe economic crisis, self-help groups were created to organize communal kitchens, infant nutrition centers, and other antipoverty activities. Though not initially highly politicized, in time these groups frequently radicalized, demanding more equitable distribution of state resources and the restoration of democracy. Finally, a third strand of the women's movement campaigned for human rights. Argentina's "Mothers of the Plaza de Mayo," regularly marched in defiance of government restrictions to demand an accounting of their missing children and grandchildren who had disappeared into the hands of the police or armed forces. Two decades after the fall of the country's military dictatorship, they continue to march weekly in front of the presidential palace, seeking information and accountability for still unresolved disappearances. In Brazil, Chile, and Uruguay, responding to state-sponsored imprisonments, torture, and assassinations by "death squads," women also formed a major component of the human rights movement. This was the most socially integrated branch of the women's movement, bringing together activists from the middle and working classes. Often they also joined forces with other human rights activists in the Catholic Church or Christian Base Communities.[46]

One of the most influential women's political movements emerged in Brazil. Several factors contributed to this phenomenon. First was the rapid expansion of women's educational opportunities from the early 1960s through the 1980s. Between 1969 and 1975 alone, while the number of men attending Brazilian universities doubled, the number of women increased fivefold. By 1980, they accounted for nearly half of the country's university students. Women also accounted for a growing proportion of Brazil's professionals, their numbers swelling from 19,000 in 1970 to more than 95,000 in 1980.[47] Often paid significantly less than their male counterparts, they became the nucleus of the new feminist movements. Their leaders were highly politicized, often having been active in leftist political parties. When military repression forced many of them into exile, they frequently resettled in Western Europe or Chile, where they were influenced by older and more sophisticated feminist organizations. Years later, when Brazil's political system began to relax, these exiles returned home to organize.

Second, in the absence of democratic elections, grass-roots movements such as tenants' associations offered the urban poor one of the only opportunities to pressure the government. In slums and shantytowns, radical priests, nuns, and parishioners—motivated by liberation theology—organized Christian Base Communities, which combined religious values with social activism. Leftist groups also helped to organize the poor. One study of neighborhood, grass-roots organizations in São Paulo, Brazil's largest city, revealed that most members and leaders were women.[48] Typically, such organizations first focused on the rank-and-file's immediate economic needs—jobs, health care, and food—rather than feminist issues. Indeed, most Church leaders were hostile to feminism while leftist groups were usually less concerned with gender divisions than with social-class tensions. In time, however, many poor women came to share "middle-class" concerns regarding household equality, domestic abuse, and other feminist issues.

In the late 1970s, the third strand of the women's movement emerged: human rights groups protesting government repression. Progressive political-party and Catholic Church activists often assumed leadership roles. Interestingly, this was one of the few instances in which women's organizations had an advantage over similar groups led by men. Because the government viewed women as inherently less political than men and, hence, less dangerous, they allowed their human rights groups greater freedom than other protest movements.

As the Brazilian military government engineered a transition to democracy in the 1980s, female voters and politicians played important roles in the PMDB, the major opposition party. However, the restoration of democracy lowered the motivation for unity among disparate wings of the women's movement and weakened them in other ways. As middle-class leaders and militants became increasingly involved in the restored democratic system, they often lost contacts with community groups representing the urban poor. Thus, ironically, in Brazil and elsewhere, the restoration of democracy demobilized many lower-income women and often weakened the women's movement, at least temporarily. More recently, however, the explosion of private voluntary groups, known as non-governmental organizations (NGOs), in LDCs worldwide has created new opportunities for women's grass-roots political participation. As their name suggests, NGOs are independent of government control. Many try to influence public policy in areas such as democratization, human rights, women's rights, environmental protection, housing, health care, and education. Compared to the earlier social movements, NGOs tend to be more specialized, more professionalized, (often) better funded, and "more respectable." The best-known groups are well financed and organized internationally, including the International Red Cross, Amnesty International, Greeenpeace, and Oxfam. But most NGOs are to be found at the local and national level, where many seek to mobilize popular support and influence government policy. In the LDCs, they have played a critical role in the expansion of civil society, particularly in democratic or democratizing societies where they often provide a political voice to otherwise powerless groups seeking reform. In countries such as Chile, Peru, India, and Thailand, they have helped expand women's political rights and economic opportunities.

Finally, a very different vehicle for grass-roots political activity has recently emerged in India, Bangladesh, Pakistan, and other South Asian nations as that region's major religions—Hinduism, Islam, and Sikhism—have become increasingly politicized (see Chapter 3). Religiously based political parties, such as India's BJP and Pakistan's Muttahida Majlis-e-Amal (a coalition of Islamic parties), have gained considerable strength. On the one hand, these parties and religious interest groups generally endorse traditional roles for women as mothers and wives and reinforce female political and social passivity. Yet for a variety of reasons, including the higher level of piety often found among women, many women have joined these political parties and movements. On the one hand, these movements have usually challenged any feminist agenda and promoted a more restricted role for women. At the same time, however, they have mobilized many women who had never before been politically active. Moreover, once such women have joined in large numbers, they sometimes have pushed these parties toward a more progressive stance on gender roles (though not in Pakistan or in other Islamic nations).[49]

Women as National Political Leaders

In political systems throughout the world (except perhaps Scandinavia and other Nordic nations), women are severely underrepresented in political leadership positions. The Third World is surely no exception. During the mid-1980s, for instance, only 6 percent of the national legislators and only 2 percent of all cabinet members in Africa were women. Despite some dramatic gains since then in many LDCs, women remain greatly underrepresented in influential government offices. Worldwide, "United Nations surveys repeatedly show that even in countries where women are active professionally, their level of responsibility as policy makers and planners [has been] low."[50] Furthermore, an examination of the relatively small number of women who have reached high leadership positions reveals that they have tended to hold posts popularly associated with female qualities. For example, most of the African women who held cabinet posts in the recent past headed ministries of education, women's affairs, health, or social welfare—areas traditionally viewed as compatible with women's "nurturing role."[51]

Nearly 30 years ago, a study of Chilean and Peruvian female political leaders revealed a pattern common to much of Latin America. Female political leaders were forced to legitimize their activism outside the home by presenting themselves as *supermadres* ("supermothers") who were using their political position to nurture their constituents (their extended family). That image had been painted eloquently years earlier by Argentina's legendary political leader, Eva Perón (Evita):

> In this great house of the Motherland [Argentina], I am just like any other woman in any other of the innumerable houses of my people. Just like all of them I rise early thinking about my husband and about my children. ... I so truly feel myself the mother of my people.[52]

Elsa Chaney's survey of 167 Chilean and Peruvian female political officials showed that half of them felt that certain government posts (such as education and health) were more appropriate for women, while others should be held by men (finance and defense, for example). Only 13 percent of the women politicians interviewed believed that gender was irrelevant to the type of political post one holds, while another 37 percent were ambivalent.[53] Of course, it is not only in developing nations that women have tended to be restricted to political positions defined by gender stereotypes. Until the 1990s, female cabinet members in the United States generally presided over such departments as Labor, Education, and Health and Human Services. More recently, however, Presidents Clinton and Bush broke that mold by appointing women as Attorney General, Secretary of State, and National Security Advisor, all previously male preserves. In the LDCs, a similarly groundbreaking appointment took place in 2002 when Michelle Bachelet was named Chile's Minister of Defense. Indeed, in much of the developing world, and particularly in Latin America, the role of women in national politics has expanded tremendously in recent years and their range of government positions has broadened.

Still, even today, female political leaders are constrained by a somewhat permeable "glass ceiling" that concentrates them at lower levels. Thus, women are generally more likely to be elected to local or state legislatures than to the national parliament. In 1993, India passed a constitutional amendment reserving one-third of the seats in all local assemblies (village councils, etc.) for women.[54] Since 1995, however, repeated efforts to extend that quota to parliament have failed.

Still, the ability of female political leaders to rise to the very top of several South Asian governments in recent decades is striking, particularly in light of women's generally lamentable position in the broader society. All three nations on the Indian subcontinent, as well as neighboring Sri Lanka, have been led by women prime ministers. The most prominent member of this group was Indira Gandhi, who served four terms as prime minister (1966–1977 and 1980–1984) and dominated Indian politics from 1966 until her assassination in 1984, when she was succeeded by her son Rajiv. In 1998, Rajiv's widow (he was assassinated as well, in 1991), Sonia Gandhi, assumed the leadership of the Congress Party. Six years later, she led the party back to power but declined the position of prime minister because of vehement opposition-party objections—objections not related to her being a woman, but rather to the fact that she was born and raised in Italy and still speaks somewhat halting Hindi.[55]

In recent decades, women have been prime ministers or presidents in Pakistan (Benazir Bhutto), Sri Lanka (Prime Minister Sirimavo Bandaranaike—the world's first female prime minister or president in the twentieth century—and her daughter, President Chandrika Kumaratunga), and Bangladesh (Prime Ministers Begum Khaleda Zia and Sheikh Hasina Wajed). Elsewhere in Asia, prominent female leaders include the Philippines' former President Corazón Aquino and recently reelected President Gloria Macapagal Arroyo, former Indonesian President Megawati Sukarnoputri, Congress Party leader, Sonia Gandhi, and Burmese opposition leader Daw Aung San Suu Kyi, winner of the 1991 Nobel Peace Prize.[56] At the same time, however, in 2004 the South Korean parliament rejected President Kim Dae Jung's nomination of a woman, Chang Sang, as that country's prime minister in that legislature's first-ever confirmation vote for that primarily ceremonial post.[57]

No other developing region matches Asia's array of female leaders, but, besides Eva Perón, Latin America has produced the current Panamanian President Mireya Moscoso Rodríguez, as well as former Presidents Isabel Perón (Argentina), Violeta Chamorro (Nicaragua), and Ertha Pascal-Trouillot (who served very briefly as Haiti's provisional president). Western hemisphere nations with female prime ministers have included Bermuda, Bolivia, Dominica, and Guyana. In Africa, women served briefly as prime ministers of the Central African Republic and Rwanda, and Maria das Neves Ceita Baptista de Sousa is currently prime minister of the Democratic Republic of São Tomé and Príncipe.

Several caveats must be raised, however, regarding the political success of these leaders. First, a number of them only served quite briefly as interim leaders. Second, most emerged from a tiny elite of highly educated, upper-class women from powerful families and, therefore, were not representative of women's societal status generally. Thus, for example, Pakistan's Benazir Bhutto and Burma's Aung San Suu Kyi were educated, respectively, at Harvard and Oxford universities. Corazón Aquino belonged to one of the Philippines' more powerful land-owning families. Finally, many of the most enduring and influential leaders, particularly in Asia, have been the wives, widows, or daughters of charismatic national leaders: Indira Gandhi was the daughter of India's legendary, first prime minister, Jawaharlal Nehru; Aung San Suu Kyi's father was the founder of modern Burma (now Myanmar); Indonesian President Megawati Sukarnoputri was the daughter of General Sukarno, that country's first president; Filipino President Gloria Macapagal Arroyo's father had also been president; Pakistani Prime Minister Benazir Bhutto's father preceded her as prime minister; and Janet Jagan was the widow of Cheddi Jagan, Guyana's first president.

A shocking number of female government leaders in the LDCs, most notably in Asia, have been the widows (or daughters) of assassinated political leaders. Sri Lankan Prime Minister Sirimavo Bandaranaike was the widow of a slain prime minister, while the country's current president, Chandrika Kumaratunga, endured the political assassinations of both her father and her husband (30 years apart). Former President Corazón Aquino, hero of the Filipino democracy movement, was the widow of an assassinated opposition leader. Bangladesh's two most recent prime ministers have been, respectively, the widow and daughter of assassinated prime ministers. In Myanmar, democracy leader Aung San Suu Kyi's father, General Aung San, was assassinated when she was a child. And in the Americas, former Nicaraguan President Violeta Chamorro was the widow of a famed newspaper editor whose assassination sparked the Nicaraguan Revolution.[58]

This does not imply that these women lacked political ability or leadership qualities. Indira Gandhi was widely recognized as one of the world's most accomplished political leaders, and Violeta Chamorro helped heal the wounds of her country's civil war. After Sri Lanka's Sirimavo Bandaranaike succeeded her assassinated husband as prime minister, she dominated that country's political system for the next three decades. Current Philippine President Gloria Macapagal Arroyo was an economics professor, finance minister, and vice president before becoming president.[59] Still, no matter how highly skilled they have been, female political leaders in the LDCs, particularly in Asia, usually have been able to reach the top of their political system only as heirs to their fathers or husbands. For now, then, a glass ceiling on government leadership remains in place for most Third World women, with the notable exception of a political or socioeconomic elite.

Reserved Seats and Quotas: Female Representation in Parliament and the Cabinet

With women accounting for slightly over half the population of most nations, gender-neutral political systems would presumably produce a comparable proportion of female political leaders in bodies such as the national legislature (hereafter referred to generically as "parliament" even when it bears other names such as "congress"). Yet, today fewer than one in six members of parliament (MPs) worldwide are female and only in a small number of countries does that proportion rise to one in three.[60] The Nordic nations of northern Europe (Denmark, Finland, Iceland, Norway, and Sweden) were far ahead of any other region, with nearly 40 percent female representation. In less-developed regions, rates vary from a high of only 19 percent in the Americas to a mere 6.4 percent in the Arab states (Table 5.3).[61]

From 1996 to 2004, the number of women MPs worldwide rose from 10.1 to 15.4 percent. Gains in the LDCs during that period were sharpest in the Arab states (still having the world's lowest rate of female representation, but nearly doubling its share in eight years) and slowest in Asia (up only slightly from 13.1 to 15.3 percent, allowing Latin America to pass it as the Third World's leader). Despite significant gains, however, women remain severely underrepresented

TABLE 5.3   The Proportion of Women in National Parliaments (Regional Averages)

Region	Single House or Lower House	Upper House or Senate	Both Houses Combined
Nordic European Countries	39.7%	—	39.7%
Latin America and North America	18.5%	18.2%	18.5%
Asia	15.5%	13.6%	15.3%
Sub-Saharan Africa	14.6%	12.8%	14.4%
Arab States	6.0%	7.5%	6.4%

Source: Inter-Parliamentary Union, *Women in National Parliaments* (May 31, 2004), http://www.ipu.org/wmn-e/world.htm.

in all parts of the world, excepting the Nordic countries. Several social, economic, and cultural factors help account for this. Pippa Norris and Joni Lovenduski have argued that the number of women in elected office depends on factors affecting "supply and demand."[62]

Supply refers to the number of women who meet the usual socioeconomic levels of public officeholders in their country. Since Third World women generally have lower levels of education, lower status, and, most important, fewer economic resources—all factors closely related to political success—they are able to "supply" fewer viable candidates for office. Indeed, Rae Lesser Blumberg's research in several regions of the world indicates that "the most important variable … affecting the level of [political] equality [or inequality] between men and women is economic power" as defined by their relative control over income and economic resources.[63] On the "demand" side (a measure of society's interest in having female political representation), cultural prejudices against women, most blatant in the Islamic states of the Middle East, further reduce female political representation.

In the past two decades, as women's educational levels have risen in most of the developing world, as they have entered the professions in greater numbers, and as cultural prejudices have diminished somewhat in many LDCs, the supply of potential women officeholders increased. However, the change accounting for the sharpest national gains in female representation in recent years has come on the demand side—the introduction of gender-based reserved seats and, especially, quotas in parliament itself or in the lists of candidates presented by competing political parties. Since 1991, gender-quota laws relevant to parliament have been passed in at least 20 countries, 14 of them LDCs. Interestingly, Latin America, a region commonly known for its *machismo*, has predominated, with 12 nations having adopted gender quotas since Argentina led the way in 1991 (soon to be followed by Bolivia, Brazil, Costa Rica, the Dominican Republic, Ecuador, Guyana, Mexico, Panama, Paraguay, Peru, and Venezuela).[64]

Legislated and voluntary attempts to raise the proportion of women in national parliaments have taken several forms. The most direct and intrusive method is to *reserve* a designated number of parliamentary seats for women. In

Bangladesh, for example, the 1972 constitution set aside 15 seats in parliament exclusively for women. That was later raised to 30 seats before the quota amendment lapsed in 2001 and the number of women MPs (elected through normal channels) plunged to six (2 percent of all seats) in the following election. A 2004 constitutional amendment reintroduced reserved seats and raised the number to 45 (13 percent of all MPs). However, women filling these "reserved seats" are not directly elected by the voters but, rather, are chosen by the regularly elected (overwhelmingly male) members of parliament. These reserved seats are divided among the nation's political parties in direct proportion to the percentage of seats each party had won in the most recently concluded national election.[65] Similarly, Morocco reserves 10 percent of its parliamentary seats for women, while Tanzania reserves 20 percent. Several other African nations, including Botswana, Rwanda, Eritrea, Sudan, Tanzania, Zimbabwe, Lesotho, Burkina Faso, and Uganda, also have reserved women's seats as did Jordan, Pakistan, and Taiwan. As of early 2003, only about a dozen countries (all of them LDCs) had similar set-asides, but that number has increased since then. Afghanistan's new constitution reserves parliamentary seats for women and it is being considered in Iraq.

Reserving seats for women is the most direct and certain means of guaranteeing greater female representation in parliament or (in cases such as India and Tanzania) in local government councils. Many democratic reformers, however, object to the practice because it creates a legal entitlement for women that men do not enjoy and because the women filling these seats often are not directly elected by the voters (as we have seen in Bangladesh).[66] Interestingly, many women's advocacy groups also oppose the practice. For one thing, the number of seats that are reserved usually is rather low (only 6 of 110 parliamentary seats in Jordan, for example). Also, while women are allowed to run in the regular parliamentary elections as well, the process of reserving seats creates its own glass ceiling if political leaders feel that such set-asides have already given women their "fair share." Political parties then feel no obligation to be inclusive when choosing their regular slate of parliamentary candidates. Furthermore, opponents argue, since the women holding reserved seats are often not directly elected but, rather, are picked by predominantly male political leaders, they are beholden to the male power structure and unlikely to challenge it. Finally, female MPs holding reserved seats lack the legitimacy that an open election confers on their fellow parliamentarians. In short, the system generally smacks of tokenism and is frequently, though not exclusively, introduced in countries such as Morocco and Jordan where women's political power is very limited, where the number of reserved seats is rather small, and where few, if any, women win regularly contested parliamentary races.[67] On the other hand, if significant numbers of seats are reserved for women, the effect can be dramatic. In Eritrea, 30 percent of the seats in both the national and regional legislatures are reserved for women. Likewise, a combination of reserved seats and viable female candidates in regularly contested races has given Rwanda's parliament the highest proportion of women in the world.

Another means of reducing female political underrepresentation is the establishment of gender quotas for the slates of parliamentary *candidates* in general elections. Quotas may take two forms. First, individual political parties may voluntarily agree to guarantee that their slate of candidates for parliament will contain a certain percentage of women. In Europe, for example, the first major gains for female parliamentary representation came in Scandinavia when that region's socialist parties (commonly the largest party in each country) agreed to gender quotas. In the Third World, the most successful example of voluntary quotas has been in South Africa's dominant party, the African National Congress (ANC).

The second type of candidate quota is legislated and either is mandatory or penalizes noncomplying parties by imposing fines or withholding government campaign funds. As we have seen, a dozen Latin American countries, and a few other LDCs, passed some form of a gender quota during the wave of democratic transitions in the 1990s. Typically, quotas of either type commit parties to nominate women in 30 percent of the parliamentary (or local) races, the figure widely believed to be a major threshold for producing government policies that are perceived as more friendly to women's interests.

The goal of quotas is purportedly to give women a greater opportunity to hold regularly elected seats rather than seats specially reserved for them. But quotas, particularly when legislatively imposed, are frequently ineffective because their objective is easily circumvented if women are simply nominated in races that they are unlikely to win. In electoral systems that choose a single legislative representative from each district (SMD), gender quotas are often undermined when political parties nominate women primarily in districts that they have little chance or expectation of winning. Similarly, in countries that elect their parliament through proportional representation—whereby parties present voters with a choice between competing lists of candidates—women are often placed at the bottom of the party's list where they are unlikely to make it into office.

In non-English-speaking electoral democracies, proportional representation (PR) is the most common electoral format. To understand how PR works, let us imagine a country with a 500-seat parliament representing 25 electoral districts (normally with roughly equivalent population sizes), each of which elects 20 MPs. Each of the national parties nominates a "party list" of 20 candidates in each district, with candidates normally ranked from 1 through 20 (closed lists). Rather than vote for a single candidate, as Americans do when they vote for the House of Representatives, under PR voters vote for one of the party lists. Seats are then allocated in proportion to the percentage of votes that each list receives. Thus if the Party X's list, for example, were to receive 40 percent votes in a particular district, they would win 40 percent of the seats in that district (i.e., eight seats). But which eight of the party's 20 candidates would go to parliament? It would be those who were ranked 1 through 8 on the party's list prior to the election. If we further imagine that a quota law requires that at least 35 percent of each party's candidates be women (i.e., at least seven in each district), the number of women who actually are elected would still depend on where they had been ranked on the party list. Since the record shows that in most countries women tend to be placed lower down on the candidate lists, even with the high quota requirement all eight of that party's victorious candidates could be men if all of the female candidates had been ranked in the bottom half of the list.

To put teeth into a legislated quota system and prevent dumping of women candidates in hopeless positions at the bottom of the party lists, countries such as

Argentina passed electoral laws requiring so-called zipper-style quotas. That means each party must not only meet its quota of female candidates, but it must also alternate male and female candidates, according to that quota percentage from the top of the list downward. In other words, if a country has a zipper-style quota of 33 percent, women candidates would have to occupy every third position on the list from the top rank on down.

In general, legally mandated quotas, of whatever type, passed since 1991 have contributed substantially to the increase in female members of parliament worldwide. In 10 Latin American countries that enacted them from 1991-1997, the number of women in parliament rose by an average of 8 percent in the very next national election.[68] However, results have been most impressive when electoral laws impose zipper-style quotas or their equivalent. For example, in the first election after Ecuador passed its 1997 zipper-style quota law, female representation in parliament jumped from 4 to 15 percent. Similarly, when Costa Rica's Supreme Court strengthened that country's quota law by insisting that women be proportionally included in competitive races, the percentage of women in the national Legislative Assembly rose from 19 percent in 1997 (already higher than in the U.S. Congress at that time) to 35 percent in 2002. Also, when the ANC took power in South Africa and then voluntarily adopted a gender quota, that country's percentage of women MPs rose from 141st in the world in 1994 to 11th in 2004. On the other hand, even though Venezuela's electoral law established a women's quota of 30 percent on each party's candidate list, the absence of regulations governing rankings helps explain why women won fewer than 10 percent of the seats in the most recent parliamentary election (2000).

Ultimately, the issue of reserved seats and candidate quotas raises another fundamental question. How much difference does increased female representation have on government policy? Women's rights advocates argue that legislatures with significantly higher female membership are more prone to address issues such as gender bias in the economy, child care, education, and equitable divorce law and are more likely to produce legislation in these areas that are beneficial to women. In fact, most analysts agree that even a substantial increase in female representation at very low levels—for example, the recent doubling of women MPs in Arab countries from 3 to 6 percent—is unlikely to affect legislative policy. Instead, as I have indicated, the evidence suggests that women usually need to achieve a critical mass of 30 percent of the seats in the national legislature in order for gender to make a difference. If representation falls substantially below that figure, women MPs either tend to be co-opted or are simply ineffective in pressing "women's issues." As representation reaches that threshold, however, parliaments are more likely to pass "women-friendly" legislation. It is for this reason that the Inter-Parliamentary Union endorses 30-percent quotas and why most quota legislation sets that mark. It is important to keep in mind, however, that while female legislators tend to be of one mind on issues such as domestic violence, they may be very split, particularly in Latin America, on other issues such as abortion.

In spite of recent gains, today there are still only 15 countries in the world that have reached that target, six of which are developing nations. Rwanda, where women constitute 49 percent of the parliament, is the only country in the world that has achieved full gender parity.[69] The other five are Cuba (36 percent),

Costa Rica (35 percent), Argentina (34 percent), South Africa (33 percent), and Mozambique (30 percent).[70]

Elections through proportional representation clearly benefit women more than single-member districts do, where effective gender quotas are much harder to legislate. Worldwide, 13 of the 14 countries with competitive elections and at least 30-percent female representation use PR exclusively and the other (Germany) uses a combination of both systems. Of the six LDCs, Costa Rica and Argentina have legally mandated quotas for all party candidate lists; Mozambique and South Africa have voluntary, party quotas; Rwanda has both legal quotas and reserved seats; and Cuba has neither, but there is only one legal party (the Communist Party) so the government and ruling party determine its nominees. Finally, of the five countries using quotas, all use zipper-style quotas or (in the case of Costa Rica) something similar. As we have noted, without a zipper-style requirement, party leaders typically undermine quota systems by relegating women to the bottom of candidate lists.

While the percentage of women in parliament is a useful measure of their influence in national politics, their share of cabinet posts is even more important. In most countries, cabinet ministers operate at the center of political power and are among the nation's most influential political figures.[71] Not surprisingly, women still hold a relatively small percentage of ministerial posts, lower even than their share of parliamentary seats. Still, as with female MPs, their numbers have grown significantly over the past two decades. Between 1987 and 2004, the percentage of women ministers worldwide more than tripled, from only 3.4 percent to 11.3 percent.[72] Once again, there is considerable regional variation. As usual, Europe has led the way, particularly the Nordic countries. Currently two European nations, Sweden and Spain, have cabinets with equal numbers of men and women. However, Latin America had the highest percentage of women ministers in the Third World (almost 18 percent), virtually equaling Europe. Africa was the next developing region with 11 percent, while Asia and the Pacific had only about 7 percent. At the same time, several LDCs were among the world leaders, including South Africa (where women currently hold 43 percent of the cabinet posts), Colombia (39 percent), and the Philippines (33 percent).

Until now, the types of cabinet posts occupied by women have still conformed to gender stereotypes. In a 1999 study of 190 countries throughout the world, the Inter-Parliamentary Union found that women were Ministers of Women's Affairs in 25 percent of the countries. They frequently headed the Ministers of Social Affairs (23 percent), Health (16 percent), Environment (15 percent), Family Affairs (14 percent), Labor (13 percent), Education, and Justice (both 12 percent)–mostly "nurturing positions." However, women held the following ministerial positions in less than 5 percent of the countries: Defense, Health, Agriculture, Science and Technology.[73] Undoubtedly, such gendering of cabinet posts has diminished somewhat since that time.

Earlier in this chapter, we noted the growing number of women prime ministers and presidents in the LDCs, most notably in South Asia. While we might assume that gains for women at the pinnacle of government would either reflect or cause broader political gains in female political representation— as it has, for example, in the Nordic countries—this has not necessarily been true in less-developed countries. Sri Lanka and Bangladesh show the most glaring inconsistencies. Women have recently served as both president and prime minister of Sri Lanka for extended periods, while Bangladesh has seen two women alternate as prime minister since 1991. Yet Sri Lanka's parliament currently has only 4.4 percent female representation, less than one-third the international average and, until reserved seats were reintroduced in 2004, Bangladesh had one of the world's lowest rates of female MPs (2 percent). Similarly, in India, having a woman dominate the political system for many years failed to generate more opportunities for women at the parliamentary level (with 8 percent of the nation's MPs, Indian women have about half the international average). In fact, during her long tenure in office, Indira Gandhi proposed little to advance women's political representation. It was only after her assassination and the succession of her son, Rajiv, that the parliament passed a 30 percent quota for women in local government.

Women and Revolutionary Change

The political, economic, and social changes brought about by Third World revolutions often present women with rather unique opportunities that merit special attention. For one thing, revolutions tend to alter or destroy many of the traditional social structures and values that had previously oppressed women. When the communists came to power in China, for example, they eliminated the last vestiges of foot binding for young women and prohibited the sale of women and girls as wives, concubines, or prostitutes.[74] At the same time, many revolutionary armies and parties create new social structures that are more open to women and offer greater opportunities for upward mobility. For example, women held important military command positions in both the Nicaraguan Sandinistas and the Salvadorian FMLN during their guerrilla struggles.

Indeed, because of their need for soldiers and their willingness to violate traditional gender roles, many guerrilla armies include significant numbers of women. For example, in the Eritrean People's Liberation Front (ELF), which engaged in a successful 30-year struggle for independence from Ethiopia, women constituted some 30 percent of the army and 11 percent of the delegates to the first ELF Congress.[75] Similarly, women made up an estimated 20 to 30 percent of the Sandinista forces in Nicaragua, perhaps 25 percent of Uruguay's Tupamaros, and a significant proportion of the FMLN guerrillas in El Salvador.[76] Because the Sandinistas and many other guerrilla armies continued to play a central political role after the revolutionary party took power, the consequences of their relatively high level of gender integration extended beyond the military struggle.

After the communist victory in China, Party Chairman Mao Zedong and the All-China Women's Federation assigned women an important role in rebuilding the nation's economy.[77] Consequently, many women who had long been confined to their homes entered the work force, not because of any feminist agenda but because the government needed to reconstruct an economy devastated by three decades of war. But while these opportunities to work outside the home were obviously beneficial, women failed to attain the occupational equality professed by the government. In both collective farms and industry, they continued to hold the less-skilled, lower-paying jobs.

Radical regimes in such countries as China, Vietnam, and Cuba try to transform traditional cultural values through education and propaganda. Combating long-standing prejudices against women is a part of that process.

But even revolutionary societies find it difficult to eradicate long-standing sexist attitudes. Although China's 1950 Marriage Law decreed that women could wed only of their own free will and granted women equal rights within the family, enforcement of those provisions has often been spotty, especially in rural areas. Furthermore, during the Maoist era (1949–1976) the government's commitment to these new values varied considerably, as the country swung back and forth between periods of ideological fervor and pragmatism. During radical phases, such as the Great Leap Forward and the Cultural Revolution, state policy supported female liberation and lambasted traditional male prejudices. In between these periods of mass mobilization and turmoil, however, when party leaders wished to restore stability, the government reverted to more traditional values, extolling the importance of motherhood and family.

Since Mao's death (1976), the government's more pragmatic policies have stressed economic growth more than gender or social class equality. As many state-owned factories phase out guaranteed lifetime employment (the "iron rice bowl") in their quest for higher efficiency, women are likely to be the first workers fired. It is in the Chinese countryside, however, that one finds the most blatant remnants of sexist values as villagers respond to stringent state policies aimed at controlling population growth in this nation of 1.4 billion people. Since the late 1970s, the government has pressured Chinese families to have only one child, denying them certain welfare benefits if they exceed that number. In rural regions, where daughters are less valued than sons, this has apparently led to significant infanticide, the murder or abandonment of female babies by parents who want their only child to be a boy.[78] Similarly, girls represent a disproportionate share of the abandoned children in rural orphanages.

Cuba's revolutionary government has also tried to improve the status of women and change traditionally sexist cultural values. In 1961 the Federation of Cuban Women (FMC) was created to mobilize women behind the revolution and give them a voice in the political process. Because Vilma Espín, the federation's leader since its founding, was Fidel Castro's sister-in-law (she is the ex-wife of Cuba's second-in-command, Raúl Castro), the FMC has had a direct line to the center of state power. Espín also had a distinguished career as a guerrilla officer in Cuba's revolutionary conflict. Officially representing 70 percent of Cuban women, the FMC encouraged them to support government-sponsored political activities and to enter the work force. Thus, during the first decade of the revolution, the proportion of women in the work force rose from 17.8 to 30.9 percent, with impressive gains in the professions.[79] In the political arena, women have been particularly active in the neighborhood-based Committees for Defense of the Revolution (CDR). The CDRs (to which some 80 percent of Cuban adults belong) promote revolutionary values, including gender equality. At their meetings, men who refuse to let their wives work or who don't put in their share of the housework may find themselves criticized for machismo (perhaps by their own wives) and chastised by their peers for such nonrevolutionary values. By the early 1980s, women represented half the local CDR leaders, 46 percent of the leaders of labor union locals, and 22 percent of the delegates to the National Assembly, the nation's congress.[80] Female representation in congress has since risen to 36 percent, one of the highest figures in the world.

But revolutions are no panacea for women's problems. Often radical rhetoric exceeds actual accomplishments. Cuba, like China, has demonstrated that even egalitarian revolutions fail to achieve full gender equality. Thus, despite their prominence in local CDR, labor unions, and the National Assembly, Cuban women have rarely penetrated the top ranks of national political leadership, such as the State Council (in effect, the president's cabinet) or the Central Committee and the Politburo of the Communist Party. Since the National Assembly routinely passes all policy proposals from the Communist Party, it is in those bodies that real power lies. An analysis in the early 1980s showed that only 8.9 percent of Central Committee members were female.[81] Cuba's Family Code (the law governing family relations), passed decades ago, requires spouses to contribute equally to domestic chores (child care, cooking, cleaning, etc.). While almost all Cuban men claim to subscribe to its regulations, most of them fail to contribute their fair share of housework. Change has been limited by ingrained male attitudes (*machismo*) and by most women's obvious reluctance to complain to their neighbors in the local CDR about their husband's noncompliance with the Code. As one observer noted, "It must take an extremely confident woman to bring her husband to public censure for failure to honor the code."[82] As in other revolutionary societies, traditional cultural values concerning gender roles are hard to change.

THE STATUS OF WOMEN: THE ROLES OF MODERNIZATION, GLOBALIZATION, AND REGIME TYPE

Our analysis has revealed that the political and economic status of Third World women are far from uniform. Their situation varies considerably from world region to region and country to country. Furthermore, even within particular countries, women's standings differ considerably, depending on their social class or ethnicity. Three factors are particularly influential: the dominant cultural values, the level of socioeconomic modernization, and the type of political regime in place.

Culture, including religious values, sets baseline boundaries around women and influence the opportunities available to them. This is most manifestly true in fundamentalist societies such as Afghanistan (even after the Taliban), Iran, Sudan, and Saudi Arabia. In the most extreme example, the Taliban government prohibited women from working outside the home and virtually confined them to their households. Beyond the terrible hardships they imposed on many women (widows with small children, for example, were denied employment), these measures also deprived one of the world's poorest nations of some of its small core of teachers and health care workers. While educational and professional opportunities exist for a female elite in Saudi Arabia, most women are marginalized from the mainstream of economic life. Political leadership in all these countries is an exclusively male preserve. Cultural restraints are more subtle in East Asia, but even in modern societies such as Singapore and South Korea women have lower than expected rates of university attendance.

Contrary to modernization theory, and true to radical feminist analysis, socioeconomic modernization has often adversely affected women in the LDCs in the short-to-medium term. In Africa, for example, the commercialization and

mechanization of agriculture have benefited male cultivators disproportionately, often at the expense of women farmers. In East and Southeast Asia, rapid
industrialization based on cheap labor has produced higher wages for some
female laborers, but exploitation of others.[83] Yet, while it may initially negatively
impact poor women, modernization's longer-term effects are generally beneficial. A growing middle class, wider educational opportunities, and higher rates
of literacy make women more aware of their rights and opportunities, while
increasing their capacity to defend these gains. Socioeconomic development
also tends to create more egalitarian values within society. It is not coincidental
that the more modernized nations of Latin America—including Argentina,
Chile, Mexico, and Uruguay—have the largest number of female political
leaders and professionals, just as the most economically advanced nations of
Europe generally have the greatest opportunities for women.

And like other political movements presented in the mass media, the feminist movement has extended into the Third World through the demonstration
effect. In many developing nations, women's rights movements have emerged
where none existed or were even conceivable a decade or two before. Educated
women in more traditional societies such as Bolivia or Jordan may be influenced by the women's movements that previously developed in more progressive, neighboring societies such as Chile or Lebanon. However, these new
movements have taken on a distinct character, distinguishing them from
Western feminism. The women's movement was born in the Western world
only four decades ago, and one can only speculate on its influence in the Third
World three decades from now.

Finally, the status of women is shaped by the type of political regime and
economic system prevailing in a country at the time. Women tend to fare more
poorly under right-wing, authoritarian military regimes such as those that dominated much of South America in the 1970s and early 1980s and to benefit more
from leftist regimes. Thus, for example, in countries such as Chile (like Sweden,
Spain, and Norway), socialist and social democratic political parties have taken
the lead in promoting increased female political representation. At the same
time, however, while women suffered under the military dictatorships in South
America, they also gained considerable political experience through social
movements for human rights and basic human services. Revolutionary regimes
that are ideologically commited to equality have championed women's rights.
However, while revolutionary change benefited women in many ways in countries such as China, Vietnam, Cuba, and Nicaragua, significant gender inequalities have remained. Sometimes, that inequality simply reflects the resiliency of
deeply entrenched cultural values or continued male dominance of the political
system. Often it is also linked the common Marxist belief that all societal
inequalities—whether related to gender, race, or religion—are derived from
class divisions. That article of faith has caused regimes such as Cuba's to underestimate gender-related problems by erroneously assuming that the destruction
of capitalism will, by itself, eventually eradicate gender discrimination.

Since full gender equality does not exist even in the most advanced industrialized democracies (only small, mostly Nordic, northern European democracies come close), it seems unlikely that socioeconomic modernization or the
spread of democratic norms will automatically bring gender equality to the
developing world. Future economic development can be expected to produce

both negative and positive consequences. In the short run, economic modernization, particularly in agriculture, will likely adversely affect many low-income
women. In countries suffering severe economic difficulties, such as debt crises, or
those experiencing civil conflict, women will doubtless continue to bear an
unequal burden. And the spread of Islamic fundamentalism in many parts of the
Middle East and Africa does not bode well for women's rights in those nations.
In the long term, however, economic modernization, higher educational levels,
and modern values of equality seem to offer Third World women their best hope.

CONCLUSION: DEMOCRACY AND THE ROLE
OF WOMEN IN SOCIETY

Since democratic ideology endorses equal political opportunity and equal
rights for *all* citizens, we might expect the Third Wave of democracy during the
final decades of the twentieth century to have advanced gender equity. Yet our
discussion of revolutionary societies revealed that their nondemocratic governments have often promoted women's rights more successfully than their
democratic counterparts. Many revolutionary regimes have established quotas
for female participation in the national legislature, improved the legal status of
women, banned oppressive traditional customs (the binding of Chinese
women's feet, for example), and, to some degree, included feminist ideals in the
new political culture. Thus, a good case can certainly be made, for example,
that the revolutionary governments of China, Cuba, and Mozambique have
advanced the cause of gender equality more effectively than the democratic
governments of Brazil, India, or the Philippines. Ironically, the transition from
communism to democracy in Eastern Europe caused a precipitous drop in the
percentage of women elected to parliament.[84]

Of course, most authoritarian governments are neither radical nor committed to women's rights. Women's causes have usually fared poorly in conservative and fundamentalist authoritarian regimes. In Afghanistan, the
Islamist Taliban government even denied women the right to work or to receive
an education outside the home and kept them veiled and confined much of the
time.[85] In countries such as Chile, Nigeria, and Pakistan, repressive military dictatorships did not restrict the role of women, but made no particular effort to
improve their status.

How did the wave of democratization that swept through the developing
world in the closing decades of the twentieth century affect women's economic
and political standing? As we have seen, women played an important role in
the struggle for democracy in several Latin American countries. Often they
were able to demonstrate for change in the streets when men could not. Yet, the
return of political parties and established interests groups (both largely male-
dominated) to political center stage during democratic transitions tended to
marginalize many grass-roots groups and NGOs in which women had played
a much larger role. Thus, as Marta Htun has observed, the restoration of
democracy had contradictory effects on women's political participation:

> The return to civilian rule and the consolidation of democratic governance ...
> created many more opportunities for women to be politically active, but also

reduced the comparative advantage of gender-specific organizations as conduits for social demands. As a result, many women who had entered politics during the struggle against authoritarian rule left gender-specific organizations for political parties and other "traditional" organizations like labor unions.[86]

Bang-Soon L. Yoon has examined the effects of democratization on gender politics in South Korea. There, too, women had played an important role in the mass protests that helped build democracy, working particularly through their labor unions. Yet the transition to democracy since the late 1980s failed to raise the comparatively small percentage of women in the National Assembly, judiciary, and bureaucracy.[87] At the same time, however, partly spurred to action by emerging women's groups, the South Korean National Assembly has become more attentive to legislation affecting women, including the Equal Employment Acts (1989 and 1995), the Child Care Act (1990), and the Law on Prevention of Family Violence and Protection of Victims (1997).

However, while democratic transitions need not lead to immediate gains for women on all fronts, and while it may even produce some setbacks, it appears that democracy, particularly when coupled with social and economic development, advances women's rights and opportunities. It is, after all, the advanced Western democracies, most notably northern European nations, that have the highest Gender Empowerment Measures (GEM). And most of the nations with the lowest GEM scores have nondemocratic regimes. Nevertheless, that correlation is primarily attributable to differences in socioeconomic development. Countries with the highest levels of education, literacy, urbanization, and industrialization (Western Europe, North America, and Oceania) are both more democratic and more egalitarian in gender-related indicators. The poorest and least developed countries in Africa and South Asia score poorly on measures of both democracy and gender equality.

Looking only at Third World nations, we find a more ambiguous relationship between democracy and gender equality. Some democracies, such as Chile and Uruguay, have relatively higher levels of equality (as measured by GEM scores), while other democracies, such as India, fare poorly. Similarly, while authoritarian nations such as Cuba score very well, others, such as Egypt and Saudi Arabia, do poorly. There is reason to believe that in the long run, democratic government will give women greater opportunities as they are able to mobilize politically, lobby government officials, and otherwise voice their concerns through democratic channels.

DISCUSSION QUESTIONS

1. Explain how the focus of research on gender in the developing world has moved from the study of oppression to the study of empowerment. What does this change reflect?
2. What occupations attract the highest proportions of Third World women? Why do many women gravitate toward those occupations?
3. Discuss the ways in which modernization has affected women of differing social status in distinct ways.

4. What is the most common characteristic of female heads of government in the Third World? To what extent has their assumption of power substantially improved the status of other women in their nations?
5. Discuss the different ways in which *quota systems* have been used to increase female representation in national legislatures and explain how quotas differ from a system of reserved seats.
6. Discuss how the percentage of women in a nation's parliament is affected by "supply and demand."
7. Compare the records of Third World democracies to those of authoritarian LDCs insofar as they promote gender equality in politics and the workplace.

NOTES

1. The informal sector, which includes a large number of street vendors and small businesses, is the part of the economy that is "unregulated by the institutions of society [most notably the state], in a legal and social environment in which similar activities are regulated" and taxed. In other words, the informal sector encompasses otherwise legal activities (not criminal operations or prostitution) but operates outside the spheres of tax collection, government labor and safety regulations, and the like. In many developing countries, it represents 30 to 50 percent of the urban workforce. See Manuel Castells and Alejandro Portes, "World Underneath: The Origins, Dynamics and Effects of the Informal Economy," in *The Informal Economy: Studies in Advanced and Developing Economies*, eds. Alejandro Portes, Manuel Castells, and Lauren A. Benton (Baltimore, MD: Johns Hopkins University Press, 1989), 12. Of course, many men work in the informal sector, but women are disproportionately represented.

2. United Nations Development Programme data cited in Jennifer L. Troutner and Peter H. Smith, "Empowering Women: Agency, Structure, and Comparative Perspective," in *Promises of Empowerment: Women in Asia and Latin America* (Lanham, MD: Rowman & Littlefield Publishers, 2004), eds. Peter H. Smith, Jennifer L. Troutner, and Christine Hünefeldt, 26.

3. *New York Times*, December 30, 1993.

4. *New York Times*, July 6, 2002 and July 17, 2002. Indeed, the trial was probably held to intimidate into silence the young brother, who had been sodomized by members of the wealthy family. The event was so extreme and so shocked Pakistani public opinion that the national government paid the victim compensation of $8,200 while bringing the perpetrators to trial. More generally, however, ordinary rape, including gang rape, is not uncommon in Pakistan, especially the province of Punjab where this took

place, and is usually not reported to the authorities. A woman is raped every two hours in Pakistan (and gang raped on an average of once every four days in Punjab), with only about a quarter of the cases being reported to the police.

5. Arturo Escobar and Sonia E. Alvarez, eds., *The Making of Social Movements in Latin America: Identity, Strategy and Democracy* (Boulder, CO: Westview Press, 1992); June Nash, "Women's Social Movements in Latin America," *Gender and Society* 4, no. 3 (September 1990): 338–353.

6. Women also were prohibited from work outside the home even if the family had no male breadwinner.

7. The World Bank, *Engendering Development* (New York: Oxford University Press and the World Bank, 2001), 58.

8. Sonia E. Alvarez, *Engendering Democracy in Brazil: Women's Movements in Transition Politics* (Princeton, NJ: Princeton University Press, 1990), 4, fn. 2.

9. Paul Cammack, David Pool, and William Tordoff, *Third World Politics: A Comparative Introduction* (Baltimore, MD: Johns Hopkins University Press, 1988), 184–193.

10. Leith Mullings, "Women and Economic Change in Africa," in *Women in Africa: Studies in Social and Economic Change*, eds. Nancy J. Hafkin and Edna G. Bray (Stanford, CA: Stanford University Press, 1976), 239–264.

11. Margo Lovett, "Gender Relations, Class Formation, and the Colonial State in Africa," in *Women and the State in Africa*, eds. Jane L. Parpart and Kathleen A. Staudt (Boulder, CO: Lynne Rienner Publishers, 1989), 37–39.

12. Ester Boserup, *Women's Role in Economic Development* (London: George Allen and Unwin, 1970), 54.

13. Ibid., 55.

14. FAO, "Gender and Food Security: Agriculture," http://www.fao.org/Gender/en/agri-e.htm.

15. For more detailed earlier data on specific LDCs and developing regions, see Esther Trenchard, "Rural Women's Work in Sub-Saharan Africa and the Implications for Nutrition," in *Geography of Gender in the Third World,* eds. Janet Henshall Momsen and Janet G. Townsend (Albany, NY: SUNY Press, 1987), 155; Marie-Angélique Savané, "Women and Rural Development in Africa," in *Women in Rural Development: Critical Issues* (Geneva: International Labour Office, 1980), 27; Boserup, *Women's Role,* 27; and Joan Mencher, "Women in Agriculture," in *Food Policy: Framework for Analysis,* eds. Charles K. Mann and Barbara Huddleston (Bloomington, IN: Indiana University Press, 1986), 39.

16. FAO, "The Feminization of Agriculture," http://www.fao.org/Gender/en/agrib2-e.htm

17. Nici Nelson, *Why Has Development Neglected Rural Women?* (Oxford, England: Pergamon Press, 1979), 4.

18. Ibid., 45–47.

19. FAO, "Gender and Food Security."

20. Leena Mehendale, "The Integrated Rural Development Programme for Women in Developing Countries: A Case Study," in *Women, Development and Survival in the Third World,* ed. Haleh Afshar (New York: Longman, 1991), 223–238.

21. Cornelia Butler Flora, "Income Generation Projects for Rural Women," in *Rural Women and State Policy: Feminist Perspectives on Latin American Agricultural Development,* eds. Carmen Diana Deere and Magdalena León de Leal (Boulder, CO: Westview Press, 1987), 212–238.

22. Claire Robertson, "Ga Women and Socioeconomic Change in Accra, Ghana," in *Women in Africa,* 111–133.

23. Gloria González Salazar, "Participation of Women in the Mexican Labor Force," in *Sex and Class in Latin America,* eds. June Nash and Helen I. Safa (New York: J. F. Bergin Publishers, 1980), 187.

24. See footnote 1 of this chapter for a detailed definition of this term.

25. Heleieth I. B. Saffioti, "Technological Change in Brazil: Its Effect on Men and Women in Two Firms," in *Women and Change in Latin America,* eds. June Nash and Helen I. Safa (South Hadley, MA: Bergin & Garvey Publishers, 1985), 110–111; Commack, Pool, and Tordoff, *Third World Politics,* 195–196.

26. *The New York Times,* June 11, 1998.

27. Cited in Alan Gilbert and Josef Gugler, *Cities, Poverty and Development: Urbanization in* the Third World, 2d ed. (New York: Oxford University Press, 1992), 104, fn. 29.

28. Johanna Son, "SOUTH-EAST ASIA: Sex Industry Thrives, But States Look Away," *InterPress News Service* (IPS) (August 19, 1998), which draws on the recent ILO study. http://www.aegis.com/news/ips/1998/IP980803.html

29. *Women and Human Rights* - U.S. Department of State report (released by the Bureau of Democracy, Human Rights and Labor U.S. Department of State, February, 2001) cited in WIN News. http://www.findarticles.com/p/articles/mi_m2872/is_2_27/ai_75099769/pg_15

30. Nici Nelson, "How Women and Men Get By: The Sexual Division of Labour in the Informal Sector of a Nairobi Squatter Settlement," in *The Urbanization of the Third World,* ed. Josef Gugler (New York: Oxford University Press, 1988), 183–203.

31. Shahnaz Kazi, "Some Measures of the Status of Women in the Course of Development in South Asia," in *Women in Development in South Asia,* ed. V. Kanesalingam (New Delhi, India: Macmillan India Limited, 1989), 19–52.

32. Boserup, *Women's Role,* 119–128.

33. New Zealand was the first country to grant women voting rights, in 1893. Female suffrage was enacted at the United States federal level in 1920 at about the same time as in most West European democracies. On the other hand, women were not able to vote in Swiss national elections until 1971, nor in the small European state of Liechtenstein until 1984.

34. On women's suffrage in Europe and the United States, see Vicky Randall, *Women and Politics: An International Perspective,* 2d ed. (Chicago: University of Chicago Press, 1987), 5, 51, 209–211; on Latin America, see Jane Jaquette, "Female Political Participation in Latin America," in *Sex and Class in Latin America,* 223; also, Francesca Miller, *Latin American Women and the Search for Social Justice* (Hanover, NH: University Press of New England, 1991), 96–101.

35. World Bank, *Engendering Development,* 57.

36. See, for example, Ellen Gruenbaum, "Sudanese Women and the Islamist State," in *Women and Power in the Middle East,* eds. Suad Joseph and Susan Slyomovics (Philadelphia: University of Pennsylvania Press, 2001), 115–125. Other chapters in the volume paint a less pessimistic picture, such as the one on Palestinian women in the political system and workplace.

37. Rama Mehta, *The Western Educated Hindu Woman* (New York: Asia Publishing House, 1970), 16–32.

38. Judith Van Allen, "Memsahib, Militante, Femme Libre: Political and Apolitical Styles of

Modern African Women," in *Women in Politics,* ed. Jane S. Jaquette (New York: John Wiley and Sons, 1974), 310.

39. Lourdes Arizpe, "Foreword: Democracy for a Small Two-Gender Planet," in *Women and Social Change in Latin America,* ed. Elizabeth Jelin (London and Atlantic Highlands, NJ: Zed Books, 1990), xv.

40. Nina Mba, "Kaba and Khaki: Women and the Militarized State in Nigeria," in *Women and the State in Africa,* 86.

41. Jaquette, "Female Political Participation," 223.

42. See, for example, JoAnn Aviel, "Changing the Political Role of Women: A Costa Rican Case Study," in *Women in Politics,* 281–303.

43. See, for example, Amy Conger Lind, "Power, Gender and Development: Popular Women's Organizations and the Politics of Needs in Ecuador," in *The Making of Social Movements,* 134–149.

44. Jana Everett, "Incorporation versus Conflict: Lower Class Women, Collective Action, and the State in India," in *Women, the State and Development,* eds. Sue Ellen M. Charlton, Jana Everett, and Kathleen Staudt (Albany: State University of New York Press, 1989), 163.

45. Armita Basu, *Two Faces of Protest: Contrasting Modes of Women's Activism* (Berkeley: University of California Press, 1992), 3.

46. Jane S. Jaquette, "Introduction" in *The Women's Movement in Latin America: Feminism and the Transition to Democracy,* ed. Jane S. Jaquette (Boston: Unwin Hyman, 1989), 6. This section draws heavily on Jaquette's book and Alvarez, *Engendering Democracy in Brazil.*

47. Sonia E. Alvarez, "Women's Movements and Gender Politics in the Brazilian Transition," in *The Women's Movement in Latin America,* 19–20; see also Alvarez, *Engendering Democracy in Brazil.*

48. Teresa Pires de Rio Caldeira, "Women, Daily Life and Politics," in *Women and Social Change in Latin America,* 47–79.

49. Patricia Jeffery and Amrita Basu, eds., *Appropriating Gender: Women's Activism and Politicized Religion in South Asia* (London: Routledge, 1998).

50. Elsa M. Chaney, *Supermadre: Women in Politics in Latin America* (Austin: University of Texas Press, 1979), 4.

51. Jane L. Parpart and Kathleen A. Staudt, "Women and the State in Africa," in *Women and the State in Africa,* 8.

52. Quoted in Chaney, *Supermadre,* 21.

53. Ibid., 141.

54. Suranjana Gupta, "Transforming Governance Agendas: Insights from Grass-roots Women's Initiatives in Local Government in Two Districts in India," in *Gender, Globalization, and Democratization,* eds. Rita Mae Kelly et al. (Lanham, MD: Rowan & Littlefield, 2001), 195–204.

55. "Sonia Gandhi turns down PM post," *BBC* (May 18, 2004) http://news.bbc.co.uk/2/hi/south_asia/3721863.stm; see also "Profile: Sonia Gandhi," *BBC* (May 18, 2004) http://news.bbc.co.uk/1/hi/world/south_asia/3546851.stm

56. San Suu Kyi rightfully should have been included in the list of Asian prime ministers since she led her National League for Democracy party to an overwhelming victory in the 1990 national elections, but the results were annulled by the military and she has been under house arrest most of the time since 1989. Few observers doubt that she would be elected handily in any free election that would be held in Myanmar (Burma's current name).

57. "Female Prime Minister Rejected," *CBS.com* (July 31, 2002) http://www.cbsnews.com/stories. Dr. Chang, a former university president, was criticized in those hearings for having claimed in her resume that her doctorate was from Princeton University, when in fact it was from Princeton Theological Seminary. Many observers, however, felt that a man would not have been rejected for the infraction since many of South Korea's male political leaders have escaped censure for far more grievous indiscretions. With less than 6 percent female representation, South Korea's parliament ranked 92nd in the world at that time in its proportion of women parliamentary members.

58. The United States had a similar pattern until recently. Vicky Randall points out that between 1917 and 1976, 73 percent of female senators, 50 percent of women congressional representatives, [and almost all female governors] were the widows of men who had held those seats. See *Women and Politics,* 132.

59. To be sure, some of the previously mentioned women leaders, most notably Isabel Perón, were far less capable.

60. For current data on this subject, see Inter-Parliamentary Union's website, www.ipu.org and IDEA (the International Institute for Democracy and Electoral Assistance), *Global Database of Quotas for Women,* http://www.quotaproject.org. Unless otherwise cited, all the data on female representation in parliament come from these two sources.

61. "The Americas" refers to Canada, the United States, and more than 30 Latin American and Caribbean nations. Thus, its two First World nations have little effect on the regional average. Moreover, while Latin America and

Caribbean legislatures had slightly lower female representation than Canada's 23.6 percent, they were actually substantially ahead of the U.S. Congress's 14.2 percent.

62. Pippa Norris and Joni Lovenduski, *Political Recruitment: Gender, Race and Class in the British Parliament* (Cambridge, England: Cambridge University Press, 1994).

63. Rae Lesser Blumberg, "Climbing the Pyramids of Power: Alternative Routes to Women's Empowerment and Activism," in *Promises of Empowerment*, 60.

64. Lisa Baldez, "Election Bodies: The Gender Quota Law for Legislative Candidates in Mexico," (Philadelphia, PA: Paper presented at the convention of the American Political Science Association, August 28-31, 2003), 32.

65. "BD women unlikely to gain more power," Internet Edition of *Dawn* (Pakistani English-language newspaper), June 11, 2004. See http://www.dawn.com/2004/06/11/int12.htm

66. As of 2003, women were appointed by another body to reserved seats in seven of 12 countries and were elected in only five. Opponents have also challenged the system in a number of countries on the grounds that it violates the principle of "equal treatment" of the sexes. Defenders, who have been supported by the courts in Mexico and elsewhere, argue that since men held most of the parliamentary seats under the previous system, they obviously have no need for equal protection.

67. For example, in Morocco's last parliamentary elections, women had 30 seats reserved, but managed to win only five more seats in the 295 regularly contested races. In Jordan's last election, six seats were reserved for women, but not a single additional woman was victorious in any of the nation's 104 regularly contested contests. The six women are appointed by the King.

68. Mala Htun, "Women and Democracy," in *Constructing Democratic Governance in Latin America*, eds. Jorge L. Domínguez and Michael Shifter (Baltimore: The Johns Hopkins University Press, 2003), 122; Mala Htun and Mark P. Jones, "Engendering the Right to Participate in Decision-Making: Electoral Quotas and Women's Leadership in Latin America," in *Gender, and the Politics of Rights and Democracy in Latin America*, eds. Nikki Craske and Maxine Molyneux (New York: Palgrave, 2002), 241.

69. In the economically developed nations, only Sweden comes close to parity with 45 percent representation in its single-House parliament. The other developed countries that have reached the 30 percent mark are, in descending order of representation, Denmark, Finland, the Netherlands, Norway, Belgium, Austria, Germany, and Iceland.

70. Among South Africa's parties, only the African National Congress has a self-imposed quota. But since it holds almost three-quarters of all seats in parliament, the total percentage of women in parliament is relatively high. See Women's Environment & Development Organization (WEDO), "Getting the Balance Right in National Parliaments. See www.wedo.org or www.wedo.org/balance.htm

71. In purely presidential systems such as in the United States, there is a separation of powers between the executive and legislative branches, thereby often excluding congressional participation in the cabinet. However, most of the world's nations have parliamentary systems (normally headed by a prime minister) which joins the two branches so that cabinet members are either exclusively or significantly drawn from the parliament. In countries using the British "Westminster" model of government, appointment to the cabinet is the pinnacle of a parliamentary representative's political career.

72. 2004 Global Summit of Women Report: *Women in [sic!] Leaders Worldwide* (June, 2004) http://www.globewomen.com/summit/2004/GSW2004Report.htm

73. Cited in Maria Escobar-Lemmon and Michelle M. Taylor-Robinson, "Women Ministers in Latin American Government: When, Where, and Why," (Paper presented at the conference on Pathways to Power: Political Recruitment and Democracy in Latin America, Clemson University, 2004), 2.

74. Delia Davin, "Chinese Models of Development and Their Implications for Women," in *Women, Development and Survival*, 32.

75. National Union of Eritrean Women, "Women and Revolution in Eritrea," in *Third World: Second Sex*, ed. Miranda Davis (London: Zed Press, 1983), 114.

76. *Envio* (Managua) 6, p. 78, quoted in Mary Stead, "Women, War and Underdevelopment in Nicaragua," *Women, Development and Survival*, 53; Randall, *Woman and Politics*, 61.

77. Bee-Lan Chan Wang, "Chinese Women: The Relative Influences of Ideological Revolution, Economic Growth and Cultural Change," in *Comparative Perspectives of Third World Women: The Impact of Race, Sex and Class*, ed. Beverly Lindsay (New York: Praeger, 1980), 99–104; see also Delia Davin, "Chinese Models of Development," in *Women, Development and Survival*.

78. John Pomfret, "In China's Countryside: 'It's a Boy! Too Often," *Washington Post* (May 29, 2001). Demographers have found an abnormally high ratio of officially reported male births to female births (as high as 117 boys nationwide for every 100 girls, with higher ratios in rural areas). Some of the discrepancy

may be caused by families who do not report the birth of daughters to local government officials, but much of it is believed attributable to infanticide (sometimes referred to as gendercide).

79. Isabel Larguia and John Domoulin, "Women's Equality in the Cuban Revolution," in *Women and Change in Latin America*, 344, 363.

80. Ibid., 360. There is extensive literature on women in revolutionary Cuba, most of it written from a strongly prorevolutionary perspective. See Margaret E. Leahy, *Development Strategies and the Status of Women* (Boulder, CO: Lynne Rienner Publishers, 1986), 91–116; Lois M. Smith and Alfred Padula, "The Cuban Family in the 1980s," in *Transformation and Struggle: Cuba Faces the 1990s*, eds. Sandor Halebsky and John M. Kirk (New York: Praeger, 1990), 176–188; and Max Azicri, "Women's Development through Revolutionary Mobilization," in *The Cuba Reader: The Making of a Revolutionary Society*, eds. Philip Brenner et al. (New York: Grove Press, 1989), 457–470. For a different viewpoint, see Julie

Marie Bunck, "The Cuban Revolution and Women's Rights," in *Cuban Communism*, 7th ed., ed. Irving Louis Horowitz (New Brunswick, NJ: Transaction Publishers, 1989), 443–465.

81. Randall, *Women and Politics*, 103.

82. Johnetta Cole, "Women in Cuba," in *Comparative Perspectives of Third World Women*, 176.

83. Linda Y. C. Lim, "Capitalism, Imperialism and Patriarchy: The Dilemma of Third World Women in Multinational Factories," in *Women, Men and the International Division of Labor*, eds. June Nash and María Patricia Fernández-Kelly (Albany, NY: SUNY Press, 1983).

84. World Bank, *Engendering Development*, 58.

85. For personal accounts by Afghan women, see Deborah Ellis, *Women of the Afghan War* (Westport, CT: Praeger, 2000).

86. Htun, "Women and Democracy," 125.

87. Bang-Soon L. Yoon, "Democratization and Gender Politics in South Korea," in *Gender, Globalization, and Democratization*, 174–176.

chapter 6

Agrarian Reform and the Politics of Rural Change

When we speak of "the people" of Africa and Asia, in large part we are talking about the peasantry—poor farmers living in a traditional culture. Despite substantial urbanization in recent decades, much of the developing world's population remains rural. According to one estimate, close to half of all Third World families earn their livelihood from agriculture.[1] It is in the countryside where some of the worst aspects of political and economic underdevelopment prevail. In nations as distinct as China and Mexico, rural annual incomes are only 20 to 25 percent as high as urban earnings. Sharp urban-rural gaps also persist in literacy, health care, and life expectancy. Rural villagers are less likely than their urban cousins to have safe drinking water, electricity, or schools.

While the proportion of the Third World's total population living in the countryside is generally substantially higher than in the First World, it varies greatly from country to country: from under one-third in Venezuela, Argentina, Brazil, and Zambia to two-thirds or more in Malaysia, Yemen, Bolivia, China, India, and much of Africa. In all, more than one billion of these rural people live in "absolute poverty," defined as suffering from inadequate housing, pervasive illiteracy, malnutrition, and high rates of infant mortality.[2] And in the world's poorest nations—including Malawi, Rwanda, the Congo, Bangladesh, and Haiti —the portion of rural inhabitants living in absolute poverty exceeds 80 percent.[3]

Given the size of the agricultural sector, we should not be surprised to find that it contributes a larger share of the Gross Domestic Product (GDP) than it does in industrialized nations. Thus, toward the end of the twentieth century, agriculture constituted 35 percent of GDP in the poorest Third World nations, 22 percent in middle-level LDCs, and 10 percent in the more advanced developing countries, compared to only 3 percent in highly industrialized countries.[4] At the same time, however, the farm population's per-capita output is far lower than the urban sector's.

In most of the developing world, political and economic power is concentrated in the cities. Consequently, government policy—on issues ranging from social expenditures to agricultural pricing—has a predictable urban bias. As noted in Chapter 1, modernization theory argues that as countries develop, modern values and institutions will spread from the cities to the countryside, and the gap between the two will narrow. Conversely, dependency theorists maintain that the links between urban and rural areas replicate the exploitative international relationship between the industrialized core (the First World) and the periphery (the LDCs).[5] What is certain is that resolving the political and economic tensions *between* urban and rural areas and reducing the vast inequalities

within the countryside, the major foci of this chapter, remain among the foremost challenges facing many developing nations.

RURAL CLASS STRUCTURES

Within the countryside, there are generally substantial disparities in access to,
and ownership of, farmland. Particularly in Latin America and parts of South
Asia, agricultural property tends to be concentrated in a relatively small number
of hands. These inequalities have contributed to rural poverty and created rigid
class systems in countries such as El Salvador, Colombia, the Philippines, and
parts of India. African nations—with notable exceptions such as South Africa,
Morocco, and Kenya—have a more equitable pattern of land distribution, though
they still suffer from sharp urban-rural gaps and intense rural poverty. Farmland
is most equitably distributed in East Asia (excepting the Philippines).

At the apex of the rural class system stand the large and powerful land
owners, sometimes known as the *oligarchy*. Major Filipino sugar growers and
Argentine cattle barons, for example, have historically exercised considerable
political power in national politics. In El Salvador, the most influential coffee
producers long dominated the country's political system . Land concentration
has been most intense in Latin America, with its tradition of large estates
(*latifundia*) dating back to the Spanish colonial era and the early years of independence. In the Philippines, Sri Lanka, Pakistan, and Bangladesh, along with
parts of India, Indonesia, and Thailand, reactionary landed elites have also
contributed to rural backwardness and poverty.

Since the middle of the twentieth century, the economic and political
power of rural landlords has declined considerably in many LDCs. In the most
extreme cases, radical revolutions in countries such as China and Vietnam
stripped landlords of their property and many were killed or sent to camps for
"political reeducation." Elsewhere, nonrevolutionary and relatively peaceful
agrarian reforms also undermined the rural elites of Peru and South Korea.[6] In
industrializing nations such as Brazil and Thailand, over time the economic
importance of agribusiness has diminished relative to the industrial and commercial sectors. Consequently, many wealthy land-owning families have diversified into other parts of the economy or have left agriculture entirely.

At the local and regional levels, however, landlords in Latin America and
much of Asia continue to exercise considerable influence. For example, upper-
caste farmers in the Indian state of Bihar and large cattle ranchers in the
Brazilian interior retain virtually unchallenged local power. At times they have
intimidated, or even murdered, peasant organizers and union leaders without
fear of legal sanctions. Such was the fate of Chico Mendes, the celebrated
Brazilian union leader who had organized Amazonian rubber-tree tappers
against the powerful ranchers who were clearing the forest and destroying the
local habitat. Despite his impressive international stature (he was honored, for
example, by Turner Broadcasting and various U.S. senators) and his links to
U.S. environmental groups, Mendes was murdered by hired gunmen. Only
after a sustained international outcry were his murderers brought to trial.

On the rung beneath the landed elite in rural society, we find middle-
sized landlords and "rich" peasants. The second group (sometimes called *kulaks*)

consists of peasants who, unlike smaller landlords, still work on the land. However, unlike poorer peasants, *kulaks* are sufficiently affluent to hire additional peasant labor to work with them. While neither middle-sized landlords nor rich peasants belong to the national power elite, they exercise considerable local political influence in countries such as India.[7] Indeed, in much of Asia, where the biggest agricultural holdings are not nearly as large as those in Latin America, middle-sized landlords are a potent political force. Their influence is typically magnified further by extended family networks. Together with rich peasants, they frequently dominate village politics.

Finally, at the bottom of the socioeconomic ladder, the rural poor—including peasants who own small plots of land, tenant farmers, and farm workers—are generally the Third World's most impoverished and powerless group. *Peasants* are defined as family farmers (mostly poor) who maintain traditional lifestyles distinct from those of city dwellers. Because they are often poor and poorly educated, many peasants lack the means to transport their crops to market themselves, lack ready access to credit, and don't know how to deal with legal proceedings that they may encounter. Consequently, they depend on merchants, moneylenders, lawyers, and government bureaucrats, all of whom frequently exploit them. Their links to the outside world—including the government, the military, the church, and the market economy—are largely dependent upon individuals and institutions outside the peasants' community.[8] Thus, as Eric Wolf has noted, "Peasant denotes an asymmetrical structural relationship between the producers of surplus [peasants] and controllers [including landlords, merchants, and tax collectors]."[9]

Poor peasants may be further subdivided into two subgroups: those who own small plots of land for family cultivation (smallholders) and the landless. The ranks of the landless, in turn, include tenant farmers (who enter into various types of rental arrangements with landlords) and hired farm laborers. It should be noted that these categories are not mutually exclusive. Smallholders, for example, may also supplement their incomes by working as farm laborers or renting land as tenants. Generally, it is the landless who constitute the poorest of the rural poor. While they represent a mere 10 percent of all agricultural families in countries such as Kenya and Sierra Leone, their numbers rise to 25 to 35 percent in Mexico, Peru, Turkey, and Cameroon, and to 50 to 70 percent in India, Bangladesh, Pakistan, the Philippines, Iraq, the Dominican Republic, and Brazil.[10] Not surprisingly, in much of Asia and Latin America, where concentration of land ownership and associated peasant landlessness are particularly notable, the issue of land reform was long at the center of rural politics.

PEASANT POLITICS

Despite their vast numbers, peasants usually play a muted role in Third World politics. Because most LDCs didn't have competitive national elections until recently those numbers do not readily convert into political influence. The peasantry's political leverage is also limited by poverty, lack of education, dependence on outsiders, and physical isolation from each other and from the centers of national power. Cultural values stressing caution and conservatism may further constrain peasant political behavior. Karl Marx's analysis of nineteenth-century European rural society questioned the peasants' capacity for political change and their revolutionary potential. Writing on the French peasantry, he derided their alleged lack of solidarity and class consciousness, and disparagingly referred to them as a "sack of potatoes." Dismayed by their apparent conservatism, he dismissed peasants as "the class that represents the barbarism in civilization."[11] In the twentieth century, Robert Redfield's classic study of Third World peasants portrayed them somewhat similarly. "In every part of the world," he argued, "generally speaking, peasants have been a conservative factor in social change, a brake on revolution."[12]

Indeed, over the years anthropological research has frequently depicted peasant political culture as fatalistic and atomized. Hence, it is claimed, they doubt the capacity of collective political action to better their own fate.[13] Discussing the reaction of Indian villagers to local government authorities, Phyllis Arora describes a sense of powerlessness resulting in political apathy. "Helplessness is ... evoked by the presence of the district officer. The peasant tends to feel that all he [or she] can do before such authority ... is petition for redress of grievances. ... In the ultimate analysis, however, ... the peasant feels at the mercy of the whims of the [political] authorities."[14] More recently, Western journalists, visiting peasant communities in China at the time of massive urban demonstrations, were struck by the villagers' lack of political involvement and their insularity from national political debate.[15]

No doubt, peasants typically are wary of radical change and respectful of community traditions. To some extent, this conservatism reflects a suspicion of outside values—a distrust frequently grounded in religious beliefs and other long-standing traditions. Indeed, the maintenance of a distinct peasant culture depends, to some extent, on the rejection of external influences. But it is important to recognize that peasant suspicion of social change is often understandable and rational. Struggling on the margins of economic survival, the rural poor have often found that the commercialization and mechanization of agriculture, as well as other aspects of rural modernization, have often had a negative impact on their lives. In rural Pakistan, for example, the introduction of tractors improved the output and income of the farmers who could afford them. As a consequence, however, many poorer tenant farmers who couldn't compete were forced off their plots, concentrating land into fewer hands.[16] Political changes may also be threatening. For example, when peasants have been organized by outside activists to challenge local injustices, they have often been ruthlessly repressed. Small wonder, then, that they are often suspicious of change, including any challenge to the power structure.

This does not mean, however, that they are incapable of standing up to landlords and government authorities who wrong them. Far from it. Examples of peasant resistance are commonplace, ranging from the most restrained to the most radical. James C. Scott has demonstrated that many peasants in Southeast Asia who appear to accept the established order actually engage in unobtrusive "everyday forms of resistance," such as theft and vandalism against their landlords, foot dragging, and false deference.[17] Elsewhere, peasants have presented their political demands more openly and aggressively. Contrary to Marx's expectations, the supposedly conservative peasantry were critical actors in most twentieth-century revolutions, including communist upheavals in Russia, China, Vietnam, and Cuba, as well as in Bolivia's and Mexico's noncommunist insurgencies.[18] More recently, they have been the backbone of guerrilla movements in the Philippines, Cambodia, Colombia, El Salvador, Peru, and Nepal. In the mid-1990s, *Zapatista* rebels from the Indian communities of Chiapas, Mexico, established a de facto zone of self-rule and forced the government to the negotiating table. And in many other LDCs, ranging from India to Ecuador, well-organized peasant groups have become influential actors in democratic political systems.

The role of the peasantry in revolutionary movements will be examined in greater detail in Chapter 8. For now, however, suffice it to say that peasants are not inherently conservative or radical. Rather, they vary considerably in their ideological propensities and their capacity for collective political action. To understand why so many peasants accept the political status quo, while others choose to resist or even rebel, we must first examine the relationship between the powerful and the weak in the countryside. Although landlords in traditional settings frequently exploit their tenants or neighboring smallholders, mutually understood boundaries normally limit the extent of that exploitation. Links between landlords and peasants are usually grounded in long-standing patron-client relationships involving reciprocal obligations. Despite the landlords' superior power, these relationships are not always exploitative. For example, land owners frequently provide their tenants with land and financial credit in return for labor on their estate. And they may fund religious festivals or serve as godparents for their tenants' children.

As long as landlords and other members of the rural power elite fulfill their obligations, peasants generally accept the traditional order despite its many injustices. However, should rural modernization and the commercialization of agriculture induce rural patrons to cease discharging their traditional responsibilities, the peasantry may conclude that the previously existing "moral economy" has failed them.[19] Eric Wolf has noted that the transition from feudal or semifeudal rural relations to capitalist economic arrangements frequently strips the peasantry of the certainty and protection afforded them by the old order. The result is often rural upheaval. Thus, he argued, the origins of communist revolutions in China, Vietnam, Cuba, and other Third World nations could be found in the threat that the growth of rural capitalism posed to the peasants' traditional way of life.[20] This in no way suggests that rural modernization and the transition to capitalism *always* radicalize the peasantry or drive them to revolutionary activity. But when peasants feel that their traditional way of life is threatened, they will resist change or at least try to channel it into forms more beneficial to their interests. How effectively they engage in collective political action and how radical or moderate their demands are depend on a variety of factors: the extent to which they perceive themselves to be exploited; how desperate their economic condition is; the degree of internal cohesion and cooperation within their communities; their ability to form political linkages with peasants in neighboring villages or in other parts of the country; the extent to which they forge political ties with nonpeasant groups and leaders; the type of outside groups with whom they ally (be it the Catholic Church in the Philippines or Maoist revolutionaries in Peru); the responsiveness of the political system to their demands; and the variety of political options that the political order affords them.

The last two factors suggest that the probability of radical peasant insurrection depends as much on the quality of a country's political system as it does on the nature of the peasantry. Given a meaningful opportunity to implement change peacefully, peasants rarely opt for revolution. Rebellion—which brings obvious dangers to their own lives and the lives of their families—is an act of desperation entered into only when other options are unavailable. It is perhaps for that reason that no democratic political system has ever been toppled by revolutionary insurgency.

In recent decades, the spread of the mass media throughout the countryside, increased rural educational levels, and the broadening of voting rights in many LDCs (such as extension of the vote to illiterates) have greatly increased the political influence of peasant voters in democratic and partly democratic countries. In countries such as India, South Korea, Nicaragua, and Ecuador, politicians must now consider the interests of the rural poor more seriously. With rising educational levels and more information at their disposal, peasants can more effectively press their demands. Still, such voting power is of little use in the single-party or no-party governments that remain in much of Africa, the Middle East, and Asia. And even in competitive party systems, the peasantry's political power is not proportional to the group's size.

Ultimately, the range of peasant political activity runs the gamut from the far Left to the far Right, from peaceful to violent. As Samuel Huntington has noted, "The peasantry ... may be the bulwark of the status quo or the shock troops of revolution. Which role the peasant plays is determined by the extent to which the existing system meets his immediate economic and material needs as he sees them."[21] In India, many peasants vote for the BJP—the conservative Hindu fundamentalist party (see Chapter 3). In Latin America, on the other hand, peasants often vote for moderately left-of-center candidates. And in countries such as China, Vietnam, Nicaragua, and Peru, still other peasants have supported revolutionary insurrections. Whatever their political inclinations, the peasants' economic and political concerns usually revolve around four broad issues: the prices they are paid for their crops, consumer prices, taxes, and the availability of land.[22] The issue of land has been the most volatile and the most critical to the political stability of many Third World nations, and it is to this issue that we now turn our attention for much of this chapter.

THE POLITICS OF AGRARIAN REFORM

In many areas of the Third World where land ownership is highly concentrated, the issue of agrarian reform has been a part of the rural political agenda. To be sure, the pressure for such reform has waxed and waned, and other models of rural development have become more popular in recent decades. Still, the issue of agrarian reform lingers. Normally, it involves redistribution of farmland from landlords to landless peasants or to smallholders who need larger plots to support their families. In other instances, it entails distribution of public property, including previously uncultivated lands. To stand a real chance of increasing agricultural production, improving rural living standards, and establishing political stability, however, government land redistribution must be accompanied by supplementary aid to its program beneficiaries. This aid includes agricultural technical assistance, commercial credit, transportation, and enhanced access to markets. Unfortunately, agrarian reform programs often fail to provide this additional support sufficiently. Furthermore, the amount of land distributed is frequently inadequate to meet the peasants' needs. Agrarian reforms introduced by revolutionary regimes sweep out the old systems of inequality, but often create new forms of land ownership or management, dominated by the state that fails to live up to the peasants' expectations. Thus, with notable exceptions such as Japan, Taiwan, and South Korea, land reform programs have often fallen short of their goals.

Patterns of Land Concentration

At the start of the twenty-first century, perhaps 100 million rural families (some 500 million people) in the developing world earn most of their income on land they do not own.[23] In addition, millions of land-owning peasants lack sufficient land to support their families adequately. In countries such as Bangladesh, Rwanda, El Salvador, and Peru, the ratio of rural families to arable land is so high that even an equitable distribution of farmland would fail to meet all the peasants' needs. But in many LDCs, where the ratio of rural families to arable land is more favorable, landlessness and land shortages are caused by the concentration of agricultural land in a small number of hands.

Maldistribution of land is most pronounced in Latin America, where large estates, sometimes measuring thousands of acres, contain a substantial proportion of the region's farmland. In Brazil, for example, a mere 2 percent of the nation's farms, each exceeding 1,000 hectares (2,500 acres), have owned more than 55 percent of all farmland.[24] Vast cattle and citrus estates have been cut out of the Amazonian interior, some covering several hundred thousand acres. In the Dominican Republic, where holdings are not nearly as vast, farms more than 50 hectares in size have constituted less than 2 percent of the nation's agricultural units; nevertheless, they have controlled more than 55 percent of the country's farmland. The largest of these estates—those exceeding 500 hectares—represented a mere 0.1 percent of all Dominican farms but held 27 percent of the nation's agricultural land. At the other end of the spectrum, peasant smallholders (owning units of 5 hectares or less) owned nearly 82 percent of the country's farms, but merely 12.2 percent of its area.[25] Similar patterns have prevailed in much of Latin America. Prior to the 1979 Sandinista revolution, an astounding 43 percent of Nicaragua's rural families were landless. Yet a mere 2 percent of the rural population owned 36 percent of the land, including about one-fifth of Nicaragua's farmland that belonged to the ruling Somoza family.[26]

With different historical traditions and far higher population density, Asia does not have agricultural estates of the same magnitude. In nations such as Indonesia, India, and Pakistan, farm holdings rarely exceed 50 hectares.[27] Still, in many cases a high proportion of farmland is concentrated in relatively few hands. For example, in Bangladesh, one of the world's most densely populated countries, the largest farms are relatively small, rarely exceeding 5 to 10 hectares. Yet less than 3 percent of the nation's rural households control more than 25 percent of the nation's agricultural land. In the Philippines, virtually identical data show 3.4 percent of the country's farms accounting for 26 percent of the land.[28]

The Case for Agrarian Reform

Given the powerful vested interests opposing land redistribution, supporters of agrarian reform have needed to justify their objectives on a variety of grounds, including social justice and equity, greater political stability, improved agricultural productivity, economic growth, and preservation of the environment. An examination of each of these arguments reveals the complexity of the debate.

Social Justice   Because of the concentration of agricultural holdings in Latin America and parts of Africa and Asia, a *prima facie* case can be made for some form of land redistribution based on social justice and human rights.[29] As noted, the millions of rural families with little or no land are among the poorest of the Third World's poor. They are frequently trapped in a web of poverty, malnutrition, and illiteracy from which few escape. Usually they are politically powerless as well, controlled by landlords or local political bosses. For them, agrarian reform is a fundamental step toward achieving greater political and socioeconomic justice.[30]

Political Stability   From the perspective of government policy makers, perhaps a more compelling potential benefit of agrarian reform has been curtailing peasant unrest. Samuel Huntington has most starkly linked reform to political stability:

> Where the conditions of land tenure are equitable and provide a viable living for the peasant, revolution is unlikely. Where they are inequitable and where the peasant lives in poverty and suffering, revolution is likely, if not inevitable, unless the government takes prompt measures to remedy those conditions.[31]

Indeed, statistical analyses indicate that the likelihood of revolutionary activity in developing countries increases where there is high inequality of land ownership and where there is a significant proportion of landless peasants.[32] Without the threat of peasant unrest, however, policy makers have tended to be relatively indifferent to the injustices of land tenure patterns. Ironically, then, the end of the Cold War, and with it the threat of communist insurrection, has reduced U.S. interest in promoting land reform, as it had done, for example, in El Salvador during the 1980s.

Productivity   One of the most hotly debated results of land reform is its effect on agricultural productivity. Opponents of reform maintain that land redistribution lowers agricultural output, thereby diminishing food supplies for the cities and curtailing export earnings. Citing "economies of scale," they argue that large agricultural units are generally more productive because they can be more easily mechanized and can use rural infrastructures (such as irrigation or roads) more effectively. Second, they insist that peasant cultivators have less education and know-how than large land owners and are, consequently, less-productive farmers.

Advocates of agrarian reform counter that, in fact, smallholders are generally more efficient producers than larger landlords. Although a growing number of land owners currently study agricultural sciences and employ modern productive techniques, many of the landed elite still farm their land ineffectively. For example, in Latin America, where land is an important source of prestige and political power, landlords have often owned more than they can efficiently cultivate. Peasant cultivators, on the other hand, tend to farm their plots very intensively because their families' living standards depend on raising productivity.

This does not mean that small, peasant-run units are *always* more efficient. Peasant beneficiaries of land reform in some regions lack necessary skills for owning their own plots. Consequently, land transfers in such cases sometimes have caused short-term declines in efficiency.[33] In such cases the beneficiaries of land reform may require supplemental government assistance as they are transformed into land owners.

The comparative efficiency of landlords and smallholders also varies according to which crop or animal is being raised. For example, production of meat, wheat, or sugar is more likely to benefit from economies of scale (that is, output per acre will usually rise significantly as the result of capital investment). On the other hand, most of the grains, tubers, fruits, and vegetables that constitute the core of Third World food consumption, along with some exports such as coffee, do best with labor-intensive cultivation on small farm units. These variations notwithstanding, data collected in Asia and Latin America reveal that labor-intensive smallholders frequently have higher yields per acre than large-scale, capital-intensive (mechanized) producers.[34]

The economic efficiency of small farms may surprise many Americans accustomed to believing that larger units are inherently more productive. But in underdeveloped rural societies with a surplus of labor (i.e., many people who are underemployed and who will work for low wages), it is often more cost effective to use family or hired labor intensively. Out of economic necessity, peasant cultivators work hard, exploiting their own family labor. On the other hand, most large estates are farmed by tenants or hired laborers, neither of whom gain from raising productivity. That difference in motivation helps explain why the agricultural yields of peasant land owners in Japan, South Korea, and Taiwan and of near-owners in China are generally over twice as high as those of Filipino tenant farmers with comparable plots of land but less motivation to raise productivity.[35]

In recent decades, the disparity between large and small units in agricultural productivity has diminished. By using more advanced technology such as high-yield seeds and complementary irrigation, some large farmers have narrowed the efficiency gap.[36] But even if the disparity was eliminated entirely, smallholding operations would still be more productive to society in another way. Owners of larger farms generally need to import a portion of their machinery, fuel, and chemicals, thereby expending some of the country's valuable foreign exchange. On the other hand, peasant farms draw upon family labor, a cheap input found in abundance. It is for this reason that the former president of the Overseas Development Council argued that "a land and capital scarce (but population plentiful) country should favor 40 two-and-a-half acre farms over a single-owner 100-acre farm in order to make optimum use of available land, labor and capital."[37]

Economic Growth   In addition to its positive effect on agricultural productivity, land redistribution often brings broader benefits to the economies of developing areas. Several countries that have implemented extensive agrarian reforms, such as Bolivia and Cuba, have slowed the tide of peasant migration to the cities. Giving peasants an economic stake in the countryside has reduced rural-to-urban migration, thereby alleviating the tremendous strain on resources in many Third World cities (see Chapter 7).

When successfully implemented, land reform improves the living standards of the rural poor. As their purchasing power increases, they consume more of their country's manufactured goods, thereby stimulating industrial growth.[38] Indeed, Japan's, Taiwan's, and South Korea's postwar economic booms followed closely on the heels of agrarian reform.[39] Agrarian reform has also contributed to relatively high income equality in Japan, Taiwan, and South Korea. That equality and pervasive purchasing power, in turn, have been a significant ingredient in the region's dramatic economic development. In contrast, Latin America's concentrated pattern of farmland ownership is partly responsible for its highly inequitable distribution of income, extensive rural poverty, reduced consumer market, and lower economic growth.

Environmental Preservation Another, more recent argument for agrarian reform in some regions relates to environmental preservation. Each year in Brazil, vast areas of the Amazonian tropical forest are destroyed as trees are deliberately burned to clear land for ranching or farming. The fires are so vast that they are believed to contribute to the *greenhouse effect* on world climate. Although a substantial portion of this burn-off is caused by large-scale farmers and ranchers, peasant settlers also contribute. Driven out of the nation's poorest regions by desperation, land-hungry peasants colonize the jungle in search of a better life. Once there, they discover that cleared jungle soil quickly loses its nutrients. Consequently, they must soon move on, clearing yet more forest land. Agrarian reform in Brazil's unforested regions would reduce landlessness and give tenant farmers a greater stake in the land they farm, thus reducing migration to the Amazonian basin.

Similar arguments have been advanced for land reform in other parts of the world. Bangladesh's severe population pressure and concentrated land ownership have forced many poor farmers to push the frontiers of farming beyond their ecologically desirable limits. In their search for farmland, landless peasants often move to unsafe coastal regions not suitable for habitation. There they often fall victim to the typhoons that periodically sweep across the region, killing thousands of people.

TYPES OF AGRARIAN REFORM

In the past century, a variety of forces brought about agrarian reform. At times reform followed foreign occupation or pressure; sometimes it resulted from peasant-based revolutions; and some reform programs were introduced by governments anxious to garner peasant support and maintain political tranquility. In each case, the underlying forces that stimulated reform have influenced the type of program that emerges.

Externally Imposed Reform

The most successful externally imposed agrarian reforms occurred in East Asia after World War II. In Japan, the U.S. occupation command limited land ownership to 10 acres, transferred 41 percent of the country's farmland from landlords to tenants, and controlled rents for the remaining tenants. The number of landless peasants was reduced from 28 percent to 10 percent of the rural population, making the countryside a bastion of stability.[40] In Taiwan and South Korea, U.S. pressure encouraged similar reforms designed to avert rural unrest. Ownership was limited to small parcels, and about one-third of each country's farmland was transferred to tenants, some 60 percent of whom became land owners.[41] In all three nations, the transformation of rural society was tremendously success-ful, raising agricultural productivity, improving rural living standards, and strengthening political stability. Consequently, East Asia's agrarian reforms have been used as benchmarks to evaluate programs elsewhere in the world.

In view of these impressive early achievements, it is striking how infre-quent and ineffective later U.S. pressures have been in stimulating Third World agrarian reform. In retrospect, it appears that there were three unique condi-tions in postwar East Asia that have not been replicated subsequently. First was the depth of American commitment to reform. Fearing that agrarian revolu-tions would spread from China to other Far Eastern nations, U.S. policy mak-ers at the start of the Cold War pushed hard for land reform as the best way to contain communism. A second unique condition was the enormous leverage that the United States could exert on those East Asian governments at the time. The Japanese were under U.S. military occupation, while the South Korean and Taiwanese governments were deeply beholden to the United States for shield-ing them militarily. In subsequent years, the United States lacked comparable influence. Although it favored land reform in South Vietnam (in the 1960s) and Central America (1980s), it was unwilling or unable to exert sufficient pressure on their conservative governments to achieve effective programs.

This leads us to East Asia's last unique characteristic: its land-owning elites were so weakened at the end of World War II that they were ill equipped to defend their own interests. The situation was most stark in Japan following its surrender to U.S. forces at the close of the war. As the occupying power, the United States could impose its will on the country's previously powerful rural landlords. Moreover, key Japanese political leaders working with the U.S. high command concurred that agrarian reform was necessary.[42] In South Korea, many landlords had collaborated with Japan during its years of occupation. Hence, when Japanese colonial rule ended at the close of World War II, the Korean landed elite had little legitimacy or political influence. And in Taiwan, the Nationalist Party government recognized that its earlier failure to imple-ment agrarian reform on the Chinese mainland had contributed to the commu-nist victory there. So, driven from the mainland to Taiwan and prodded by the United States, the government was ready to modernize the countryside.

In the decades that followed, U.S. efforts on behalf of land reform were far less effective. In Southeast Asia and Central America, large landlords used their extensive political power to obstruct rural reform. At the same time, when peasant unrest developed in countries such as South Vietnam and El Salvador, the United States lacked the leverage or the will to promote real reform in the face of determined opposition by conservative elites.

Revolutionary Transformation

From the Mexican and Chinese revolutions through more recent insurgencies in the Philippines and El Salvador, most twentieth-century insurrections were peasant based (Chapter 8). Consequently, agrarian reform was a fundamental rallying cry in both Marxist revolutions (China, Vietnam, Cuba, and Nicaragua) and non-Marxist upheavals (Mexico, Bolivia, and Algeria). In the 1930s and

1940s, for example, the Chinese communists gained considerable peasant support by transferring land to the rural poor. Following their victories in Nicaragua, Vietnam, and Cuba, revolutionary parties in those countries also implemented radical agrarian reforms.

After coming to power in 1949, the Chinese communists distributed almost half of the country's arable land to about 60 million peasant households, comprising over half the nation's population. Like the U.S.-sponsored reforms in East Asia (Japan, South Korea, and Taiwan), China's agrarian reform initially disbursed the land to peasant smallholders. But soon convinced that privately owned peasant plots would reintroduce rural inequalities and class divisions, the government pressured the peasantry to join state-sponsored cooperatives.[43]

Because they have fully vanquished the rural upper class, revolutionary governments are freer to redistribute large quantities of land. In countries such as Cuba, Nicaragua, and Vietnam, property belonging to the defeated rural aristocracy was either converted to state farms or distributed to peasant smallholders. Similarly, following their anticolonial revolutions, Algeria and Kenya redistributed farmland belonging to ousted European settlers. In Mexico, some 40 percent of peasant families benefited from agrarian reform, receiving more than 40 percent of the country's agricultural and forest areas. Eighty percent of Bolivia's farmland was transferred to three-fourths of its rural families.[44]

Revolutionary agrarian reform programs are more likely to introduce collective or cooperative farms than the peasant smallholdings promoted in the East Asian model, though many have involved a mixture of both. While even some non-Marxist revolutions have distributed land through cooperatives (Mexico, for example), communist regimes have been most committed to collective farming. Some revolutionary governments, such as Cuba's, have maintained private farming alongside the larger collectivized sector but have generally encouraged peasant land owners to sell their property to the state. Others, however, harshly repressed peasants resisting forced collectivization of their plots into state farms or state-dominated cooperatives, often with tremendous loss of life. Eric Wolf points out the irony of forced collectivization in countries such as the Soviet Union (where, under Joseph Stalin, millions died of state-enforced famine), China, and Vietnam. Peasants, he notes, supported or even fought for radical revolutions in hopes of getting plots of land for their families. Yet after risking their lives to bring the revolution to power, they were often coerced into collectivizing their farms.[45] Ethiopia later enforced similarly unpopular land collectivization programs.

China illustrates the dangers of forced collectivization, not only when the peasants are coerced into joining collective farms but years after. As we have noted, a brief period of family farming soon gave way to collectivized farming. The process reached its apex during the Great Leap Forward (1958 to 1961), when huge agricultural communes were created. Overcentralization of decision making and poorly informed government policies caused huge declines in the availability of food. In the massive famine that resulted, some 20 to 25 million people died of starvation or disease.[46] Although the government then backed away from the commune experiment, collective farming was emphasized again during the Cultural Revolution (1966 to 1976).

The communists' preference for collective farming, whether on state farms or on cooperatives under state direction has several motives. A fundamental objective was to establish state control over agriculture so that government administrators could dictate which crops were grown and what their selling price would be. In China, for example, the government required agricultural communes to concentrate on the production of basic food grains such as rice and wheat, which were then sold to the general public at controlled prices. From a political standpoint, collectivization was seen as a means of controlling the peasantry's individualistic impulses and reorienting them to work for the public good. Arguing that private farming inevitably leads to inequalities between villagers and creates a bourgeois mentality among peasant smallholders, government leaders initially dismissed family farming as an undesired form of capitalism.[47] Finally, supporters of collectivized agriculture maintained that large, centrally controlled farms were more efficient than smallholdings. In fact, large state farms *are* often more efficient in one respect. They facilitate government delivery of social service. Thus, it is generally easier to deliver clean water, medical care, and schools to large collective farms than it is to provide these services to widely scattered private farms. However, the assumption that large state farms are more efficient producers than peasant smallholding was, with some exceptions, quite erroneous. In fact official production data from Cuba, Ethiopia, Nicaragua, and China demonstrate that, for most crops, private peasant plots have *higher* yields per acre than collective farms do.[48]

Peasant plots are generally more productive than collective farms for the same reason that they tend to outperform large private farms in capitalist LDCs. Because their standard of living is tied directly to how much they produce, peasant smallholders are highly motivated to work intensely and to do whatever it takes to raise output. On the other hand, state farm employees receive the same wage no matter how hard or how little they work. Small wonder that a number of years ago the Cuban government admitted that the average state farm worker, while being paid to work an eight-hour day, actually worked on that job about four hours daily. Government research revealed that they spent the remaining time taking breaks or, in some cases, illegally working for nearby private farmers.

In recent decades, faced with growing evidence that peasant smallholdings are more productive than collective farms, many of the remaining communist governments have set aside their ideological preferences and accepted more pragmatic policies. When Deng Xiaoping succeeded Mao Zedong as China's political leader, he introduced the "Responsibility System," which converted China's farm communes back to peasant-controlled, private farms.[49] In what amounted to a second agrarian reform (or as one expert called it, "a second revolution"), large communal farms were broken up and distributed to the peasants living on them. The ensuing "unleashing [of] the entrepreneurial talents of China's peasants" led to striking gains in farm productivity. From 1980 to 1984 alone, the value of agricultural output rose an astonishing 40 percent.[50] That surge was a major factor contributing to a spectacular improvement in rural living standards from the early 1980s to the mid-1990s. More recently, other Marxist and reformed-Marxist regimes in Asia, most notably Vietnam, have also decollectivized agriculture.

In Nicaragua, Sandinista agrarian reform officials initially preferred state farms to any other agricultural unit. They saw peasant-run cooperatives as next best and ranked private smallholdings last. Not surprisingly, surveys showed that the peasants' preferences were exactly the opposite. During the economic crisis of the 1980s, the government, which was generally more pragmatic and less ideologically rigid than most Marxist regimes, conceded that peasant farms were more efficient. Moreover, as it fought a bitter civil war with the Contras (U.S.-backed anti-revolutionary guerrillas), the government realized that giving land to family farms would give peasant recipients incentive to support the Sandinista army. Consequently, the regime altered its priorities to accommodate peasant preferences.[51] Cuba never eliminated private farming but until recently used various incentives and pressures to convince peasants to sell their farms to the state. During the country's severe economic crisis in the 1990s, however, Castro's government converted many of Cuba's centrally run agricultural cooperatives into units based on family-run farms.

Moderate Reformism

Most agrarian reform programs are not introduced by foreign intervention or revolution. Countries such as Egypt, Iran, India, Bangladesh, Zimbabwe, Chile, Venezuela, and Peru have redistributed agricultural land in a variety of ways. In each case, however, the government introduced reform as a means of soliciting peasant support. Following the Cuban revolution, the United States and various Latin American governments concluded that rural reform was needed in the region in order to contain the spread of peasant unrest. Chile, Venezuela, and Peru all enacted moderate land reform programs in the 1960s. Twenty years later, the challenge of guerrilla insurgency prompted limited agrarian reform in El Salvador.

Elsewhere, the driving force for change has been the enfranchisement of growing numbers of peasants, caused either by the abolition of literacy requirements for voting or rising rural literacy rates. Once minor players in the electoral process, peasants have often been transformed into an important voting constituency wooed by competing political parties. Running on platforms calling for agrarian reform, Chile's Christian Democratic Party, Peru's *Acción Popular*, and Venezuela's *Acción Democrática* all won national elections in the past with the help of broad peasant support. Once in office, all these governments introduced land reforms of varying size.[52] Similarly, in Asia, some mix of incipient rural unrest and electoral politics contributed to agrarian reforms in the Philippines and parts of India, including the states of Kerala and West Bengal.[53]

Moderate reformism has one obvious advantage. It is relatively free of the violence and excesses often associated with revolutionary programs. But with rare exceptions, its scope is far more limited than either externally induced redistribution or revolutionary change. In Latin America, for example, the most extensive land redistribution followed revolutions in Cuba, Bolivia, Nicaragua, and Mexico.[54] In comparison, most moderate reform in the region has been more modest. Similarly, reformism in Asia (Bangladesh, Thailand, the Philippines, and India) has also produced meager results when compared to revolutionary land redistributions in China and Vietnam.

Reformism generally produces a less-sweeping agrarian transformation because the government must deal with landed elites who are still strong enough to limit the scope of change.[55] For example, reformist programs generally grant monetary compensation to landlords who have lost property. This means that the scope of land redistribution is limited by the scarcity of government funds. In addition, bureaucratic obstacles and court challenges frequently slow the pace of agrarian reform to a crawl.

One notable exception to this pattern was implemented in Peru from 1968 to 1979. There, a sweeping reform was implemented in the absence of either external pressure or internal revolution. A left-of-center, nationalist military government led by General Juan Velasco expropriated most of the country's large agricultural and ranching estates, turning them over to the peasants and farm laborers who had been working there. The military regime was able to sweep aside objections from the nation's rural oligarchy, a group despised by Velasco and his team. In all, approximately 40 percent of the country's farmland was transferred to 30 percent of all peasant families.[56] Initially, most of the land was organized as cooperatives, but subsequently, as administration and labor problems arose, most of the co-ops were subdivided and converted to peasant family smallholdings.[57]

Ultimately, however, the military's agrarian reform failed to reduce Peru's pervasive rural poverty. What it did accomplish was to destroy the once-considerable power of the land-owning class and thereby transform the country's political and economic structure. The virtually unchallenged power of a military dictatorship, like the might of a revolutionary regime, allowed the government to ignore the demands of the rural aristocracy in a way that a democratic government never could. However, no other military government in Latin America was equally dedicated to comprehensive rural change.[58]

In contrast, democratic governments, no matter how committed to helping the peasantry, cannot launch that type of frontal assault on the landed elite. For example, Venezuela's democratically elected *Acción Democrática* government, elected with strong backing from peasant voters, introduced a relatively ambitious agrarian reform. But because of political and financial restraints, much of the land transferred was previously uncultivated public property in the nation's jungle regions. Although this transfer permitted the government to sidestep landlord objections, such land was typically of marginal quality and not easily accessible.

The Limits of Agrarian Reform

While the experiences of Taiwan, South Korea, Cuba, and China demonstrate that agrarian reform can substantially improve peasant living standards, few programs elsewhere have matched their success. Peru illustrates how even sweeping change initiated by a well-intentioned government may not achieve its objectives. The proportion of national farmland turned over to the peasantry was quite high compared to other agrarian reforms in Latin America, even comparable to revolutionary transformations in Cuba, Mexico, and Nicaragua. Powerful Andean and coastal landlords who had once dominated the countryside were stripped of their land and the accompanying power. Yet these radical changes failed to improve peasant living standards as expected. The military's attempts at rural political change were often heavy-handed and counterproductive. But even if the program had been better executed, expropriating the nation's largest haciendas and plantations wouldn't have provided enough land to satisfy the peasants' needs. There simply wasn't enough arable farmland. Ultimately, fewer than one-third of the rural families in need received any land, and the poorest of the poor were frequently overlooked.[59] Even the program's beneficiaries generally discovered that their added land was insufficient for alleviating their deep poverty.

While the Peruvian military government narrowed appreciably the gap between rich and poor in the countryside, it did nothing to bridge the more important gulf between rural and urban living standards. As in most LDCs, the nation's economic structure had long favored the urban population over the peasantry. While urban poverty is widespread, the average income of city dwellers as a whole remains several times higher than the rural population's. Consequently, a substantial improvement in peasant living standards is impossible without a shift of wealth and government resources from urban areas to the countryside. Given the tremendous political clout of the urban upper class, middle class, and organized working class, such a transfer of wealth and resources was something not even the Peruvian armed forces were prepared to implement. Absent that transfer, agrarian reform merely redistributed poverty within the countryside.

Revolutionary agrarian reforms have limitations as well. Mexico still suffers from substantial rural poverty and landlessness, despite a reform that affected half the nation's peasants and a similar proportion of agricultural land. Beginning in the 1930s, reform beneficiaries were organized into *ejidos*, cooperative units designed to channel state aid to the peasantry and increase their productivity. Following World War II, however, government agricultural policy changed in favor of larger commercial farms, failing to channel adequate credits, infrastructure, or technology to the *ejidos*. As a consequence, poor farmers were unable to compete in the marketplace. Many lost their farms and poured into the nation's cities or across the border to the United States. Since 1970, the government has developed several programs designed to bolster peasant agriculture. While these programs have had some positive impact, they were cut short after 1982 by the country's debt crisis and severe economic recession.[60] Current government policy encourages the privatization of the *ejidos'* communal property. In the long run, this may benefit the most productive peasants, who will be able to buy and sell land more readily, but it may also force less-competitive peasants off their farms into Mexico's already overcrowded cities.

The shortcomings of reform efforts in Mexico and Peru do not suggest that agrarian reform is without value. Rather, they indicate that redistribution of land must be supported by additional government measures if it is to be effective. Evidence from elsewhere in Latin America and from South Asia indicates that successful reform programs usually require some degree of peasant organization and mobilization.[61] That is to say, the state is more likely to provide land recipients with needed technical assistance, infrastructure, education, and financial credit if it is pressured to do so by effective peasant organizations. Government also needs to allow peasants a fair price for their crops.[62] The administrative apparatus governing reform must be simple, and peasant beneficiaries must be given a strong role in the decision-making process. In countries where the landed elites maintain substantial political power, landlords losing property must receive reasonable payments if the program is to be politically viable. At the same time, peasant beneficiaries must be asked only to pay an amount they can sustain if the program is to be economically feasible for them.[63] Where possible, Third World governments must reduce the tremendous gap that typically separates urban and rural living standards.

Even the most intelligently executed reform programs, however, will not be equally successful in each country. In nations such as Peru, El Salvador, and Bangladesh, there simply isn't enough quality land to fully satisfy peasant needs. In such cases, alternative employment needs to be created for the rural poor in other sectors of the economy. Ultimately, each nation's agrarian-reform package must be carefully designed to meet its own specific needs.

OTHER APPROACHES AND ISSUES

Since the 1970s, agrarian reform has become more infrequent, with a few notable exceptions, such as Nicaragua, El Salvador, and, in a more controversial form, Zimbabwe. Critics on the Right have long believed it undermines allegedly more efficient, large-scale agribusiness. Critics on the Left have found the fruits of moderate reformism disappointing, claiming that it has benefited capitalists and state bureaucracies more than it has the peasantry.[64] And powerful urban interests fear agrarian reform will curtail agricultural production. In many ways, rural pressure for reform has diminished. Increasing numbers of peasants have migrated to the cities, no longer demanding change in the countryside. Most governments now attach less importance to peasant agriculture than to large, export-oriented commercial farming, which earns the nation foreign exchange. While modest land redistribution programs continue in some LDCs, for now at least, efforts at rural reform have shifted to other issues and other types of programs.

Crop Pricing

In addition to the problem of access to land, peasants often have suffered from unfavorable government price policies. Anxious to ensure a supply of cheap food for their urban populations, many governments, particularly in Africa and the Middle East, imposed price controls on basic commodities such as rice, potatoes, and sugar. Price controls were also meant to promote industrialization by providing workers with cheap food, thereby helping employers to keep wages down and permitting more capital investment.[65] But by holding crop prices below their free-market levels, these controls further impoverished peasant producers.

In Africa, governments also commonly controlled the price of export crops, extracting the difference between what they paid farmers and the higher world-market price as a de facto tax. One early study found that African farmers often received less than two-thirds, and in some cases less than half, of the value of their export crops.[66] Although designed to provide the urban poor and the middle class with cheaper food and to generate government revenues from exports, price controls ultimately had perverse effects. They particularly damaged poor farmers and reduced the supply of basic foods by creating disincentives to production. In Egypt, for example, when the government controlled the price of basic food grains, large landlords either evaded government controls or, more commonly, reduced the supply of badly needed grains by switching to other, uncontrolled crops. Peasants were less capable of switching crops and thus suffered declining incomes.[67] Throughout Africa, price controls reduced food output by driving many farmers out of business and removing production incentives for the rest. For decades, per-capita food production has declined, and the continent has become increasingly dependent on food imports and foreign aid. While there is no single cause for that deterioration, one study of African famine argues that government price controls and inefficient government bureaucracies aggravated the problem.[68]

Unfortunately, once governments embarked on the path of commodity price regulation, they were soon caught in a conflict between short-term political pressures and long-term production needs. The immediate effect of price deregulation was a sharp increase in food prices. Governments that removed price controls (often in response to external pressures from the IMF) frequently faced urban protests and riots by irate urban shoppers. Not surprisingly, for many years few administrations were willing to risk such unrest, particularly since the urban middle class, a group adversely affected by price hikes on food, is usually a vital pillar of government support. In the long run, however, better crop prices should stimulate greater food production, ultimately leading prices to decline again, though not necessarily to their prior low. More recently, as many developing nations have been introducing neoliberal economic policies (eliminating government economic intervention), more and more are eliminating price controls (see Chapter 10).[69]

CONCLUSION: DEMOCRACY AND RURAL REFORM

For decades government development policies in most LDCs have emphasized industrial growth and urban modernization, often to the detriment of the rural sector. In many cases the consequences have been stagnant agricultural production, rising food imports, rural poverty, and heavy rural-to-urban migration. In some instances, rural poverty has led to peasant insurrection. Most notably in Africa and Latin America, pro-urban government biases, along with the forces of capitalist development, have driven many peasants into the rural or urban working class in a process known as *proletarianization*.[70] Pessimistic scholars have predicted the inevitable spread of large mechanized farms to the detriment of peasant family farming.

More recently, research in countries such as Bolivia, Ecuador, and Colombia has revealed that, in at least some regions, innovative peasants have adapted skillfully to the forces of rural capitalism and modernization. Many have taken advantage of new commercial opportunities to compete successfully in the marketplace.[71] In Africa and Asia, peasant smallholders remain an even greater component of rural society. Rather than abandoning the peasantry as a relic of history, Third World governments and international agencies need to promote balanced economic and political development that gives proper weight to the rural sector and its peasant population.

The relationship between democracy and rural reform is somewhat paradoxical. On the one hand, democratic governments such as Venezuela, which carried out agrarian reform and other forms of assistance to the rural poor, broadened their base of political support. As we noted earlier, experts such as Samuel Huntington argued during the Cold War that agrarian reform was a Third World nation's best defense against revolution. However, the fact remains that the most far-reaching land reforms in the past century were not carried out by democratic governments but by revolutionary regimes in China, Vietnam, Mexico, Bolivia, Cuba, and Nicaragua. Other significant redistribution of land took place under military governments in Peru and Egypt. South Korea's and Taiwan's reforms were implemented by authoritarian governments under pressure from the United States. By contrast, in democratic countries such as Brazil, India, and, more recently, the Philippines, landlords have been sufficiently powerful as a lobbying group and pillar of major political parties that they have blocked substantial reforms from becoming law.

With the threat of communist revolution no longer facing most developing nations, the prospect of major land redistribution in the Third World currently seems remote. But if the LDCs are to prevent unmanageable rural-to-urban migration and potential rural violence, their governments will have to find other ways to improve the lives of the rural poor.

DISCUSSION QUESTIONS

1. Third World peasants have frequently been described as conservative or apolitical, yet they have been major players in revolutionary movements. How can those two images be reconciled?
2. What are the major arguments that have been raised for and against agrarian reform programs in the developing world?
3. Describe the different types of agrarian reform programs that have been introduced. Briefly discuss some of the advantages and disadvantages of each type of reform.
4. What are the major reasons why major agrarian reform programs are unlikely in the foreseeable future?
5. How have government crop-pricing policies often disadvantaged the rural producer and inhibited production?

NOTES

1. This figure is extrapolated from Prosterman and Riedinger's estimate in the mid-1980s that 60 percent of the developing world's population was agricultural at that time. Roy L. Prosterman and Jeffrey M. Riedinger, *Land Reform and Democratic Development* (Baltimore, MD: Johns Hopkins University Press, 1987), 1.

2. Published statistics on the proportion of rural poverty in any country are usually imprecise. They often vary greatly from study to study and should be treated as educated estimates designed to serve as guideposts. Occasionally the data clash with the "commonsense" observations of experts who have studied the region. In the decade since these U.N. data were collected, the populations of most of the countries studied

have increased, the percentages of their populations living in the countryside have dropped, and the actual number of persons living in rural poverty (as opposed to the percentage) has risen.

3. Figures are extrapolated from earlier data in M. Riad El-Ghonemy, *The Political Economy of Rural Poverty* (London: Routledge and Kegan Paul, 1990), 302–303, 17–19. The data were adapted from the United Nations Food and Agricultural Organization, *The Dynamics of Rural Poverty* (Rome: 1986).

4. Merilee S. Grindle and John W. Thomas, *Public Choices and Policy Change: The Political Economy of Reform in Developing Countries* (Baltimore, MD: Johns Hopkins University Press, 1991), 46.

5. Alain de Janvry, *The Agrarian Question and Reformism in Latin America* (Baltimore, MD: Johns Hopkins University Press, 1981), 7–60.

6. The terms *agrarian reform* and *land reform* are often used interchangeably. Technically, land reform refers only to the redistribution of land to needy peasants or laborers. Agrarian reform is a broader term that encompasses financial and technical aid, infrastructure, and the like that are normally needed to go with land redistribution if it is to be effective.

7. Marcus Franda, "An Indian Farm Lobby: The Kisan Sammelan," in *The Politics of Agrarian Change in Asia and Latin America*, ed. Howard Handelman (Bloomington: Indiana University Press, 1981), 17–34.

8. George Foster, "Introduction: What Is a Peasant?" in *Peasant Society*, eds. Jack Potter, George Foster, and May Diaz (Boston: Little, Brown, 1967); Teodor Shanin, "The Nature and Logic of the Peasant Economy," *Journal of Peasant Studies* 1, nos. 1–2 (1974).

9. Eric R. Wolf, *Peasants* (Upper Saddle River, NJ: Prentice Hall, 1966), 10.

10. Prosterman and Riedinger, *Land Reform and Democratic Development*, 41.

11. Karl Marx, *Capital*. Quoted in Teodor Shanin, "Peasantry as a Political Factor," *Sociological Review* 14 (March 1966): 6.

12. Robert Redfield, *Peasant Society and Culture: An Anthropological Approach* (Chicago: University of Chicago Press, 1965), 77.

13. See, for example, Oscar Lewis, *La Vida* (New York: Random House, 1966); George M. Foster, "Peasant Society and the Image of the Limited Good," *American Anthropologist* 67 (April 1965): 293–315.

14. Phyllis Arora, "Patterns of Political Response in Indian Peasant Society," *Western Political Quarterly* 20 (September 1967): 654.

15. See, for example, *New York Times*, July 4, 1993.

16. Ronald J. Herring and Charles R. Kennedy Jr., "The Political Economy of Farm Mechanization Policy: Tractors in Pakistan," in *Food, Politics and Agricultural Development: Case Studies in the Public Policy of Rural Modernization*, eds. Raymond F. Hopkins, Donald J. Pachula, and Ross B. Talbot (Boulder, CO: Westview Press, 1979), 193–226.

17. James C. Scott, *Weapons of the Week: Everyday Forms of Peasant Resistance* (New Haven, CT: Yale University Press, 1986).

18. One of the most insightful books on the role of the peasantry in twentieth-century revolutions is Eric R. Wolf, *Peasant Wars of the Twentieth Century* (New York: Harper & Row, 1969).

19. James C. Scott, *The Moral Economy of the Peasant: Rebellion and Subsistence in Southeast Asia*

(New Haven, CT: Yale University Press, 1976); James C. Scott and Benedict J. Kirkvliet, *How Traditional Rural Patrons Lose Their Legitimacy* (Madison: University of Wisconsin, Land Tenure Center, 1975).

20. Wolf, *Peasant Wars*.

21. Samuel P. Huntington, *Political Order in Changing Societies* (New Haven, CT: Yale University Press, 1968), 375.

22. Ibid.

23. That is probably a conservative estimate extrapolated from figures presented over a decade ago in Roy L. Prosterman, Mary N. Temple, and Timothy M. Hanstad, "Introduction," *Agrarian Reform and Grassroots Development: Ten Case Studies*, eds. Prosterman, Temple, and Hanstad (Boulder, CO: Lynne Rienner Publishers, 1990), 1.

24. Hectares, rather than acres, are the standard measurement of farmland area in most of the world. One hectare is equivalent to 2.47 acres; Anthony L. Hall, "Land Tenure and Land Reform in Brazil," in *Agrarian Reform and Grassroots Development*, 206.

25. Carrie A. Meyer, *Land Reform in Latin America: The Dominican Case* (New York: Praeger, 1989), 38.

26. Rupert W. Scofield, "Land Reform in Central America," in *Agrarian Reform and Grassroots Development*, 154–155.

27. D. P. Chaudhri, "New Technologies and Income Distribution in Agriculture," in *Peasants, Landlords and Governments: Agrarian Reform in the Third World*, ed. David Lehmann (New York: Holmes and Meier, 1974), 173; Howard Handelman, "Introduction," *The Politics of Agrarian Change*, 4.

28. F. Tomasson Jannuzi and James T. Peach, "Bangladesh: A Strategy for Agrarian Reform," and Jeffrey Riedinger, "Philippine Land Reform in the 1980s," in *Agrarian Reform and Grassroots Development*, 84, 91.

29. Henry Shue, *Basic Human Rights: Subsistence, Affluence, and U.S. Foreign Policy* (Princeton, NJ: Princeton University Press, 1980). For a discussion of the moral issues, see Joseph S. Nye, Jr., "Ethical Dimensions of International Involvement in Land Reform," in *International Dimensions of Land Reform*, ed. John D. Montgomery (Boulder, CO: Westview Press, 1984), 7–29.

30. Keith Griffin, *Land Concentration and Rural Poverty*, 2d ed. (London: Macmillan, 1981), 10.

31. Huntington, *Political Order*, 375.

32. Bruce M. Russet, "Inequality and Instability: The Relation of Land Tenure to Politics," *World Politics* 16 (April 1964): 442–454; Prosterman and Riedinger, *Land Reform*, 24.

33. William Thiesenhusen, "Introduction," *Searching for Agrarian Reform in Latin America*, ed. William Thiesenhusen (Boston: Unwin Hyman, 1989), 18.

34. Ibid., 16–20; Peter Dorner, *Latin American Land Reforms in Theory and Practice* (Madison: University of Wisconsin Press, 1992), 21–29; R. Albert Berry, "Land Reform and the Adequacy of World Food Production," in *International Dimensions*, 63–87.

35. Riedinger, "Philippine Land Reform," 19.

36. Dorner, *Latin American Land Reforms*, 23–25; Berry, "Land Reform," 72; Michael R. Carter and Jon Jonakin, *The Economic Case for Land Reform: An Assessment of 'Farm Size/Productivity' Relations and Its Impact on Policy* (Madison: University of Wisconsin, Department of Agricultural Economics, 1989), quoted in Dorner, *Latin American Land Reform*.

37. James Grant, "Development: The End of Trickle Down," *Foreign Policy* 12 (Fall 1973): 43–65.

38. Bruce F. Johnston and John W. Mellor, "The Role of Agriculture in Economic Development," *American Economic Review* 51 (September 1961): 566–593.

39. Dorner, *Latin American Land Reforms*, 29–31.

40. Ronald P. Dore, *Land Reform in Japan* (London: Oxford University Press, 1959); Mikiso Hande, *Modern Japan* (Boulder, CO: Westview Press, 1986), 347–348.

41. Shirley W. Y. Kuo, Gustav Ranis, and John C. H. Fei, *The Taiwan Success Story: Rapid Growth with Improved Distribution in the Republic of China, 1952–1979* (Boulder, CO: Westview Press, 1981); Gregory Henderson, *Korea: Politics of the Vortex* (Cambridge, MA: Harvard University Press, 1968).

42. Dore, *Land Reform in Japan*, 147–148.

43. John W. Bruce and Paula Harrell, "Land Reform in the People's Republic of China: 1978–1988," *Land Tenure Center Research Paper No. 100* (University of Wisconsin-Madison, 1989), 3–4; Vivienne Shue, *Peasant China in Transition—The Dynamics of Development Toward Socialism, 1949–56* (Berkeley: University of California Press, 1980).

44. Thiesenhusen, *Searching for Agrarian Reform*, 10–11.

45. Wolf, *Peasant Wars*. Collectivization refers to an involuntary consolidation of peasant farms into larger, state-dominated collective farms.

46. Harry Harding, *China's Second Revolution* (Washington, DC: Brookings Institution, 1987), 12; Suzanne Ogden, *China's Unresolved Issues* (Englewood Cliffs, NJ: Prentice Hall, 1989), 46–50; Nicholas Lardy, *Agriculture in China's Modern Economic Development* (Cambridge, England: Cambridge University Press, 1983).

47. There were exceptions to this pattern, particularly outside the Third World. Poland and Yugoslavia, for example, did not collectivize agriculture during the communist era. Cuba and especially Nicaragua had private farms alongside a larger collectivized sector.

48. For a crop-by-crop analysis of state and private sector farm productivity in Cuba, see Nancy Forster, "Cuban Agricultural Productivity," in *Cuban Communism*, 7th ed., ed. Irving Louis Horowitz (New Brunswick, NJ: Transaction, 1989), 235–255.

49. Nicholas Lardy, "Agricultural Reforms in China," *Journal of International Affairs* (Winter 1986): 91–104. The program was announced in 1978 but was not implemented for two years.

50. Harding, *China's Second Revolution*, 106.

51. Forrest D. Colburn, *Post-Revolutionary Nicaragua: State, Class and the Dilemmas of Agrarian Policy* (Berkeley: University of California Press, 1986), and Laura J. Enríquez, *Harvesting Change: Labor and Agrarian Reform in Nicaragua* (Chapel Hill: University of North Carolina Press, 1991), offer contrasting analyses.

52. David Lehmann, "Agrarian Reform in Chile, 1965–1972: An Essay in Contradictions," in *Peasants, Landlords*, 71–119; Marion R. Brown, "Radical Reformism in Chile: 1964–1973," in *Searching for Agrarian Reform*, 216–239.

53. Riedinger, "Philippine Land Reform," and Ronald Herring, "Explaining Anomalies in Land Reform: Lessons from South India," in *Agrarian Reform and Grassroots Development*, 15–75; K. N. Raj and Michael Tharakan, "Agrarian Reform in Kerala and Its Impact on the Rural Economy," and Ajit Kumar Ghose, "Agrarian Reform in West Bengal," in *Agrarian Reform in Contemporary Developing Countries*, ed. Ajit Kumar Ghose (New York: St. Martin's Press, 1983), 31–137.

54. Thiesenhusen, "Introduction," *Searching for Agrarian Reform*, 1–41; Meyer, *Land Reform in Latin America*, 4. Thiesenhusen and Meyer each calculate the percentage of farmland redistributed and the percentage of rural families benefiting. Although they use somewhat different time periods and Meyer analyzes a wider sample of nations, they arrive at very similar rankings.

55. de Janvry, *The Agrarian Question*.

56. Howard Handelman, "Peasants, Landlords and Bureaucrats: The Politics of Agrarian Reform in Peru," in *The Politics of Agrarian Change*, 103–125; Cristóbal Kay, "The Agrarian Reform in Peru: An Assessment," in *Agrarian Reform in Contemporary Developing Countries*, 185–239.

57. Michael Carter and Elena Alvarez, "Changing Paths: The Decollectivization of Agrarian Reform Agriculture in Coastal Peru," in *Searching for Agrarian Reform*, 156–187.

58. Agrarian reforms enacted by the Ecuadorian and Panamanian militaries were far more modest.

59. Howard Handelman, "Peasants, Landlords and Bureaucrats," 103–125; Kay, "The Agrarian Reform in Peru," 185–239.

60. Merilee S. Grindle, *Searching for Rural Development: Labor Migration and Employment in Mexico* (Ithaca, NY: Cornell University Press, 1988); Grindle, "Agrarian Reform in Mexico: A Cautionary Tale," in *Agrarian Reform and Grass-roots Development*, 179–204; Steven E. Sanderson, *The Transformation of Mexican Agriculture* (Princeton, NJ: Princeton University Press, 1986); Frank Meissner, "The Mexican Food System (SAM)—A Strategy for Sowing Petroleum," and M. R. Redclift, "The Mexican Food System (SAM)—Sowing Subsidies, Reaping Apathy," *Food Policy* 6, no. 4 (November 1981): 219–235.

61. Ronald J. Herring, "Explaining Anomalies in Agrarian Reform: Lessons from South Asia," in *Agrarian Reform and Grassroots Development*, 73.

62. Thiesenhusen, "Conclusions," in *Searching for Agrarian Reform*, 483–503.

63. Prosterman and Riedinger, *Land Reform and Democratic Development*, 177–202.

64. de Janvry, *The Agrarian Question*; Merilee S. Grindle, *State and Countryside: Development Policy and Agrarian Politics in Latin America* (Baltimore, MD: Johns Hopkins University Press, 1986).

65. Charles Harvey, ed., *Agricultural Pricing Policy in Africa* (London: Macmillan, 1988), 2.

66. Robert H. Bates, *Markets and States in Tropical Africa: The Political Basis of Agricultural Policy* (Berkeley: University of California Press, 1981), 29; see also Michael J. Lofchie, *The Policy Factor: Agricultural Performance in Kenya and Tanzania* (Boulder, CO: Lynne Rienner Publishers, 1989), 57–59.

67. Marvin G. Weinbaum, *Food, Development, and Politics in the Middle East* (Boulder, CO: Westview Press, 1982), 61.

68. Michael F. Lofchie, "Africa's Agricultural Crisis: An Overview," and Robert H. Bates, "The Regulation of Rural Markets in Africa," in *Africa's Agrarian Crisis: The Roots of Famine*, ed. Stephen K. Commins, Michael F. Lofchie, and Rhys Payne (Boulder, CO: Lynne Rienner Publishers, 1986), 3–19, 37–54.

69. Neoliberalism rejects much of the state intervention in the economy that was prevalent in many developing economies and instead favors free-market mechanisms. For a more extensive discussion of these issues, see Chapter 10.

70. de Janvry, *The Agrarian Question*; David Goodman and Michael Redclift, *From Peasant to Proletarian: Capitalist Development and Agricultural Transitions* (Oxford, England: Basil Blackwell, 1981).

71. This is most impressively demonstrated in Nola Reinhardt, *Our Daily Bread: The Peasant Question and Family Farming in the Colombian Andes* (Berkeley: University of California Press, 1988). See also Lesley Gill, *Peasants, Entrepreneurs and Social Change: Frontier Development in Lowland Bolivia* (Boulder, CO: Westview Press, 1987).

chapter 7

Rapid Urbanization and the Politics of the Urban Poor

Each day, in the villages of Bangladesh, China, Kenya, Egypt, and Bolivia, thousands of young men and women pack up their meager belongings and board buses, trucks, or trains for the long trip to Dhaka, Shanghai, Nairobi, Cairo, or La Paz. Often they travel alone, sometimes with family or friends. They are a part of one of the largest and most dramatic tides of human migration in world history. In China alone, some 300 million rural villagers are expected to migrate to urban centers over the next two to three decades. Despairing of any hope for a better life in the countryside and seeking new opportunities for themselves and their children, millions of villagers leave the world they have known for the uncertainties of the city. In Africa, these legions of migrants have been augmented by millions of refugees fleeing civil war and famine. In the aftermath of Rwanda's ethnic genocide, the country's urban population grew by an astounding 11.6 percent *annually* from 2000 to 2005. Between 2003 and 2030, it will climb from only 18.3 percent of the nation's total to 58.5 percent.[1]

Most maintain close links with their rural roots long after they have migrated. Some come intending to accumulate savings and eventually return to their villages. "Others alternate between city and country in a permanent pendular pattern."[2] Indeed, in many parts of West Africa and Southeast Asia, more than half the urban migrants are temporary, including those who repeatedly circulate between village and city.[3] In China, where until recently government restrictions made it very difficult to migrate, most new migrants (some 100 million people) live in a bureaucratic limbo without assurance of permanence. Known as China's "floating population," these relatively temporary migrants number 100 million people or more. Some stay permanently, though most others do not. Although not officially counted as part of the urban population (since their residency documents restrict them to their home villages), they actually account for about one-fifth of China's urban residents at any given time.[4] In contrast, Latin America's cityward migrants tend to settle permanently. But whatever their initial aspirations, migrants continue to crowd the urban slums and shantytowns they have come to call home. Swelled by both internal (natural) population growth and the influx of migrants in recent decades, many Third World cities have mushroomed in size and will continue to do so in the coming years (see Tables 7.1 to 7.3). In the past half century, the magnitude of that expansion has placed tremendous strains on the developing world's large cities. In Latin America, national capitals such as Caracas (Venezuela) and Lima (Peru) once doubled their populations every 12 to 15 years. African cities, though

TABLE 7.1   Percentage of the Population in Urban Areas by Region, 2003–2030

Region	Percentage Urban 2003	Projected Percentage Urban 2030	Projected Annual Urban Growth (percent) (2000–2005)	Projected Annual Rural Growth (percent) (2000–2005)
Developed Regions	48.3	60.8	0.5	−0.5
Less Developed Regions	42.1	57.1	2.8	0.5
Africa	38.7	53.5	3.6	1.3
Asia	38.8	54.5	2.7	0.4
Latin America and the Caribbean	76.8	84.6	1.0	−0.3

Source: United Nations, Department of Economic and Social Affairs, Population Division, "Urban and Rural Areas, 2003," http://www.un.org/esa/population/publications/wup2003/2003 Urban_Rural.pdf.

starting from a smaller base, expanded at an even faster pace. Between 1960 and 1983, Kinshasa (Congo) grew by nearly 600 percent and Abidjan (Côte d'Ivoire) by more than 800 percent.[5] Today, a number of cities in the LDCs continue to double their populations in less than two decades (Table 7.3). In 1970, Third World cities contained 675 million people. That figure grew to 1.9 billion by the year 2000 and is expected to reach some 4 billion in 2025.[6] There is some debate among demographers as to what proportion of this growth has been caused by internal increase and what percentage has been the product of rural-to-urban migration. The evidence indicates that about half the urban population explosion has come from each of those two sources, with a higher proportion attributable to migration in Africa and a greater percentage to natural increase in Asia.[7] As a consequence, the world's developing nations, not long ago predominantly rural, will probably be half urban within a decade and nearly 60 percent urban by 2030 (see Table 7.1).

Latin America is by far the most urbanized region in the developing world (Table 7.1). In 2003, the portion of its population living in cities (77 percent) almost equaled that of the United States or Western Europe.[8] With more than 17 million people today, Mexico City is already one of the world's largest metropolitan areas (Table 7.3), and Sao Paulo (Brazil) and Buenos Aires (Argentina) are not far behind. To be sure, poorer Central American countries such as Honduras are still less than half urban, but in Chile, more than 87 percent of the population now lives in cities (Table 7.2).

Africa and Asia are considerably less urban (each currently less than 40 percent). But their cities have grown at a far more rapid rate in recent decades, particularly in Africa. In 1960, Casablanca (Morocco) and Cairo (Egypt) were the only cities on that continent with populations of more than one million. Twenty-three years later, nine cities exceeded that size.[9] As Table 7.3 indicates, in many Sub-Saharan African metropolises—such as Addis Ababa (Ethiopia) and Lagos (Nigeria)—populations continue to explode. Indeed, Lagos expected to have a

TABLE 7.2 Percentage of the Population in Urban Areas by Country, 1970–2030

Country	% Urban 1970	% Urban 2003	% Urban 2030 (estimate)
Ethiopia	9%	16%	29%
Morocco	35	58	73
Mozambique	6	36	60
Bangladesh	8	24	39
Thailand	13	32	47
Chile	75	87	92
Honduras	29	46	60
Mexico	59	76	83

Source: United Nations Development Programme, *Human Development Report, 1998* (New York: Oxford University Press, 1998), 174–175. Reprinted by permission; United Nations, Department of Economic and Social Affairs, Population Division, "Urban and Rural Areas, 2003," http://www.un.org/esa/population/publications/wup2003/2003Urban_Rural.pdf.

population of nearly 25 million by 2015, making it perhaps the world's largest megacity. In all, between 2000 and 2005, African cities have grown at an average annual rate of 3.6 percent, while Latin America—its most rapid rural-to-urban migration behind it—has been experiencing annual urban growth of only 1.0 percent (Table 7.1). The proportion of people residing in cities, however, varies considerably from country to country. At one end of the spectrum, Ethiopia remained only 16 percent urban in 2003. But urbanization was far more advanced in North African countries such as Morocco, with more than 58 percent of its population then in cities (Table 7.2).

Many of Asia's largest countries—including Bangladesh, India, Pakistan, and Thailand—are still at least two-thirds rural. Yet huge cities such as Jakarta (Indonesia), Karachi (Pakistan), New Delhi, Mumbai—formerly Bombay—and

TABLE 7.3 Population of Third World Cities, 1995–2015

City	Population	
	1995	2015 (estimate)
Mexico City	16,562,000	19,180,000
Tegucigalpa	995,000	2,016,000
Santiago	4,891,000	6,066,000
Cairo	9,690,000	16,530,000
Casablanca	3,101,000	4,835,000
Addis Ababa	2,431,000	6,578,000
Lagos	10,287,000	24,640,000
Bangkok	6,547,000	9,844,000
Dhaka	8,545,000	19,486,000

Source: United Nations Development Programme, *Human Development Report, 1998* (New York: Oxford University Press, 1998), 174–175. Reprinted by permission.

Calcutta (all in India) now have populations exceeding 10 million. During the second half of the twentieth century, their populations leapfrogged past New York, London, and Los Angeles. While Bangladesh is now only about 20 to 25 percent urban, the population of its megacity, Dhaka, is in the process of more than doubling between 1995 and 2015, reaching nearly 20 million people in the coming decade (Table 7.3).

THE POLITICAL CONSEQUENCES OF URBAN GROWTH

In fact, the Third World's enormous *rate* of urban growth since the middle of the twentieth century is not without precedent. According to one estimate, the proportion of the LDCs' total population living in cities grew from 16.7 percent in 1950 to 28.0 percent in 1975 (and 42 percent in 2003). But from 1875 to 1900, the West's urban population increased from 17.2 to 26.1 percent, a percentage change of similar magnitude.[10] What makes the current urban explosion unique, however, is the sheer volume of people involved. The *total* population of the developing world is much larger today than that of nineteenth-century Europe and North America, and it is growing at a more rapid rate. So, it is one thing for a nineteenth-century European city to grow from 80,000 to 400,000 people in a 25-year period. It is quite another for Seoul (South Korea) to mushroom from one million to nearly seven million, for Kinshasa (Congo) to spiral from 400,000 to more than 2.5 million, or Lagos from 10 million to more than 25 million in the same number of years. Massive population shifts such as these obviously pose especially daunting challenges to urban housing, sanitation, education, and transportation needs.

This chapter examines two important aspects of urban politics in the developing world. First, it looks at the problems that exploding urban populations present to political leaders and government planners. Specifically, it asks how poor countries can provide city dwellers with needed jobs, housing, sanitation, and other services, while also protecting them from crime. What is the government's role in those areas, and how do state policies interact with private sector activities and self-help efforts? Second, we examine the political attitudes and behavior of city dwellers in the LDCs, focusing particularly on the politics of the urban poor. To what extent do the inhabitants of urban shantytowns and slums have political orientations that are distinct both from those of the rural poor and those of the urban middle and upper classes? Is rapid urbanization likely to contribute to political development, or does it carry the seeds of political instability?

THE STRUGGLE FOR EMPLOYMENT

Contemporary Third World urbanization differs from the West's earlier experience not only in its magnitude but also in its economic context. The nineteenth-century urban revolution in Europe and North America occurred at the dawn of an era of unprecedented industrialization and economic growth. Modern capitalism was coming of age and could accommodate, indeed needed, the wave of migrant and immigrant laborers. By contrast, the economies of most contemporary LDCs have failed to provide sufficient employment to their growing urban work force.

To be sure, many people do find jobs, and some low-income workers achieve impressive upward mobility. For example, one study of Howrah, an industrial city in West Bengal, found that "several hundred men who started with almost nothing now own factories large enough to employ twenty-five [or more] workers," placing them "among the richest people in the community."[11] Similar examples can be found in much of the developing world. But these are exceptional cases. Many others have achieved more modest success. For most of the urban poor, however, economic survival remains an ongoing struggle. Even during Mexico's economic boom in the 1960s and 1970s, the country's expanding modern sector was able to provide new employment for only about half the people seeking to enter the urban work force. The debt crisis and severe recession that gripped Africa, Latin America, and parts of Asia in the 1980s exacerbated the problem, as industrial employment in many countries plummeted. Hyperinflation in many Sub-Saharan African countries has meant that even people who are regularly employed rarely have salaries or wages high enough to support their families.

Most of those unable to find work in the formal sector of the urban economy (factories, the civil service, modern commercial enterprises) and those whose formal-sector paychecks cannot feed or house their families have turned to the informal economy for employment. As noted in Chapter 5, that sector is defined as the part of the economy that is "unregulated by the institutions of society [most notably the state], in a legal and social environment in which similar activities are regulated" and taxed.[12] A large proportion of the workers in the informal economy are self-employed in occupations ranging from garbage recyclers to shoe shine boys, street vendors, mechanics, electricians, plumbers, and drivers of unlicensed taxis.

Of course, informal sector activity is not limited to the developing world. In recent years, cities like New York, Los Angeles, and Milan have seen substantial expansion in the number of unlicensed street vendors, underground garment manufacturers, and other illegal or unlicensed activities. In the Third World, however, the informal economy represents a far greater proportion of all urban employment. During the 1970s, for example, it constituted some 35 percent of the urban work force in Malaysia; 44 percent in Nairobi (Kenya); 45 percent in Jakarta; and 60 percent in urban Peru.[13] In many countries, those percentages rose significantly as a result of the economic crises of the 1980s and late 1990s.

In the vast garbage dumps of Cairo, hordes of entrepreneurs can be found sifting through the refuse looking for marketable waste. At night, on the streets of Rio de Janeiro and Nairobi thousands of prostitutes search for customers. On the commercial boulevards of Manila (Philippines) and Mexico City, an army of street vendors sells food, household appliances, and bootleg audiotapes. In Lagos and Lahore (Pakistan), shoemakers and carpenters, working out of their homes, sell their wares to appreciative clients. All belong to the informal economy. While it was once assumed that people working in this sector were particularly impoverished, we now know that their earning power varies greatly, and that some have higher incomes than factory workers.[14] To cite one admittedly atypical example, during Nicaragua's runaway inflation in the 1980s, street vendors selling Coca-Cola earned more in a few hours than government white-collar employees made in a week. A more representative study of Montevideo (Uruguay) found that laborers in the formal and informal sectors made fairly comparable incomes.[15]

The informal economy's merits and faults have been debated extensively. Critics point out that its workers are not protected by minimum wage laws and lack access to government health and welfare programs. Proponents respond that the informal economy not only employs vast numbers of people who would otherwise have nothing, but it also contributes a substantial proportion of the Third World's consumer goods and services. In a book that has been very influential in Latin American political circles, Peruvian author Hernando de Soto argues that Third World governments should cease trying to regulate and license the informal sector and instead allow it to flourish and expand.[16]

While the informal sector represents concrete, small-scale efforts by the poor (and not-so-poor) to create employment, the government's involvement in the job market has usually been more indirect. Only in communist countries such as China and Cuba is the state a primary urban employer. Because they consider employment to be a fundamental worker's right, until recently many communist governments created as many jobs as necessary to achieve full, or nearly full, employment, no matter how economically inefficient many of these jobs might be. Often they also restricted migration, prohibiting people from moving into cities unless they already had employment lined up there (though these regulations have been totally ineffective in China as of late). Governments in capitalist LDCs, on the other hand, reject the role of "employer of last resort" and do not limit urban migration. They may occasionally institute public works projects specifically designed to create employment, but such efforts are normally quite limited.

Instead, nonsocialist, Third World governments primarily influence urban employment indirectly through their broader national macroeconomic policies.[17] In their efforts to stimulate economic growth, they hope to generate employment over the long run. Two areas of economic policy particularly influence job creation: industrialization strategy and the containment of inflation. Differences in government industrialization policies led to very different employment outcomes in Latin America and East Asia.

Starting as early as the 1930s and 1940s, some Latin American governments began stimulating economic development through import-substituting industrialization (ISI).[18] The governments of Argentina, Brazil, and Mexico, for example, created tariff walls and fiscal stimuli to nourish local industries that produced consumer goods for the domestic market. Items such as clothing, appliances, and sometimes even automobiles, which had previously been imported, were instead manufactured locally. One of ISI's many goals was to create industrial employment for the urban working class. Consequently, from the 1940s into the 1970s, labor unions and industrialists, despite their differences on a host of other issues, united behind state policies supporting ISI.

Many comparatively well paid, blue-collar jobs were created, but their numbers remained rather small relative to the vast army of unskilled laborers. Domestic markets simply weren't large enough to generate a sufficient number of industrial jobs, and the region's highly protected industries, facing little external competition, had few incentives to improve product quality or manufacturing efficiency. As a consequence, their products were unable to compete in the international market. By the late 1970s, Latin America's industrial economies began to stagnate (see Chapter 10).

In contrast, East Asian governments in Hong Kong, Singapore, South Korea, Taiwan, Thailand, and Malaysia, which had first stimulated industrialization through import-substituting policies (ISI), soon lowered or removed protective tariffs, forcing domestic manufacturers to compete with foreign imports. That competition forced firms to produce goods whose quality and price made them competitive, not only at home but in the export market. Though the East Asian export-led model was initially based on the exploitation of a poorly paid work force, the region's labor-intensive industries eventually generated so many jobs that they drove up local wage scales. More recently, Latin American countries such as Brazil, Chile, Colombia, and Mexico have sought to emulate East Asia's export-led model, with some degree of success.[19] But while these countries have increased their industrial exports considerably in the past 20 years, job creation has still lagged behind because Latin American export industries tend to be more capital-intensive and less labor-intensive.

Beginning in the early 1980s, many LDCs faced the dual problems of rampant inflation and stagnant economic growth. Because solutions to each of those problems often conflicted, at least in the short run, governments had to decide which challenge to tackle first and how to confront it. Encouraged or pressured by the International Monetary Fund (IMF), the World Bank, and private lenders, many heavily indebted African and Latin American countries adopted macroeconomic policies designed to slash inflation rates first. To do so, they reduced (or tried to reduce) large budgetary and trade deficits by slashing government spending and public sector employment, devaluating the national currency, and privatizing state enterprises (selling them to private investors). In the late 1990s, East and Southeast Asian governments were forced to devalue their currencies as well.

Although stabilization and adjustment policies such as these may be beneficial in the long run (their record is somewhat mixed), they always drive unemployment up sharply in the short run. And while austerity programs in countries such as Argentina, Ghana, Morocco, and Peru have curtailed inflation, they have been slow or unable to reinvigorate employment. In the 1990s, government economic adjustment policies in Thailand, Indonesia, and Malaysia caused substantial unemployment and declining living standards.

Government policy also affects the urban employment market in yet another important way, by expanding or contracting state bureaucracies and semiautonomous, state-owned enterprises known as *parastatals*. Throughout Africa, government bureaucracies and parastatals have traditionally employed far more people than they needed. Ten people often do the work of six. They have been overstaffed for two important political reasons: they provide work for potentially volatile white- and blue-collar workers unable to find jobs in the weak private sector, and they are a source of patronage for government or political party supporters. For example, at the start of the 1990s, some 40 percent of all government employees in Sierra Leone were "ghosts," employees on the government payroll who never showed up for work. The government's inclination to hire an excessive number of bureaucrats, pervasive throughout the Third World, primarily benefits the urban middle class rather than the poor, who lack the necessary education for these positions. However, parastatals (including agricultural marketing operations, electric power plants, telephone companies, railroads, and other state enterprises) employ both blue- and white-collar workers, thereby benefiting working-class and middle-class constituencies.

In recent decades, the IMF and other international lenders have induced debt-ridden African governments to pare their payrolls substantially. As a result, in countries such as Ghana and Uganda, the government fired thousands of ghost employees.[20] Austerity measures in Latin America also have required sharp cuts in government employment. In addition, many parastatals were sold to private investors, who had no incentives to maintain unneeded workers. Following the sale of Mexico's state steel industry, for example, the new private owners laid off more than half the work force.[21]

Thus, for the foreseeable future, the shrinking state sector will offer little relief for the growing number of urban job seekers. For decades, the expansion of labor-intensive industries in the private sector provided substantial private sector employment in East and Southeast Asia. The region's 1997 economic crisis led to widespread plant closings. But in recent years that region's economy has begun to recover. On the other hand, manufacturing in Latin America has often been more capital-intensive, generating fewer jobs. In Africa, where most economies have performed rather poorly for decades and the size of the industrial sector has remained fairly limited, the informal sector will continue providing a substantial proportion of urban employment.

THE STRUGGLE FOR HOUSING AMONG THE URBAN POOR

Of all the problems facing the urban poor, particularly the wave of new immigrants, none is more serious than finding adequate housing. With many metropolitan areas doubling in size every 10 to 20 years, private-sector housing cannot possibly expand fast enough to meet the need. Moreover, most of the new homes and apartment houses built for sale or rental privately are designed for the middle and upper classes, since low-income housing is not profitable enough to attract much investment. At the same time, while many Third World governments have invested in public housing, little of it reaches the poor. So, lacking adequate options in either the private or state sectors, a large segment of the urban poor live in squatter settlements and other forms of "self-help" (occupant-built) housing sometimes referred to as "spontaneous shelter."[22] Many others crowd into existing urban slums. The poorest city dwellers, lacking even the resources to rent or build, are left homeless, residing in doorways, unused construction material, or the like.

In all, the total number of shantytown residents, slum dwellers, and homeless account for over half the population of Third World cities. A number of years ago, a United Nations report on "Shelter and Urbanization" estimated that 100 million people worldwide were homeless (a figure that has likely risen since). In Cairo, several hundred thousand people, with nowhere else to go, live in cemetery tombs. Half the people of Ankara (Turkey) and about one-third of the populations of Manila and São Paulo live in squatter settlements and other forms of spontaneous shelter. For many of these people, sanitary conditions are particularly problematic. Another United Nations report calculated that close to 20 percent of the Third World's urban inhabitants have no access to clean water, and almost 30 percent lack sanitation facilities. Although the *percentage* of the urban population lacking those vital services has fallen since then, their absolute numbers have risen as a result of rapid urban growth. Less than one-third of the inhabitants of São Paulo and New Delhi are served by sewage systems, while in Karachi that portion drops to 20 percent. Tap water is equally hard to come by, reaching only half the population of Acapulco (Mexico) and one-third of Jakarta. Those who lack running water must either purchase it from private vendors (water tankers) at high prices or drink unsafe water. An estimated 100,000 inhabitants of Bangkok (Thailand), for example, obtain their drinking water from canals and other waterways that are dangerously polluted by industrial and human waste.[23] In recent years, many urban slum neighborhoods have gained access to electricity, potable water, and sewage facilities. All too often, however, such gains fail to keep up with the rate of urban growth.

Today, the availability of basic urban services in low-income neighborhoods varied considerably from region to region. For example, a recent study of eight low-income neighborhoods in Latin America—Rio de Janeiro and Aracajo (Brazil) and Santiago and Temuco (Chile)—found that nearly all of the inhabitants had running water and electricity. On the other hand, a parallel study of eight poor, African neighborhoods—in the cities of Abidjan and Man (Côte d'Ivoire) and Nairobi and Kisumu (Kenya)—revealed that almost all the residents had to buy their drinking water in cans (a minority had nearby wells, while virtually no families had tap water in their homes). Similarly, very few homes in any of the eight African neighborhoods had electricity, which was either unavailable or too expensive.[24] In light of these glaring needs, most developing nations have sought appropriate state responses.

Public Housing and the Role of the State

Throughout the developing world, many governments have constructed public housing to alleviate housing shortages. In China, workers in state enterprises are assigned apartments linked to their employment. Cuba's revolutionary regime has built large apartment blocks housing 25,000 to 40,000 persons on the outskirts of its largest cities.[25] During Venezuela's petroleum boom, the government constructed as many as 34,000 urban housing units annually.[26] In the 1960s and 1970s, various African governments established housing agencies with far more limited resources. One of the continent's most ambitious programs was in the Côte d'Ivoire, where some 40,000 units were constructed during the 1970s, almost all in the capital city of Abidjan. By the close of that decade, the Kenyan government was building more than 3,000 units annually.[27]

In time, however, it has become clear that public housing cannot provide sufficient shelter for the poor and, in some cases, it actually worsens their plight. In the capital cities of India, Senegal, and Nigeria, for example, many government housing projects were designed to eradicate urban blight. Prior to their construction, "unsightly" squatter settlements or slums have been demolished so that the city could become more aesthetically pleasing to the political elite, urban planners, middle-class residents, and foreign tourists. But rarely did the slum dwellers who had been evicted from their homes subsequently secure residence in the newly constructed public housing projects. Even those who were given alternate housing were usually relocated on the edges of town, far removed from their workplace. Diana Patel describes how Zimbabwe's government periodically ousted the same squatters from their settlements in different parts of the nation's capital, in effect "chasing them around town." Many government planners, viewing these shacks through middle-class lenses, believed that unless the squatters could afford "decent" urban housing with plumbing and multiple rooms for their families, they would be better off returning to the countryside.[28]

Even when new public housing projects are not built on the ruins of shantytowns and slums, they generally don't help the needy. In order for the government to recoup its construction costs, it must sell or rent the new housing units at higher rates than the urban poor can afford. Consequently, the state is faced with two options: it can subsidize rents and mortgages to bring the cost down to a level that the poor can afford, or it can rent or sell the dwellings to those who can better afford them, namely the middle class.

Despite its obvious potential as a welfare benefit for the poor, subsidized housing has several drawbacks. First, it is simply too costly for most developing nations to sustain even if they would like to do so. For example, following the Cuban revolution, the government committed itself to a variety of programs designed to serve workers and the poor—including public health, education, and housing. "Early housing policies reflected Fidel Castro's belief that nothing was too good for the working class."[29] Housing projects such as Santiago's José Martí provided schools, day-care centers, theaters, clinics, and stores for its 40,000 inhabitants. But by lavishing excessively "luxurious" housing on early recipients, the government soon ran out of funds for the many others needing shelter. Thus, the East Havana project, planned for 100,000 dwelling units, ultimately contained only 1,500. Even though it lacked adequate resources itself, the government discouraged or prohibited private and self-help housing (i.e., units built by the owner) until recently.[30] Not surprisingly, Cuba, like most Marxist regimes, has suffered chronic housing shortages.[31]

Second, in many LDCs subsidized housing has become a political plum allocated on the basis of connections (rewarding government supporters) rather than need. Political patronage plays an important role, with policemen, government bureaucrats, teachers, and activists in the ruling party being the first served.[32] As a consequence, residents in state housing are generally middle-class. They not only can better afford the rents, thereby reducing the magnitude of government housing subsidies, but also have the political influence to acquire this valuable resource.

Singapore and Hong Kong are among the very few cities that have constructed extensive, low-income public housing. But they are very atypical in two respects. First, because they are unusually densely populated and have very little unused land on which to expand, high-rise projects are the only possible means of housing large numbers of people. Second, the two cities are among the Third World's most affluent cities and, hence, can afford the cost of extensive subsidized housing. With the exception of the oil-rich Gulf states, other developing nations lack the budgetary resources to make a serious dent in their housing shortage. Consequently, most analysts feel that limited state funds would be better spent helping a larger number of beneficiaries in a less costly way. Macroeconomic policy changes have further reduced the scale of public housing in recent decades, as many LDCs have reduced the role of the state in providing social services and housing (see Chapter 10).

Spontaneous Housing

For years, many social scientists and urban planners have maintained that the most effective remedy for housing shortfalls in Third World cities is spontaneous (or self-help) shelter—the very shantytowns and squatter settlements that are so frequently viewed as a blight. In cities throughout the developing world, the poor have built their own homes, sometimes with hired or volunteer assistance. While living in these dwellings, many proprietors, particularly in Africa, also rent space to tenants. In some cases, the owners are squatters, living on land that has been occupied illegally, though often with the compliance of government authorities.[33] Others, residing in so-called "pirate settlements," have purchased their lots from land speculators but lack ownership titles because their community fails to conform to government zoning requirements.[34]

Spontaneous housing settlements range in size from a few isolated homes to a community of many thousands. For example, on the dried-up marshlands outside Mexico City, the municipality of Netzahualcóyotl began as a pirate settlement in the 1940s. By 1970 it housed 600,000 people.[35] An organized protest eventually induced the government to provide badly needed urban services and grant the squatters legal title to their homes. Elsewhere, up to 40 percent of Nairobi's population and one-fourth to one-third of the inhabitants of Jakarta, Karachi, and Lima live in squatter settlements.[36] These homes, argued John F. C. Turner, have erroneously been viewed as a problem, when in fact they are a major part of the solution to urban housing needs.[37] Rather than build public housing, he insisted, Third World governments can serve many more people by removing legal and political obstacles to spontaneous housing settlements and helping their residents upgrade the dwellings they have built.

Self-built homes have several important advantages over public housing.[38] First, they actually serve the poor, whereas most public housing does not. Second, they afford occupants the opportunity to upgrade their homes continuously. For example, in Lima's vast network of shantytowns, one can observe many wood and straw shacks whose owners are building brick walls around them, slowly constructing a better home as funds become available. Third, precisely because they are self-built, these homes better address the needs and desires of their owners than do units built by government planners. Finally, squatter settlements have the "churches, bars and neighborhood stores that help create a sense of community" that is too often lacking in large, impersonal, public housing projects.[39] Given these advantages, proponents of spontaneous housing argue that the state's most constructive role would be to stop evicting illegal squatters, and grant them land titles and other assistance needed to improve their homes. In 2003, Brazil's reformist government announced plans to give several million urban squatters title to their homes. Proponents of the plan expect that it will give millions of families greater access to utilities, mail delivery, and credit. Many obstacles, however, including problems of competing ownership claims, remain to be ironed out.[40]

Sites-and-Services Programs

Other analysts who favored a more active role for the state viewed the Turner thesis as a convenient excuse for governments that didn't wish to spend funds on the poor. Championing self-help housing, charged these critics, merely perpetuated the status quo and allowed the state to direct its limited housing resources toward the middle class.[41]

Ultimately, however, many Third World governments, the World Bank, and other foreign aid donors have pursued a middle ground between providing expensive, fully built public housing units and a laissez-faire policy that leaves the government with little role to play. In countries as diverse as Colombia, India, Malawi, and Turkey, the state has sold or rented parcels of land to the poor with basic services such as running water, sewage, and electricity. Purchasers then build their own homes on the sites as they do with spontaneous housing. In some cases, governments provide credit, technical assistance, or low-cost construction materials.[42]

These "sites-and-services" programs have several obvious advantages. First, they allow the government to steer self-built housing to locations that are safer and more environmentally sound. By contrast, unregulated spontaneous shelters in Caracas illustrate the dangers of unzoned squatter settlements. There, more than half a million people live on precarious hillsides in shacks that are sometimes washed away during the rainy season by mudslides. Second, in contrast to many sprawling squatter communities, inhabitants of sites-and-services settlements have electricity, sanitation, and other needed services from the outset. Finally, although occupants must purchase their sites, the lots are far more affordable than are fully built, state housing units. The government can further assist residents by providing them with cheap credit and construction materials.

Critics of sites-and-services programs note that even these relatively inexpensive lots are too costly for the poorest of the poor. While conceding that the communities developed on these sites are often healthier, safer, and more aesthetically pleasing, some scholars point out that they still fail to help the poorest of the poor, who can't afford them. In addition, they charge that these programs draw away the most talented and successful residents of unaided slums and shantytowns, thereby leaving the older communities bereft of leadership. Finally, they note that governments tend to locate sites-and-services projects in remote areas of town in order to remove the poor from downtown business areas. As a consequence, their inhabitants are far removed from their jobs and from important urban facilities.[43]

Such criticisms notwithstanding, we have seen that sites-and-services programs have some clear advantages over unaided spontaneous shelters and clearly benefit the poor more than fully built public housing does. Unfortunately, these programs often have not been self-financing (i.e., government income from the rent or sale of lots has not covered costs). Consequently, during the periodic economic crises that LDCs have faced over the years, many governments have abandoned them, once again leaving the poor to fend for themselves. Finally, in time, both sites-and-services programs and unregulated squatter settlements have faced a growing obstacle—as a consequence of increasing urban sprawl, cities have ever-diminishing space for any type of self-built housing.[44]

The Struggle Against Urban Crime

Rising crime rates are a problem in cities throughout the developing world.[45] There, as in developed countries, crime's origins lie in poverty, discrimination, income inequality, inadequate schools, and broken families. Its victims are to be found in all social classes—poor, middle class, and, less frequently, rich. However, throughout the world the urban poor contribute disproportionally to both criminal activity and its victims. The confluence of poverty, inequality, and social decay helps explain why violent crime rates in Africa and Latin America are generally substantially higher than in Western Europe, Japan, and other economically advanced nations. Not all countries or regions fit this pattern, however. For example, the rates of homicide and rape are much higher in the United States than in most other economically advanced countries and exceed those of developing countries such as South Korea, Singapore, Kuwait, and Argentina (Table 7.4). Conversely, the violent crime rate in Asia, despite its considerable poverty, is substantially lower than in the United States and somewhat lower than in Western Europe.[46] One explanation for these anomalies may be that income *inequality* promotes crime as much as or more than the *absolute* rate of poverty. Countries such as the United States, South Africa, and Brazil—with particularly high levels of income inequality—tend to have higher violent crime rates than countries with comparable or even lower average incomes but less inequality.

As Table 7.4 reveals, many African and Latin American countries suffer from very high crime rates, where the problem is most pronounced in their urban centers. South Africa, with one of the world's more inequitable income distributions (a vestige of its *apartheid* past), has an urban homicide rate about 13 times that of the United States and about 50 times Britain's. It also has the world's highest incidence of rape.[47] El Salvador's homicide rate peaked in 1995 at 139 per 100,000—roughly 25 times the U.S. rate and 150 times higher than Spain's.[48] Rio de Janeiro is among the world's leaders in robbery and sexual

TABLE 7.4   Cross-National Homicide Rates (1992–1997)

Country	Homicide Rate (per 100,000 people)
United States	5.70
Canada	2.16
Spain	0.95
South Korea	1.62
Singapore	1.71
Taiwan	8.12
Kuwait	1.01
Argentina	4.51
Brazil	19.04
Mexico	17.58
Colombia	64.60
South Africa	75.30

Source: "International Violent Death Rates," http://www.guncite.com/gun_control_gcgvintl.html; http://www.guncite.com/gun_control_gcgvinco.html.

assaults, while Bogotá (Colombia), Kingston (Jamaica), Kampala (Uganda), and Gaborone (Botswana) all suffer from exceptionally high levels of violent crime.

Furthermore, in many developing countries "government crime" in the form of corruption also afflicts the average citizen. In many Mexican cities, for example, the police will not respond to a homeowner's report of a burglary unless he or she has previously paid the local policeman a small monthly bribe for protection. In polls conducted during the late 1990s, only 0.1 percent of Britains and 0.2 percent of Americans indicated that they either had been asked to pay a bribe to a government official (often policemen) during that year or expected to be asked to pay one before the end of the year. That proportion rose to 19.5 percent in Kampala (Uganda), 29.9 percent in Jakarta (Indonesia), and 59.1 percent in Tirana (Albania).[49] The situation is even more precarious when police are closely linked to violent criminal activities. In 2004, hundreds of thousands of citizens marched in Buenos Aires (Argentina) and Mexico City to protest extensive police involvement in their cities' alarmingly high (and rising) rates of kidnapping. In Buenos Aires, the extent of criminal activity by the police is so great that it has resisted the best efforts of reformist President Néstor Kirchner to clean it up. As one Argentine sociologist has explained:

> Each division dedicates itself to the area of crime that it is supposed to be fighting. The robbery division steals and robs, the narcotics division traffics drugs, auto theft controls the stealing of cars and the chop shops, and those in fraud and bunco defraud and swindle.[50]

All too sadly the same can be said of police forces in many other Third World capitals. Rampant crime and, especially, widespread police corruption not only threaten the security of all the urban inhabitants (regardless of economic status), but undermines the government's legitimacy.

The Politics of the Urban Poor: Conflicting Images

How do the urban poor react politically to their daily struggle for jobs, shelter, and personal safety? Their political attitudes and behavior, like those of the peasantry, have been depicted in sharply conflicting ways.[51] When political scientists and sociologists first noted the flood of cityward migration and urban growth in the developing countries, many viewed the sprawling slums and squatter settlements as potential hotbeds of unrest or revolution. In one of the most influential early works on Third World politics, James Coleman warned that, "there exist in most urban centers elements predisposed to anomic activity."[52] Samuel Huntington maintained that the first generation of urban migrants was unlikely to challenge the existing order, but their children often would: "At some point, the slums of Rio and Lima are likely to be swept by social violence, as the children of the city demand the rewards of the city."[53] And economist Barbara Ward, taking note of shantytown poverty and the rise of radical urban movements, insisted,

> unchecked left to grow and fester, there is here enough explosive material to produce ... bitter class conflict ... erupting in guerrilla warfare, and threatening, ultimately, the security even of the comfortable West.[54]

As we will see, the urban poor have, indeed, contributed to several recent Third World revolutions. In addition, rioting over food prices and bus fares has shaken such cities as Algiers, Caracas, and Santo Domingo. Nonetheless, the urban conflagrations that many expected have been rare. Most of the poor have shunned violence. And voters in the slums and squatter settlements of the LDCs have been as likely to support right-wing or centrist political candidates as radicals. Indeed, initial expectations of a violent or radicalized urban lower class were largely based on erroneous premises. To be sure, many urban migrants came to the cities with raised expectations and heightened political sensitivities. But horrendous as the slums of Cairo, Calcutta, or Karachi may appear to the Western observer, migrants often find them preferable to their previous dwellings in the countryside. In fact, the urban poor are far more likely than their rural counterparts to enjoy electricity, sewage, tap water, and schools. In many countries, urban migration provides an escape from semifeudal social controls or ethnic civil war. Small wonder that surveys of migrants to Ankara, Baghdad, Bogotá, Mexico City, Rio de Janeiro, and other cities have indicated that most respondents feel better off in their urban hovels than they had in their rural villages.[55] A study of 13 low-income neighborhoods in Bogotá, Valencia (Venezuela), and Mexico City revealed that between 64 and 76 percent of those surveyed believed that their settlement was "a good place to live," while only 11 to 31 percent felt they lived in a "bad place."[56] Undoubtedly, severe economic recession since the early 1980s, which sharply lowered urban living standards in Africa, Latin America, and parts of Asia, gave slum dwellers a more jaundiced view of their condition. Yet survey research in Latin America has usually indicated that even when the urban poor do not feel their own lives have improved, most remain optimistic about the future and about prospects for their children.[57]

When early expectations of urban radicalism and violence generally failed to materialize, some scholars jumped to opposite conclusions. For example, based on his studies of low-income neighborhoods in Mexico and Puerto Rico, anthropologist Oscar Lewis concluded that most of the urban poor are prisoners of a "culture of poverty." Lewis described a sub-proletariat that lacks class consciousness, economic and political organization, or long-term aspirations. While distrustful of government, they feel powerless and fatalistic about effecting change. The culture of poverty, Lewis argued, is inherently apolitical and, hence, quite unlikely to generate radical or revolutionary activity.[58]

A related body of literature described the urban poor as "marginal"— outside the mainstream of the nation's political and economic life. Consequently, it was argued, there is a political vicious cycle in which the poor's exclusion leads to increased apathy on their part, which, in turn, further isolates them. They demonstrate a "lack of active participation due to the fact that … marginal groups make no decisions; they do not contribute to the molding of society."[59] Like the victims of Lewis's culture of poverty, marginals allegedly show little class consciousness or capacity for long-term collective action.

While it may be true that many poor urbanites, often with good reason, feel incapable of advancing their lives or influencing the political and economic system, survey research suggests that they don't necessarily suffer from the apathy or helplessness that scholars such as Lewis ascribed to them. Levels of fatalism and optimism undoubtedly vary from place to place and from time period to time period, depending on both the community's cultural values and its socioeconomic experiences. That is, those living in a country that has been enjoying rapid economic growth, some of which has percolated down to the urban slums and shantytowns, should logically be more optimistic about the future than are those in stagnant or inequitable economies. When poor urbanites in Côte d'Ivoire and Kenya—two very impoverished African countries—were asked if they believed that "when a person is born, the success he/she is going to have is already decided" (an obvious measure of fatalism), nearly 60 percent of them strongly agreed and an additional 11 percent agreed somewhat. In Brazil, a much more economically developed country (but one with enormous economic gaps between rich and poor), only about 15 percent strongly agreed, but some 30 percent agreed somewhat. Finally, in Chile, which has experienced the most rapid economic growth in Latin America since the start of the 1990s and has enjoyed a sharp decline in urban poverty, only 4 percent of the respondents strongly agreed and only 15 percent agreed somewhat.[60] In short, the level of fatalism or optimism among the urban poor varies considerably across nations and seems to correspond to objective economic conditions more than to any culturally embedded values.

Just as initial predictions of radicalism and violence among the urban lower class have proven to be greatly exaggerated, so too have assertions that the poor are invariably apathetic and fatalistic. To be sure, most low-income communities are not highly politicized. In his study of the poor in Guatemala City, Bryan R. Roberts found that "they claim to avoid politics in their local work, and to them the term 'politician' is synonymous with deceit and corruption."[61] Such perceptions are not the result of apathy or fatalism, however, but stem rather from the realistically "perceived impracticality of changing the existing order" in most Third World countries and, in some cases, such as Guatemala, from a repressive political climate.[62] On the other hand, when given the opportunity to organize (i.e., when their political activity is not repressed) and when there is a realistic chance of attaining some benefits from the political system, many low-income communities, or at least an activist minority within them, have seized the opportunity. Studies of Caracas, Lima, and Rio, for example, have revealed a number of poor neighborhoods with extensive political cooperation and organization. Moreover, their community leaders often have a keen sense of how to manipulate the political environment.

In time, social scientists came to question the concepts of marginality and the culture of poverty.[63] In the previously mentioned survey of poor neighborhoods in four African cities (in Côte d'Ivoire and Kenya) and four Latin American cities (in Brazil and Chile), political attitudes and levels of political interest and knowledge varied considerably. In all four countries a majority of the people surveyed responded that they were not interested in politics. The portion of those expressing "no interest" ranged from 51 percent in Brazil to 62 and 63 percent in Côte d'Ivoire and Chile.[64] The Chilean figures are noteworthy since 25 to 30 years earlier the shantytowns of Chile's largest cities were among the most politicized and radicalized in the world. But 17 years of repressive military dictatorship, during which many left-wing political activists were jailed or killed, had led many Chileans to disengage themselves from politics.

Yet, despite their professed disinterest, many of the urban poor in these four countries were rather well informed and communicative about politics. In Chile, Côte d'Ivoire, and Kenya roughly half of them reported talking occasionally with other people "about the problems which [their] country has to face today." In Brazil, that proportion rose to almost two-thirds. And about half of those surveyed in Chile and Côte d'Ivoire claimed that they regularly followed political news. In Brazil and Kenya that portion fell to about one-third. When asked to name important government leaders, they were generally quite knowledgeable. In all four nations, most were able to name the president of the country (ranging from 69 percent in Brazil to 94 and 96 percent in Kenya and Chile). Moreover, about half the respondents in Chile and Kenya, and two-thirds in Brazil and Côte d'Ivoire could also name the mayor of their town. Most impressively, more than 70 percent of the poor Kenyans and Ivorians could name the president of at least one *other* African country, while almost half the Chileans could name the president of another Latin American country. One suspects that these figures exceed the percentage of middle-class Americans who can name the president of Mexico or the prime minister of Canada. In short, these low-income city dwellers seemed to have a greater interest in politics then they were willing to admit. Or, perhaps, the question regarding their level of political interest had a different meaning to them than it did to the people conducting the survey.

On the negative side of the ledger, in all four countries the urban poor tended to take a rather dim view of their political system and of their elected representatives. More than 80 percent of those surveyed in each of the four countries believed, that "those we elect to parliament lose touch with people pretty quickly," with that number peaking at 94 percent in Chile. When asked whether they believed that "public officials care what people like me think, " a significant majority in all of the eight cities said "no." The number who believed that public officials *do* care ranged from a low of 15 percent in Chile to a high of 40 percent in Côte d'Ivoire. Perhaps most surprisingly, Ivorians, living in a country that is not democratic, were most positive about their public officials (the poll took place prior to the outbreak of serious violence in that country). On the other hand, Chileans, who live in the most democratic and politically responsive of the four nations, were least likely by far to believe that their government officials care about them and were also least likely to believe that their parliamentary representative keeps in touch with their poor constituents. Perhaps Chileans had harbored unrealistically high expectations of their restored, democratic, political leaders when the 17-year Pinochet dictatorship ended in 1990. Another important factor is that Chilean parties, once renowned for their strong linkages to the lower classes, have become more elitist and distant since the return of democracy.

Thus, even that limited sample of Third World cities reveals a wide variety of political attitudes among the urban poor. Similarly, while the slums or squatter settlements of, say, Santiago in 1973 or Tehran (Iran) in 1979 may boil with unrest, the same neighborhoods may be tranquil or even passive years later. Clearly, a more nuanced view of Third World urban politics requires us to ask: Under what circumstances do the poor organize politically? What goals do they seek, and how do they pursue them? What factors determine whether their political organization is peaceful or violent, conservative or radical, reformist or revolutionary?

FORMS OF POLITICAL EXPRESSION
AMONG THE URBAN POOR

Political scientists have long understood that the urban poor tend to be better politically informed and more politically active than their rural counterparts. Indeed, early scholarship on the Third World used a nation's level of urbanization as an indirect indicator of its level of political participation.[65] Lower-income city residents have higher levels of literacy than do peasants, greater exposure to the mass media, and more contact with political campaigns and rallies. But this does not mean that most of them are highly politicized. To the contrary, many are uninterested, apathetic, or even fatalistic about political events.[66] Nor does it even mean that political activists in the community are radical, indignant about their economic conditions, or prone to violent protest. What it does mean is that the urban poor generally vote in higher numbers than the peasantry. And it means that many low-income neighborhoods and communities, having intelligently assessed what kinds of benefits they can reasonably hope to extract from the political system, have organized to secure them. Contrary to initial expectations that the disoriented and frustrated urban poor would riot and rebel, they have tended, instead, to be rather pragmatic and careful in their political behavior.

Individual Political Behavior

For most slum and shantytown dwellers, opportunities for individual political activity are rather restricted. Until recently, voting has had a limited political impact in most developing nations. Even with the impressive spread of Third World democracy during the past decades, most countries in Africa and the Middle East, and many in Asia, continue to be dominated by a single party, with controlled or unbalanced elections. Many regimes in those regions, as well as in parts of Asia, restrict mass political participation. After an authoritarian interlude, competitive elections have returned to almost all of Latin America and have spread to much of Asia and parts of Africa as well, but their relevance to the poor often remains unclear.

   An alternative, often more fruitful, type of individual political activity takes the form of *clientelism*. As many observers have noted, members of the urban lower class often seek to advance their interests by attaching themselves to a patron within the government, a powerful political party, or an organized movement.[67] Clientelism (i.e., patron-client relationships) involves "the dispensing of public resources as favors by political power holders/seekers and their respective parties, in exchange for votes or forms of popular support."[68] While offering concrete advantages to the less-powerful partner (the client), it is at its heart "a strategy of elite controlled political participation fostering the status quo."[69] Among the urban poor, potentially frustrated or radicalized individuals and groups can be co-opted into the political system with the lure of immediate, if limited, gains.

   Patron-client relations, of course, also were typical of American big-city political machines in the late nineteenth and early twentieth centuries. Political parties aided recently arrived immigrants or Black migrants from the South by offering them jobs, Christmas turkeys, or assistance with local authorities, all in exchange for their support at the polls. Today, in countries throughout the Third World, the poor secure credit, government or parastatal employment, and other economic goods from the governing political party or local government strongman. Even in countries with competitive elections, such as India, Uruguay, and the Philippines, political bosses garner votes and volunteers primarily through patronage.

For most of the urban poor, however, collective rather than individual activity appears to be the most productive form of political participation. Many low-income neighborhoods have organized rather effectively to extract benefits from the political system. Not surprisingly, one of their most common goals is to secure land titles for their homes along with basic services such as sanitation, sewage, tap water, schools, and paved streets.

Collective Goals: Housing and Urban Services

On the outskirts of Lima, Peru, several million people live in squatter communities once known as *barriadas* and more recently called *pueblos jóvenes* ("young towns"). Typically, these settlements were born out of organized invasions of unoccupied land—either government property or land whose ownership had been in dispute:

> Some invasions involve relatively small groups of families who join together on an informal basis shortly before the occupation of the land. Others involve hundreds of families and are planned with great care. The leaders of these invasions often organize well before the invasion occurs and meet many times to recruit members, choose a site and plan the occupation itself.[70]

Although these land seizures were obviously illegal, David Collier's early research found that nearly half of them (involving more than 60 percent of Lima's squatter population) were conducted with explicit or tacit government approval.[71] While the authorities didn't want this phenomenon to get out of hand, they understood that permitting a controlled number of invasions onto low-value land (much of it public) enabled the poor to build their own homes with little cost to the state and defused a potentially explosive situation. There were political benefits to be gained as well. By protecting the invaders from police eviction, a political leader or governing party could garner future electoral support from that community. In many cases, squatters paid off local authorities prior to their invasions.

When Peru's leftist military regime seized power, it was anxious to mobilize the urban poor but, at the same time, to reduce spontaneous grass-roots political activity. The generals issued an urban reform law legalizing most existing squatter communities. They also tried to mobilize, yet control, the poor through SINAMOS, a state-controlled political organization for the rural and urban masses. However, they took a tougher stance against new land invasions. Henry Dietz's study of six poor neighborhoods in Lima demonstrates that community leaders in several locations were quite adept at moving from premilitary, competitive electoral politics to the new rules of enlightened authoritarianism.[72] Mobilized neighborhoods used an impressive array of political tactics to secure assistance from the military regime. These tactics included working through SINAMOS, enlisting the aid of a sympathetic Catholic bishop whom the church had assigned to the shantytowns, gaining the support of foreign nongovern-mental organizations (NGOs), publishing letters in leading newspapers, pres-suring local government bureaucrats, and directly petitioning the president.

Lima's squatter settlements have long attracted the interest of political scientists and anthropologists because of their unusually high level of political activity. But research elsewhere in Latin America has found similar ties between poor neighborhoods and the state.[73] For example, in her study of low-income neighborhoods in Mexico City, Susan Eckstein described how powerful community leaders tied themselves to the then-ruling party (the PRI) and became the links between the government and the grass roots. Because these community organizations were controlled from the top down and tended to be short-lived, Eckstein was skeptical about how much the poor really gained by operating through Mexico's clientelistic system. Still, she conceded that over the years poor neighborhoods had successfully petitioned the government for water, electricity, local food markets, schools, public transportation, and the like.[74] Following the National Action Party's presidential victory in 2000 and Mexico's transition to democracy, Mexico's low-income neighborhoods have been forced to establish new clientelistic relationships.

The politics of low-income neighborhoods throughout the developing world tends to resemble Peru's and Mexico's in two important respects: the scope of the group's claims and its relationship to the national political system. Studies of urban politics in India, Pakistan, the Philippines, and other LDCs repeatedly show the demands of the poor to be quite limited and pragmatic.[75] At times they are defensive, simply asking not to be evicted from illegal settle-ments. Frequently, their political objectives focus on housing. However, as John Turner suggested, squatters and slum dwellers rarely want the government to build homes for them, desiring instead the means to do it themselves.[76] Some neighborhoods may ask for a medical clinic, a market, or a preschool lunch pro-gram. None of these objectives, however, involve a fundamental challenge to the political system or a major redistribution of economic resources.

Such limited demands are intimately related to the nature of political organization in low-income neighborhoods. Political inputs from the poor are filtered through patron-client linkages to the state, powerful political parties, and political bosses. Organizations may be based in particular neighborhoods; they may be tied to ethnic, religious, or racial identities; or they may simply be formed around powerful political figures. In the slums of Madras, India, where politics is closely linked to the film industry, clientelistic organizations grow out of local fan clubs for politically active movie stars.[77] Whatever its base, patron-client politics inherently reinforces the status quo. In return for votes or other forms of political support, the state delivers some of the goods or services that residents need. In many cases, a neighborhood's rewards are very paltry. Elsewhere, political systems are far more generous. In either case, however, the state engages in "divide and rule" politics, as poor urban districts compete with each other for limited government resources.[78]

Critics of clientelistic politics stress how limited are the benefits that accrue to slums and shantytowns through these relationships. While some communities gain water, electricity, or medical clinics, many others are left out.

Moreover, even successful neighborhoods find it difficult to maintain pressure on the system for extended periods of time because their political organizations generally atrophy after a number of years. Consequently, as Alan Gilbert and Peter Ward charge, "The main aim of community-action programs is less to improve conditions for the poor ... than to legitimate the state ... to help maintain existing power relations in society."[79] As an alternative to clientelism, its critics favor a more independent, and perhaps more radical, form of mobilization that would raise the urban poor's political consciousness and, hopefully, lead to more sweeping redistributive policies benefiting far more people.

Other analysts, however, hold a more positive view of clientelism. While recognizing its shortcomings, they point out the benefits that it brings are clearly better than nothing. Viewed in the broader context of society's tremendous inequalities, paved streets, clean drinking water, a clinic, or a food market may not seem like sufficient gains to a middle-class observer. But they are usually greatly appreciated by the low-income neighborhoods that badly need them. A radical regime might redistribute more to the poor, but today that is not a viable option in most LDCs.[80]

The benefits of clientelism vary from country to country, depending on the nature of its political system and the health of its economy. In relatively open and democratic systems, the poor have broader opportunities to organize, demonstrate, petition, and vote. Clearly, their capacity to *demand* rewards from the state is greater than under authoritarian regimes. However, the benefits clientelistic systems can allocate to low-income neighborhoods are also constrained by the state's economic resources. During their petroleum booms, the Mexican and Venezuelan governments could be more generous to the urban poor. Even in more difficult economic times, the Mexican government has used revenues from the sale of state enterprises to finance public works projects in urban slums. Conversely, the impoverished dictatorships of Sub-Saharan Africa have neither the economic resources nor the political will to aid their slums and squatter settlements.

During the 1980s, a number of independent, grass-roots organizations emerged in the poor neighborhoods of Brazil, Chile, Mexico, and several other Latin American countries. Known as "new social movements," they avoided clientelistic linkages with the government or political parties, keeping independent even of leftist parties. For example, following Mexico City's immense earthquake in 1985, slum dwellers, frustrated by the ineptitude of the government's reconstruction efforts, formed an effective network of self-help associations. In Monterrey, radicalized squatters in the community of *Tierra y Libertad* (Land and Liberty) hijacked several buses, forcing the public transport company to extend its routes further into their neighborhood.[81] Ultimately, however, these independent movements had limited longevities. By the 1990s they were being overshadowed by President Carlos Salinas's public works network for low-income neighborhoods known as the National Solidarity Program. Using traditional clientelistic techniques, his administration won their support by establishing new schools, clinics, and the like through government-affiliated neighborhood groups.

Whatever the merits or limits of clientelism, its scope and range refute prior assumptions about the politics of the urban poor. On the one hand, the sometimes delicate and complex patron-client negotiations that they often require demonstrate that many neighborhood leaders are more politically skilled than some outside analysts had assumed. While many slum dwellers suffer from fatalism and excessive individualism, others are capable of sophisticated political organization and tough bargaining with the state. On the other hand, the poor rarely engage in the kind of revolutionary activity, violent upheavals, or radical politics that some political scientists had expected. During the 1980s, when living standards declined precipitously in much of the Third World, there was some increase in protest activity.[82] But the extent of rioting and social unrest remained surprisingly limited. Similarly, the slums of Bangkok and Kuala Lampur (Malaysia) have remained politically peaceful despite East Asia's recent financial crisis. To be sure, Indonesia's economic slide produced widespread urban rioting that toppled the Sukarno dictatorship in 1998. But it was primarily university students, not the poor, who demonstrated against the government. Jakarta's slum dwellers more often vented their fury, instead, against the affluent Chinese minority.

Radical Political Behavior

While most of the Third World's urban poor have favored moderate and pragmatic forms of political expression, there have been important exceptions. In some countries, such as Chile in the early 1970s, Peru in the 1980s, and El Salvador since the mid-1990s they have voted in substantial numbers for Marxist political candidates. And in a few cases, urban slum and shantytown dwellers have been important players in revolutionary upheavals. In 1970, Salvador Allende, candidate of Chile's leftist Popular Unity (UP) coalition, became the developing world's first democratically elected Marxist president. Allende received considerable electoral support in the *campamentos* (squatter settlements) that ring the capital city of Santiago. In addition, a number of *campamentos* were organized by the UP or by the MIR (Leftist Revolutionary Movement), a movement to the left of the UP that periodically engaged in armed action.[83] In 1983, the poor of Lima played a major role in electing a Marxist mayor, Alfonso Barrantes. These examples, as well as the Communist Party's electoral successes in several Indian cities, indicate that the poor do support radical political parties under certain circumstances. Those parties must have a realistic chance of winning at the local or national level and, with it, the possibility of delivering benefits to their supporters. Thus, even radical voting is often based on very pragmatic calculations. Not long after supporting Barrantes for mayor, Lima's poor rejected him for the post of national president, seeing even his moderate Marxism as not viable at the national level.[84]

More often, the urban poor are attracted to charismatic populists (left- or right-wing) such as the current president of Venezuela, Hugo Chávez or to moderate (non-Marxist) leftists such as Brazilian President Luiz Inácio Lula da Silva. Squatters or slum dwellers are even less likely to embrace urban guerrillas or other revolutionary movements. Teodoro Petkoff, a former leader of the Venezuelan communists' urban guerrilla wing noted that even residents of Caracas's poor barrios who belonged to leftist unions rejected the guerrillas. Blue-collar workers often elected communist union representatives in those days, Petkoff observed, because they felt that union militants would deliver more at the bargaining table. But when it came to voting for national office, they were more prone to support the two mainstream parties (Social Democrats and Christian Democrats) or even the former right-wing dictator, all of whom had a better track record of delivering rewards to their supporters.[85] Talton Ray's study of barrio politics explains why the inhabitants were unlikely to support the armed insurrection of the Armed Forces of National Liberation (Fuerza Armada de Liberación Nacional/FALN):

> The FALN's urban guerrilla warfare proved to be a grave tactical error ... [creating a] mood of revulsion ... in the barrios. Terrorist activities struck much too close to home. ... Almost all of the murdered policemen [killed by the FALN] were barrio residents.[86]

In the 1980s and 1990s, Peru's *Sendero Luminoso* (Shining Path) guerrillas had some success in the shantytowns of Lima. However, in view of Sendero's terror and intimidation tactics against both the peasantry and the urban poor, there is reason to believe that the group inspired more fear and acquiescence than support. When the popular vice-mayor of one of Peru's largest and most radical shantytowns, Villa El Salvador, tried to keep the Shining Path out of her community, she was brutally assassinated. In any event, Sendero activists in both the countryside and urban slums were more often students and teachers, rather than the poor themselves.

This is not to suggest that the urban poor never support revolutions. Josef Gugler notes that during the second half of the twentieth century, in four of the Third World's revolutions—Bolivia, Cuba, Iran, and Nicaragua—the cities played a central role.[87] However, in all but Nicaragua, where the urban poor's mass demonstrations were crucial, other social classes took the lead in the cities: miners, blue-collar workers, artisans, the lower-middle class, and the national police in Bolivia; students and university graduates in Cuba; theology students and petroleum workers in Iran. In contrast, Douglas Butterworth's study of the former inhabitants of a Havana slum, *Las Yaguas*, found that most were barely aware of Fidel Castro's existence during his rise to power.[88]

CONCLUSION: FUTURE URBAN GROWTH AND DEMOCRATIC POLITICS

While the *rate* of urbanization has slowed in parts of the Third World, *absolute increases* in urban populations will be greater than ever in the coming decades (Table 7.3). Thus, governments will have to heed urban needs, including those of the poor. Still, even with the best-intentioned public policies, developing economies will be hard pressed to provide sufficient jobs, housing, sanitation, and social services. Economic crises such as Latin America's and Africa's in the 1980s and East Asia's in the late 1990s have made the task all the more difficult. Urban crime, pollution, and AIDS will add tremendously to the burdens on the political-economic systems. In countries such as South Africa, Guatemala, and Iraq, the fall of authoritarian regimes has led to a surge in crime.

Given the current weakness of the radical Left, however, and the tendency of the poor to engage in adaptive behavior, urban discontent is more likely to express itself in occasional rioting than in mass insurrection or revolution. Perhaps the one exception may be in the Middle East, where segments of the urban lower and middle classes may turn to militant Islamic fundamentalism, as many have already done in Iran, Algeria, and Egypt. Elsewhere, crime and drug usage are more likely than radical politics to threaten stability in the proximate future. In the long run, Third World governments may be able to cope with these problems if they can generate sustained economic growth. In the short term, however, the possibility of increased state repression persists in many countries as the military and middle class become fearful of urban crime and disorder.

We have noted previously that poor urban neighborhoods generally receive more government assistance from democratic governments than from authoritarian ones. In countries where there has been an enduring transition to democracy, the urban poor will have to refine their strategies for securing state resources. By the same token, if newly democratic governments are to endure, they will need to become more responsive to the poor and more cognizant of the vast inequalities that plague Third World cities. Studies of urban slums and shantytowns generally suggest that while the poor are not as radical or even potentially radical as once thought, they are not necessarily committed to democratic values either. Faced with rising crime rates and economic barriers they may become disillusioned with democracy (Chapter 2). Democratic governments will have to prove to them that they are more helpful than prior authoritarian regimes. And political institutions of all kinds need to spread democratic cultural values.

DISCUSSION QUESTIONS

1. How have Third World governments been involved in providing urban housing? To what extent have such efforts benefited or hurt the urban poor?
2. Describe the advantages and limitations of spontaneous housing. In what ways are sites-and-services programs an improvement over spontaneous housing? Are there disadvantages to sites-and-services programs?
3. Discuss the political orientations of the urban poor. What does survey research tell us about the way that the urban poor look at their present circumstances and their view of the chances of improving them?
4. Discuss the role of clientelism or patron-client relationships in the politics of the urban poor.
5. Discuss the growth of urban crime in the Third World, the major obstacles to reducing crime rates, and the possible political consequences of rising crime rates.
6. Is rapid urban growth (linked to migration) beneficial or harmful for developing democratic government?

NOTES

1. United Nations, Department of Economic and Social Affairs, Population Division, "Urban and Rural Areas, 2003," http://www.un.org/esa/population/publications/wup2003/2003Urban_Rural.pdf
2. Stella Lowder, *The Geography of Third World Cities* (New York: Barnes and Noble, 1986), 19.
3. Sally Findley, "The Third World City," in *Third World Cities*, eds. John Kasarda and Allan Parnell (Newbury Park, CA: Sage Publications, 1993), 14–16.

4. Thus, while China officially has an urban population of about 500 million (or 39 percent of the nation's total), in fact, when the floating population is added in, there are really over 600 million city dwellers. See, Beatriz Carrillo Garcia, "Rural-Urban Migration in China: Temporary Migrants in Search of Permanent Settlement," *Portal* 1, no. 2 (July 2004): 1-12; also, Arianne M. Gaetano and Tamara Jacka (eds.), *On the Move: Women and Rural-to-Urban Migration in Contemporary China* (New York: Columbia University Press, 2004).

5. R. A. Obudho, "Urbanization and Urban Development Strategies in East Africa," in *Urban Management*, ed. G. Shabbir Cheema (New York: Praeger, 1993), figures extrapolated from Table 4.2, p. 84.

6. Cheema, "The Challenge of Urban Management," in *Urban Management*, 2.

7. David Drakakis-Smith, *Urbanization, Housing and the Development Process* (New York: St. Martin's Press, 1980), 6; Samuel Preston, "Urban Growth in Developing Countries," in *The Urbanization of the Third World*, ed. Josef Gugler (New York: Oxford University Press, 1988), 14–15, using earlier data, indicates a higher percentage of increase due to natural growth; Findley, "The Third World City," 15, using more recent data, indicates a higher percentage of increase due to migration.

8. United Nations, Department of Economic and Social Affairs, Population Division, "Urban and Rural Areas, 2003."

9. Obudho, "Urbanization and Urban Development Strategies," 84.

10. John V. Graumann, "Orders of Magnitude of the World's Urban and Rural Population in History," *United Nations Population Bulletin* 8 (1977): 16–33, quoted in Preston, "Urban Growth," 12.

11. Raymond Owens, "Peasant Entrepreneurs in an Industrial City," in *A Reader in Urban Sociology*, eds. M. S. A. Rao, Chandrashekar Bhat, and Laxmi Narayan Kadekar (New Delhi, India: Oriental Longman, 1991), 235.

12. Manuel Castells and Alejandro Portes, "World Underneath: The Origins, Dynamics and Effects of the Informal Economy," in *The Informal Economy: Studies in Advanced and Developing Economies*, eds. Alejandro Portes, Manuel Castells, and Lauren A. Benton (Baltimore, MD: Johns Hopkins University Press, 1989), 12.

13. Om Prakash Mathur, "Managing the Urban Informal Sector," in *Urban Management*, 179. The data are drawn from International Labor Organization (ILO) studies.

14. Alan Gilbert and Josef Gugler, *Cities, Poverty and Development*, 2d ed. (New York: Oxford University Press, 1992), 98. Gugler argues elsewhere that the composition of the informal economy is so diverse that it is not clear whether it can really be referred to as a single sector.

15. Alejandro Portes et al., "The Informal Sector in Uruguay," *World Development* 14 (1986), 727–741.

16. Hernando de Soto, *The Other Path* (New York: Harper & Row, 1989), translated from the Spanish edition.

17. Dennis Rondinelli and John Kasarda, "Job Creation Needs in Third World Cities," in *Third World Cities*, 92–120.

18. Macroeconomic policy will be discussed in far greater detail in Chapter 10. The reader wishing to better understand the economic analysis offered briefly in this section is referred to that chapter.

19. Stephan Haggard, *Pathways from the Periphery* (Ithaca, NY: Cornell University Press, 1990).

20. Richard Sandbrook, *The Politics of African Economic Recovery* (New York: Cambridge University Press, 1993), 60–61.

21. *New York Times*, October 27, 1993.

22. While squatter settlements or shantytowns can accurately be called poor neighborhoods, not everyone living in them is poor. Data from Istanbul, Rio, Caracas, and elsewhere show that some shantytown residents are white-collar workers or well-paid blue-collar workers. Better-off residents may live there because rents elsewhere are too high. Others have enjoyed upward mobility since settling there but stay because of attachments to friends and community.

23. Statistics in the preceding paragraphs come from Om P. Mathur, "foreword" in Kamlesh Misra, *Housing the Poor in Third World Cities* (New Delhi, India: Concept Publishing Company, 1992), 6–8; Gilbert and Gugler, *Cities, Poverty and Development*, 115.

24. Silvia Schmitt, "Housing Conditions and Policies," in *Poverty and Democracy*, eds. Dirk Berg-Schlosser and Norbert Kersting (London and New York: Zed Books, 2003), 61. In each of the four countries (Brazil, Chile, Côte d'Ivoire, Kenya) the study examined two poor, urban neighborhoods in the nation's capital and two in smaller cities.

25. Fred Ward, *Inside Cuba Today* (New York: Crown, 1978), 36–38.

26. Howard Handelman, "The Role of the State in Sheltering the Urban Poor," in *Spontaneous Shelter*, ed. Carl V. Patton (Philadelphia: Temple University Press, 1988), 332–333.

27. Richard Stern, "Urban Housing in Africa: The Changing Role of Government Policy," in *Housing Africa's Urban Poor*, eds. Philip Amis and Peter Lloyd (Manchester, England: Manchester University Press, 1990), 36–39.

28. Diana Patel, "Government Policy and Squatter Settlements in Harare, Zimbabwe," in *Slum and Squatter Settlements in Sub-Saharan Africa*, eds. R. A. Obudho and Constance Mhlanga (New York: Praeger, 1988), 205–217.

29. Handelman, "The Role of the State," 339.

30. Some experts call Cuba's construction of microbrigade housing (houses built by teams of

worker volunteers) self-help. But they are built by groups under state direction who don't design the homes and don't conform to much of the self-help model discussed later in the chapter.

31. Gilbert and Gugler, *Cities, Poverty and Development*, 139.

32. Susan Eckstein, *The Poverty of Revolution: The State and the Urban Poor in Mexico*, 2d ed. (Princeton, NJ: Princeton University Press, 1988); Henry Dietz, *Poverty and Problem Solving Under Military Rule* (Austin: University of Texas Press, 1980), 41; Howard Handelman, *High-Rises and Shantytowns* (Hanover, NH: American University Field Staff, 1979), 17; B. Sanyal, "A Critical Look at the Housing Subsidies in Zambia," *Development and Change* 12 (1981): 409–440.

33. David Collier, *Squatters and Oligarchs* (Baltimore, MD: Johns Hopkins University Press, 1976).

34. Gilbert and Gugler, *Cities, Poverty and Development*, 123.

35. Alan Gilbert and Peter Ward, *Housing, the State, and the Poor* (New York: Cambridge University Press, 1985), 86–87.

36. Diana Lee-Smith, "Squatter Landlords in Nairobi," in *Housing Africa's Urban Poor*, 177; Douglas Butterworth and John Chance, *Latin American Urbanization* (New York: Cambridge University Press, 1981), 147; Collier, *Squatters and Oligarchs*, 27–28.

37. John F. C. Turner, "Barriers and Channels for Housing Development in Modernizing Countries," *Journal of the American Institute of Planners* 33 (May 1967): 167–181; John F. C. Turner and Robert Fichter, eds., *Freedom to Build* (New York: Macmillan, 1972); see also William Mangin, "Latin American Squatter Settlements: A Problem and a Solution," *Latin American Research Review* 2, no. 3 (1967): 65–98.

38. Gilbert and Gugler, *Cities, Poverty and Development*, 117–130; Carl Patton, "Prospects for the Future," in *Spontaneous Shelter*, 348–355.

39. Handelman, "The Role of the State," 328.

40. *The New York Times* (April 19, 2003).

41. Peter Nientied and Jan van der Linden, "Approaches to Low-Income Housing in the Third World," in *The Urbanization of the Third World*, 138–156; R. Burgess, "Petty Commodity Housing or Dweller Control? A Critique of John Turner's Views on Housing Policy," *World Development* 6 (1978): 1105–1133.

42. Handelman, *High-Rises and Shantytowns*; A. A. Laquian, "Whither Site and Services," *Habitat* 2 (1977): 291–301; Thomas Pennant, "The Growth of Small-Scale Renting in Low-Income Housing in Malawi," in *Housing Africa's Urban Poor*, 196–200.

43. Ernest Alexander, "Informal Settlement in Latin America and Its Policy Implication," in *Spontaneous Shelter*, 131–133; Drakakis-Smith, *Urbanization, Housing and the Development Process*, 141–142; Jorge Hardoy and David Satterthwaite, *Shelter, Need and Response* (New York: John Wiley, 1981); Lisa Peattie, "Some Second Thoughts on Sites-and-Services," *Habitat International* 6 (Winter 1982): 131–139.

44. Gilbert and Ward, *Housing, the State and the Poor*.

45. Portions of this section are drawn from Howard Handelman, *The Security and Insecurities of Democracy in the Third World* 12, no. 1 (Milwaukee: University of Wisconsin-Milwaukee, Global Studies Perspectives: Occasional Paper Series of the Center for International Education, 2004).

46. Andrew Morrison, Mayra Buvinic, and Michael Shifter, "The Violent Americas: Risk Factors, Consequences, and Policy Implications of Social and Domestic Violence," in *Crime and Violence in Latin America*, eds. Hugo Frühling and Joseph Tulchin (Washington, D.C.: Woodrow Wilson Center Press, 2003), 96.

47. Jeffrey Herbst, "The Nature of South African Democracy: Political Dominance and Economic Inequality," in Theodore K. Rabb and Ezra N. Suleiman, eds., *The Making and Unmaking of Democracy: Lessons from History and World Politics* (New York and London: Routledge, 2003), 220-221.

48. For the Salvadorian rate see Laura Chincilla, "Experience with Citizen Participation in Crime Prevention in Central America," in *Crime and Violence*, eds. Fruhling and Tulchin, 209. The U.S. and Spanish data are in Table 7.4 of this chapter.

49. All the crime and corruption data in this paragraph come from the UNDP, *Human Development Report 2000*, 220-221.

50. *New York Times* (August 4, 2004).

51. Joan Nelson, *Access to Power* (Princeton, NJ: Princeton University Press, 1979), chap. 4; Howard Handelman, "The Political Mobilization of Urban Squatter Settlements," *Latin American Research Review* 10, no. 2 (1975): 35–72; Gilbert and Gugler, *Cities, Poverty and Development*, chap. 7.

52. James Coleman, "Conclusion: The Political Systems of Developing Nations," in *The Politics of Developing Areas*, eds. Gabriel Almond and James Coleman (Princeton, NJ: Princeton University Press, 1960), 537. Anomic activity is action not governed by social practices and values.

53. Samuel Huntington, *Political Order in Changing Societies* (New Haven, CT: Yale University Press, 1968), 283.

54. Barbara Ward, "Creating Man's Future Goals for a World of Plenty," *Saturday Review* 9 (August 1964): 192.

55. Joan Nelson, *Migrants, Urban Poverty, and Instability in Developing Nations* (Cambridge, MA: AMS Press and the Harvard University Center for International Affairs, 1969), 18–20; Eckstein, *The Poverty of Revolution*, 41.

56. Gilbert and Ward, *Housing, the State and the Poor*, 215.

57. Ibid., 57–61.

58. Oscar Lewis, *The Children of Sanchez* (New York: Random House, 1961), and *La Vida* (New York: Random House, 1966).

59. Jorge Giusti, "Organizational Characteristics of the Latin American Urban Marginal Settler," *International Journal of Politics* 1, no. 1 (1971): 57.

60. Barbara Happe and Sylvia Schmit, "Political Culture," in *Poverty and Democracy*, eds. Berg-Schlosser and Kersting 130.

61. Bryan R. Roberts, *Organizing Strangers: Poor Families in Guatemala City* (Austin: University of Texas Press, 1973), 299.

62. Alejandro Portes and John Walton, *Urban Latin America* (Austin: University of Texas Press, 1976), 108.

63. Janice Perlman, *The Myth of Marginality* (Berkeley: University of California Press, 1976); William Mangin, "The Role of Regional Associations in the Adaptation of Rural Migrants to Cities in Peru," in *Contemporary Cultures and Societies of Latin America*, eds. Dwight Heath and Richard Adams (New York: Random House, 1974).

64. Happe and Schmit, "Political Culture," 125. All of the survey results that follow come from that chapter (pp. 121–152) or from Norbert Kersting and Jaime Sperberg, "Political Participation," 153–180.

65. Karl Deutsch, "Social Mobilization and Political Development," *American Political Science Review* 55 (September 1961): 493–514; Daniel Lerner, *The Passing of Traditional Society* (Glencoe, IL: Free Press, 1958).

66. Of course, even in highly educated industrialized democracies such as the United States, many citizens are also apolitical. Moreover, that political apathy extends to members of the middle class.

67. Gilbert and Gugler, *Cities, Poverty and Development*, 180–187; S. N. Eisenstadt and L. Roninger, *Patrons, Clients and Friends* (New York: Cambridge University Press, 1984).

68. A. Bank, "Poverty, Politics and the Shaping of Urban Space: A Brazilian Example," *International Journal of Urban and Regional Research* 10, no. 4 (1986): 523.

69. *Ibid.*

70. Collier, *Squatters and Oligarchs*, 41.

71. Ibid., 44.

72. Dietz, *Poverty and Problem-Solving under Military Rule.*

73. Wayne Cornelius, *Politics and the Urban Poor in Mexico* (Stanford, CA: Stanford University Press, 1975); Gilbert and Ward, *Housing, the State and the Poor*, 189–196.

74. Eckstein, *The Poverty of Revolution*, chap. 3.

75. Frans Schuurman and Ton van Naerssen, *Urban Social Movements in the Third World* (New York: Routledge, 1989).

76. Turner, "Barriers and Channels."

77. Joop de Wit, "Clientelism, Competition and Poverty: The Ineffectiveness of Local Organizations in a Madras Slum," in *Urban Social Movements*, 63–90.

78. Jan van der Linden, "The Limits of Territorial Social Movements: The Case of Housing in Karachi," in *Urban Social Movements*, 101.

79. Gilbert and Ward, *Housing, the State and the Poor*, 175.

80. Marxist governments often redistribute significant resources to the poor soon after taking power. However, with the notable exception of China, leftist regimes generally have a poor record of economic growth. In Nicaragua, for example, the urban poor benefited initially from Sandinista welfare programs but then saw their standard of living deteriorate sharply due to the U.S.-backed Contra war as well as to poor economic management by the Sandinistas. In other revolutions, such as Cuba's or Vietnam's, where counterrevolutionary activity has been less extreme, experts differ sharply regarding how the urban poor have fared in the long run.

81. Vivien Bennet, "The Evolution of Popular Movements in Mexico Between 1968 and 1988," in *The Making of Social Movements in Latin America*, eds. Arturo Escobar and Sonia Alvarez (Boulder, CO: Westview Press, 1992); Menno Vellinga, "Power and Independence: The Struggle for Identity and Integrity in Urban Social Movements," in *Urban Social Movements*, 151–176.

82. Susan Eckstein, *Urbanization Revisited: Inner-City Slum of Hope and Squatter Settlement of Despair* (Storrs: University of Connecticut and Brown University Occasional Papers in Latin American Studies, 1989), 14.

83. Handelman, "The Political Mobilization of Urban Squatter Settlements: Santiago's Recent Experience," *Latin American Research Review* 10, no. 2 (1975): 35–72.

84. Henry Dietz, "Political Participation in the Barriadas: An Extension and Reexamination,"

Comparative Political Studies 18, no. 3 (1985): 323–355.

85. The author's conversations with Petkoff in 1976 and 1978. Petkoff left the Communist Party to help found a democratically oriented Marxist party called MAS. He was subsequently elected to Congress on the MAS ticket and in the late 1990s held a powerful cabinet position.

86. Talton Ray, *The Politics of the Barrios of Venezuela* (Berkeley: University of California Press, 1969), 132–133.

87. Josef Gugler, "The Urban Character of Contemporary Revolutions," in *The Urbanization of the Third World*, 399–412.

88. Douglas Butterworth, *The People of Buena Ventura* (Urbana: University of Illinois Press, 1980), 19–20.

chapter 8

Revolutionary Change

The opening decades of the twentieth century ushered in the Mexican and Russian revolutions. The closing decades witnessed the collapse of Soviet communism, the transformation of the Chinese and Mexican revolutions, and the weakening of Cuba's revolutionary government.[1] No era in world history has encompassed more revolutionary upheaval. Yet as the twenty-first century begins, the force that had once promised, or threatened, to transform the face of the Third World appears to be spent, at least for the time being.

Karl Marx, the foremost prophet of revolution, expected these upheavals to take place in industrialized European nations where the organized working class would rise up against the oppressive capitalist system. Instead, modern revolutionary movements have been largely a Third World phenomenon, fought primarily by the peasantry. And even Europe's internally generated communist revolutions—Russia and Yugoslavia—occurred in countries where capitalism and industrialization were relatively underdeveloped. The remaining communist regimes in Central Europe were installed by Soviet military intervention, not through indigenous uprisings.

In the Third World, the appeal of revolutionary change has been its promise of rapid and sweeping solutions to the problems of underdevelopment. It pledged to end colonial rule, terminate dependency, protect national sovereignty, reduce social and economic inequalities, accelerate economic development, mobilize the population, and transform the political culture. Not surprisingly, many of the LDCs' poor and oppressed, along with numerous intellectuals and alienated members of the middle class, have found revolutionary platforms and ideologies quite appealing.

Some revolutionary governments—in China, Cuba, and Mexico, for example—were able to deliver on a number of their promises. Under Mao Zedong's leadership, the Chinese Communist Party redistributed land to the peasantry, industrialized the economy, and transformed the country into a world power. Fidel Castro's government implemented extensive land reform, a vast adult literacy campaign, and significant public health programs. Mexico's revolutionary party reestablished national sovereignty over the country's natural resources, initiated agrarian reform, and transformed the nation into a Third World industrial power.

Often, however, these gains have come at great cost, including political repression, considerable human suffering, and rampant corruption. As a result of their revolution, the Chinese people now enjoy far better medical care, more education, and better living conditions than ever before. At the same time, however, some 30 million people starved to death in the 1950s due to the mistaken experiments of Mao's Great Leap Forward. Millions more suffered humiliation, imprisonment, or death (for some 400,000 people) during the ultra-radical period called the Cultural Revolution (1966 to 1976). Most communist governments had their *gulag* for real and imagined political opponents. In Vietnam, many suspected dissidents were sent to "reeducation" camps, and in Cuba a smaller, but still significant, number were imprisoned.

In the most unfortunate cases—Angola, Mozambique, Kampuchea (Cambodia)—huge portions of the population died as the result of civil war or the regime's brutality, with little or nothing positive to show for it.[2] In Kampuchea, the fanatical Khmer Rouge government killed more than a million people, including much of the country's educated class, while accomplishing nothing for its people. Over the years, even some of the more idealistic revolutionary regimes were transformed into corrupt bureaucracies, run by a new generation of opportunistic *apparatchiks* (party or government bureaucrats) who had never risked anything for the revolution's ideals.

After examining the meaning of revolution and classifying different types of twentieth-century revolutions, this chapter will discuss the causes of revolutionary upheavals, their principal sources of leadership and support, and the policy objectives of their leaders once in power. Finally, it will discuss the decline of the revolutionary model at the end of the twentieth century.

DEFINING REVOLUTION

Scholars have argued endlessly about what constitutes a revolution and whether particular upheavals such as the American Revolution or Iran's Islamic Revolution were, in fact, true social revolutions.[3] Thus, Chalmers Johnson notes, "half the battle will lie in answering the question, 'What is revolution?'"[4] In its broadest and least precise usage, the term is applied to any nonlegal, nondemocratic, or violent overthrow of government. Peter Calvert offers perhaps the most open-ended definition when he maintains that revolution is "simply a form of governmental change through violence."[5] Such a definition, however, seems too broad since it encompasses military coups and other upheavals that do little more than change the heads of government. Most scholars insist on a more rigorous definition, arguing that revolutions must involve fundamental political, economic, and social change. Thus, Samuel P. Huntington has suggested:

> A revolution is a rapid, fundamental, and violent domestic change in the dominant values and myths of society, in its political institutions, social structure, leadership and government activity and policies. Revolutions are thus to be distinguished from insurrections, revolts, coups and wars of independence.[6]

To be sure, the distinctions that Huntington proposes in the last sentence are not always easily made. For example, many "wars of independence" (sometimes called "wars of national liberation") such as Algeria's and Angola's are generally considered authentic social revolutions because they ushered in fundamental societal change.[7] On the other hand, Theda Skocpol accepts Huntington's starting definition but narrows it by claiming that "social revolutions are accompanied and in part effectuated through [massive] class upheavals."[8] She adds:

Social revolutions are set apart from other sorts of conflicts by the combination of two coincidences: the coincidence of societal structural change with class upheaval; and the coincidence of the political with social transformation.[9]

Skocpol concedes that according to her more restrictive, class-based definition, only "a handful of successful social revolutions have ever occurred." The most clear-cut cases are the three she has studied in great detail: France (1789), Russia (1917), and China (1911 to 1949). Other, less-restrictive definitions of revolution would apply to Mexico, Bolivia, Cuba, Nicaragua, Algeria, Ethiopia, Mozambique, Angola, Eritrea, Vietnam, Cambodia, Turkey, and Iran, among others. What is common to all of them is that insurgency brought sweeping changes to the country's political, economic, and social systems.

Because revolutions involve a fundamental transfer of political and economic power, rather than a mere change in political leaders (as is the case in most military coups), they are invariably violent. Not surprisingly, government officials and social classes that have long held (and often abused) power and that now face uncertain futures normally fight bitterly to stay on top. Should the revolutionaries triumph, old elites are removed from power, new ones are installed, and at least in some respects, their political, economic, and social participation broadens to include those further down the social ladder. This does not imply that revolutionary governments are democratic. They virtually never are. But they are usually more broadly participatory and egalitarian than the regimes that they have toppled.

I classify as a revolution any insurgency that brings about these kinds of comprehensive political and socioeconomic changes. The upheaval may be rooted in class struggles (China and Nicaragua), as Skocpol insists, or, contrary to Huntington, it may be a war of national liberation (Algeria and Angola), as long as it overturns critical political and economic institutions and changes the country's underlying power structure. In fact, the borderline between nationalist and class-based revolutions is often difficult to discern. The Vietnamese revolution most clearly combined anticolonial and class struggle.[10] But even primarily class-based revolutions, such as China's, Mexico's, Cuba's, and Nicaragua's, had important nationalist, anti-imperialist components to them.

Revolutions may be Marxist (China, Russia, Vietnam, Kampuchea, and Cuba), partially Marxist (Nicaragua), or non-Marxist (Mexico, Bolivia, Libya, and Iran). Marxism was particularly appealing to many revolutionaries because it promised the redistribution of economic resources, the ideological rigor, and the new set of political myths that they sought. But the revolutionary's vision of social justice need not be tied to communism. It may also come from nationalism, Islam, or a number of other ideologies or religions.

Revolutionaries generally come to power either through mass uprisings featuring strikes, protest marches, and street riots (Russia, Bolivia, and Iran), through guerrilla warfare (China, Vietnam, and Cuba), or through a combination of both (Nicaragua). There have also been a few elite revolutions in which military officers or upper-level bureaucrats have overthrown the regime and instituted far-reaching socioeconomic changes that far transcended the objectives of mere coups.[11] Primary examples include Mustafa Kemal Ataturk's revolt in Turkey in 1919, Gamal Abdel Nasser's officers' revolt in Egypt in 1952, and Peru's "revolution from above" in 1968, all led by progressive military officers (see Chapter 9).

UNDERLYING CAUSES OF REVOLUTION

Just as experts have failed to agree on a common definition of revolution, they have also been divided on the causes of revolutionary insurrection. Some theories focus on broad historical trends, including changes in the world order that make revolution likely or even inevitable. Other explanations center on weaknesses in the *ancien régime* (the outgoing political system), examining factors that caused the prerevolutionary state to fall. And yet others focus on the major players in Third World revolutions, particularly the peasantry, seeking the factors that cause them to revolt.

Inexorable Historical Forces

Karl Marx viewed revolution as an unstoppable historical force growing out of class inequalities that are rooted in the unequal ownership of the means of production. Those who command the economic system, he argued, control the state as well. Over time, however, subordinate classes will become alienated from the political-economic system and will attain sufficient political skills and vision (class consciousness) to overthrow the existing order. Thus, Marx maintained, the 1640 British Revolution (or Civil War) and the French Revolution (1789) were each led by the ascendent *bourgeoisie* (property owners, including capitalists) who toppled the old order controlled by the aristocracy and landed oligarchy. Both revolutions were part of a broader European transition from agrarian feudalism to industrial capitalism. Although Marx believed that this new capitalist order presented a more advanced and more productive historical stage, he maintained that it depended on the exploitation of the working class (proletariat). In time, he predicted, as the exploitation of the proletariat became more apparent and as workers developed sufficient class consciousness, they would overthrow capitalism and install revolutionary socialism.[12]

More than any other revolutionary theorist, Marx influenced the course of history, since most of the twentieth century's major revolutionary leaders— including V. I. Lenin, Mao Zedong, Ho Chi Minh, Ché Guevara, and Fidel Castro—fervently believed in his ideology. His writings evoked the centrality of class struggle in most revolutionary movements. But as even sympathetic analysts have noted, "He was, first and foremost a nineteenth-century man" whose ideology was closely linked to the era in which he lived.[13] "Marx's theoretical approach," wrote one contemporary Marxist sociologist, "enabled him to explain the past but failed him in his predictions."[14] Indeed, *no* country has ever had the succession of revolutions that he predicted, first capitalist, then socialist.[15] Instead, the major locus of modern revolution has been the Third World—not advanced capitalist nations—and the major protagonists have been peasants rather than industrial workers.

Mao Zedong, the father of the Chinese Revolution, accepted Marx's view of revolution as part of a historical dialectic.[16] Like other Third World Marxists, he viewed capitalist exploitation and resulting class conflict as the root cause of communist upheavals. However, the Chinese communists' military defeats in the 1920s convinced him that its orthodox commitment to proletariat revolution was not viable in a country in which the working class constituted such a small percentage of the population. Consequently, he reinterpreted Marxist revolutionary strategy to make it more applicable to China and other parts of the developing world. Mao developed a theory of peasant-based struggle and a military strategy designed to encircle and conquer China's cities following a period of protracted rural guerrilla conflict.[17] The success of his strategy in the world's most populous country and its widespread application elsewhere in the Third World made Mao the most influential twentieth-century practitioner of revolutionary warfare.

In Vietnam and Cuba, Ho Chi Minh and Ché Guevara refined Mao's vision of "peoples' war" to make it more compatible with conditions in Southeast Asia and Latin America. While all of them demonstrated that communist revolutions could take place in countries that are not highly industrialized (Cuba came closest to Marx's ideal), those leaders still adhered to Marx's theory of history and his vision of class struggle.

Regime Decay

Even before the collapse of the Soviet bloc, it had become obvious that there was no *inevitable* march toward revolution and that, in fact, successful revolutions are rather rare and unique. Theta Skocpol argues that neither the repression of the masses nor the skills of revolutionary leadership alone can bring about successful social revolutions. These factors may be necessary, but they are not sufficient. Rather, true revolutions succeed only when the state is undermined by international pressures such as war, economic competition, or an arms race. Modernization of Britain and other European powers, she contends, created severe military and economic pressures on less-developed countries within and outside Europe. Some of those states, such as royalist France, czarist Russia, and imperial China, were less able to adjust to these challenges and, hence, became more susceptible to revolutionary challenges.[18]

In the Russian case, excessive military entanglements, foreign indebtedness, and a disastrous entry into World War I undermined the czarist state. Successive military defeats in two wars—first by the Japanese (1905) and then by the Germans (1917)—did in the regime. Similarly, China's Manchu dynasty, having been fatally weakened first by European and then Japanese imperialism, was toppled easily by Guomindang (Nationalist) forces in 1911. Elsewhere, stronger regimes were able to withstand comparable challenges, but the Russian and Chinese states were too weak to marshal sufficient economic and military resources. Ultimately, peasant rebels led by "marginal elites" (university students and middle-class professionals alienated from the system) toppled the old order.[19] Ironically, just as military competition undermined the czarist government and set the stage for the Russian Revolution, some 70 years later the Soviet-American arms race weakened the Soviet Union and contributed to its collapse.

Thus, Skocpol and others have argued that the primary factor contributing to revolutionary transformation is not the revolutionaries' strategy, tactics, or zeal, but rather the internal rot of the decaying old order. For example, Japan's invasion of China prior to World War II undercut the legitimacy of the Guomindang (Nationalist) government. The Japanese occupation demonstrated that the Nationalists were too corrupt and incompetent to resist a foreign threat, while the Chinese communists' People's Liberation Army was far more effective in that regard. When the Chinese revolutionary war resumed after World War II, many of the areas in which the communists won major military victories were the same ones in which they had organized mass resistance against the Japanese.[20]

In fact, military defeats have frequently delegitimized the regime in power, setting the stage for subsequent revolutions. Thus, the destruction of the Ottoman empire in World War I and the Japanese capture of British, French, and Dutch colonies in Asia (Burma, Vietnam, and Indonesia) during World War II all undermined the imperial or colonial governments and led, respectively, to the "Young Turks" military revolt in Turkey and independence movements in South and Southeast Asia.[21] Similarly, Egypt's defeat in a war with Israel (1948–1949) helped precipitate Colonel Nasser's revolution from above.

War has the additional effect of disrupting peasant life, forcing many of them to seek a new social structure and physical protection by the revolutionary forces. For example, in accounts of life in rural China during its civil war and the Japanese invasion, "one is struck by the number of peasants ... who had their routines upset through the [war-related] death of their kin before they joined revolutionary organizations."[22]

But governments may be undermined by factors other than military defeat. In Cuba and Nicaragua, prolonged dictatorships became obscenely corrupt. Fulgencio Batista rose from the rank of army sergeant in 1933 to become Cuba's dominant political actor over the next two decades. Under his administration and those of others he dominated, corruption infested all ranks of government. Batista's links to the American mafia helped turn Havana into a playground for affluent tourists seeking gambling and prostitution. For decades, members of the ruling Somoza dynasty commandeered a huge share of Nicaragua's economy, while their personal army, the National Guard, engaged in graft like intercepting and selling United States relief supplies sent after the nation's capital (Managua) was leveled by an earthquake.

A further factor undermining the legitimacy of both dictatorships was their subservience to the United States and their affronts to national pride. Because both countries had been occupied for years by the U.S. military early in the twentieth century and had subsequently remained in the American sphere of influence, this was a particularly sensitive issue. Nicaragua's hated National Guard was first headed by Anastasio Somoza, Sr., during the U.S. Marine occupation. Decades later, in the years preceding their revolution, Nicaraguans derisively referred to his son President Anastasio Somoza, Jr., a graduate of West Point, as "the last Marine." In both Cuba and Nicaragua, the combination of rampant corruption and injuries to nationalist sensibilities united people across class lines—from peasants to students to business people—against the government. Lacking any real commitment to the regime, Batista's undisciplined army offered surprisingly little resistance to Fidel Castro's rather small guerrilla force. In Nicaragua, the National Guardsmen, knowing that they faced popular retribution if they lost power, put up a stronger fight against the Sandinista revolutionaries but also fell relatively quickly.[23]

Revolutionary opportunities may also develop when the economy deteriorates, standards of living decline, and the government is unable to meet long-standing economic responsibilities to its population. For example, support for China's Guomindang government was eroded by runaway inflation. Declining living standards helped spark the Kenyan rebellion against British colonialism. Thus, maintains Charles Tilly, one cause of revolution is "the sudden failure of government to meet specific obligations which members of the subject population regarded as well established and crucial to their welfare."[24]

While Skocpol, Tilly, and others emphasize the decay of state authority at the *national* level, revolutions can also be linked to the breakdown of authority at the *grass-roots* level. We observed earlier (Chapter 6) that a web of patron-client relationships linking peasants to their landlords and other local power brokers helps maintain stability in the countryside. Peasants will tolerate considerable injustice if the local landlord or the village political boss compensates by providing villagers with needed benefits: secure access to land, credit, protection from the police, and the like. However, if the expansion of market forces makes rural patrons unwilling or unable to continue providing benefits that peasants had come to expect, then their authority will likely break down. At this point, the state may try to replace the traditional patrons by providing social services such as credit, technical assistance, schools, and clinics. If, however, government authorities also fail to satisfy the peasants' needs, the rural poor may turn to revolutionary groups as their new patrons and protectors.

Challenge from Below

While revolutionary movements generally succeed only against discredited or weakened governments, they must also mount a well-organized and politically coherent challenge from below. Without that, the old regime, weak though it may be, will either cling to power (the Third World has many incompetent and discredited governments that linger on) or the society may collapse into disorder or even anarchy.

Charles Tilly contends that three things must happen before a revolutionary movement can succeed: first, the revolutionaries must establish themselves as an "alternative sovereignty"; that is, the rebel leadership must convince its would-be supporters that it can function as a viable alternative government. Second, significant portions of the population must support that revolutionary alternative. Finally, the established government must be unable to suppress the revolutionary opposition.[25] For example, following the collapse of Russia's czarist regime, the Bolsheviks (Communist Party) established a network of workers' soviets (local political committees) to challenge the sovereignty of Alexander Kerensky's moderate provisional government. Asia's protracted guerrilla wars also illustrate the phenomenon of alternative sovereignties. During the Chinese Revolution, the People's Liberation Army (the Communist Party's military arm) controlled "liberated zones" in which the communists distributed land to the peasants, organized support, and demonstrated their ability to govern. The same was true of South Vietnam's National Liberation Front (Viet Cong).

Knowing these broad preconditions for successful revolutionary activity, we still must ask what causes a revolution to break out in a particular place and time? Samuel Huntington maintains that the probability of a successful insurrection is determined by the balance of power between the capabilities of government political institutions, on the one hand, and the level of antigovernment political and social mobilization, on the other. Most revolutions, he notes, occur neither in highly traditional societies nor in modern nations. Rather, they are most likely to erupt in modernizing countries—those in transition from traditional culture to modernity.[26] As greater urbanization, increased education and literacy, and expanded mass-media communication stimulate mass political mobilization, civil society (the network of organized groups independent of government control) makes increased demands on the political system. Unless the governing regime can create appropriate institutions capable of accommodating this increased political participation in a timely manner, the system will become overloaded and, hence, more unstable.

Huntington then distinguishes two distinct revolutionary patterns: a *Western* model in which "the political institutions of the old regime collapse followed by the mobilization of new groups into politics and then by the creation of new [revolutionary] political institutions" (i.e., regime decay precedes a full challenge from below); and an *Eastern* revolutionary model that "begins with the mobilization of new groups into politics and the creation of new [revolutionary] political institutions and ends with the violent overthrow of the political institutions of the old order." The French, Russian, and Mexican revolutions fit the Western model, while communist revolutions in China and Vietnam followed the Eastern model.[27]

James C. Davies shifts our attention from the broad historical-social forces that make revolution possible to the question of why particular individuals choose to join a revolt or a revolution. He asserts that, contrary to what we might expect, people rarely rebel when they are experiencing prolonged or permanent suffering. "Far from making people revolutionaries, enduring poverty makes for concern with one's solitary self or solitary family, at best a resignation, or mute despair at worst."[28] To uncover the source of political upheavals, Davies combines economic and psychological explanations. Unlike Marx, Skocpol, or Tilly, his analysis lumps together mass revolutions with local uprisings and military "revolutions from above." Drawing upon historical data ranging from Dorr's Rebellion (an 1842 uprising in Rhode Island) to the Egyptian military revolution of 1952, he concludes that each upheaval was preceded by a period of sustained economic growth followed by a sharp downturn. A diagram of that growth and subsequent downturn (Figure 8.1) produces what Davies called the "J-curve."[29] As a country's economy grows for a period of time, he suggests, people's expectations rise correspondingly (parallel to the long side of the J). However, those expectations continue to rise even after the economy enters a downturn. What emerges is "an intolerable gap between what people want and what they get."[30] Davies argues that the American and French revolutions, the American Civil War, the rise of German Naziism, student unrest in the United States during the 1960s, and the African American civil rights movement can all be explained by economic J-curves as well.[31]

Using twentieth-century data from 17 LDCs, Raymond Tanter and Manus Midlarsky confirmed Davies's thesis in Asia and the Middle East but not in

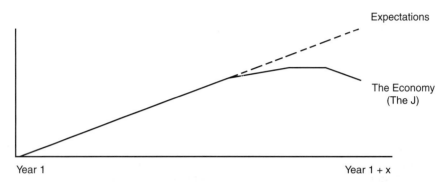

FIGURE 8.1   Davies's Psychological Model Showing the Gap Between People's Expectations and Economic Reality

Latin America. Interestingly, their Asian and Middle Eastern cases also indicated that the higher the rate of economic growth prior to a downturn and the sharper the slide immediately preceding a revolution, the longer and more violent the upheaval will be.[32]

Davies's theory is one of the most influential, psychologically based explanations of revolutionary behavior. There is, however, an important limitation to his findings. His conclusions were based entirely on countries in which revolts or revolutions had taken place. That raises the question of whether there are countries that experienced a J-curve in their economies (growth followed by a downturn) yet did not have social upheavals. In fact, Davies admits that there are. For example, he notes the absence of mass unrest in the United States during the Great Depression, a devastating economic downturn. The same holds true for many Latin American countries that enjoyed strong economic growth in the 1960s and 1970s followed by a precipitous decline in the 1980s. Argentina had a comparable cycle in the 1990s to 2001. Thus, as Davies concedes, his theory identifies common but not sufficient conditions for unrest. Although a J-curve often leads to revolution, it does not necessarily do so.

Ted Gurr has also developed a psychological model examining the gap between expectations and reality. Like Davies, he examines various types of civil violence, not just revolution. Gurr argues that "the necessary precondition for violent civil conflict is relative deprivation defined as [the] actors' perception of the discrepancy between their value expectations [i.e., what people believe they deserve from life] and value capabilities ... conditions that determine people's perceived chances of getting ... what they ... expect to attain."[33] In other words, *relative deprivation* is the gap between what people want or expect from life and what they actually get.

Unlike Davies's theory, however, Gurr's notion of relative deprivation is not solely economic. Thus, he posits that there is a high probability of civil unrest if many people are deprived of some benefit they have come to expect, or if they have suffered a blow to their status and their preferred social order. For example, although Westerners admired the Shah of Iran's attempts to modernize the dress and status of Iranian women (removing the veil), many of these changes violated the "preferred social order" of the nation's Shi'ite majority. This, as we have seen, helped set the stage for the Islamist revolution. Furthermore, adds Gurr, the closer people are to attaining their goals, the greater will be their frustration if they fail to achieve them. Note, for example, the growing radicalization of Palestinians as the once-promising peace process between Israelis and the PLO seemed to break down, and with it their dreams of a Palestinian state.

Finally, Gurr maintains that the type of civil violence that a country experiences will depend on which segments of society are experiencing relative deprivation. If the poor alone feel frustrated, there may be political "turmoil" (spontaneous, disorganized violence) but not a revolution. Only if important portions of the middle class and the elite—more educated and politically experienced individuals who can provide political leadership—also suffer relative deprivation can there be revolutionary upheaval (organized, instrumental violence).

Causes of Revolution: A Summary

None of these theories of revolution offers a single "correct" explanation. For one thing, they often focus on different aspects of the question. For example, while Gurr and Davies ask why individuals join revolts or revolutionary movements, Skocpol focuses on the international economic and military factors that have weakened the state prior to successful revolutionary insurrections.

Clearly, revolutions are never inevitable and, in fact, successful revolutions are rare. While the causes of unrest may lie in relative deprivation and the regime's loss of legitimacy, the ultimate success or failure of revolutionary movements also depends on the relative military and political capabilities of the contending forces. Only by comparing the political-military strength of those who rebel with the state's capacity to defend itself can we understand why some revolutionary movements succeed while others fail.

As we have seen, revolutions often occur after a country has been defeated or badly weakened in war (Russia, China, Turkey, and Egypt) or after its government has been ousted temporarily (Europe's colonial regimes in Asia during World War II). They may also take place when a government is particularly corrupt (Cuba and Nicaragua) or subservient to foreign powers (China, Mexico, and Nicaragua). In all of these cases, the incumbent regime lost its legitimacy. Thus, the Russian czarist and Chinese Guomindang governments both fell when they proved incapable of defending their people's sovereignty. Similarly, Cuba's President Batista lost his legitimacy when he turned Havana into "the brothel of the Caribbean." So too did the Shah after his Westernization program offended Iran's Islamic mullahs. British, French, and Dutch colonial rule in Asia was secure as long as the indigenous population believed that Europeans were more powerful than they were and also better equipped to govern. When the Japanese ousted the colonial governments of Burma, Malaysia, Vietnam, and Indonesia, they demonstrated that Asians could defeat Europeans militarily. Once the European powers lost their aura of invincibility, they were unable to reestablish colonial rule after World War II.

Finally, the very authoritarianism of many Third World governments may ultimately undermine them. Cuba's Fulgencio Batista, the Shah of Iran, and Nicaragua's Anastasio Somoza, Jr., illustrate that point. Because their governments had never been legitimized through free and honest elections, they could not convincingly claim to represent the people. Ignoring that problem during

the Cold War, the United States frequently supported authoritarian governments in countries such as El Salvador, Nicaragua, Chile, Zaire (Congo), South
Korea, Iran, and Pakistan. Responding to criticisms by human rights groups,
Washington argued that, whatever their faults, these repressive governments
were the last remaining fire walls against communist subversion and the rise of
totalitarianism. In truth, however, a democratic government offers the best
inoculation against revolution. Indeed, no consolidated democracy has ever
been toppled by a revolution.[34]

LEVELS OF POPULAR SUPPORT

Ché Guevara, the leading military strategist of the Cuban Revolution, once
observed that those who undertake revolutions either win or die. Though perhaps overstating his point, Guevara's remark highlights the tremendous risk
revolutionary fighters take, be they poor peasants or radicalized university students. Rebels almost always face superior fire power and a range of repressive
state institutions (the police, the military, special intelligence units, etc.). Not
surprisingly, most of the time the insurgents lose. One study counted 28 guerrilla movements in Latin America from 1956 to 1990. Of them, only two succeeded (Cuba's July 26th movement and Nicaragua's Sandinistas).[35] Asia and
Africa are also littered with the corpses of dead revolutionaries and failed
insurgencies. Even victorious revolutions, such as Vietnam's and China's, leave
behind vast numbers of fallen rebel fighters and supporters. Those who survive
often return home to devastated villages and suffering families. Not surprisingly, then, individual peasants, workers, students, and professionals do not
take lightly the decision to join a revolutionary force.

What portion of the population must support a revolution if it is to succeed? What types of people are most likely to join the movement? The answer
to the first question is ambiguous. There is no fixed or knowable percentage of
the population that must support an insurrection in order for it to triumph.
Following World War II, a majority of Ukrainians probably favored a separatist
movement fighting Soviet control, yet that uprising was crushed anyway by the
powerful Soviet army. On the other hand, insurgencies elsewhere have succeeded with the active support of less than 20 percent of the civilian population.

Any evaluation of popular sentiment during a revolutionary upheaval
needs to identify at least five different groups: first, there are those who
strongly support the government and believe that their own fates are linked to
the regime's survival. Government officials, military officers, land owners, and
businesspeople with close links to the state normally fall in this category. It may
also include ethnic groups tied to the regime (such as the Hmong people of
Laos), people ideologically committed to the political system, and an assortment of others with a vested interest in preserving the status quo.

A second group in society also supports the government but more condi-
tionally. For example, during the 1960s, most Venezuelans supported the government's battle against Marxist guerrillas. Even though many of them shared
the guerrillas' disapproval of Venezuela's severe inequalities, sprawling urban
shantytowns, and rural poverty, they were repelled by the rebels' use of violence
and their failure to work within the country's recently achieved democratic
framework.[36] Because the government's public support was broad but thin

(i.e., many Venezuelans were conditional supporters), it could easily have lost its advantage had it used the repressive anti-guerrilla tactics so widely employed elsewhere in Latin America.

A third, often critical, segment of the population supports neither the revolutionaries nor the government. Its members are generally alienated and probably dislike both sides. In the 1980s and 1990s, many Peruvian Indian peasant communities were victimized by the *Sendero Luminoso* (Shining Path) guerrillas, an extremely fanatical and brutal, revolutionary Marxist movement. At the same time, these villagers were often also brutalized by the Peruvian army, which flagrantly violated the peasants' human rights. Not surprisingly, most peasants feared and hated both sides. Caught in the middle, for their own preservation they avoided taking sides, though some did join government-supported defense militias.

A fourth group—drawn primarily from the peasantry, workers, urban poor, and alienated members of the middle class who sympathize with the revolutionary cause—occasionally lends support to the insurgents but do not actually join them. For example, sympathetic peasants in China, Cuba, and Vietnam offered intelligence information, food, and shelter to rebel guerrillas. In countries such as China and El Salvador, where the guerrillas controlled "liberated zones" for long periods of time, these support networks were very extensive. In other countries where the revolution was fought primarily through urban street protests rather than guerrilla war (Iran) and in revolutions with important urban and rural components (Mexico, Nicaragua), revolutionaries depended on the sympathy and occasional support of the urban poor, workers, and the middle class.

Finally, there is a relatively small portion of the population that fully involves itself in the revolutionary struggle. In Cuba, Mexico, and Nicaragua, for example, committed students, teachers, and professionals assumed leadership positions. In those countries, as well as in China, Vietnam, and El Salvador, many peasants (including women and teenagers) become the revolution's foot soldiers. Given the enormous risks involved for the participants and their families, it is not surprising that only a small portion of the people took up arms. Some peasants joined out of desperation, because their village had been destroyed by the armed forces or because they feared being drafted into an army they despised. Others were attracted by the revolutionaries' promises of a more just social order.

One can only guess the proportion of a country's population in each of these five groups at a particular point in time. Public opinion surveys in countries that are divided between warring factions are unlikely to elicit honest responses. But we do know that if they are to succeed, revolutionary movements must attract a core of firmly committed activists willing to risk their lives for the cause, as well as a larger circle of sympathizers. How large their numbers must be depends on the extent of government decay and loss of legitimacy. It also depends on how well-armed and committed government troops are, how effectively those troops fight, and how much foreign support they have. Thus, for example, Fidel Castro's small rural force of only a few hundred troops (supported by a comparable number of urban guerrillas) defeated Batista's much larger but dispirited army. On the other hand, El Salvador's FMLN—a far larger and better-equipped guerrilla army—could not unseat a government that was bolstered by extensive American economic and military aid. Yet even the United States' commitment of massive military assistance and hundreds of thousands of American troops could not save the South Vietnamese government from the Viet Cong and its North Vietnamese allies.

The people in the second category (mild government supporters) and the third (neutrals) are equally important targets for any revolutionary movement. In developing countries with substantial urban populations, governments can maintain power in the face of considerable peasant unrest and rural guerrilla activity as long as they control the cities and retain the support of the urban middle class, particularly civil servants, businesspeople, and professionals. These middle-class groups are not normally radical, but they can become disenchanted with particularly corrupt, repressive, or ineffectual regimes. In Iran, the tide turned in favor of the revolutionary mullahs when Tehran's bazaar shopkeepers lost confidence in the Shah's government.

Nicaragua's revolution also illustrates this point. Because the Somoza family had expropriated such a large share of the national economy, its greed not only damaged the poor but hurt the business community as well. As the Sandinista uprising spread and the National Guard became increasingly repressive, Nicaragua's private sector grew increasingly alienated from the government. Prominent business leaders—including the head of the country's Coca-Cola bottling plant, the nation's most prominent newspaper owner, and the directors of several important banks—demanded Anastasio Somoza, Jr.'s, resignation and organized business shutdowns to express their opposition. While most of these people were wary of the Sandinista movement (which made no secret of its leftist ideology), they shared its desire to oust the Somoza regime.[37]

While flying from Panama to Miami during the height of the insurrection, this author found himself seated next to the chief executive of an important Nicaraguan agrochemical plant. In the course of our conversation about events back home, he declared, "Somoza has to go. He's too damned corrupt and he's wrecking the country." "But what if reformist business leaders such as yourself have to share power with the [Marxist-oriented] Sandinistas after he falls?" I asked.[38] "I don't like those guys," he replied, "but if sharing power with them is what it takes to get rid of Somoza, then we'll have to do it." In the face of such broad ideological and cross-class opposition to the government, it was just a matter of time before the Somoza regime fell.

In short, if a revolutionary movement is to gain power, there must be wide-scale disaffection with the government, a disaffection that reaches beyond the ranks of the poor and the oppressed to the heart of the middle class and the business community. It is neither likely nor necessary for a large portion of those sectors to actively support the insurrection. For the revolution to succeed, it is only essential that some of them, including a highly committed core, do so, while many others, like the Nicaraguan business executive on the plane, simply cease supporting the government.

PEASANTS AS REVOLUTIONARIES

Let us now turn our attention to the ranks of committed revolutionary supporters, particularly the last group, revolutionary activists. With rare exception, Third World revolutions have been fought primarily by peasants. The Chinese Red Army and the Viet Cong, for example, consisted overwhelmingly of the rural poor. Indeed, almost all African and Asian revolutionary movements have been overwhelmingly rural in character. And even in Latin America's revolutions, where the urban populations often played key roles, peasants were also very important. Consequently, it is important to ask, "What factors induce peasants to risk joining a revolution, and what types of peasants join?"

Why Peasants Rebel

In our analysis of Third World rural society (see Chapter 6), we noted that traditional peasant culture tends to be rather conservative. Since early economic modernization frequently affects them negatively, they have good reason to cling to tradition. But the intrusion of market forces into their communities sometimes so unsettles their world that it radicalizes them as they struggle to protect what they have. For one things, increasing numbers of subsistence farmers (peasants producing primarily for their family's consumption) in a modernizing economy are induced or pressured to enter the commercial market for the first time. Once involved in commercial agriculture, however, they must deal with fluctuations in the price of their crops, including volatile shifts that they are ill-equipped to handle.

At the same time, rural landlords, whose precapitalist exploitation of local peasants had been somewhat constrained by their neofeudal obligations, now viewed their tenants merely as factors of production in the new market economy. In Latin America, many landlords who had previously funded their peons' *fiestas* or lent them money when they were ill, concluded that such expenditures were no longer financially prudent in the more competitive market environment. Other landlords entering the commercial market decided to mechanize production and evict tenant farmers from their land.

For all of these reasons, rural society's transition from neofeudal to capitalist production precipitated many of the twentieth century's Third World revolutions.[39] James Scott notes that the pain peasants suffered during that transformation was not merely economic or physical but also a *moral pain*. To be sure, the precapitalist rural order had its share of grave injustices, but those inequities were somewhat mitigated by a web of reciprocal obligations between landlords and peasants and among peasants. It is the collapse of that "moral economy," Scott argues, that drives many peasants to revolution.[40] Similarly, as noted in Chapter 6, Eric Wolf insists that in countries as disparate as Cuba, Mexico, Algeria, Vietnam, and China, most peasant participants in revolutionary movements were not trying to create a new socialist order. Rather, they were seeking to restore the security of their old way of life.

Which Peasants Rebel

Even in a single country or region, peasants are not a homogeneous mass. Some of them, called *kulaks*, own larger plots of land and employ other peasants to work their farms with them. Others are landless or own extremely small plots. And still others work as wage laborers on large estates or rent parcels of land from the landlord, paying their rent in cash, labor, or sharecropping.[41] Each group has distinct political and economic needs.

Those peasants most threatened by the economic modernization of the countryside are the ones most likely to join local revolts or broader revolutionary movements. Analyzing data collected from 70 developing nations over a 22-year period, Jeffrey M. Paige found that the peasant groups most likely to join insurgencies are wage laborers and sharecroppers who work for landlords who, in turn, lack financial resources outside of their land.[42] Not only are these peasants particularly vulnerable to changing economic conditions, but their landlords are also less likely to grant them financial concessions because they depend exclusively on their farmland for their incomes. Research on Latin American guerrilla movements reveals that squatters (poor farmers illegally occupying land) and other peasants who face eviction from the land they cultivate are also more prone to rebel.[43]

But even peasants with more secure access to the land feel threatened by declining crop prices. For example, in Peru's Ayacucho province, the birthplace of the Shining Path guerrilla movement, peasants experienced declining terms of trade for two decades; that is, the cost of the goods they consumed had been rising faster than the price of the crops that they sold. Caught in an ongoing financial squeeze, they felt increasingly insecure and, hence, became more receptive to the Shining Path's appeals.[44]

All of the peasants who are prone to support revolutions, then, have one element in common—they are threatened by the prospect of losing their land and/or their livelihood. Conversely, the most conservative peasants are those with secure title to their land holdings and relatively stable prices for their crops. It is for this reason that many analysts maintain that the best protection against rural revolution is an agrarian reform program that distributes land, secure titles, and support services to the peasantry.

Peasant insurrections are also more likely to develop in areas that previously had historical traditions of rebellion. For example, the revolutionary forces in China, Vietnam, Cuba, Mexico, and Nicaragua all received their greatest support in regions that had traditions of peasant resistance, what one author calls a "rebellious culture."[45] Fidel Castro's home province of Oriente, known as "the cradle of the Cuban Revolution," had a long history of unrest dating back to nineteenth-century slave revolts against their owners and against Spanish colonial rule. China's Hunan province (Mao Zedong's home) and the area around the Sandinista stronghold of León also had rebellious traditions. Some revolutionary movements take root in areas without a record of prior rebellions but with a tradition of lawlessness and hostility toward the legal authorities. For example, Mexican revolutionary leader Pancho Villa operated in a region known for cattle rustling and other forms of social banditry. And Villa himself was a bandit turned revolutionary. Similarly, Castro's July 26 guerrillas based themselves in the Sierra Maestra mountains, a region with a history of smuggling, marijuana production, and banditry.

REVOLUTIONARY LEADERSHIP

Although peasants furnish the foot soldiers for revolutions, they rarely provide their highest leaders. They may stage spontaneous uprisings or even more extensive revolts on their own, but they usually lack the organizational and political skills needed to conduct a broader social revolution. Consequently, both upper- and mid-level revolutionary leaders are typically people with more education and greater political experience. To be sure, there are exceptions. Mexico's Emiliano Zapata was a horse trainer from a peasant family who only became literate as an adult.[46] Pancho Villa was also of humble origins. More recently, the Colombian Revolutionary Armed Forces (FARC) guerrillas in Colombia have largely been led by peasants.[47] Ultimately, however, their lack of political experience usually proves costly. For example, Villa and Zapata jointly conquered Mexico City, the nation's capital, but then left it because neither man was equipped to run the country.

More typically, then, the top revolutionary leadership comes from middle-class or even upper-class origins. In Latin America, for example, "they are drawn disproportionately from the intelligentsia, not only highly educated, but also largely involved in the production of theories."[48] Trained as a librarian, China's Mao Zedong was the son of a rural grain merchant. In Vietnam, Ho Chi Minh, the son of a rural school teacher, practiced a number of professions, including photography, while living in Paris and becoming a French Communist Party activist. Fidel Castro received a law degree at the University of Havana, where he was a leader in student politics. His father, a Spanish immigrant, had started life in Cuba as a worker, but eventually became a well-to-do land owner. Castro's comrade, Ché Guevara, was a doctor whose mother came from an aristocratic Argentine family and whose father was an architect. Similarly, most of the nine *comandantes* who directed Nicaragua's Sandinista revolution came from solid middle- or upper-class families and were well educated. For example, President Daniel Ortega and his brother, Defense Minister Humberto Ortega, were the sons of an accountant-businessman. Luis Carrión, the son of a millionaire, had attended an American prep school. Only one *comandante*, Henry Ruiz, came from a poor urban family, and none were of peasant origin.[49] Finally, a Vietnamese Communist Party study of nearly 2,000 party activists (conducted after World War II, at the start of their long revolutionary struggle) revealed that 74 percent of them were either intellectuals or were from bourgeois families, while only 7 percent were workers, and 19 percent came from peasant families.[50] These are noteworthy statistics for a party trying to speak for the country's peasantry and working class.

Not surprisingly, a larger number of lower-ranking revolutionary leaders are of peasant or working class background. The rural poor have been most broadly represented at all leadership levels in Asian nations such as China, Vietnam, and Kampuchea, where they account for most of the country's population. Both during their two-decade revolutionary struggle and once in power, the Chinese Communist Party and the Red Army provided peasant activists with unprecedented opportunities for upward mobility. Virtually from the date of its formation, the party offered peasants and children of peasants—heretofore at the bottom of the social ladder—preference for admission. And as late as 1985, decades after the communists took power, one-third of all Communist Party members were peasants (some 25 percent of whom were illiterate).[51] Similarly, many of the lower- and middle-level guerrilla leaders in El Salvador and Peru were of peasant origin, although they had often left their villages to become teachers, health workers, or the like.

The educational and social gap separating aspiring revolutionary leaders and the peasant rank-and-file can be a considerable problem unless the leaders have a firm understanding of the local culture. Although Mao Zedong became an urban intellectual, his rural upbringing had given him an understanding of village life. Fidel Castro was certainly no peasant, but his childhood on his father's farm had familiarized him with the region's rural poor. And in Venezuela, several of the FALN commanders were sons of local landlords who traded on their father's patron-client ties to the local peasants.[52]

On the other hand, aspiring guerrilla activists who come to the countryside from the city, or from other regions of the country, other countries, or other ethnic backgrounds are often rejected by the rural poor. Given their history of exploitation, peasants tend to be understandably wary of outsiders. The wider the linguistic, cultural, or racial gaps between would-be revolutionary leaders and the local villagers, and the greater the peasants' prior suspicion of outsiders, the harder it is for organizers to break through that wall of distrust. In Cuba, where racial and ethnic divisions were relatively less severe, Ché Guevara—a White, urban, middle-class Argentinian—was accepted by the peasants of the Sierra Maestra. So when he later ventured to Bolivia to spread the revolution, Guevara may have been ill-prepared for the substantial mistrust its Aymara Indian peasants felt toward White outsiders such as him. There he was killed by an anti-guerrilla unit of the Bolivian armed forces, which was aided by the CIA and by local villagers who saw no reason to risk their safety for an outside agitator. Similarly, Hector Béjar, a failed Peruvian guerrilla leader, later wrote candidly in his memoirs about how he—a coastal, White journalist and poet—was unable to gain the trust of the highland Indians whom he had hoped to lead.[53]

REVOLUTIONARIES IN POWER

While many comparative studies have examined the causes of revolution, there is less cross-national research on the *policies* revolutionary regimes implement once in office. Perhaps guerrilla fighters in the hills have inspired more interest and romanticization (or fear) than have revolutionary bureaucrats in the corridors of power. The record suggests that Third World revolutions in the developing world have accomplished more than their detractors admit but less than their supporters claim.

A primary objective of Marxist and many non-Marxist revolutionary governments alike has been greater socioeconomic and political equality. That quest usually begins with the struggle for power itself, when revolutionary leaders use egalitarian appeals to garner support from downtrodden peasants and workers. Recognizing the critical importance of that support, Mao Zedong wrote that the peasantry is to the guerrilla army what water is to fish. To win their loyalty, the Red Army treated China's peasants with greater respect than had other military forces or governments.[54] Similarly, in Cuba, "the army's brutal treatment of the peasants" contrasted with "Castro's policy of paying for the food purchased from the peasants ... and putting his [mostly urban] men to work in the ... fields."[55]

Once in power, revolutionary governments continue to emphasize equality. In addition to redistributing land and other economic resources, they introduce egalitarian cultural reforms as well. For example, at meetings of Cuba's

Committees for the Defense of the Revolution (CDRs), men may be pressured to share household tasks with their spouses. Efforts at economic and social egalitarianism have been more limited in non-Marxist revolutions. Still, insurgencies such as Bolivia's and Mexico's have somewhat improved the social status of their rural populations, including indigenous peoples.

As we have seen, revolutions open up new channels of upward social mobility for peasants and workers who previously had few such opportunities. To be sure, most of the higher government and party posts are generally held by people from middle-class backgrounds. Nor do many party members from ethnic minorities hold the most powerful political positions. Thus, for example, there have been relatively few Blacks in Cuba's Communist Party politburo or ethnic minorities in China's. But many revolutionary activists from humble backgrounds *do* hold lower- and mid-level political positions that they could never have attained under the old order. Revolutionary parties and mass organizations such as Cuba's CDRs may give peasants and workers a greater sense of participation in the political system.

Finally, revolutions usually decrease their nation's level of economic inequality, though the degree of change varies from country to country. Agrarian reform programs in China, Vietnam, Bolivia, Cuba, Mexico, and Nicaragua redistributed land from the rural oligarchy to the peasantry.[56] Many Marxist regimes provided guaranteed employment, state-supported medical care, subsidized housing and food, and other egalitarian measures, while at the same time establishing more equitable income distribution than in other LDCs at comparable stages of economic development. On the other hand, more moderate revolutions in Bolivia and Mexico failed to reduce economic inequality.

To be sure, notable inequalities persist even in radical revolutionary societies. Disparities between rural and urban populations may be reduced but not eliminated. As China implements free-market reforms, income inequality has increased dramatically. In Cuba and Vietnam, professionals and skilled workers still earn much higher salaries than do peasants or unskilled blue-collar workers, even though that gap has narrowed. At the same time, a new form of inequality often seeps in, as newly entrenched party and government officials begin to appropriate special perquisites for themselves and their families. Many years ago, Milovan Djilas, a disillusioned former leader of Yugoslavia's communist government, complained about the rise of a "new class" in revolutionary regimes, an elite of party officials who enjoy special privileges and a better standard of living.[57] Today in China, the foremost Communist Party leaders are well known for their lavish lifestyles, while the children of the party cadre are despised for their arrogance and corruption. Despite these problems, however, revolutionary governments such as Cuba's and Vietnam's have reduced the general level of social inequality.

Another major revolutionary objective has been mass political mobilization. As Samuel Huntington notes, "a full-scale revolution involves the rapid and violent destruction of existing political institutions, the mobilization of new groups into politics, and the creation of new political institutions."[58] Thus, in China, Vietnam, Cuba, and Nicaragua, government incentives and pressures induced a large portion of the population to join revolutionary support groups.[59] At one time, close to 90 percent of Cuban adults belonged to their neighborhood Committees for the Defense of the Revolution (CDRs). In the

1980s, substantial portions of the Nicaraguan population joined Sandinista Defense Committees (CDSs).

At its best, mass political mobilization has increased the government's capacity to build the economy by mobilizing volunteer labor or spreading labor discipline. At times, revolutionary support groups have also helped combat sexism, racism, and criminality. At worst, these groups have been used as vigilantes against alleged counterrevolutionaries and as agents of thought control. At CDR meetings, members are familiarized with the current government political position, encouraged to volunteer for projects such as planting neighborhood gardens, and imbued with greater revolutionary consciousness.[60] But in Mao Zedong's China, mass mobilization often involved brutal political campaigns that called upon citizens to root out and punish alleged enemies of the revolution. Hundreds of thousands were persecuted, jailed, or killed during the government's Anti-Rightist Campaign (1957) and its Cultural Revolution (1966–1976).[61]

Mass mobilization can be used either to activate citizens who support the revolution's goals or to isolate and persecute those who do not. Most revolutionary regimes are led by a dominant party, such as the Chinese Communist Party or the Mexican PRI, which stands at the center of the mobilization process. Opposition parties are either prohibited or are only tolerated in a weakened condition. Among Marxist governments, only Nicaragua's Sandinistas allowed themselves to be voted out of office. Elsewhere, a number of non-Marxist revolutionary parties have lost favor over time. They may resort to fraud when faced with the prospect of losing (Mexico until 2000), cancel elections that the opposition is expected to win (Algeria), or hand over the reins of power and become just another competing party (Bolivia and, very recently, Mexico).

In short, while revolutionary regimes claim to speak for the people and often do in many respects, we have noted that they are hardly ever democratic. Because they view themselves as the *only* legitimate voice of the popular will and the *only* representatives of the general good, most radical regimes tend to regard opposition groups as enemies of the people who should not be afforded political space. Nicaragua's Sandinista government, a rare exception, allowed opposition parties and interest groups to function, though they were occasionally harassed. Although the opposition newspaper, *La Prensa*, was periodically censored or briefly shut down, it continued to vigorously, and sometimes outrageously, attack the government right up to the time its publisher, Violeta Chamorro, was elected the nation's president. For the most part, however, even communist governments that have opened up their economies to free-market reforms (China and Vietnam) have maintained their repressive political structure and remained intolerant of opposition voices.

While the first generation of revolutionary leaders often comes to power full of idealism, either its own members or the generation that succeeds it generally succumbs in some way to the corruptions of power. In Vietnam and China—where the large private sector still depends on the government for licenses, raw materials, and the like—bribing the right state official is often a requirement for doing business.[62] Cubans, who once felt that their revolutionary officials had a higher standard of honesty than preceding governments, were shocked by the "Ochoa affair," which revealed that high-ranking military and security officers were involved in the drug trade. Government corruption on a lesser scale has since become far more pervasive as a result of the severe economic scarcities of the 1990s. And after the Sandinistas left office, disillusioned Nicaraguans learned that top party officials had kept for themselves some of the luxurious mansions that had been confiscated from the Somoza regime. It is not that these revolutionary regimes are more corrupt than other Third World governments; often they are less so. It is just that some of their followers, many of whom made considerable sacrifices for their cause, had expected more.

CONCLUSION: REVOLUTIONARY CHANGE AND DEMOCRACY

Throughout the twentieth century, revolutionary change was an important force in much of the Third World. That influence was most pronounced in Asia, where the Chinese Revolution transformed the lives of one-fifth of humanity and where revolutionary conflicts in Vietnam, Laos, and Cambodia involved France and then the United States in major wars. Elsewhere in Asia, failed communist insurgencies affected the Philippines and Malaysia. Most of Africa's revolutions have been wars of national liberation from European colonialism (Algeria, Kenya, and Namibia, among others) or secessionist wars (including Biafra, Eritrea, and southern Sudan). Class-related revolutions in Africa (such as Ethiopia's) were generally initiated from above by military officers. Latin America had two non-Marxist insurrections (Bolivia and Mexico), two Marxist revolutions (Cuba and Nicaragua), and a number of unsuccessful revolutionary movements (Argentina, Colombia, El Salvador, Guatemala, Peru, Uruguay, and Venezuela). Both the revolutions and the failed insurgencies had spillover effects in neighboring countries. For example, the Cuban Revolution spawned various agrarian reform programs elsewhere in Latin America, most designed to avert "another Cuba." The Nicaraguan Revolution inspired both agrarian reform and intensified government repression in neighboring El Salvador. However, today the appeal of revolution, particularly Marxist revolution, has waned considerably. Indeed, today's world is a veritable graveyard of failed insurrections. The Soviet Union, once the fountainhead of communism, lies in ruins, and its most important successor state, Russia, struggles to overcome the errors of its Marxist-Leninist past. Communism is equally discredited in Eastern and Central Europe, where it held sway until recently. Cuba's government, like Nicaragua's before it, has seen its impressive initial gains in education, health care, and social equality eroded by its deteriorating economy. And in many other recently fallen or still-surviving Marxist and neo-Marxist revolutions, the scorecard of successes and failures is far more disheartening. Countries such as Afghanistan, Angola, Cambodia, Ethiopia, Mozambique, and Myanmar have suffered enormous devastation with little or nothing to show for it.

Evaluating the quality of revolutionary change in the more successful revolutions is not easy, for it is influenced by the analyst's ideological lens and by the difficulty of isolating the effects of revolutionary policy from a host of other overlapping factors. For example, critics of the Chinese Revolution argue that the socioeconomic gains attained under Mao were achieved in spite of his radical policies, not because of them. They further insist that the country's rapid economic growth under Deng Xiaoping demonstrates the advantages of free-market reforms. Others maintain that Cuba's substantial progress in health care and education since its revolution has been no more substantial than Costa Rica's and was accomplished in part because of massive Soviet aid until the end of the 1980s.

On the other hand, more sympathetic observers note that Cuba achieved impressive educational and welfare progress in the face of the U.S. economic embargo, and that the American-backed Contra war (coupled with a trade embargo) destroyed the Nicaraguan revolution's earlier economic and social accomplishments. China's market-based economic boom, others insist, could never have been achieved without the educational advances produced under revolutionary socialism. Neither side can definitively prove its position because too many potentially determining factors make it impossible to establish clear causal relationships.

In any event, it is likely that the age of revolution is drawing to an end in the Third World. The demise of Soviet and Central European communism exposed more clearly the deficiencies of Marxism-Leninism. So too have China's and Vietnam's introduction of free-market (capitalist) components into their economic systems.[63] As communism has been discredited even among some of its once-fervent supporters, it is unlikely to find adherents willing to risk their lives fighting for its ideals. Marxist ideology, once chic among Third World intellectuals and political activists, has become far less fashionable.[64] At the end of the 1980s, facing defeat by its mujahadeen opponents, Afghanistan's People's Democratic Party renounced its Marxist ideology in a failed effort to maintain power. One of its leaders dismissed the party's long-standing communist stance by claiming that it had been adopted at "a time when Marxism-Leninism was quite in fashion in underdeveloped countries." In Angola, where the governing party made a similar ideological conversion, the president explained that continuing to support the Marxist-Leninist model "would be rowing against the tide [of capitalist democracy]."[65] Similar transformations have occurred within Nicaragua's Sandinista party and El Salvador's FMLN, both former revolutionary movements that subsequently transformed themselves into democratic socialist political parties. In his 2001 campaign for the presidency, Sandinista leader Daniel Ortega insisted that Jesus Christ, not Marx, was his first inspiration when he led the country's revolution more than 20 years earlier. Modifying his earlier leftist views, he declared that "in this new context, to which we had to adjust, the market economy plays its role."[66]

How many revolutionary upheavals will take place in the coming years is hard to predict, and the answer may be partly an issue of semantics (that is, how we choose to define a revolution). However, now that colonialism has come to an end in Africa and Asia, there are few possibilities for wars of national liberation as we have known them. There still may be other mass-based revolutions in societies that suffer from severe socioeconomic inequalities, sharp rural-urban divisions, or repressive governments. However, as we have noted, the collapse of the Soviet bloc, the abandonment of Marxist economics in China and Vietnam, the failure of the Nicaraguan revolutionary government, and Cuba's current economic crisis have all substantially diminished the appeal of revolutionary Marxism. Thus, El Salvador's FMLN guerrillas ended their 12-year struggle, signed a peace treaty that promised some of the reforms that they had long fought for, and converted themselves into one of the leading political parties in the congress. Marxist guerrilla groups continue to battle in Colombia (where their considerable income from cocaine trafficking, kidnapping, and extortion help make them a formidable military force), Nepal, and a few other places. But their prospects are quite uncertain.

Future insurgencies are most likely to occur in Africa, the Middle East, and parts of Asia. Conceivably, there also will be scattered uprisings by indigenous peoples (Indians) in Latin America, as there already have been in Bolivia, Ecuador, and Peru. Fundamentalist Islamic upheavals are certainly possible in some of these regions. Whether these struggles can properly be called revolutions, however, is debatable. They satisfy neither Huntington's nor Skocpol's definitions. Hence, it is probably more accurate to call them civil wars, secessionist rebellions, religious uprisings, or ethnic conflicts rather than revolutions. Successful revolutions, in the sense that Skocpol or even Huntington defines them, appear unlikely in the foreseeable future.

DISCUSSION QUESTIONS

1. What are some of the major factors that have led to the collapse of state power and the rise of revolutions?
2. What factors account for the declining likelihood of further Third World revolutions?
3. Discuss some of the psychological theories of revolution (i.e., the theories of James C. Davies or Ted Robert Gurr).
4. What segments of the population are more likely to support revolutionary movements, and how much support do such movements need in order to succeed?
5. Discuss some of the major accomplishments and failures of revolutionary governments.

NOTES

1. China's Leninist regime remains in place, but the principles of Marxist economics and class politics have been abandoned.

2. In Angola and Mozambique, most of the killing was carried out by counterrevolutionary forces. For the hundreds of thousands of innocent civilians butchered, however, it mattered little which side killed them.

3. One classical study of historical change argues that the American War of Independence was not a revolution. See Barrington Moore Jr., *The Social Origins of Dictatorship and Democracy* (Boston: Beacon Press, 1966), 112. For a contrary view, see J. Franklin Jameson, *The American Revolution Considered as a Social Movement* (Boston: Beacon Press, 1956), 16–20, 32–35.

4. Chalmers Johnson, *Revolution and the Social System* (Stanford, CA: Hoover Institution, 1964), 2.

5. Peter Calvert, "Revolution: The Politics of Violence," *Political Studies* 15, no. 1 (1967): 2; and

Revolution and Counter Revolution (Minneapolis: University of Minnesota Press, 1990).

6. Samuel P. Huntington, *Political Order in Changing Societies* (New Haven, CT: Yale University Press, 1968), 264. A similar definition was offered decades earlier in Sigmund Neumann, "The International Civil War," *World Politics* 1, no. 3 (April 1949): 333–334, fn. 1.

7. Norman R. Miller and Roderick R. Aya, *National Liberation: Revolution in the Third World* (New York: Free Press, 1971).

8. Theda Skocpol, "France, Russia, China: A Structural Analysis of Social Revolutions," *Comparative Studies in Society and History* 18, no. 2 (1976): 176.

9. Theda Skocpol, *States and Social Revolutions: A Comparative Analysis of France, Russia and China* (Cambridge, England: Cambridge University Press, 1979), 4.

10. John Walton distinguishes between the handful of "great revolutions" that satisfy Skocpol's definition and a larger number of "national revolts" that are based on class and nationality and that he feels are not particularly distinguishable from social revolutions. John Walton, *Reluctant Rebels* (New York: Columbia University Press, 1984), 1–36.

11. Ellen Kay Trimberger, "A Theory of Elite Revolutions," *Studies in Comparative International Development* 7, no. 3 (1972): 191–207; Ellen Kay Trimberger, *Revolution from Above: Military Bureaucrats and Development in Japan, Turkey, Egypt and Peru* (New Brunswick, NJ: Transaction Books, 1978).

12. Karl Marx and Frederick Engels, *Manifesto of the Communist Party* (New York: International Publishers, 1948).

13. A. S. Cohan, *Theories of Revolution* (London: Thomas Nelson and Sons, 1975), 72.

14. Irving M. Zeitlin, *Marxism: A Re-examination* (Princeton, NJ: Princeton University Press, 1967), 142.

15. In other words, no Marxist revolution has taken place in a country where capitalism was entrenched. By the end of the twentieth century, in a complete turnabout of Marxist theory, communist regimes in the Soviet Union and Central Europe were falling to capitalism. It is still too early to know what form that transition will ultimately take in Russia and other former Soviet republics.

16. Marx's use of "dialectic," which he drew from the German philosopher G. W. F. Hegel, indicated that major ideas or historical forces (the thesis) are inevitably opposed by opposing ideas or forces (the antithesis), and out of this struggle emerges a "synthesis" that draws upon both sides.

17. Stuart R. Schram, *The Political Thought of Mao Tse-tung* (New York: Praeger, 1969).

18. Skocpol, *States and Social Revolutions*.

19. Skocpol, "France, Russia, China."

20. Chalmers Johnson, *Peasant Nationalism and Communist Power* (Stanford, CA: Stanford University Press, 1962).

21. Johnson, *Revolution and the Social System*.

22. Joel Migdal, *Peasants, Politics and Revolution* (Princeton, NJ: Princeton University Press, 1974), 252.

23. Ramón L. Bonachea and Marta San Martín, *The Cuban Insurrection, 1952–1959* (New Brunswick, NJ: Transaction Books, 1974); Jorge L. Domínguez, *Cuba: Order and Revolution* (Cambridge, MA: Belknap Press of Harvard University Press, 1978), 93–95; John A. Booth,

The End and the Beginning: The Nicaraguan Revolution (Boulder, CO: Westview Press, 1982).

24. Charles Tilly, *From Mobilization to Revolution* (New York: Addison-Wesley, 1978), 204–205.

25. Charles Tilly, "Does Modernization Breed Revolution?" *Comparative Politics* 5, no. 3 (April 1974): 425–447.

26. Huntington, *Political Order in Changing Societies*, 265.

27. Ibid., 266. Not all Asian revolutions followed the Eastern model, nor did all Latin American insurgencies conform to the Western model. The collapse of the Chinese imperial regime in 1911 fit the Western model, while the Cuban Revolution (1959) followed the Eastern model, at least in part.

28. James C. Davies, "Toward a Theory of Revolution," *American Sociological Review* 27, no. 1 (February 1962): 7.

29. More precisely, the economic pattern he describes can be graphed as the letter "J" tipped over (Figure 8.1), with the long side representing the period of economic growth and the rounded part depicting the downturn.

30. James C. Davies, "Toward a Theory of Revolution," reprinted along with other articles on the causes of revolution in *When Men Revolt and Why*, ed. James C. Davies (New York: Free Press, 1971).

31. Ibid., and James C. Davies, "Revolution and the J-Curve," in *Violence in America: Historical and Comparative Perspectives, A Report Submitted to the National Commission on the Causes and Prevention of Violence*, eds. Hugh Davis Graham and Ted Robert Gurr (New York: New American Library, 1969), vol. 2, 547–577.

32. Raymond Tanter and Manus Midlarsky, "A Theory of Revolution," *Journal of Conflict Resolution* 11, no. 3 (1967): 264–280.

33. Ted Robert Gurr, "Psychological Factors in Civil Violence," *World Politics* 20, no. 2 (1967–1968): 252–253; see also Ted Robert Gurr, *Why Men Rebel* (Princeton, NJ: Princeton University Press, 1970).

34. The only case where a communist regime replaced a democratic government is in postwar Czechoslovakia. But that communist government took power through a Russian-backed coup, not through revolutionary insurgency.

35. Timothy P. Wickham-Crowley, *Guerrillas and Revolution in Latin America* (Princeton, NJ: Princeton University Press, 1992), 312. Revolutions and guerrilla wars are not synonymous, of course. In recent decades, however, virtually all revolutionary struggles have been fought by guerrillas in Latin America and other parts of the Third World.

36. One defining event, a guerrilla attack on a tourist train, alienated most Venezuelans. Ultimately, several guerrilla leaders renounced violence and, following a government amnesty, entered electoral politics. Teodoro Petkoff, a former guerrilla who has since enjoyed a distinguished career as a congressman, cabinet minister, and presidential candidate, told me in a 1978 interview that the Left's violent tactics had been a major error and had cost it considerable support.

37. Booth, *The End and the Beginning*.

38. Such an alliance was being discussed in the U.S. press and government circles. Neither Nicaraguan businessmen nor the State Department harbored any illusions that they could keep the *Sandinistas* out of power at that point. However, they and the Carter administration hoped that the *Sandinistas* were not strong enough to hold power on their own. In fact, after the Somoza regime was ousted, the *Sandinista*-led government did initially include progressive business leaders, but they soon parted ways.

39. Eric R. Wolf, *Peasant Wars of the Twentieth Century* (New York: Harper & Row, 1969). For a discussion of similar factors in the capitalist transformation of Europe, see Karl Polanyi, *The Great Transformation* (New York: Rinehart, 1957).

40. James C. Scott, *The Moral Economy of the Peasant: Rebellion and Subsistence in Southeast Asia* (New Haven, CT: Yale University Press, 1976); James C. Scott and Benedict J. Kirkvliet, *How Traditional Rural Patrons Lose Legitimacy* (Madison: University of Wisconsin, Land Tenure Center, 1975).

41. Sharecroppers are tenant farmers who pay their rent by giving the landlord a percentage of their crop.

42. Jeffrey M. Paige, *Agrarian Revolution: Social Movements and Export Agriculture in the Underdeveloped World* (New York: Free Press, 1975), chaps. 1–2. Sharecroppers are defined in endnote 42.

43. Wickham-Crowley, *Guerrillas and Revolution*, chap. 6.

44. Cynthia McClintock, "Sendero Luminoso: Peru's Maoist Guerrillas," *Problems of Communism* 32, no. 5 (September–October 1983): 19–34.

45. Wickham-Crowley, *Guerrillas and Revolution*, 246–250; Wolf, *Peasant Wars*.

46. John Womack Jr., *Zapata and the Mexican Revolution* (New York: Vintage, 1968).

47. Wickham-Crowley, *Guerrillas and Revolution*, 145.

48. Ibid., 213; Alvin Gouldner, *The Future of Intellectuals and the Rise of the New Class* (New York: Seabury Press, 1979), 53–73.

49. Dennis Gilbert, *Sandinistas: The Party and the Revolution* (New York: B. Blackwell, 1988); for detailed information on the social backgrounds and occupations of a substantial number of Latin American guerrilla leaders, see Wickham-Crowley, *Guerrillas and Revolution*, 327–339.

50. Thomas H. Green, *Comparative Revolutionary Movements* (Upper Saddle River, NJ: Prentice Hall, 1974), 18.

51. Of course the percentages of peasants and illiterates in the party were still well below their proportions in the general population, but they were higher than in most LDCs.

52. Wickham-Crowley, *Guerrillas and Revolution*, 143.

53. Hector Béjar, *Peru 1965: Notes on a Guerrilla Experience* (New York: Monthly Review Press, 1970).

54. Among the many writings on Maoist ideology and strategy, see Stuart R. Schram, *The Political Thought of Mao Tse-tung* (New York: Praeger, 1963); Arthur Cohen, *The Communism of Mao Tse-Tung* (Chicago: University of Chicago Press, 1964); Cohan, *Theories of Revolution*, 93–110.

55. Sebastian Balfour, *Fidel Castro* (New York: Longman, 1990), 49.

56. Peasants have been most pleased when they received individual family plots and far less satisfied when agrarian reform converted the old agricultural estates into cooperatives or state farms.

57. Milovan Djilas, *The New Class* (New York: Praeger, 1957).

58. Huntington, *Political Order in Changing Societies*, 266.

59. See, for example, William J. Duiker, *The Communist Road to Power in Vietnam*, 2d ed. (Boulder, CO: Westview Press, 1996).

60. Richard R. Fagen, *The Transformation of Political Culture in Cuba* (Stanford, CA: Stanford University Press, 1969); Domínguez, *Cuba: Order and Revolution*.

61. There is a voluminous literature on the Cultural Revolution. Liang Heng and Judith Shapiro, *Son of the Revolution* (New York: Vintage, 1983), offers a moving personal account of both the Anti-Rightist Campaign and the Cultural Revolution. See also K. S. Karol, *The Second Chinese Revolution* (New York: Hill and Wang, 1974); Jean Esmein, *The Chinese Cultural Revolution* (New York: Anchor Books, 1973); and

Lowell Dittmer, *Liu Shao-ch'i and the Chinese Cultural Revolution* (Berkeley: University of California Press, 1974).

62. Liang Heng and Judith Shapiro, *After the Nightmare* (New York: Collier, 1986).

63. Nicholas Nugent, *Vietnam: The Second Revolution* (Brighton, England: In Print Publishers, 1996), chaps. 5–6.

64. On this theme, see Forrest Colburn, *The Vogue of Revolution in Poor Countries* (Princeton, NJ: Princeton University Press, 1994).

65. Both quotations come from Colburn, *The Vogue of Revolution*, 89.

66. *The New York Times*, September 6, 2001.

chapter 9

Soldiers and Politics

For many years, in much of the developing world—most notably in Latin America, Africa, and the Middle East—military governments were very common. As democracy has advanced in much of the Third World, military rule has become increasingly rare. However, in countries such as Libya and Pakistan, military rulers still preside and in many other developing nations the armed forces continues to exert considerable political influence.

Of course, even the most advanced governments are occasionally headed by men emerging from the military ranks. American President Dwight Eisenhower, French President Charles de Gaulle, and Israeli Prime Minister Ariel Sharon all used distinguished military careers as stepping stones to the leadership of their nations. But each of them entered politics as a private citizen, having first retired from the armed forces. Moreover, their accessions to high office were achieved through democratic elections.

What has distinguished Third World politics over the years is the extent to which the military has intruded either as the governing body or as a dominant interest group. Unlike their counterparts in industrialized democracies, soldiers in the LDCs have often rejected the dividing line between military and political activity. A pronouncement by the Indonesian armed forces prior to their assumption of power in the 1960s illustrates that perspective well:

> The army, which was born in the cauldron of the Revolution, has never been a dead instrument of the government, concerned exclusively with security matters. The army, as a fighter for freedom, cannot remain neutral toward the course of state policy, the quality of government, and the safety of the state.[1]

To be sure, there are countries such as India, Malaysia, Kenya, Tunisia, Mexico, and Costa Rica where the military has not penetrated deeply into politics for decades. But until the 1980s, such restraint was the exception rather than the rule. Indeed, until recently the military's political involvement in most of the Third World was so pervasive that it was almost a defining characteristic of political underdevelopment.

One study of military intervention revealed that 59 developing nations experienced 274 attempted coups between 1946 and 1970. Twenty-three of those countries were subjected to five or more takeover attempts in that period. Bolivia and Venezuela led the way with 18 attempted coups each.[2] At the start of the 1980s, almost every country in South America—most notably Argentina, Brazil, Chile, and Peru—was governed by the armed forces. Through the rest of that decade the military dominated politics in much of Africa, including Algeria, Ghana, Nigeria, and Sudan. Starting in Egypt in 1952—North Africa's first coup d'état—and General Mobutu's 1960 takeover in the Congo (Kinshasa)—the first in Sub-Saharan Africa—that continent's politics was particularly dominated by the armed forces. From 1958 to 1984, there were more than 62 coups and 60 failed attempts in Sub-Saharan Africa, affecting more than 80 percent of the nations in that region.[3] In 1982-1983 alone, Upper Volta (now Burkina Faso) experienced three military takeovers in only nine months! On average during the 1980s, 65 percent of Africa's population was governed by the armed forces. Noting the absence of electoral change in the region until the 1990s, one observer argued that "coups had become the functional equivalent of elections, virtually the sole manner of ousting incumbent political leaders."[4]

Military dominance was not quite as obvious in Asia where India, Sri Lanka, and Malaysia, among others, were able to maintain relatively democratic civilian governments, while in the Philippines, Singapore, Taiwan, and China authoritarian civilian rulers controlled the armed forces. Still, for much of the 1970s and 1980s, Pakistan, Bangladesh, Thailand, South Korea, and Indonesia experienced long periods of military dominance.

Although several Islamic nations in North Africa (including Algeria, Libya, and Sudan) frequently have been controlled by the armed forces or by military strongmen, indirect military dominance is more common in the Middle East. Presidents Husni Mubarak of Egypt and Syria's recently deceased strongman, Hafez Assad (succeeded by his civilian son), entered politics as military men. Elsewhere in the region, monarchies in Morocco, Jordan, Saudi Arabia, Kuwait, and the smaller Gulf states have, at least until now, successfully controlled the military.

The last 20 to 25 years have seen a marked decline in the number of military coups and military regimes. Nowhere has that been more dramatic than in Latin America where democratically elected civilian government has become the norm. In 1990, the last extended period of military rule in that region came to an end when General Augusto Pinochet's 17-year dictatorship was replaced by a freely elected government. In a remarkable turnabout for the region, armed forces coups have virtually ended in the region as it has enjoyed its longest period of democratic governance during its history. In Asia, military regimes have been toppled in countries such as Thailand, Indonesia, Bangladesh, and South Korea. Today, the military regimes in Pakistan and Myanmar stand out as exceptions to the rule. Even in Africa, where military government remains more pervasive, important transitions to civilian government have taken place in nations such as Nigeria and Ghana.

Since the 1980s, as the number of military-run governments has declined, the armed forces continue to wield considerable political influence over many civilian regimes. Frequently, they are able to veto the decisions of elected civilian officials in policy areas such as external defense, domestic security, or even the selection of certain government officials.[5] In some countries, military leaders protect their own budget, determine who serves as defense minister, or control military promotions. Thus, although Guatemala has experienced elected government since 1985, any civilian president still hesitates to pursue a policy that threatens the army's interests. Similarly, when Corazón Aquino served as Philippine president, she regularly consulted on major issues with her military chief of staff, General Fidel Ramos, who later succeeded her as president.[6] Elsewhere, however, in countries once dominated by the military (such as Argentina and Brazil) civilian governments have established considerable control over the armed forces.

In order to examine military involvement in Third World politics and changing civil-military relations, this chapter explores a series of interrelated questions: What has accounted for the high level of armed-forces political involvement? How do the structures of military regimes differ from one another? What do the armed forces hope to accomplish when they seize power? How successful have military regimes been in achieving their political and economic goals? Is military rule generally beneficial or detrimental to economic and political development? What factors have increasingly induced military regimes to step down in recent decades? What political role do the armed forces continue to play after the establishment or reestablishment of civilian rule? How can long-standing or recently established civilian governments best control the military?

THE CAUSES OF MILITARY INTERVENTION

Two alternative perspectives have often been proposed to explain the frequency and nature of military intervention in developing countries. The first focuses on the internal characteristics of the armed forces themselves. The second stresses the broader political environment in which the generals operate, most notably the weakness of civilian regimes.

The Nature of the Armed Forces

In early research on Third World politics, many political scientists maintained that the armed forces enjoyed greater organizational cohesion and clarity of purpose than did civilian political institutions, hence their proclivity to intervene. As one leading analyst concluded, "The ability of officers to intervene in domestic politics and produce stable leadership is [directly] related to internal [military] social cohesion."[7] Recognizing the importance of understanding the military's inner workings, scholars examined the officer corps' class origins, educational level, ideological orientations, and internal organization. These factors all seemed to affect the probability of military involvement in politics and help determine the officers' goals.

Obviously, military politics are greatly influenced by the officers' education and training. In his highly influential book *The Soldier and the State*, Samuel Huntington argued that a country wishing to keep the military out of politics must impart professional values to its officers.[8] Ideally, as military training and techniques become more sophisticated, officers develop specialized and complex military skills, while distancing themselves from politics. Under those circumstances, he claimed, "a clear distinction in role and function exists between military and civilian leaders."[9] However, Huntington warned subsequently, such a division of function will only develop if military training is addressed toward external threats such as war with other nations. Should the focus of military education shift toward internal warfare—controlling guerrilla unrest or other civil insurrection—professionalization will not suffice to keep the military out of politics.[10]

Building on this theme, Alfred Stepan distinguished between "old" and "new" military professionalism. The former, typical of developed countries such as the United States, emphasizes skills appropriate to "external security." As military officers are trained to repel foreign enemies, Stepan agreed, they can be expected to remove themselves from domestic politics. In many developing nations, however, military training (new professionalization) has primarily prepared officers for internal warfare against class- or ethnically-based insurgencies.

Following the Cuban Revolution, Latin American generals and U.S. policy makers shared a common concern over leftist guerrilla movements in the region. Training of Latin American officers at home and in the United States emphasized counterinsurgency techniques as well as "civic action" programs (e.g., road and school construction) designed to "win the hearts and minds" of the local population. American policy makers claimed that such preparation would provide the military with a professional mission and thereby remove it from national politics. Almost invariably, however, teaching officers to deal with *internal* security threats involved them in the study of domestic political and economic issues, thereby drawing them into the political arena.[11]

In a recent historical study of civilian relations with the military in a variety of national settings, Michael Desch found that the level of civilian control over the armed forces is related to the degree of external threat that the country faces from a foreign adversary and the extent of domestic threat from internal upheaval. He argues that civilian control over the military is likely to be strongest when the country faces a high external threat and a low internal threat. Conversely, civilian control is generally weakest when the country faces a low external threat and a high internal threat.[12]

The Nature of Civil Society

Although research into the internal structure and dynamics of the armed forces is very instructive, it fails to tell the entire story. That is to say that the likelihood and nature of military intervention in politics cannot be ascertained merely by evaluating factors such as military cohesion, size, or ideological orientation. There is, for example, surprisingly little correlation between the military's size or firepower and its propensity to topple civilian governments. Indeed, Africa, home to some of the world's smallest armed forces, has had one of the highest incidences of military rule. West Africa's first coup was carried out in Togo by an army of 250 men and a small number of retirees from the former French colonial force. "In Dahomey, General Sogol [sic] who had come to power by a coup d'état, was [later] overthrown by sixty paratroopers."[13] Several other military takeovers in the region were also executed by small and poorly armed units. In the closing years of the twentieth century, of nearly 45 African countries, 35 had military forces of fewer than 30,000 and 23 of those had fewer than 10,000 men.[14] By way of contrast, the armed forces of China, India, Israel, Sweden, and the United States have never attempted coups despite their large size, strong internal cohesion, and considerable military prowess.

Ultimately, then, the military's propensity to intervene in politics is less a function of its own capabilities than of the weaknesses of civilian political institutions. As Huntington has insisted, "The most important causes of military intervention in politics are not military, but political and reflect not the social and organizational characteristics of the military establishment but the political and institutional structure of society."[15] Hence, the second group of explanatory theories focuses its attention on the fabric of civil society.

If a civilian government enjoys substantial popular, elite, and political party support, maintains stability, and presides over a healthy economy, it is probably relatively immune to coups. Conversely, "in times of uncertainty and the breakdown of [civilian political] institutions, soldiers come into their own; when there is no other effective organization of society, even a small, weak army may take command over a large, unorganized mass."[16] In his classic study of civil-military relations, *The Man on Horseback*, Samuel E. Finer maintained that national political cultures could be ranked according to the following three criteria:[17]

1. The extent of public support for the procedures used to transfer political power and for the corresponding belief that only those procedures are legitimate.
2. The degree of public awareness regarding the individuals and institutions holding sovereign authority, and the degree to which the population believes that no other person or group can legitimately hold that power.
3. The strength of civil society. That is, the extent to which the populace is organized into groups such as labor unions, business associations, or churches that act independently of the government.

The higher a nation's political culture ranks on each of these three dimensions, argued Finer, the lower the likelihood of military intervention. In short, countries are most capable of maintaining civilian rule when there is a wide consensus on the legitimacy of civilian government along with independent organized groups capable of defending that principle—even taking to the streets if need be.

When the government retains widespread citizen loyalty, even if coups are attempted, they will usually fail. A Second World example demonstrates well what can happen when the civilian government enjoys greater legitimacy than its military opponents. In 1991, when Soviet generals and hard-line communist civilian officials staged a coup aimed at ousting Soviet President Mikhail Gorbachev, thousands of civilians joined Russian President Boris Yeltsin in defending the Russian parliament with their bodies. At the same time, key commanders of troops sent to take Moscow and St. Petersburg refused to support the rebellion. Thus, the coup d'état failed badly because Yeltsin and Gorbachev had sufficient legitimacy to survive. In contrast, the legitimacy of civilian regimes in many developing nations has been low. Consequently, disgruntled military leaders have been more inclined to overthrow them, while loyalist troops and civilians have been less likely to risk their lives defending them.

A variety of factors may either enhance or undermine a government's legitimacy. From an institutional perspective, civilian regimes stand most firmly when they are supported by broadly based political parties. Where party systems are deeply entrenched in the fabric of society and elicit widespread support, the likelihood of military intervention is greatly diminished.[18] Indeed, a country's susceptibility to coups is less influenced by its level of democracy than by the degree to which its party system penetrates and organizes society. Thus, authoritarian governments in Mexico, Cuba, Taiwan, and China (all now or once dominated by a single party) have controlled the military as effectively as have democratic party systems in Jamaica and India. When placed under sufficient stress, however, not even a strong party system can fully immunize a political system from military interference. For example, during most of the twentieth century, vibrant, competitive parties in Uruguay and Chile shielded those countries from the pattern of military takeovers that plagued most of Latin America. By 1973, however, growing class conflict and political polarization had undermined the political order in both countries, ushering in authoritarian military regimes.

Civilian governments are most vulnerable when they are unable to maintain political stability, during periods of economic decay (particularly runaway inflation), or when they are widely perceived as corrupt. All these circumstances undermine their legitimacy and often increase popular expectations that military rule could improve conditions. In nations such as Nigeria, Thailand, and Pakistan, soon after taking power military leaders declared their intention to root out widespread corruption. Following severe economic and political crises in Argentina, Brazil, Chile, and Uruguay, the new military authoritarian regimes set out to crush leftist movements, restore social order, and reinvigorate the economy.

As modernization theory would lead us to believe, countries that are more socioeconomically developed are less likely to suffer military takeovers than their poorer neighbors.

> Countries with per-capita GNPs of $1,000 or more [in 1995 dollars] do not [usually] have *successful* coups; countries with per-capita GNPs of $3,000 or more [normally] do not have coup *attempts*. The area between $1,000 and $3,000 per-capita GNP is where unsuccessful coups occur, while successful coups ... were [most common] in countries with per-capita GNPs under $500.[19]

In short, a nation's propensity for military intervention correlates strongly with the nature of its political institutions, its political culture, and its level of economic development. Yet these factors alone do not account for all the variations in civil-military relations. Elite values and behavior also play an important role. For example, India and Costa Rica, with political and socioeconomic circumstances comparable to those of their neighbors have far less military intervention. The explanation may lie in the values of their political elites: elected officials and government bureaucrats, as well as political party, business, and labor leaders.

India illustrates this point well. Adjoining several countries with histories of military intervention (Pakistan, Bangladesh, Myanmar, Thailand), it has been governed exclusively by civilians since independence. There is little to suggest that the Indian public, largely rural and illiterate, has a political culture more modern or informed than that of its neighbors. Nor, until the 1990s, was its economy much more advanced (indeed it has trailed Thailand). It appears, however, that India's political elite subscribes to the principle of civilian control more strongly than its neighboring counterparts.

Elite values, however, may change more quickly than do entire political cultures. In a process of "political learning," a nation's civilian leaders may learn from prior experience how better to avert military coups. Venezuela was governed by the military for much of the first half of the twentieth century. From 1959 into the mid-1990s, nearly four decades of elected government transformed the country into one of Latin America's most stable democracies until the legitimacy of its political establishment was undermined in the 1990s.[20] While a number of factors contributed to the prolonged period of civilian dominance, one critical element was a change in the attitudes of political elites following the collapse of Venezuela's first experiment with democracy (1945 to 1948). Recognizing that political polarization had precipitated the 1948 military coup, leaders of the major political parties agreed to moderate their political conflict. In 1958, the leading democratically oriented political parties signed the Pact of Punto Fijo, increasing interparty cooperation and setting the basis for civilian political dominance.[21] Viewed as a model for democratic reform in the region, Venezuela was one of the only Latin American countries to avoid military rule in the 1970s and 1980s. Subsequently, political pacts, often modeled after Punto Fijo, helped terminate civil wars and establish democratic government in several Central American countries.

By the end of the 1980s, however, Venezuela's deep economic crisis and its pervasive government corruption had severely eroded civilian support for the political parties that had dominated government since the interparty pact. Two unsuccessful coup attempts in 1992 received considerable popular approval and turned coup leader, Lieutenant Colonel Hugo Chávez, into a national hero, at least among the poor. Elected government has survived, but Chávez, who spent two years in jail for his coup activity, easily won the 1998 presidential elections. The two political parties that had signed the Punto Fijo pact and had dominated Venezuelan politics for the next 40 years were practically wiped off the electoral map. Since then, Chávez has subverted some of the country's democratic institutions and given the armed forces a much greater foothold in politics (though a 2004 referendum on his presidency indicated that a substantial majority of the population continues to support his populist economic reforms). Still, while not a panacea, political pacts in Venezuela and elsewhere have often been a valuable tool for establishing more stable civilian government.

PROGRESSIVE SOLDIERS AND MILITARY CONSERVATIVES

Having examined the factors promoting or inhibiting military intervention, we will now examine the political behavior and policies of military regimes once they have established control. Given the disorder and conflict that characterize so many Third World civilian governments, we must ask whether military rule produces greater political stability and socioeconomic development, at least in the short run. Also, once in office, are the generals and colonels likely to be a force for progressive change or defenders of the status quo? Some of the early modernization theorists felt strongly that the armed forces could contribute to development. Marion J. Levy was impressed by the military's alleged rationality, disciplined organization, and commitment to modern values. Taking their critics to task, he maintained that the armed forces might be "the most efficient type of organization for combining maximum rates of modernization with maximum levels of stability and control."[22] Lucian W. Pye also saw the military as one of the best-organized national institutions in otherwise "disorganized transitional societies." It was, said Pye, at the forefront of technical training and a leader in imparting the values of citizenship.[23] For Manfred Halpern, the Middle Eastern military was "the vanguard of nationalism and social change."[24]

Positive evaluations such as these predominated in the early modernization literature.[25] They were based to some extent on an idealized vision of the professional soldier: trained in modern organizational skills; nationalistic; and above narrow tribal, class, and regional interests. At times these writings reflected the authors' strong preference for order and stability, coupled with the assumption that the military could bring order out of political and economic chaos. Occasionally, they drew on a few military success stories and projected them onto a larger screen. One early model was the Turkish military revolt led by Mustafa Kemal (Ataturk) in 1922. During the next two decades, Ataturk and his followers modernized the country before eventually turning it over to civilian rule.[26] Another frequently cited military reformer was Egypt's Colonel Abdul Gamal Nasser, who rose to power in the 1950s seeking to reform his country's social and economic institutions while strengthening its military. Subsequent reformist militaries elsewhere in the developing world have often been labeled "young Turks" or "Nasserites."

Over the years a wide array of soldiers have seized power, promising to modernize their country through industrialization, greater labor discipline, expanded education, agrarian reform, or other fundamental changes. In countries such as Upper Volta, Libya, and Peru, left-wing militaries have promoted economic redistribution, greater state intervention in the economy, mass mobilization, and a struggle against imperialism. Conversely, conservative generals in Brazil, Chile, Indonesia, and South Korea repressed mass political participation while encouraging investment by domestic and multinational corporations.

Why have some military regimes championed the poor, while others have supported wealthy corporate and land-owning interests? To find the answer, we must examine the class origins of the officers' corps, a nation's level of socioeconomic development, and the class alliances that emerge in the political system. Research in various parts of the developing world frequently has shown that officers tend to come from middle-class backgrounds, at least in Asia and Latin America. Typically, their fathers were officers, shopkeepers, merchants, mid-sized land owners, teachers, or civil servants.[27] Not surprisingly, then, military regimes have commonly identified with the goals and aspirations of their nation's middle class.

But what are those goals, and what political ideologies and government policies have emerged from them? In the least developed Third World countries, officers often have viewed economic elites, including large land owners and multinational corporations, as the source of their country's backwardness. The middle class frequently resents those same elites for obstructing its own rise to political and social prominence. In such a setting, both groups may perceive the relatively unmobilized lower class as a potential ally in the battle against the oligarchy. For example, soon after taking office, Peruvian General Juan Velasco blamed the traditional land-owning class and Peru's international economic dependency for the nation's underdevelopment. In the following years, the military's ambitious land redistribution, shantytown reform, expropriations of property belonging to multinational corporations, expansion of the state economic sector, and mass mobilization greatly altered the country's political and economic landscape. Elsewhere, "General Omar Torrijos of Panama railed against oligarchical control and encouraged the lower class to participate in politics."[28] Muammar Qadhafi's government in Libya and a number of Marxist military regimes in Africa were cut from a similar cloth.

As a country modernizes, however, and as lower-class mobilization inten-sifies, the military confronts a changing political panorama. Urbanization, the spread of secondary and university education, and the development of more complex economies all enlarge and strengthen the middle class, enabling it to wrest a share of political power from the economic elites. At the same time, industrialization increases the size of the working class and enhances the trade union movement. Urbanization also creates a growing and sometimes militant shantytown population. And the commercialization of agriculture often trig-gers unrest in the countryside (see Chapter 6). Not surprisingly, the middle class (having achieved a share of political influence) and its military partners now come to see the more activated and politicized lower classes as a threat rather than a useful ally.

If the Left has enjoyed considerable mass support and there has been growing political unrest, the military is even more likely to ally itself with the economic elite and to repress mass mobilization. In Chile, the election of Salvador Allende's Marxist government and the accompanying mobilization of workers, peasants, and urban poor polarized the country along class lines. In nearby Uruguay, the Left's electoral appeal was not as strong, but labor-indus-trial conflict was intense, and the Tupamaros, a potent urban guerrilla force, were engaged in a campaign of political kidnappings and other forms of vio-lence. In both countries, the perceived threat of mass mobilization and an ascendent Left caused the military to topple long-standing democracies.

In short, then, the more underdeveloped a country is and the weaker is its middle class, the greater has been its likelihood of developing a progressive military.[29] However, notes Eric Nordlinger, "the soldiers who have power in countries with an established middle class ... act as more or less ardent defend-ers of the status quo."[30] Similarly, Samuel Huntington observes:

> In the world of the oligarchy, the soldier is a radical; in the middle class world, he is a participant and arbitrator; as mass society looms on the horizon he becomes the guardian of the existing order. ... The more advanced a society becomes, the more conservative and reactionary becomes the role of the military.[31]

More recently, the armed forces in Pakistan and Algeria have stood as a barrier to mass mobilization by Islamic Fundamentalists.

THE GOALS OF MILITARY REGIMES

Having observed the range of ideological orientations among military govern-ments, we now examine their structures and associated political-economic goals.

Personalistic Regimes

In the world's least developed countries—those with low levels of military pro-fessionalization, limited popular political participation, extensive political cor-ruption, and little semblance of representative government—military officers frequently seize power for their own personal enrichment and aggrandize-ment. Their governments tend to be personalistic; that is, they are led by a single charismatic officer with a strong personal following. In order to bolster his support, however, the leader allows some government plunder to pass on to the military or civilian clique surrounding him. "Legitimacy is secured through patronage, clientelistic alliances, [and] systemic intimidation."[32]

In Latin America, personalistic dictatorships were most common in the less developed political systems of Central America and the Caribbean. One of the most prominent examples was the Somoza dynasty in Nicaragua. As leader of the country's National Guard, General Anastasio Somoza, Sr., overthrew the government in 1937, primarily seeking his own enrichment. Governing a small and impoverished nation, he amassed a fortune of several hundred million dollars using state resources to purchase construction firms, urban real estate, electrical power plants, air and shipping lines, cement factories, and much of the nation's best farmland. Following Somoza's 1956 assassination, his political and financial empire passed to his two sons, who ruled the country in succession until the 1979 Sandinista revolution.[33] Other personalistic regimes in the Americas included the Batista government in Cuba (eventually toppled by Fidel Castro's revolutionary army) and Alfredo Stroessner's extended dictatorship in Paraguay. Batista had links to the mafia's gambling and prostitution operations in Havana. Stroessner and his associates enriched themselves by collaborating with international smugglers and drug dealers.[34]

Personalistic military regimes also have been common in Sub-Saharan Africa, sometimes led by upwardly mobile junior officers or even enlisted men such as Ghana's Flight Sergeant Jerry Rawlings and Liberia's Sergeant-Major Samuel Doe. While some, like Rawlings, were well intentioned, most have done little to develop their countries. The most infamous personalistic dictators in the continent have been Uganda's Idi Amin Dada and the Central African Republic's Jean-Bédél Bokassa. Enamored as much of power as of wealth, Amin played upon and exacerbated Uganda's ethnic divisions during his brutal eight-year reign (1971 to 1979). He not only expelled the country's sizable Asian population but also murdered thousands of other civilians, most notably members of the previously influential Langi and Acholi tribes. Seeing enemies at every turn, he even executed one of his wives and had another tortured. In an attempt to maintain absolute control over the armed forces, he purged or executed a large portion of the officers' corps, eventually creating an army composed largely of foreign troops (principally Sudanese and Zairean).[35]

Equally megalomaniacal, the Central African Republic's Marshal Bokassa unleashed a reign of death and terror on his country following his takeover in 1965. Plundering the treasury of one of the world's more impoverished nations, he concluded that the presidency was not a sufficiently exalted position, so he lavished millions on his own coronation as the country's new emperor. In time, Amin and Bokassa so outraged the world community that they were ousted through external intervention. Amin fell to a Tanzanian invasion, while Bokassa was toppled by a French-sponsored coup.[36]

Because most personalistic dictators lack a meaningful ideology or policy program to legitimize their regime, they typically must share some of the spoils of state plunder with their military and civilian supporters in order to maintain themselves in office. For example, Zaire's President Mobutu, once Africa's most enduring military dictator (1965–1997), made himself one of the richest men on earth while opening up the floodgates of corruption to benefit his military and civil service. In this manner, he kept himself in office for decades while bank-rupting the national government and destroying a once-dynamic economy. By the late 1990s, however, as the Zairean economy collapsed, his government unraveled, falling rapidly to a rebel force who, unfortunately, proved just as corrupt once they were in control.[37] More recently, warlords in Sierra Leone and Liberia have overthrown the government with few goals other than looting the country. In Nicaragua, the Somoza dynasty maintained the National Guard's critical support by allowing its officers to share in the regime's plunder. In the most egregious example, following an earthquake that devastated the nation's capital, Guard officers appropriated relief supplies sent from the United States and sold them for a profit.[38]

Institutional Military Regimes

As Third World political and economic systems modernize, corresponding changes take place in military institutions and attitudes. Frequently officers attend advanced military academies at home or abroad. Sometimes they enroll in specialized seminars with civilian leaders, establishing links with politicians, businesspeople, or academics. Through these programs they become more deeply exposed to their country's political and economic problems.

When these "new soldiers" seize power, they are likely to govern collec-tively rather than vest authority in the hands of a single leader. To be sure, some institutional military regimes have been dominated by a single figure, such as Libya's Muammar Qadhafi, Indonesia's Suharto, Syria's Hafez Assad, and Chile's Augusto Pinochet. Like purely personalistic dictators, these men may be motivated by "covert ambition, fear, greed and vanity."[39] Still, even in such cases, a substantial number of officers hold influential government positions, and there is a degree of institutional decision making. In Indonesia, for exam-ple, active and retired military officers at one time held nearly half the positions in the national bureaucracy and some two-thirds of provincial governorships.[40] In a like manner, the Argentine military dominated top positions in almost all government ministries during its most recent period in office. Furthermore, regime goals are broader than any single leader's ambitions.

Institutional military governments have generally been headed by collegial bodies such as Niger's Supreme Military Council or Myanmar's Revolutionary Council. Comparable councils or juntas have governed Algeria, Argentina, Brazil, Ethiopia, Thailand, Uruguay, and a host of other countries.[41] Typically, one active or retired officer serves as president and wields the most influence. Often, however, his term of office is limited. For example, presidents of military gov-ernments in Argentina and Brazil were restricted by their colleagues to a single term. In some countries, including South Korea, Brazil, and Indonesia, the armed forces tried to legitimize their rule by forming a government political party that ran candidates in tightly controlled elections. Often, candidates retire from active duty before standing for office. And in Egypt and Syria, military and civilian elites have joined together to form a ruling political party.[42]

Institutional military regimes can be as repressive and brutal as person-alistic dictatorships—sometimes more so. Their day-to-day governing style, however, is more bureaucratic and sophisticated, commonly drawing on the tal-ents of highly trained civilian technocrats.[43] Moreover, unlike self-aggrandizing personalistic leaders, they are more likely to support the aspirations of the middle class (from which most officers have sprung), more prone to espouse a coherent political ideology, and more likely to champion nationalistic causes.

Most institutional military governments pursue four broad objectives, or at least profess to do so. First, whatever their real motivations, they usually justify their seizure of power by denouncing the alleged corruption of the government they have ousted. Thus, when Bangladesh's Lieutenant General Hussain Muhammad Ershad led a 1982 army coup, he charged that the outgoing administration had "failed totally because of [its] petty selfishness … and unbounded corruption."[44] Similar proclamations have been made by incoming military leaders in Uruguay, Pakistan, Thailand, and much of Africa. All promised to clean up the mess.

A second goal—one rarely publicly articulated or acknowledged—is the advancement of military corporate interests. As Ruth First observed in Africa, while coup leaders may claim to have acted for the good of the nation or another broad political purpose, "when the army acts, it generally acts for army reasons."[45] When officers are unhappy with their salaries, defense budgets, or the level of arms purchases, they usually respond. They also react negatively to civilian "interference" in military affairs, such as deviating from normal officer promotion practices or lessening the armed forces' autonomy.

Ever since the 1960s—a decade featuring coups in Togo, Ghana, Mali, Congo-Brazzaville, and Algeria—African armies have frequently taken power to protect themselves from competing military units (such as presidential guards), to increase their troop strength, to raise their salaries, or to augment their budgets.[46] In South Asia, repeated coups in Bangladesh were motivated by similar desires for greater military spending and by resentment against civilian interference in military promotions.[47] In Southeast Asia, while "neglect of [military] corporate interests" by civilian governments has only been "a background factor contributing to a general sense of alienation [among the armed forces] rather than an immediate cause of intervention," several coups in that region were partially motivated by armed forces concerns over the defense budget.[48]

A third common goal is the maintenance or restoration of order and stability. Institutional coups often have occurred when the country has experienced or anticipates civil unrest, guerrilla activity, or civil war. For example, the army first involved itself deeply in South Korean politics when the administrations of Syngman Rhee and Chang Myon were challenged by student and labor unrest (though other factors also played a role). Thailand's many coups in past decades frequently followed strikes and street demonstrations in Bangkok.

Military officers are particularly troubled by radical challenges to the political and economic order and by threats to the safety and integrity of the armed forces. During the early 1960s, Indonesia's civilian president, Sukarno, moved his regime leftward and became increasingly dependent on the country's large Communist Party, much to the discomfort of his conservative military command. Their fears were raised further in 1965, when a small group of leftist officers assassinated Lieutenant General Achmad Yani and five other officers, claiming these men had been plotting a coup against Sukarno. The top military command responded with a massive attack against the communists, eventually killing some half a million alleged party supporters. Many Indonesian civilians used the chaos as an opportunity to loot and kill members of the country's relatively prosperous Chinese minority. Two years later, army leader General

Suharto ousted Sukarno and established a military dictatorship that lasted more than 30 years (until 1998).[49]

Similarly, in Argentina, Brazil, Chile, and Uruguay, military dictatorships lasting up to two decades were prompted by the generals' fear of leftist unions, guerrillas, and radical political parties.[50] In 1992, the Algerian armed forces terminated parliamentary elections that seemed sure to bring victory to the FIS, a group of militant Islamic fundamentalists.

A final important goal of many institutional military regimes has been to revive and stimulate the economy. As we have noted, coups frequently follow periods of rampant inflation, labor conflict, and economic stagnation. For example, a statistical analysis of military intervention in 38 Sub-Saharan African governments over a two-decade period revealed that coups were most likely to occur after an economic downturn.[51] Similar patterns have been found in Asia and Latin America.

Third World militaries are particularly committed to industrialization. For one thing, industrial growth can provide them with arms and supplies that previously needed to be imported. In the least developed countries, such production may be limited to food, uniforms, or rifles. On the other hand, in countries such as Brazil, Indonesia, and South Korea, highly advanced arms industries now produce planes, tanks, and sophisticated weaponry for both domestic consumption and export. Even when it has no direct military payoff, industrialization contributes to national pride and international prestige. Small wonder, then, that many Latin American and Asian countries have seen a political alliance between industrialists and the armed forces.[52]

Having reviewed the goals of institutional military governments in general, we now focus on two distinct regime types that have received considerable attention in recent years: the bureaucratic authoritarian regime and the revolutionary military regime.

Bureaucratic Authoritarian Regimes Beginning with the Brazilian coup d'état of 1964, through the Argentine military takeovers of 1966 and 1976, to the 1973 coups in Uruguay and Chile, four of the most socioeconomically developed countries in South America succumbed to authoritarian rule. Chile and Uruguay had also been the most long-standing democracies in the region, free of military domination for decades. Thus, their coups contradicted the widely held assumption that both socioeconomic development and the creation of a strong party system limit military intervention.

Once in power, these regimes endured longer than typical military governments in the region, lasting between 12 years (Uruguay) and 21 (Brazil).[53] Political party activity was suspended for extended periods, labor unions and other grass-roots organizations were crushed, strikes were prohibited, and many suspected political dissidents were jailed and often tortured. In Argentina and Chile, thousands of people were murdered or "disappeared" (unofficially taken away and never to be seen again).

In a series of provocative writings, Argentine political scientist Guillermo O'Donnell referred to these military governments as "bureaucratic authoritarian (BA) regimes." Compared to previous military dictatorships, they had a more extensive bureaucratic structure that included like-minded civilian technocrats. They penetrated more deeply into the spheres of civil society, were especially closely linked to multinational corporations (MNCs), and were especially repressive.[54] O'Donnell focused on the closely related economic and political factors that explained the rise of these BA regimes in the most developed area of Latin America. First, he argued, economic growth in these countries had come to a relative standstill because they had developed as far as they could with their available capital and technology. Further growth would require heavy investment in capital goods industries and new technologies, both of which could only be provided by multinational corporations. But MNCs (as well as domestic companies) had been reluctant to invest in these countries because of frequent labor strife, civil unrest, and leftist electoral strength. All of these conditions, in turn, largely resulted from economic stagnation, high inflation, and declining living standards for workers.

The military became deeply alarmed at the growing radicalism and political polarization of society. In Argentina, Chile, and Uruguay, urban guerrillas added to the perceived threat. The goals of the new BA regimes, then, were to crush leftist political parties, unions, and guerrilla movements; limit wages; create a "stable environment for investment"; and work closely with MNCs and domestic big business to control inflation and reinvigorate the economy. Beyond repressing the Left, the generals sought to depoliticize society and exclude the population from political participation for a prolonged period. At the same time, many of them wished to extend the role of the private sector and roll back state economic activity such as welfare programs, minimum wage guarantees, and public ownership of economic resources. Many of these objectives, of course, were consistent with the goals of other institutional military regimes articulated earlier. But these entailed a more precise and elaborate "game plan" and a far more sweeping restructuring of society. Still, despite many predictions that Latin America's BA regimes would become a model for the more industrialized LDCs, they proved to be an exception to the general pattern in which military takeovers are more likely in the least economically developed Third World nations.

Revolutionary Military Regimes   In a number of developing nations, the military pursued goals diametrically different from those of the conservative BA regimes. Rather than excluding most of the population from the political system, they instead *extended* political and economic participation to formerly excluded groups. Normally, however, that participation was tightly controlled by an authoritarian political structure.[55]

In Africa, a number of Marxist, military regimes laid out a program of cultural nationalism, anti-imperialism, peasant and working-class political mobilization, expansion of the state's economic role, and redistribution of economic resources to the poor.

Revolutionary soldiers have usually been led by radicalized officers from the junior ranks. In a speech outlining the goals of Upper Volta's military government, Captain Thomas Sankara articulated the Marxist rhetoric typical of such regimes:

> The triumph of the Revolution ... is the crowning moment of the struggle of the Volta People against its internal enemies. It is a victory against international imperialism and its internal allies. ... These enemies of the people have been identified by the people in the forge of revolutionary action. They are: the bourgeoisie of Volta

[and] ... reactionary forces whose strength derives from the traditional feudal structures of our society. ... The People in our revolution comprises: The working class ... the petty bourgeoisie ... the peasantry ... [and] the lumpen proletariat.[56]

Similarly radical declarations have been made by military regimes in Ethiopia, the Sudan, Somalia, Congo-Brazzaville, Benin (formerly Dahomey), and Madagascar. Like other African military regimes, however, these governments have been led by men lacking significant political experience or advanced education, though they tended to be more educated than the officers who preceded them. Consequently, their Marxist ideals were "self-taught, ideologically immature and crude, and riddled with inconsistencies."[57] For some, Marxism simply expressed their strong nationalism and distaste for the European nations that had colonized the continent. But for others, revolutionary rhetoric came almost as an afterthought, a means of justifying their seizure of power and authoritarian control. Thus, the government of Colonel Mengistu in Ethiopia, perhaps Africa's most prominent radical military regime, did not embrace Marxism-Leninism until it had been in office for three years. In Dahomey, General Mathieu Kerekou declared his government Marxist and created "revolution committees" simply as a pretext for spying on the civil service.[58]

Outside of Sub-Saharan Africa, at various times leftist (though not Marxist) military regimes have governed in countries as disparate as Libya, Myanmar, Panama, and Peru. Peru's military came to power, seeking to curtail the influence of the traditional rural oligarchy and incorporate the peasantry, working class, and urban poor into the political system.[59] And military regimes in Panama and Ecuador introduced comparable, though far more modest, reform programs.

THE ACCOMPLISHMENTS AND FAILURES OF MILITARY REGIMES

How successfully have military governments achieved their goals and how well have they served their country? Little needs to be said about personalistic military dictatorships. With a few notable exceptions, they are rarely seriously interested in benefiting their country. Even those with broader goals have patently self-serving objectives. Thus, it would be impossible to argue seriously that dictators such as Batista (Cuba), Somoza, Jr., (Nicaragua), Stroessner (Paraguay), Amin (Uganda), or Bokassa (Central African Republic) contributed to the long-term political or economic growth of their nation. Consequently, the analysis in our next section focuses exclusively on the record of institutional military governments.

Combating Corruption

Let us first look at one of the most commonly professed objectives of institutional regimes—eliminating government corruption. Because government malfeasance is so pervasive in the Third World, denouncing corruption is a convenient means of legitimizing the armed forces' unconstitutional seizure of power. Yet most soldiers in office prove every bit as corrupt as their predecessors, or more so. To be sure, a few military regimes have been quite honest, but they are the exceptions. As one leading scholar has observed:

> Every Nigerian and Ghanaian coup ... has had as its prime goal the elimination of deeply ingrained corruption from society. Yet, not one military administration has made truly consistent efforts in that direction ... or for that matter remained immune to it itself. ... [Elsewhere in Africa] in two ... military regimes—Guinea and Burkina Faso—nepotism and accumulation of wealth commenced the very day the officers' hierarchy took office.[60]

Ironically, the continent's constant military intervention has tended to increase corruption in the civilian governments that are ousted. "The fear that [civilian] power may not last encourages the incoming politicians to grab what is grabbable."[61] In Asian nations such as Thailand and Indonesia, the military's record has been equally disappointing. Indeed, Harold Crouch has noted that "often military officers have already become entangled in this web [of corruption] even before the coup takes place."[62] In those few military governments that avoid *gross* corruption, the more modest lure of contraband automobiles and tax-supported vacation homes often proves irresistible. In short, even military governments that take office with noble intentions generally are soon corrupted.

Defending Corporate Interests

When it comes to pursuing their second major objective—advancing their own corporate interests—not surprisingly, military governments have been more successful, at least in the short term. More often that not, military rule enhances the nation's defense budget. Unfortunately, however, those expenditures draw government resources away from badly needed social and economic programs.

Typically, military governments increase spending on armaments, military salaries, military housing, and luxurious officers' clubs. In much of Asia, officers have benefited from "lucrative public sector employment, foreign postings, and preferential treatment in the disbursal of governmental contracts."[63] After leading a coup in Libya, Colonel Qadhafi insured his officers' loyalty by doubling their salaries, making them the highest paid army in the Third World. In their first five years in office, Uruguay's generals raised the military and security share of the national budget from 26.2 percent to more than 40 percent.[64] A parallel "bias in favor of army, police and civil-service salaries and benefits can be observed in practically every military regime in Africa."[65]

Throughout the LDCs, even when soldiers do not actually govern, the mere specter of intervention has often led civilian governments to bestow salary hikes and expensive weapons systems on the armed forces. For example, it would be very imprudent of elected leaders in the Philippines or Thailand to slash their country's defense budget. Even Malaysia and Singapore, with no history of coups d'état, pay their officers generously to keep them out of politics.[66] Similarly, Colombia and Venezuela, two of Latin America's most long-lived civilian governments (though military involvement in politics has risen sharply in both since the 1990s), have supported healthy defense budgets aimed at keeping the generals at bay.

But, although military rule may enlarge military budgets, it also damages the armed forces in the longer term by reducing their institutional cohesion. Eventually, generals and admirals begin to squabble over resource allocation and other policy issues. As new economic and political challenges arise, they drive a wedge between the officers in command. Furthermore, even military regimes that took power with considerable popular support usually lose their legitimacy as they confront difficult economic and social problems. As a consequence, in some regions, most notably Sub-Saharan Africa, internal coups (one faction ousting another) have produced a series of unstable military governments. Elsewhere however, particularly as of late, the armed forces have generally returned to the barracks to avoid further internal divisions, restoring the government to civilian hands.

Patterns in Military Spending

The military's budgetary gains, however, are frequently the nation's loss. Third World military outlays are frequently higher than their country can afford, thereby reducing badly needed social and economic investment. Countries in South America that have not fought an international war in decades, waste fortunes on naval vessels and state-of-the-art combat jets. And in Africa, home to many of the world's poorest countries, military expenditures are especially disproportionate to economic capacities. Thus, in the 1980s, despite having per-capita national incomes that were substantially less than half of Latin America's, African governments spent one-third more per soldier.[67] Africa's defense outlays did decline unevenly from 1991 to 1998, but they shot up sharply after that.[68] Currently, defense consumes a disproportionate share of that continent's Gross Domestic Product (GDP) and limits expenditures for education, health, and other social needs. In the 1990s, military budgets were particularly large in countries that were engaged in domestic or international warfare such as Uganda, Rwanda, Sudan, and Angola. Angola, one of the world's poorest nations, spent 6.7 percent of its 1996 GNP on defense, more than twice the worldwide average.[69] In 1999, Eritrea, also an extremely impoverished country, devoted an astounding 37.5 percent of its GDP to military expenditures.

Table 9.1 reveals that, while some developing nations have tightly limited their military spending, others have enormous military budgets relative to their resources, particularly those facing external military threats or civil war. The table compares health, education, and military spending in four groups of countries: highly industrialized democracies (the United States and Japan), relatively wealthy Third World nations (Kuwait and Singapore), middle-income developing nations (Mexico, Ghana, and Jordan), and extremely poor developing nations (Burundi, Ethiopia, and Eritrea). The second column indicates what percentage of the nation's 2002 GDP was devoted to public welfare, defined here as the combined national expenditures on health and education. The next column shows the proportion of GDP spent on the armed forces. And the last column compares those two expenditures, presenting welfare spending as a percentage of military outlays. For example, column four indicates that in 2002 the United States spent almost three times as much on health and education as on the military (297 percent). In contrast, Eritrea spent slightly less than a third as much (32 percent) on public welfare as it did on the military.

TABLE 9.1   Public Welfare (Health and Education) versus Military
Spending as a Percentage of GDP in 2002

Country	Health and Education (% of GDP)	The Military (% of GDP)	Health and Education Spending as % Military Spending
United States*	10.1	3.4	297%
Japan*	9.5	1.0	950
Kuwait*	n/a	10.4	n/a
Singapore*	4.8	5.2	92
Mexico**	6.9	0.5	1380
Ghana**	6.3	0.6	1050
Jordan**	9.2	8.4	109
Burundi***	6.6	5.2	126
Ethiopia***	5.0	7.6	66
Eritrea***	7.6	23.5	32

n/a, not available; *High-income Countries; **Middle-income countries; ***Low-income countries.
Source: Stockholm International Peace Research Institute (SIPRI) 2004.

As column three of the table indicates, there are wide variations in spending patterns within both the relatively affluent nations and the poorer countries. Impoverished Eritrea devoted an enormous portion of its GDP—more than 23 percent—to the military (though still far less than it did in 1999 or 2000). That was probably the highest percentage in the world and about 6 to 7 times the international average. Military expenditures also consumed a very high percentage of the GDP in Kuwait (10.4%), Jordan (8.4%), and Ethiopia (7.6%), and a smaller, but considerable, share in Burundi and Singapore (both at 5.2%). All of these countries faced hostile or potentially hostile neighbors, while two (Ethiopia and Burundi) also confronted domestic ethnic unrest. All had governments that were to some degree authoritarian. On the other hand, the armed forces consumed a mere 1 percent or less of the GDP in Mexico and Ghana. Both nations have recently democratized and face no significant external or domestic military threats.

Column four—comparing public welfare with military spending—is particularly revealing. Clearly the poorest nations (Burundi, Ethiopia, and Eritrea) have the greatest need for health and educational expenditures and can, therefore, least afford high military outlays. Yet, Eritrea and Ethiopia spent far more on the armed forces than on public welfare and Burundi devoted a much higher relative share to the armed forces than did the United States, Japan, Mexico, or Ghana.

Throughout the developing world, only civilian governments with strong control over the armed forces and low security threats have reduced military budgets substantially. As the third wave of democracy strengthened the legitimacy and authority of newly elected governments in the 1980s and 1990s, a number of LDCs made such cuts. For example, following the restoration of democracy in Argentina, military spending was nearly halved from 1983 to 1987.[70] From 1985 to 1993, defense expenditures as a share of GNP fell from

TABLE 9.2   Trends in Estimated Regional Military Expenditures, 1994–2003[a]

Region	1994	1999	2003	% Change
Africa[b]	9.2	9.9	11.4	+24%
Central America	3.5	3.4	3.3	−5%
South America	17.6	20.1	21.8	+24%
East Asia	101	105	125	+24%
South Asia	12.0	14.6	16.9	+41%
Middle East[c]	47.1	50.3	70	+48%

[a]Figures are in billions of dollars (U.S.) at constant 2000 prices and exchange rates.
[b]African data excludes Angola, Benin, Republic of Congo, Democratic Republic of Congo, Liberia, and Somalia.
[c]Middle East data excludes Iraq.
Source: Stockholm International Peace Research Institute (SIPRI) 2004. http://web.sipri.org/contents/milap/milex/mex_wnr_table.html.

2.9 percent to 1.7 percent in Argentina, from 6.8 percent to 2.1 percent in Chile, and from 4.4 percent to 1.6 percent in El Salvador.[71] Elsewhere in Central America, there were significant cuts in spending and military manpower as well. More recently (1997-2003), military expenditures in Cambodia fell from 4.6 percent of GDP to an estimated 2.7 percent.

In general, however, the decline in Third World military governments during the 1980s and 1990s has not seemed to produce a widespread cut in defense spending, at least not since the mid-1990s. However, in some regions, military budgets grew only modestly. Thus, as Table 9.2 indicates, from 1994 to 2003, Central America made the most progress as military expenditures fell from $3.5 billion to $3.3 billion, controlling for inflation—a small, but impressive, reduction for a region that until recently had been immersed in civil war. Expenditures in Africa, South America, and East Asia all rose by an identical 24 percent, still a relatively small increase of about 2 percent annually. South Asia and the Middle East had by far the largest increases, a total of 41 and 48 percent respectively. The South Asian outlays reflect military tensions between Pakistan and India, while the growth in the Middle East resulted from Arab-Israeli tensions and fears of Iraq during Saddam Hussein's rule.

Because these data do not compare expenditures in democratic countries (including newly democratized nations) with those of military regimes, they fail to tell us whether democracy influenced military spending. Clearly, however, they suggest that defense expenditures were also influenced by factors other than regime type (democratic or authoritarian), particularly the level of international or domestic conflict in the region. Only in Central America did there seem to be a clear "democracy dividend," linked to the end of civil wars.

Elsewhere, Ethiopia slashed the size of its armed forces, Africa's largest, from 438,000 in 1991 to 120,000 in 1996, while Mozambique and Nigeria also made sizable cuts. However, in countries such as Chad and Sudan, troop strength has grown substantially.[72] And Ethiopian military outlays have rebounded sharply since 1997. Authoritarian governments such as Myanmar's and North Korea's continue their massive military expenditures, but so too do democracies such as India, South Korea, and Taiwan, all with hostile neighbors. Still, democratization seems to have at least opened up opportunities for limiting military expenditures.

Establishing Stability

Military officers almost always react negatively to popular unrest and political instability. For one thing, disorder violates their hierarchical view of society. Furthermore, it frequently threatens the interests of their middle-class and industrialist allies. In other instances, it poses an imminent danger to the military itself. The Generals and Colonels of Latin America, for example, have been keenly aware that Marxist revolutions in Cuba and Nicaragua destroyed the old military establishment. In Cuba a number of Batista's officers faced the firing squad and many Nicaraguan National Guardsmen were imprisoned or had to flee the country. In Chile and Brazil, leftist movements threatened the officers' hierarchical control of the armed forces. Similarly, the generals in Algeria felt endangered by the growing strength of Islamic fundamentalism. Even "revolutionary soldiers" in Ethiopia, Libya, and Peru preferred change dictated from the top with tight controls on mass mobilization.

In many respects, military governments are particularly well suited for controlling civil unrest. They can use force with impunity to combat guerrilla insurrections, disperse street demonstrations, and ban strikes. In some cases, their extensive intelligence agencies, such as South Korea's KCIA and Chile's DINA, enabled them to penetrate deeply into society and control dissent. The Argentine, Chilean, and Uruguayan armies used mass arrests, torture, and death squads to crush potent urban guerrilla movements. In Indonesia, the military destroyed one of the world's largest communist parties and later decimated various separatist movements.

But order was only restored at a tremendous cost in human suffering. Some 20,000 to 30,000 people died in the Argentine army's "dirty war" against the Left, while many more were imprisoned and tortured. Students and other young people were the primary victims, many of them incorrectly identified as part of the radical opposition. In Chile, thousands of intellectuals and professionals fled the country, devastating one of the Third World's most advanced university systems and artistic communities. Some 3,000 Chileans died; many others were the victims of torture.[73] During Indonesia's "year of living dangerously," perhaps 500,000 communists and ethnic Chinese were massacred, while some 150,000 other people died subsequently (largely from starvation) in the army's struggle against East Timorian separatists.[74]

Moreover, *in the longer term*, the military has not been particularly successful in providing political stability. To be sure, in several Asian and Latin American countries, state repression, coupled with technocratic development policies, have either co-opted or decimated opposition groups. In South Korea, sharply improved living standards and a gradual political transition paved the way to stable, elected government. And in Argentina, Chile, and Uruguay, the BA regimes' brutality against radical movements convinced political leaders on both sides of the ideological spectrum (but especially the Left) to moderate their positions so as not to provoke further military intervention.

But these "successes" are the exception. Despite their brute strength, the length of the armed forces' hold on power has been surprisingly limited. Eric Nordlinger's pioneering study of military governments found that, on average, they dissolved in five to seven years.[75] Karen Remmer's later work on 12 South American military regimes between 1960 and 1990 showed four to be quite durable (12 to 35 years); the remaining eight, however, averaged less than seven years in office.[76] Moreover, military rule, no matter what its accomplishments, ultimately impedes the maturation of political parties and other civilian institutions necessary for long-term stability.

In Africa, more often than not, coups have only led to further coups, preventing development as it turns politics into a Hobbesian game. The brutal regime of Sergeant Samuel Doe exposed Liberia to a devastating civil war and a more sinister dictator who spread bloody conflict to nearby Sierra Leone. Military rule in Ethiopia and the Sudan only exacerbated ethnically based civil wars. Elsewhere, extended suppression of dissident groups in countries such as Myanmar will likely lead to greater upheavals after those regimes fall.

Economic Development

Earlier we noted that coups often follow economic recessions or severe inflation. Consequently, newly installed military governments commonly hope to impose fiscal discipline and revitalize the economy. In South Korea, Indonesia, Brazil, and Chile, for example, conservative military regimes curtailed union activity in order to suppress wage demands. Reduced strike activity and weaker unions were expected to lower inflation and attract multinational investment.

Proponents of military dictatorships assert that they can more readily make economic decisions consistent with the broad national interest because they need not pander to special interest groups. Critics counter that soldiers lack the expertise to manage an economy. Even when well intentioned, they tend to allocate excessive funds to defense and to wasteful chauvinistic projects. Examining the economic performance of specific military governments provides evidence to support both sides of the debate. South Korea demonstrated that a military government can oversee a very successful economic development program. Following General Park Chung Hee's seizure of power in 1961, the armed forces governed the country for more than 25 years. During that period, the Republic of Korea was transformed from an underdeveloped nation into one of the world's most dynamic industrial economies.[77] Moreover, sustained economic growth was accompanied by very equitable distribution of income. Indeed South Korea is often cited as a model of well-executed economic modernization.

Elsewhere in Asia, Indonesia's military also presided over rapid economic growth from the mid-1960s to late 1990s. During the 1970s and early 1980s, a portion of the country's extensive petroleum revenues were plowed back into labor-intensive export industries. At the same time, rural development programs and mass education improved income distribution and, coupled with economic growth, substantially reduced the number of Indonesians living in poverty. Nearby Thailand, governed by the military for much of the last

70 years, also participated in the region's economic boom.[78] However, excessive borrowing, "crony capitalism" (plentiful government loans and contracts to politically connected businesspeople), and corruption brought on a severe financial crisis in East and Southeast Asia beginning in 1998 (see Chapter 10). Sharp declines in production, plant closings, currency devaluations, and inflation all eradicated many of the gains the population had enjoyed in the preceding decades.

Two of Latin America's major bureaucratic-authoritarian regimes—Brazil and especially Chile—also had relatively successful economic records, though not without problems. After several false starts, Chile's probusiness, export-oriented policies ushered in a period of strong economic expansion with low inflation. Those achievements, however, were preceded by a period of severe economic hardship, with the poor being forced to bear a disproportionate share of the sacrifice. Under Chile's military dictatorship, as with other BA regimes, income distribution deteriorated. After the restoration of democracy in 1990, the civilian governments of Patricio Aylwin and Eduardo Frei maintained high growth rates while using targeted programs to reduce the number of Chileans living in poverty. Antipoverty programs continue under the current presidency of Ricardo Lagos in the face of more difficult economic challenges.

Brazil's BA regime achieved dramatic economic growth during the late 1960s and 1970s, turning the country into an important industrial power. The benefits of that growth, however, were very poorly distributed, leaving many of the poor worse off. Moreover, Brazil's "economic miracle" was built on excessive foreign borrowing, making the nation the Third World's largest external debtor. Unlike Chile, civilian rule has not appreciably improved the economy since the military stepped down in 1985. Initially, continued deficit spending and poor planning brought back the hyperinflation that the generals had vowed to eradicate. President Fernando Henrique Cardoso brought inflation under control in the 1990s, but economic growth has been weak and the country's financial structure unstable. Cardoso's successor, President Lula da Silva, has vowed to alter the economic model introduced by the military in an attempt to better serve the needs of the poor, though he has maintained conservative fiscal policies.

Other Latin American military governments, including the BA regimes in Argentina and Uruguay, generally performed poorly in the economic sphere. They spent excessively on defense, borrowed too much, suffered from corruption, and lacked a grasp of development economics. In Africa, the armed forces' economic record has generally ranged from poor to disastrous.

Moving beyond the evidence from individual cases such as these, some analysts have offered more systematic statistical analyses. Examining data on economic indicators such as growth rates and inflation, they have compared the economic performance of military and civilian governments throughout the Third World or in particular regions. Such comparisons, however, face a number of methodological problems. It is very difficult to control for the myriad of other factors that might explain why one set of governments has performed better than another.[79] For example, if we were to compare the performance of specific military regimes with the civilian governments that preceded or replaced them, we would be analyzing their economic records during different time periods when international economic conditions unrelated to regime type—such as oil prices or U.S. demand for Third World imports—had changed. Moreover, the outgoing regimes may have pursued erroneous economic policies whose effects only manifested themselves under the successor regime. For example, the poor economic performance of many restored Latin American democracies in the 1980s was often related to the excessive deficit spending and borrowing of their military predecessors.

Generally, statistically controlled cross-national analyses have found little difference between the economic growth rates of the two types of regimes. Karen Remmer's analysis of Latin America, however, indicates that economies frequently decline right after the military has stepped down. She suggests, quite reasonably, that since there is a lag time between when economic policies are introduced and the effects that they have, it would appear that the outgoing military governments, rather than their civilian successors, were responsible for the quick decline in performance.[80] It is worth noting that the military rulers with the best economic performance—South Korea, Indonesia, and Chile—recognizing the limits of their own skills, pursued the policy recommendations of civilian advisers.[81]

◆

MILITARY WITHDRAWAL FROM POLITICS

Once the armed forces have become entrenched in the political system, dislodging them is normally no easy task. Military withdrawal is sometimes induced by domestic upheavals (Indonesia) or by external intervention (Uganda). More often, however, the armed forces have voluntarily relinquished power for one or more of the following reasons: having accomplished their major objectives, they see no value in retaining power; deteriorating economic conditions make continued rule unappealing; extended rule undermines internal military cohesion; or, the regime becomes so unpopular that staying in office would reduce the military's legitimacy as an institution.

Many military governments came into office as "caretakers" whose goal was to restore stability or solve a particular problem and then quickly return control to civilians. In Ecuador, for example, the armed forces frequently ousted elected leaders whom they considered too demagogic, too populist, or too incompetent. After ruling relatively briefly, they then voluntarily stepped down.

Since the perpetrators of institutional coups took power with expectations of augmented military budgets and accelerated economic growth, their interest in governing, not surprisingly, wanes when the economy turns sour. In countries such as Peru, Uruguay, and Thailand, economic downturns have convinced military governments to step down. Economic declines may also aggravate internal divisions within the armed forces.

In Sub-Saharan Africa, governing may also aggravate ethnic divisions within the army, particularly when officers from one tribe or religion dominate top government positions. For example, in Nigeria, the armed forces' entrance into the political arena unleashed four internal coups in a 10-year span, with ethnic tensions playing a role. Two heads of government and a number of other senior officers were killed in the military's internal struggles. Some military governments, fearing a deterioration in military cohesiveness of that sort, have preferred to step down, leaving the country's problems to civilians.

Finally, just as military coups are most likely when civilian governments lack legitimacy, the army is most likely to return to the barracks when its own legitimacy declines. This happens most dramatically when the soldiers have been defeated in war. For example, following its humiliating defeat by Britain in the Falklands (or Malvinas) war, the Argentine military regime was forced to step down. Similarly, in Pakistan, the military had to transfer power to its leading civilian critic, Zulfiqar Ali Bhutto, after it lost East Pakistan (now Bangladesh) in a war with India.

Of course, there are other ways military regimes lose legitimacy. In Uruguay, economic decay and public revulsion against the political repression so weakened the military government that it unexpectedly lost a national referendum that it was sure it could tightly control.[82] Eventually, popular discontent induced the generals to negotiate a return to civilian government. In the 1990s, in Thailand, massive student-led prodemocracy demonstrations convinced the armed forces to withdraw.

While some combination of these factors has accounted for the withdrawal of most military regimes, they have not guaranteed that the armed forces would stay out. Indeed, until the 1980s, the soldiers were likely to return. Talukder Maniruzzaman examined 71 instances of military withdrawal from office in the Third World from 1946 to 1984.[83] In 65 percent of these cases, the armed forces were back in power within five years.[84]

Since the early 1980s, however, those military regimes that have stepped down have been more prone to stay out of office. Except for Sub-Saharan Africa—where in late 2003 military regimes remained in such nations as the Republic of Congo, Ecuatorial Guinea, Central African Republic, Togo, Côte d'Ivoire, Chad, Uganda, Rwanda, and Libya—there has been a dramatic decline in Third World armed forces rule. For example, as of 2005, the Latin American nations of Argentina, Ecuador, Brazil, Guatemala, and El Salvador, all with long histories of armed forces' intervention, have enjoyed anywhere from 16 to 27 years without military government. In South Korea, decades of military dominance came to an end in 1993.[85] Even in Africa, military rulers in several countries, including Nigeria, Ghana, Benin, and Congo-Brazzaville, have been replaced by elected civilian governments.[86]

In some cases, the military's legitimacy was undermined by years of repressive or corrupt rule. Thus, Argentina's elected governments since the mid-1980s have been able to reduce the country's formidable armed forces to one-third their previous size. Elsewhere, as in Mozambique, El Salvador, and Nicaragua, peace treaties ending long civil wars mandated sharp reductions in the size of the military. In other countries, however, the military has maintained its share of the government budget.

Ultimately, if the armed forces are to acquiesce to their removal from the center of national politics, they will need to find new roles to justify their existence. This is particularly true in countries that face no serious external threat. In Latin America and much of Africa, for example, wars between nation-states, as opposed to civil conflict, have been quite rare. In assigning the military new roles, however, new civilian governments must be careful not to involve it in tasks that may draw it back into politics—a danger some analysts see in the Latin American armed forces' growing involvement in combating the drug trade.

New Roles for the Armed Forces

Many of the proposed "new roles" for the military are not really entirely new. They include combating drug trafficking (in parts of Latin America, the Caribbean, and Asia), antiterrorist activity, emergency relief efforts (following natural disasters), and construction of infrastructure such as roads. Unfortunately, in the past some of these activities have brought as many new problems as solutions. In Mexico, Colombia, the Caribbean, and Central America, antidrug efforts have often corrupted the armed forces, as officers changed from enforcers to well-paid protectors of the drug cartels. In Mexico, for example, there have even been gun fights between antidrug units and other soldiers that had been paid off to protect drug bosses. Furthermore, the armed forces have often used their mandates to combat terrorism and other forms of internal subversion as carte blanche to violate human rights and crush peaceful and legitimate political opposition groups.

During the Cold War, U.S. training programs for Third World officers often stressed democratic norms. However, the training missions' strong emphasis on combating guerrilla movements and other perceived subversive threats was sometimes understood to mean that security objectives justify repressive tactics, human rights violations, and interference in national politics. With the end of the Cold War, however, the United States began to deliver a more unambiguous message. During the mid-1990s, for example, a directive sent to U.S. military commanders stationed overseas called on them to encourage foreign armed forces "to consider roles … that are supportive of civilian control and respectful of human rights and the role of law."[87] During the Clinton administration, the International Military Education and Training program (IMET) increasingly emphasized those values.[88] If democracy is to survive and advance in the LDCs, the military must pursue its new roles in a manner that reinforces, rather than subverts, civilian control and strengthens the military's respect for human rights and civil liberties. This will be no small task.

Finally, one other new role for Third World militaries merits mention. In recent years countries such as Argentina, India, Pakistan, and Uruguay have supplied United Nations peacekeeping forces for trouble spots such as Bosnia, Cambodia, and Afghanistan. This represents a very different military role and holds great promise for supporting international peace efforts. In addition, West African regional peacekeeping forces have recently been sent to Liberia and Sierra Leone. But there is some potential for mischief since regional powers such as Nigeria may use these interventions as a means of extending their own influence and pursuing their foreign policy agendas.

CONCLUSION: DEMOCRACY AND THE MILITARY

By definition, the spread of democracy has reduced the number of Third World military governments. This does not mean that the specter of military takeovers has disappeared. By one count, there were 30 to 40 coup attempts in the 1980s and early 1990s.[89] As we have noted, direct military intervention persists as a problem in Africa and even in Latin America, where the greatest progress has been made. There also have been relatively recent coup attempts in countries such as Ecuador and Venezuela.

Even in democratically elected governments, the armed forces often still exercise considerable political influence in certain policy areas and may remain outside civilian control. For example, in Chile, where General Pinochet's outgoing dictatorship was able to dictate the terms of the 1989 transition to democracy, the new constitution afforded the armed forces considerable influence. The military was granted amnesty for most of its human rights violations, including the murder of some 2,000 to 3,000 civilians. The elected civilian president lacked the authority to remove the military's chief of staff, and the armed forces named several appointed members of the nation's senate. General Pinochet himself was appointed senator for life. It was to be some nine years before a Spanish judge indicted Pinochet for human rights violations, and he was placed under an extended house arrest during a medical visit to England. Only then did the Chilean armed forces lose their aura of invincibility, and only then was Chile's civilian government able to more forcefully assert its control over the military and expand trials for human rights violations.

If democracy is to be consolidated, merely restoring civilian government is not enough. The military must be placed securely under civilian control, and the generals must unconditionally accept the authority of freely elected presidents and prime ministers who govern by the rules of the "democratic game" (respecting civil liberties and the legitimacy of political activity by opposition groups). Long accepted in the advanced industrialized democracies and in a small number of LDCs such as India, Costa Rica, and Jamaica, these attitudes and behaviors have begun to take root in a growing number of developing nations since the inception of the third wave of democratization. Still, in many LDCs much remains to be done to enshrine civil-military relationships that sustain democracy.

Stable and secure democratic government requires a professionalized military that is committed to staying out of domestic politics. In other words, there must be both "a high level of … professionalism and recognition by military officers of the limits of their professional competence" and "subordination of the military to the civilian political leaders who make the basic decisions on foreign and military policy" as well as domestic policy.[90] Officers must define their professional role as defending their country from potential external threats and must recognize that their involvement in national politics will only divide the armed forces and diminish their professional capacity. But just as the generals and colonels must keep out of national politics, civilian political leaders must respect the military domain and not attempt to politicize the armed forces. All too often, aspiring political leaders who are unable to gain office through legitimate channels have approached the armed forces for support. As David Mares has noted:

> If civilians are willing to accept democracy as a value, it is hard to see how a professional military would be drawn into politics. And if civilians, especially powerful corporate groups, do not accept the rules of the democratic game, it is difficult to see how democracy could be consolidated whether or not the military intervenes.[91]

Even the most successful military regimes inhibit political development. They do so because their very rationale for taking office is "the politics of antipolitics."[92] With their hierarchical perspective and their distaste for disorder, soldiers believe in a managed society. Most reject the give and take of political competition and the compromises inherent in politics. Consequently, they

> fail to see the functional aspects of the great game of politics: They severely restrict the free flow of the political process and force would-be politicians into a long period of hibernation. ... The opportunity for gaining political skills by a people once under a military regime is likely to be continually postponed with the arrival of every new military regime.[93]

DISCUSSION QUESTIONS

1. What factors influence the likelihood of military intervention in Third World politics?
2. What are the major types of military regimes, and what are their goals?
3. What are the major strengths and weaknesses of military governments?
4. What factors induce the armed forces to withdraw from politics?
5. What effect, if any, has the growth of Third World democracy had on military spending?

NOTES

1. Harold Crouch, *The Army and Politics in Indonesia* (Ithaca, NY: Cornell University Press, 1978), 345.

2. William Thompson, "Explanations of the Military Coup," Ph.D. dissertation, University of Washington, Seattle, 1972, 11. Quoted in Amos Perlmutter, *The Military and Politics in Modern Times* (New Haven, CT: Yale University Press, 1977), 115.

3. Claude E. Welch, "Military Disengagements from Politics?: Incentives and Obstacles in Political Change," in *Military Power and Politics in Black Africa*, ed. Simon Baynham (New York: St. Martin's Press, 1986), 89–90; Steven Thomas Seitz, "The Military in Black African Politics," in *Civil-Military Interaction in Asia and Africa*, eds. Charles H. Kennedy and David J. Louscher (Leiden, The Netherlands: E. J. Brill, 1991), 65, 67.

4. Samuel Decalo, *Coups and Army Rule in Africa* (New Haven, CT: Yale University Press, 1990), 2.

5. Harold A. Trinkunas, "Crafting Civilian Control in Argentina and Venezuela," in *Civil-Military Relations in Latin America*, ed. David Pion-Berlin (Chapel Hill: University of North Carolina Press, 2001), 161-193.

6. When Aquino's term ended, Ramos, running as a civilian, was democratically elected as her successor. During his term in office he increased the military's institutional influence in government. See Jeffrey Riedinger, "Caciques and

Coups: The Challenge of Democratic Consolidation in the Philippines," in *Democracy and Its Limits*, eds. Howard Handelman and Mark Tessler (Notre Dame, IN: Notre Dame University Press, 1999), 176-217.

7. Morris Janowitz, *Military Institutions and Coercion in the Developing Nations: Expanded Edition of the Military in the Political Development of New Nations* (Chicago: University of Chicago Press, 1977), 105.

8. Samuel P. Huntington, *The Soldier and the State: The Theory and Politics of Civil-Military Relations* (New York: Vintage Books, 1964).

9. Samuel P. Huntington, "Civilian Control of the Military: A Theoretical Statement," in *Political Behavior: A Reader in Theory and Research*, eds. Heinz Eulau, Samuel Eldersveld, and Morris Janowitz (New York: Free Press, 1956), 380–381.

10. Samuel P. Huntington, "Patterns of Violence in World Politics," in *Changing Patterns of Military Politics*, ed. Samuel P. Huntington (New York: Free Press, 1962), 19–22.

11. Alfred Stepan, "The New Professionalism of Internal Warfare and Military Role Expansion," in *Armies and Politics in Latin America*, rev. edit., eds. Abraham Lowenthal and J. Samuel Fitch (New York: Holmes and Meier, 1986), 134–150. See also Jose Nun, "The Middle-Class Military Coup Revisited," in ibid., 59–95, for similar arguments.

12. Michael C. Desch, *Civilian Control of the Military: The Changing Security Environment*, (Baltimore: The Johns Hopkins Press, 1999).

13. Ruth First, *The Barrel of a Gun: Political Power in Africa and the Coup D'état* (London: Allen Lane/Penguin Press, 1970), 208, 4.

14. Michel Louis Martin, "Operational Weaknesses and Political Activism: The Military in Sub-Saharan Africa," in *To Sheathe the Sword: Civil-Military Relations in the Quest for Democracy* (Westport, CT: Greenwood Press, 1997), 89.

15. Samuel P. Huntington, *Political Order in Changing Societies* (New Haven, CT: Yale University Press, 1968), 194.

16. Robert Wesson, "Preface," *New Military Politics in Latin America*, ed. Robert Wesson (New York: Praeger, 1982), v.

17. Samuel E. Finer, *The Man on Horseback: The Role of the Military in Politics*, 2d ed. (London: Penguin Books, 1976), 78–82.

18. Huntington, *Political Order in Changing Societies*.

19. Samuel P. Huntington, "Reforming Civil-Military Relations," in *Civil-Military Relations and Democracy*, eds. Larry Diamond and Marc F. Plattner (Baltimore: The Johns Hopkins University Press, 1996), 9. Italics added. However, during the 1970s countries such as Argentina, Chile, and Uruguay suffered successful coups despite having per-capita GNPs well above $1,000.

20. For a cautiously optimistic look at Venezuelan democracy and the role of the military written only a year before former coup leader Lt. Colonel Hugo Chávez's election as president, see Gisela Gómez Sucre and María Dolores Cornett, "Civil-Military Relations in Venezuela," in *Civil-Military Relations*, ed. David R. Mares, (Boulder, CO: Westview Press, 1998), 59–75.

21. Terry Karl, "Petroleum and Political Pacts: The Transition to Democracy in Venezuela," in *Transitions from Authoritarian Rule*, eds. Guillermo O'Donnell, Philippe C. Schmitter, and Laurence Whitehead (Baltimore, MD: Johns Hopkins University Press, 1986), 196–219. See also Felipe Aguero, "The Military and Democracy in Venezuela," in *The Military and Democracy*, eds. Louis W. Goodman, Johanna S. R. Mendelson, and Juan Rial (Lexington, MA: Lexington Books, 1990), 257–276.

22. Marion J. Levy Jr., *Modernization and the Structure of Societies* (Princeton, NJ: Princeton University Press, 1966), vol. 2, 603.

23. Lucian W. Pye, "Armies in the Process of Political Modernization," in *The Role of the Military in Underdeveloped Countries*, ed. John J. Johnson (Princeton, NJ: Princeton University Press, 1962), 69–89.

24. Manfred Halpern, *The Politics of Social Change in the Middle East and North Africa* (Princeton, NJ: Princeton University Press, 1963), 75, 253.

25. One of the most influential was Morris Janowitz, *Military Institutions and Coercion in Developing Nations* (Chicago: University of Chicago, 1977). For a summary of those writings and further references, see Henry Bienen, "The Background to Contemporary Study of Militaries and Modernization," in *The Military and Modernization*, ed. Henry Bienen (Chicago: Atherton, 1971), 1–33; First, *The Barrel of a Gun*, 13–20.

26. Daniel Lerner and Richard D. Robinson, "Swords and Plowshares: The Turkish Army as a Modernizing Force," in *The Military and Modernization*, 117–148.

27. Eric A. Nordlinger, *Soldiers in Politics: Military Coups and Governments* (Englewood Cliffs, NJ: Prentice Hall, 1977), 32–37.

28. Karen L. Remmer, *Military Rule in Latin America* (Boston: Unwin Hyman, 1989), 3.

29. It is not invariable that the armed forces of the least developed nations are reform oriented. Often, coups in Africa and other very poor areas are motivated solely by the self-interest of their military leaders. While the military has often been progressive in the less developed nations of South America, Africa, and the Middle East, it has been quite reactionary in Central America and the Caribbean, where it has been co-opted by the upper class.

30. Eric Nordlinger, *Soldiers in Politics*, 173; also Huntington, *Political Order*, chap. 4.

31. Huntington, *Political Order*, 221.

32. Decalo, *Coups and Army Rule in Africa*, 133.

33. John Booth, *The End and the Beginning: The Nicaraguan Revolution*, 2d ed. (Boulder, CO: Westview Press, 1985).

34. Some relatively personalistic dictators, like Argentina's Juan Perón, have introduced broader social programs. Perón sought to industrialize the country and benefit the working class. Even benevolent personalistic regimes such as his, however, still have suffered from extensive corruption and overconcentration of power in the hands of one person.

35. Decalo, *Coups and Army Rule in Africa*, 139–198.

36. On personalistic dictatorships in Africa, military and civilian, see Robert Jackson and Carl Rosberg, *Personal Rule in Africa* (Berkeley: University of California Press, 1982).

37. David J. Gould, *Bureaucratic Corruption and Underdevelopment in the Third World* (New York: Pergamon Press, 1980), xiv; Michael J. Schatzberg, *The Politics of Oppression in Zaire*

(Bloomington: Indiana University Press, 1988). Mobutu changed the name of his country from the Congo to Zaire. After he was overthrown, the name was changed back to the Congo.

38. Richard Millet, *Guardians of the Dynasty* (Maryknoll, NY: Orbis, 1977).

39. Decalo, *Coups and Army Rule in Africa*, 11. Decalo argues that in Africa personalities, more than broad socioeconomic or political variables, explain military intervention. See also his *Psychoses of Power: African Personal Dictatorships* (Boulder, CO: Westview Press, 1989).

40. Edward A. Olsen and Stephen Jurika Jr., "Introduction," and Harold W. Maynard, "The Role of the Indonesian Armed Forces," in *The Armed Forces in Contemporary Asian Society*, eds. Edward A. Olsen and Stephen Jurika, Jr. (Boulder, CO: Westview Press, 1986), 18, 207–208.

41. In some cases such councils have been mere facades, with one person really in power. Thus, it is not always easy to distinguish between personalistic and institutional military regimes. Ultimately, the determining factor is where real power resides rather than the formal structures.

42. Amos Perlmutter, *Political Roles and Military Rulers* (London: Frank Cass, 1981).

43. Guillermo O'Donnell, *Modernization and Bureaucratic-Authoritarianism: Studies in South American Politics* (Berkeley: University of California Press, 1973).

44. Jeffrey Lunstead, "The Armed Forces in Bangladesh Society," in *The Armed Forces in Contemporary Asian Society*, 316.

45. Ruth First, *Power in Africa* (New York: Pantheon Books, 1970), 20.

46. First, *The Barrel of a Gun*, 429.

47. Craig Baxter and Syedur Rahman, "Bangladesh's Military: Political Institutionalization and Economic Development," in *Civil-Military Interactions*, 43-60.

48. Harold Crouch, "The Military and Politics in South-East Asia," in *Military-Civilian Relations*, 291.

49. Crouch, *The Army and Politics in Indonesia*.

50. Remmer, *Military Rule in Latin America*, 3–31.

51. Seitz, "The Military in Black African Politics," in *Civil-Military Interaction*, 61–75.

52. John J. Johnson, *The Military and Society in Latin America* (Stanford, CA: Stanford University Press, 1964); O'Donnell, *Modernization and Bureaucratic-Authoritarianism*.

53. Argentina's two military regimes lasted seven years each (1966 to 1973 and 1976 to 1983), with a three-year hiatus of unstable civilian government. The Pinochet government in Chile lasted from 1973 to 1990. While the Chilean dictatorship was not as long-lived as Brazil's,

Pinochet himself ruled far longer than any of the military presidents in those four countries.

54. Guillermo O'Donnell, "Corporatism and the Question of the State," in *Authoritarianism and Corporatism in Latin America*, ed. James Malloy (Pittsburgh: University of Pittsburgh Press, 1977). The most complete analysis of O'Donnell's rather difficult theories is contained in David Collier, ed., *The New Authoritarianism in Latin America* (Princeton, NJ: Princeton University Press, 1979); and an excellent critique is found in Karen L. Remmer and Gilbert W. Merkx, "Bureaucratic-Authoritarianism Revisited," *Latin American Research Review* 17, no. 2 (1982): 3–40.

55. For a discussion of the difference between inclusionary and exclusionary regimes and their relationship to democracy and authoritarianism, see Remmer, *Military Rule in Latin America*, 6–17.

56. "The Political Orientation Speech Delivered by Captain Thomas Sankara in Ouagadougou, Upper Volta on 2 October, 1983," in *Military Marxists in Africa*, eds. John Markakis and Michael Waller (London: Frank Cass, 1986), 145–153 (selected portions).

57. Samuel Decalo, "The Morphology of Radical Military Rule in Africa," in *Military Marxist Regimes*, 123.

58. Thomas S. Cox, *Civil-Military Relations in Sierra Leone* (Cambridge, MA: Harvard University Press, 1976), 14.

59. Kevin Middlebrook and David Scott Palmer, *Military Governments and Political Development: Lessons from Peru* (Beverly Hills, CA: Sage Publications, 1975).

60. Samuel Decalo, "Military Rule in Africa: Etiology and Morphology," in *Military Power and Politics in Black Africa*, 56, 58.

61. J. Bayo Adekanye, "The Post-Military State in Africa," in *The Political Dilemma of Military Regimes*, eds. Christopher Clapham and George Philip (London: Croom Helm, 1985), 87.

62. Crouch, "The Military and Politics in South-East Asia," in *Military-Civilian Relations*, 292–293.

63. Charles H. Kennedy and David J. Louscher, "Civil-Military Interaction: Data in Search of a Theory," in *Civil-Military Interaction*, 5.

64. Howard Handelman, "Uruguay," in *Military Government and the Movement towards Democracy in South America*, eds. Howard Handelman and Thomas Sanders (Bloomington: Indiana University Press, 1981), 218.

65. Decalo, *Coups and Army Rule in Africa*, 20.

66. Harold Crouch, "The Military in Malaysia," in *The Military, the State*, 130–131.

67. Claude E. Welch Jr., "From 'Armies of Africans' to 'African Armies': The Evolution of Military Forces in Africa," in *African Armies: Evolution and Capabilities*, eds. Bruce E.

Arlinghaus and Pauline H. Baker (Boulder, Co: Westview Press, 1986), 25.

68. Elisabeth Sköns et al., "Military Expenditures," in *The Stockholm International Peace Research Institute (SIPRI) Yearbook 2000: Armaments, Disarmament and International Security* (Oxford: Oxford University Press, 2000). Summarized on the SIPRI website (http://www.sipri.se/).

69. *Electronic Mail & Guardian* (Johannesburg, South Africa) October 16, 1997: http://www.mg.co.za

70. J. Samuel Fitch, *The Armed Forces and Democracy in Latin America* (Baltimore, MD: The Johns Hopkins University Press, 1998), 77–78.

71. Juan Rial, "Armies and Civil Society in Latin America," in *Civil-Military Relations*, 57.

72. Michel Louis Martin, "Operational Weaknesses and Political Activism," in *To Sheathe the Sword*, 89.

73. Pamela Constable and Arturo Valenzuela, *A Nation of Enemies: Chile under Pinochet* (New York: W. W. Norton, 1991).

74. Of course, many military regimes are not particularly repressive. However, it is precisely those that seize power to restore order in highly polarized societies that normally are the most brutal.

75. Nordlinger, *Soldiers in Politics*, 139.

76. Remmer, *Military Rule*, 40.

77. Jueng-en Woo, *Race to the Swift* (New York: Columbia University Press, 1991).

78. For a somewhat more critical view, particularly of income distribution and welfare in Indonesia, see "Military Regimes and Social Justice in Indonesia and Thailand," in *Civil-Military Interaction*, 96–113; see also the chapters on South Korea, Indonesia, and Thailand in James W. Morely, eds., *Driven by Growth* (New York: M. E. Sharpe, 1992).

79. For a discussion of the problems involved in evaluating the economic performance of Latin America's military governments, see Karen L. Remmer, "Evaluating the Policy Impact of Military Regimes in Latin America," in *Armies and Politics*, 367–385; Remmer, *Military Rule*, chap. 4.

80. Remmer, *Military Rule*, 197–200; see also, Robert W. Jackman, "Politicians in Uniform: Military Governments and Social Change in the Third World," *American Political Science Review* 72, no. 4 (1978): 1262–1275; Seitz, "The Military in Black African Politics." There are, of course, cases, such as Chile in the 1990s, when the econ-

omy picks up after the civilians take over and, assuming the improvement comes early, it seems reasonable to give the outgoing military government some credit for the progress.

81. Edward A. Olsen, "The Societal Role of the ROK Armed Forces," in *The Armed Forces in Contemporary Asian Society*, 95–96.

82. Howard Handelman, "Prelude to the 1984 Uruguayan Election: The Military Regime's Legitimacy Crisis and the 1980 Constitutional Plebiscite," in *Critical Elections in the Americas*, eds. Paul Drake and Eduardo Silva (San Diego: University of California Press, 1986).

83. In all of these cases military rulers were succeeded by civilians. There are, of course, also many instances of military governments giving way to another military government as the result of internal coups or other intramilitary conflict.

84. Talukder Maniruzzaman, *Military Withdrawal from Politics: A Comparative Study* (Cambridge, MA: Ballinger Publishing, 1987), 21, 24–25.

85. South Korea's first democratic presidential election had been held in 1987, but the victor, Roe Tae Woo, was a former military strongman. Thus, full civilian government did not come until Kim Young Sam assumed the presidency in 1993. On Korea's transition, see Byung-Kook Kim, "Korea's Crisis of Success," in *Democracy in East Asia*, eds. Larry Diamond and Marc F. Plattner (Baltimore, MD: Johns Hopkins University Press, 1998), 113–132.

86. Michael Bratton and Nicolas van de Walle, *Democratic Experiments in Africa* (New York: Cambridge University Press, 1997), 197–203.

87. Quoted in Louis W. Goodman, "Military Roles Past and Present," in *Civil-Military Relations and Democracy*, 32. The discussion that follows of "new roles" for the military draws on Goodman's chapter.

88. Joseph S. Nye Jr., "Epilogue: The Liberal Tradition," in *Civil-Military Relations*, 153–154.

89. Samuel P. Huntington, "Reforming Civil-Military Relations," 8.

90. Ibid., 3–4.

91. David R. Mares, "Civil-Military Relations, Democracy, and the Regional Neighbors," in *Civil-Military Relations*, 18.

92. Brian Loveman and Thomas M. Davies Jr., eds., *The Politics of Antipolitics: The Military in Latin America*, 2d ed. (Lincoln: University of Nebraska Press, 1989).

93. Ibid., 6.

chapter **10**

The Political Economy of Third World Development

Virtually every Third World government, except the most corrupt and incompetent, wishes to promote economic development. Economic growth coupled with a reasonably equitable income distribution offers the promise of improved living standards and, presumably, increased popular support for the ruling regime.[1] It also provides added tax revenues, thereby augmenting government capacity. And economic development can enhance a nation's military strength, diplomatic influence, and international prestige. But the obvious benefits of growth should not obscure the many difficult questions that surround economic development. For example: How is growth to be achieved, and how can the sometimes conflicting goals of economic development be reconciled? How should the inevitable sacrifices required for generating early economic development be shared? How can economic development be achieved without doing irreparable harm to the environment?

The optimism expressed by early modernization theorists regarding Third World economic development seemed ill-founded during the 1980s in the face of sharp economic declines in Africa and Latin America.[2] In South Asia, Sub-Saharan Africa, and other developing regions, the war on poverty often seemed unwinnable. On the other hand, dependency theory's pervasive pessimism about the limits of development in the periphery seemed to have been belied by East Asia's spectacular growth from the 1960s into the 1990s, though that region's deep economic crisis at the end of the 1990s complicated the picture somewhat.

In recent decades, scholarship on the Third World has often focused on its *political economy*. Martin Staniland defines this field as the study of "how politics determines aspects of the economy, and how economic institutions determine the political process," as well as "the dynamic interaction between the two forces."[3] This chapter focuses on several important economic issues: What should the role of the state be in stimulating and regulating economic growth and industrialization in the LDCs? What are the major strategies for development? How should countries deal with the deep economic inequalities that persist, or even increase, during the modernization process? How should they cope with the environmental problems often associated with economic growth?

THE ROLE OF THE STATE

The question of the state's proper economic role has been at the center of political and economic debates for hundreds of years, first in Western industrial economies, and more recently in the Third World. During the sixteenth and seventeenth centuries, major European powers were guided by the philosophy of *mercantilism*, which viewed a nation's economic activity as a means of enhancing the political power of the state and its monarch. Government, consequently, was viewed as "both source and beneficiary of economic growth."[4] That perspective was sharply challenged by the eighteenth-century Scottish political economist Adam Smith, who favored a minimized state that allowed market forces a relatively free hand. The following century, Karl Marx, reacting to the exploitative nature of early capitalism, proposed assigning the state a dominant role, at least initially, through ownership of the means of production and the centralized direction of the economy. Finally, in the twentieth century, Sir John Maynard Keynes, responding to the Great Depression, advocated a substantial degree of government economic intervention but rejected Marxist prescriptions for state ownership and centralized planning.

Today, the collapse of the Soviet bloc's centrally controlled "command economy" and the poor economic performance of the remaining communist nations (except China and Vietnam, which have largely abandoned Marxist economics) have discredited the advocates of state-dominated economies. At the same time, however, no government embraces full *laissez faire* (i.e., allowing market forces a totally free reign, with no government intervention). All countries, for example, no matter how capitalistic, have laws regulating banking, domestic commerce, and international trade. Most have introduced some environmental regulation. In the real world, then, governments must decide where to position themselves between the extreme poles of laissez faire and a command economy.

For a number of reasons, that choice is particularly contentious in the LDCs. The fragile nature of many Third World economies, their high levels of poverty, their poor distribution of wealth and income, their extreme dependence on international market forces, and their endangered natural environment have encouraged many governments to assume an active economic role. Moreover, many developing nations also lack a strong entrepreneurial class and substantial private capital for investment. As a consequence, their governments have often built the steel mills, railroads, or sugar refineries that the private sector could not or would not. More recently, governments have been called upon to protect the environment against the ravages of economic development. Not surprisingly, then, state economic intervention traditionally has been more pronounced in Africa, Latin America, and much of Asia than in the West. In recent decades, however, a worldwide trend toward "neoliberal" (free enterprise) economic policies has sharply reduced government economic intervention in both the developing and developed world.[5]

This chapter discusses a number of alternative models prescribing the role of the state in Third World economies, ranging from command economies such as North Korea's to very limited state intervention in Hong Kong. In considering these alternatives, the reader should keep in mind that these are ideal types. Few countries fit any of these models perfectly (Cuba's Marxist government, for example, permits private farming and a variety of small businesses), and many nations have tried some mix of these approaches. Moreover, other models exist, so the options discussed below are not exhaustive.

The Command Economy

Marxism began as a critique of capitalism in the Western world during the early stages of industrial development. Inherently, argued Marx, capitalism produces an inequitable distribution of wealth and income because those who control the means of production (industrialists, landlords) exploit those who work in them (the working class, peasants). One of Marxism's appeals to its supporters, then, has been its promise of great equality and social justice. In modern times, economy inequality has tended to intensify as countries have moved from the lower to the middle levels of development.[6] Consequently, it is not surprising that Marxist ideology initially appealed to many Third World leaders and aspiring leaders who were troubled by the deep injustices in their own economic systems. That argument was particularly persuasive in Latin America and parts of Africa, where there are the greatest disparities between rich and poor.

A second assertion made by Third World Marxist regimes was that only they could free their country from the yoke of dependency. Since many dependency theorists believe that an exploitative relationship between core industrial nations and peripheral LDCs is an inevitable outcome of capitalist trade and investment, they have felt that only a socialist economy could achieve economic independence and development.

Finally, another of communism's appeals has been its belief in centralized state control over the economy. A command economy, initially established in the Soviet Union, has two central features. First, the means of production are primarily owned and managed by the state. That includes factories, banks, major trade and commercial institutions, retail establishments, and, frequently, farms. While all communist nations have allowed some private economic activity, the private sector has been quite limited, aside from communist nations such as China, which have largely abandoned Marxist economics in recent years. Second, decisions concerning production are not set by market forces but rather by centralized state plans.

Interestingly, Marxists have viewed market (capitalist) economies as anarchistic because they leave the most fundamental decisions over the allocation of resources and the determination of prices to the whims of supply and demand. Thus, Adam Przeworski has satirized the orthodox Marxists' attitude toward capitalism's "invisible [guiding] hand": People in Britain and the United States get up each morning and find their newspapers or milk cartons already sitting outside their doors without even knowing who delivered them. However, Przeworski noted wryly, Marxists continued to insist that the paper or milk carton couldn't possibly have arrived there without a central planner guaranteeing its delivery.[7] He countered that under a centrally planned economy not only wouldn't home delivery be reliable, but there would be constant shortages of paper, cartons, and milk. Indeed, the collapse of Soviet and Eastern European communism revealed the organizational failures of centralized, command economies.

In fact, the flaws of command economies are now so obvious as to hide their earlier accomplishments. By dictating the movement of people and resources from one sector of the economy to another, communist countries such as the Soviet Union and China were able to jump-start their industrial takeoffs. During the 1920s and 1930s, "entire industries were created [in the USSR], along with millions of jobs that drew peasants away from the countryside and into higher-paying jobs and higher living standards."[8] Western estimates of Soviet economic performance during its industrialization phase indicate that between 1928 and 1955, GNP grew at a robust average annual rate of roughly 5 percent.[9] During the early decades of its revolution, China also moved quickly from a backward agrarian economy to a far more industrialized society. According to one leading authority, between 1952 and 1975, China's economy grew at an average annual rate of 8.2 percent, while industrial output surged ahead at 11.5 percent annually.[10] These rates far exceeded the norms in either capitalist developing nations or industrialized democracies.[11] Other analysts believe that China's growth rates could not have been that high because of the setbacks of the Great Leap Forward and the Cultural Revolution. Still, all agree that compared to India, Pakistan, and most LDCs, China's growth during that period, like the Soviet Union's decades earlier, was extremely impressive. Small wonder that the Soviet and Chinese models (though in many ways different from each other after 1966) were attractive to many Third World leaders.

Finally, command economies have generally made great strides toward reducing income inequalities. Indeed, it is here that communist LDCs most clearly outperform their capitalist counterparts. In Cuba, for example, the revolution brought a substantial transfer of income from the richest 20 percent of the population to the poorest 40 percent.[12] The poor also benefited from an extensive land reform program, subsidized rents, and free health care, though some of those gains were undermined in the 1990s, following the loss of Soviet economic assistance. Equality was further advanced through mass adult literacy programs and the expansion of education. Nor was Cuba unique in this respect. Cross-national, statistical comparisons indicate that communist countries as a whole have more equal income distribution than do capitalist nations at similar levels of development.[13]

Eventually, however, the weaknesses of command economies overshadow their accomplishments.[14] In the absence of indicators of consumer demand, state planners have little basis for deciding what to produce and how much. Moreover, factory and farm managers in centrally controlled economies are rewarded for meeting their output quotas, with little concern for product quality. Even in the best of circumstances, to be at all efficient, a centralized, command economy would need a highly skilled and honest bureaucracy equipped with sophisticated and accurate consumer surveys. None of these qualities exist in Third World bureaucracies. Moreover, in command economies, inefficient state bureaucracies have been given inordinate power and, as Lord Acton warned, "Power tends to corrupt, and absolute power tends to corrupt absolutely."

Analysts of Chinese politics observe that the price of doing business for local business entrepreneurs is bribing government officials (cadres) or their adult children.[15] Elsewhere as well, command economies have been known for their large privileged class of state and party bureaucrats (*apparatchiks*), who have enjoyed perquisites unavailable to the rest of the population. While the Soviet Union and China experienced impressive bursts of growth in the early decades of their revolutions, each eventually lost momentum as their economies became more complex and, hence, harder to control centrally. Moreover, command economies are more adept at building heavy industries such as steel mills or constructing public works projects—endeavors more typical of early industrialization—than they are at developing sophisticated, high-tech production techniques or producing quality consumer goods. The Soviet Union, for example, turned out impressive military hardware and powerful space rockets but was unable to produce a decent automobile or home washing machine.

By the late 1970s (in China) or the 1980s (the USSR), with both economies deteriorating, their leaders (Deng Xiaoping and Mikhail Gorbachev) recognized the need for economic decentralization and reduced state economic control. China's subsequent transition to *market socialism* (a mixture of free market and socialist economics) has produced one of the world's fastest growing economies. However, in the Soviet Union and its major successor state, Russia, reforms resulted in an economic collapse that lasted for nearly a decade. The fall of Soviet bloc communism and China's remarkable economic transformation have inspired market-oriented reforms in other command economies. Vietnam, for example, has transferred state farmland to the peasantry and freed prices from state controls. Elsewhere in Asia and Africa, governments such as Myanmar and the Congolese Republic have privatized much of the state sector and reduced government economic controls. The end of Soviet aid has undercut some of Cuba's earlier gains in health care, nutrition, and education. Stripped of its primary benefactor, it too has been forced to accept limited free-market innovations.

For many former communist nations in Eastern and Central Europe, the demise of their command economies has so far failed to improve living standards and has often sharply lowered them. In some cases, the economic order previously imposed by government authorities was removed without adequate free-market incentives to replace it. In a sense, the "stick" driving the economy forward disappeared before workable "carrots" had been developed to replace it. Workers who accepted Spartan living conditions in return for guaranteed employment, controlled prices, and free social services (what the Chinese call the "iron rice bowl") find themselves stripped of these guarantees with no compensatory gains. Only in China, where many state controls remain in place, has the transition toward free-market economics raised living standards substantially.

Latin American Statism

Even in capitalist Third World countries, the state has often played a major economic role, seeking to be an engine of economic growth. In the period between the two World Wars, many Latin American nations first pursued state-led industrialization. That process accelerated during the Great Depression of the 1920s and 1930s, when countries in the region had difficulty finding markets for their food and raw material exports and, consequently, lacked foreign exchange for industrial imports. Argentina, Brazil, Chile, Uruguay, and Mexico were among the early leaders in the push toward industrialization.

Unlike communist countries, Latin American nations left most economic activity in the hands of the private sector and did not centralize control over the economy. But their governments often owned strategically important enterprises and invested in industries that failed to attract sufficient private capital.

Consequently, prior to the recent privatization of state enterprises, many of the region's railroads, airlines, petroleum industries, mines, steel mills, electric power plants, telephone companies, and armaments factories were state owned.

Two aspects of state ownership in the region contradict popular stereotypes. First, many government takeovers were not opposed by the domestic private sectors. One reason was that the most important nationalizations—including the petroleum industries in Mexico and Venezuela, mining in Chile and Peru, and railroads in Argentina—affected companies that had been owned by foreign corporations rather than local capitalists. Second, the newly state-owned petroleum industries, railroads, and utilities provided private-sector industries with cheaper, subsidized transportation, power, and other needed resources. In fact, until the 1980s, conservative governments in the region were as likely to expand government ownership as were left-leaning or populist regimes. For example, during the 1960s and 1970s, Brazil's right-wing military regime substantially increased the size of the state sector.

Along with its ownership of many essential enterprises, the state also played a pivotal role in fomenting private-sector industrial growth. In Latin America's largest economies, the government initiated import-substituting industrialization (ISI) programs in the early to mid twentieth century. ISI (discussed more extensively later in this chapter) sought to replace imported consumer goods with products that were manufactured domestically.[16] Although import-substituting firms were almost always privately owned, government economic policies and programs were essential for stimulating industrial growth. These included protective import tariffs and quotas, favorable exchange rates, subsidized energy and transport, and low-interest loans.

In Argentina, Brazil, Colombia, Mexico, and elsewhere, such government-supported development policies were quite successful. From 1945 to 1970, rates of investment in Latin America were higher than in the Western industrial powers, and from 1960 to 1980, the region's manufacturing output grew faster as well.[17] Virtually every Latin American country began manufacturing basic consumer goods such as textiles, clothing, packaged food, and furniture. Larger nations such as Argentina, Brazil, and Mexico established automotive industries, steel mills, and other heavy industries. Although the largest manufacturing plants were usually foreign owned, local entrepreneurs also played an important role in the region's industrial expansion. In time, industrialization altered the region's demographic and class structures. Massive rural migration to the cities transformed Latin America into the Third World's most urbanized region (see Chapter 7). Many blue-collar jobs were created and the size of the middle class expanded substantially.

But hidden beneath these accomplishments, state-sponsored ISI also promoted economic inefficiencies and inequalities. While its nurturing of industrialization was helpful, perhaps necessary, in the early stages of economic development, government protection and stimuli were employed too broadly and for too long. Rather than serving as a finely calibrated tool for getting industrialization off the ground, ISI became a politically motivated juggernaut. With industrialists, the middle class, and organized labor all united behind these policies, elected officials were unwilling to wean established industries from government support and protection long after they should have become more self-sufficient. Inefficient domestic industries received excessive protection;

trade and fiscal policies designed to promote industrialization often harmed agricultural exports; and the income gap widened both between the urban and rural populations and between skilled and unskilled workers.

Mexico illustrates both the initial accomplishments and subsequent weaknesses of statism in the region. From the mid-1930s to 1970, the national government accounted for 35 to 40 percent of the country's total investment.[18] At the same time, the state-owned petroleum and railroad enterprises provided private industry with subsidized energy and transport (i.e., both were priced below their free-market values).[19] Government trade and labor policies protected Mexican companies from foreign competition and held down wages as a means of stimulating further investment. As a consequence, between 1935 and 1970, industrial output grew at an average annual rate of nearly 10 percent, and GNP rose 6 percent annually, making Mexico one of the world's fastest growing economies.[20] During the 1970s and early 1980s, however, the role of the state in the economy took on a life of its own and grew enormously.[21] By the mid-1980s, the government operated nearly 1,200 state enterprises (*parastatals*). Mexico's "economic miracle" had left the countryside and urban poor behind, creating a highly unequal distribution of income and substantial pockets of poverty. When the state petroleum company discovered vast new oil reserves in the 1970s and the price of petroleum more than tripled, the government came under intense political pressure to use its oil bonanza not just to help the poor, but to provide subsidies for consumers of all classes, further subsidize private industry, and create new jobs in the parastatals. Quite quickly, spiraling government expenditures exceeded new petroleum revenues and contributed to huge fiscal deficits and enormous foreign indebtedness.

In general, Latin America's development model introduced two important areas of inefficiency, both of which are also common elsewhere in the developing world. First, the many state-owned enterprises were frequently overstaffed and poorly run. It is not that all state enterprises are inherently inefficient. Advanced industrialized nations such as France and Norway have often operated state enterprises quite effectively. But few, if any, Third World governments have the skilled and disciplined personnel needed to perform at that level. Furthermore, in the face of high rates of unemployment and underemployment, governments are under great political pressure to hire more personnel than the enterprises need. Consequently, Third World parastatals have tended to be substantially overstaffed.[22] At the same time, these enterprises have also faced political pressures to sell the public consumer goods and services at highly discounted prices. For example, prior to 1991, Argentineans rode the state railroads for a nominal fee and received highly subsidized electricity. Elsewhere in the region, governments have subsidized or controlled gasoline prices, urban bus fares, and food prices.[23] Ultimately, the combination of money-losing parastatals, consumer subsidies, and subsidies to private-sector producers helped bankrupt many Latin American governments. By 1982 virtually every government in the region was deeply in debt and experiencing severe fiscal problems.

A second important weakness of Latin America's development model was the inefficiency it encouraged in the private sector. To be sure, governments throughout the world have effectively used protectionist measures to help infant industries get started during the early stages of industrialization.

Typically, a wall of high tariffs and import quotas has protected early domestic manufacturers of consumer goods from foreign competition. But over time, the level of protection needs to be scaled back or domestic firms will have little incentive to become more productive and internationally competitive. Instead, Latin American protectionism, rather than serving as a temporary stimulus, became embedded in the economy.

Starting in the 1980s, almost all Latin American nations, forced by the region's severe debt crisis and economic depression, sharply reversed their earlier statist policies. In Mexico, the de la Madrid and Salinas administrations (1982 to 1994) shut down or privatized more than 80 percent of the country's 1,155 state enterprises, including the national airline, telephone companies, and banks.[24] In Chile, the transition to a slimmed-down state began under the dictatorship of General Augusto Pinochet (1973 to 1990). But when democracy was finally restored, the new governing coalition (led first by the Christian Democrats and then the Socialists) continued many of Pinochet's economic policies, which they had once denounced.

While these reductions in public-sector activity may have been necessary, they were implemented at great human cost. Throughout Latin America, millions of workers lost their jobs, as parastatals either experienced massive layoffs after privatization or were simply shut down. In Mexico alone, an estimated 400,000 jobs were eliminated in the course of the government's economic restructuring. For example, more than half the workers formerly employed in state steel mills were laid off when their companies privatized.[25] Similar layoffs took place in Argentina, Chile, Peru, and Venezuela. At the same time, reduced protectionism in much of the region opened the door to a surge of imported consumer goods, thereby reducing sales and employment by local firms that were unable to compete. Finally, the elimination or reduction of government consumer subsidies sharply increased the cost of basic necessities such as food staples, gasoline, public transportation, and electricity.

In Mexico and Argentina, just as in Chile, populist and leftist parties that had once been the leading advocates of government economic intervention reluctantly conceded that the state sector had grown too unwieldy and had to be cut back.[26] Excessive government spending, coupled with the state's inability or refusal to make the middle and upper classes pay their fair share of taxes, resulted in massive fiscal deficits and runaway inflation. Only by substantially cutting budgetary deficits since the 1980s have Latin America's governments been able to control inflation that had reached annual rates of 1,000 to 10,000 percent in Argentina, Brazil, Nicaragua, and Peru. The debt crisis and the related economic recession contributed to a sharp decline in Latin American living standards from the early 1980s to the early 1990s (the "lost decade"). In Peru and Venezuela, for example, real incomes fell by nearly 40 percent.[27] Since the start of the 1990s, the region has experienced an irregular recovery. High inflation rates, which had severely eroded living standards, have been brought under control and some countries have enjoyed bursts of economic growth. But living standards have only recovered slowly, countries such as Venezuela, Brazil, and, especially Argentina have suffered severe economic crises, and growth elsewhere in the region has slowed in recent years.[28] Thus, while most analysts agree that Latin America's level of state economic interventionism and protectionism had to be reduced, neoliberal reforms designed to scale down government have failed to generate higher living standards in the region except in Chile.

East Asia's Developmental State

While Latin America has been struggling since the early 1980s, a number of East and Southeast Asian economies have grown at a phenomenal rate during most of that period. South Korea, Taiwan, Hong Kong, and Singapore (known as the "little tigers") and China (now the world's second largest economy) have received the most attention. For one thing, their impact on world trade has been enormous. China is now one of the United States' leading trading partners and the world's greatest exporter of manufactured goods. But other Southeast Asian economies—Thailand, Malaysia, and Indonesia—have also grown dramatically. From the mid-1960s until the region's recent economic crisis, Taiwan, South Korea, Singapore, Hong Kong, Thailand, Malaysia, Indonesia, and China all grew at annual rates ranging from 4 to 10 percent, and China and South Korea sometimes exceeded 10 percent.[29] In fact, from 1960 to the late 1990s, these economies grew almost three times as fast as Latin America and five times as fast as Sub-Saharan Africa.[30] While some East and Southeast Asian economies suffered setbacks during the financial crisis of the late 1990s, they have since resumed their high rates of growth. Moreover, the benefits of East and Southeast Asia's rapid growth were relatively equitably distributed, with a far narrower gap between the rich and poor than one finds in Latin America or Africa.

With the partial exception of Communist China (which has developed a mixed socialist and free-market economy), East and Southeast Asian countries have largely tied their growth to the free market. More than in other Third World regions, productive capacity has been largely owned by private enterprise, with a relatively smaller state sector.[31] Not surprisingly, this has led conservative economists to hail the East Asian economic miracle as a triumph of unfettered capitalism, a testimony to keeping government out of the economy.[32]

But many scholars specializing in East Asian economies argue that, to the contrary, governments in that region were key players in stimulating economic growth.[33] Examining the causes of Japan's spectacular postwar economic resurgence, Chalmers Johnson first formulated the notion of the *developmental state*.[34] The meaning of that term is best understood by comparing the role of government in East Asia's high-growth capitalist nations (Japan, South Korea, Singapore, and Taiwan) to its function in Western nations during their early industrial expansions some 150 years before. The early developing Western nations established *regulatory states* in which "government refrained from interfering in the marketplace, except to insure certain limited goals" (e.g., antitrust regulations, protection of consumer rights), while the East Asian developmental states "intervene actively in the economy in order to guide or promote particular substantive goals" (e.g., full employment, export competitiveness, energy self-sufficiency).[35]

Japan's powerful Ministry of International Trade and Industry (MITI), Johnson notes, directed that country's postwar industrial resurgence. Subsequently, South Korea, Taiwan, Singapore, Indonesia, and other industrializing nations in East and Southeast Asia adopted many aspects of Japan's state-guided, capitalist development model.[36] Typically, each country had a powerful government ministry or agency "charged with the task of planning, guiding and coordinating industrial policies."[37] They included South Korea's Economic Planning Board, Taiwan's Council for Economic Planning and Development, and Singapore's Economic Development Board, all modeled after MITI. Under the developmental state, there was far more extensive and direct government economic intervention than in the West, targeting either whole economic sectors (such as agriculture or industry), whole industries (such as computers, automobiles, or electronics), or particular companies (such as South Korea's Hyundai).[38]

Developmental states did not always implement identical policies. For example, the bonds between government and big business have been tighter in South Korea than in Taiwan, while state enterprises were more important in Taiwan than in Korea. In Singapore, government control over labor has been more extensive than in the other two countries.[39] But in all of them, the state played an important role, guiding the private sector toward targeted economic activities and stimulating growth in areas that the government wished to expand. Sometimes government planners have even pressured particular industries or companies to specialize in certain products and abandon others.

For the most part, East Asian state intervention was more indirect than it had been in Latin America, but, at least until recently, it was significant nonetheless. Among the tools governments have used to sway private-sector activity have been tax policy, control over credit, and influencing the price of raw materials. For example, when the South Korean and Taiwanese governments wished to develop the electronics, computer software, and automobile industries, they intervened aggressively, rather than leave it to the marketplace. They established related research institutes; granted firms in targeted industries preferential access to credit; temporarily required companies that had been importing those targeted products to switch to domestic manufacturers; and offered trade protection to new industries for limited periods of time. South Korea temporarily banned all imports of computers when it promoted that industry, and Taiwan did the same for textiles.[40]

While the East Asian development model's tremendous success has won it widespread admiration, some observers have remained skeptical about its applicability elsewhere. One concern is the model's apparent political requirements. Chalmers Johnson notes that most developmental states have been authoritarian—or what he calls "soft authoritarian"—during their major industrialization push.[41] Other analysts have felt that authoritarian or semi-authoritarian rule (including the ability to repress or control labor unions and to direct management) was an essential component of the region's early economic growth. Taiwan and South Korea industrialized under authoritarian governments, though both have subsequently become democracies. The governments of Malaysia, Singapore, and Indonesia have all repressed democratic expression to varying degrees. Since its return to Chinese rule, Hong Kong, a former British colony, has curbed its brief experiment with democracy. Of course, Japan, the original developmental state, is a democracy, but since the 1950s, its government has been largely dominated by one political party (the Liberal Democrats). Thus, we are left to wonder how the developmental state would perform under the democratic pressures now spreading across the Third World.

Another important question is the transferability of East Asian political and economic practices to other parts of the Third World.[42] The developmental state seems to require qualities that are in short supply elsewhere in the developing world: a highly skilled government bureaucracy and close cooperation between business, labor, and agriculture. In Indonesia, for example, a team of skilled government economists known as "the Berkeley Boys" (most of them had doctoral degrees from the University of California at Berkeley) oversaw that country's economic development. Similarly, South Korea's highly trained state technocrats worked closely with the country's dominant business conglomerates (*chaebols*), such as Hyundai and Samsung.[43] Similar cooperation between sophisticated government planners and big business, unchallenged by a relatively docile working class, has contributed to the economic surges elsewhere in East and Southeast Asia. Outside of Asia, however, only Chile's "Chicago Boys" (economists trained at the University of Chicago) brought a comparable set of skills and enjoyed a similar cooperation with the business community.

Some have argued that East Asia's Confucian culture—featuring nationalism, close cooperation between different sectors of society, and a strong work ethic—has been a critical ingredient in the region's rapid economic growth.[44] If that is true, then a development model that has worked in that part of the world may not transfer well to other cultures. Of course, similar cultural explanations have been put forth to explain the West's economic takeoff. Long ago, Max Weber credited the birth of capitalism to the Protestant work ethic. But such cultural explanations have always aroused considerable controversy. Critics point out, for example, that not all of Asia's star economic performers have Confucian cultures. Rapidly growing Malaysia and Indonesia, for example, are predominantly Muslim. A more telling criticism of the cultural thesis points out that Confucian culture has been around for centuries, while the East Asian economic "miracle" is only a few decades old.[45] Ironically, before the region's takeoff, some Western scholars attributed East Asia's poverty, in part, to Confucian culture.

In fact, it is implausible that there is something so uniquely Asian about the developmental state that it cannot be reproduced elsewhere. But few African, Latin American, or Middle Eastern nations currently offer promising conditions for its growth. Most still lack both a highly professional, merit-based bureaucracy and a spirit of cooperation between key economic actors that would allow them to replicate the East Asian model. And even in Asia, the economic crisis of the late 1990s revealed serious weaknesses in the developmental state model. In countries such as Indonesia, intense government involvement in the economy helped create "crony capitalism" in which the government provided well-connected investors with insider opportunities. Elsewhere, excessive government regulation stifled competition within the private sector. The developmental state has been fine-tuned since East Asia's financial crisis. Indeed, current free-trade regulations and neoliberal prescriptions from the World Trade Organization (WTO) mean that future industrial development in the LDCs will require somewhat less intervention than the initial Japanese model.

The Neoclassical Ideal

Quite unlike the preceding models, the neoclassical (or neoliberal) ideal assigns government a very limited economic role.[46] The state, it argues, should provide certain fundamental "public goods" such as national defense, police protection, a judicial system, and an educational system. It can also supply a physical infrastructure, including sewers and harbors, when it is not feasible for private capital to do so, and perhaps allocate enough resources to the very poor to meet their basic needs.[47] But, say neoclassical analysts, most Third World governments have injured their economies by moving far beyond that limited role. These critics attribute Africa's and Latin America's economic development problems to excessive state intervention, at least in the past, while they credit East Asia's success to their governments' allegedly limited role.

Neoclassical economists insist that free-market forces should determine production decisions and set prices without government interference. Consequently, they have criticized government policies designed to stimulate industrial growth in the LDCs: protective tariffs and import quotas that restrict free trade and thereby drive up prices to the consumer; artificial currency exchange rates that distort the prices of exports and imports; state subsidies to producers and consumers; and government controls on prices and interest rates. All of these measures, argue the neoclassicists, distort the choices made by producers, consumers, and governments. Only when these artificial constraints are removed will the economy "get prices right" (i.e., let them be determined by free-market forces).

During the past two decades the neoclassicists (also known as neoliberals) have largely won the debate against advocates of extensive state intervention. As we have observed, governments throughout Africa and Latin America have liberalized their economies in recent years, deregulating the private sector, removing trade barriers, and freeing prices. Government subsidies for industry and for consumers have been reduced, often out of financial necessity. And many state enterprises have been privatized. In part, these changes resulted from pressures that international lending agencies such as the World Bank and the International Monetary Fund (IMF) have exerted on the LDCs. But they have also sprung from the growing conviction of Third World governments that earlier statist models have failed. Still, the growing consensus that government intervention had gotten out of hand does not mean that the neoclassical model has triumphed. While conservative economists and politicians often depicted the East Asian economic miracle as proof positive of what free enterprise can do if government doesn't intervene in the economy, leading specialists on the region such as Stephan Haggard and Alice H. Amsden disagree. They insist that government intervention has been a fundamental ingredient of industrial growth in that region.[48] Far from "following the market," Robert Wade maintains, the state has actively "governed the market."[49] So, while the neoclassicist's criticisms of statist policies ring true, they take their case too far in prescribing a hands-off state.

In fact, the only East Asian economy that has nearly conformed to the neoclassical model has been Hong Kong's, and its recent absorption into Communist China does not seem to have altered that. As the least regulated economy in the area, it is often cited as a success story for unrestricted capitalism. But Hong Kong is such a unique case that it may not offer many lessons for other countries. For one thing, it is rather small and it consists mostly of a single city with no rural population to speak of. Like Singapore, it hasn't had to deal with rural poverty or the related problems that are so daunting in most Third World countries. Initially, its wealth was tied to its location as a major port for Asian trade and an outpost of the British empire. Other LDCs obviously don't enjoy such benefits.

Some of the strongest criticisms of neoclassical economics have come from environmentalists. From their perspective, even a modified policy of laissez faire, acknowledging some state responsibility for the environment, is totally inadequate. As Richard Albin notes, "The idea that private interest, operating within unfettered markets, will tend to produce a close approximation of the socially optimal allocation of resources, was close to the truth when output (population, too) was so much smaller."[50] Nevertheless, he argues, as world population and pollution reach dangerous levels, society can no longer afford to let free-market mechanisms allocate penalties for pollution. Such remedies would come far too late. Further discussion of economic growth and the environment follows later in this chapter.

Finding a Proper Role for the State

Political scientists and economists will long continue to debate the state's proper role in Third World economies. As time goes on, new models will undoubtedly emerge. Still, some areas of agreement have emerged in recent decades. On the one hand, the level of government intervention in both the command economies and Latin American statism was surely excessive. At the same time, the extremely limited government role advocated by the neoclassicists is unrealistic and inadequate in most countries. East Asia's developmental state model has been the most successful, at least until the late 1990s. But it is unclear whether it can be replicated elsewhere. Indeed, a model that succeeds in one country or region will not necessarily work in another. Countries vary greatly in size, human capital, natural resources, and the like. Thus, cookbook formulas will likely prove inadequate. As we have noted, the strong hand of the stereotypical developmentalist state—as implemented in Japan, South Korea, Singapore, and Taiwan—would have to be modified to meet current trade regulations under the World Trade Organization (WTO). Finally, new crises—such as the oil shocks of the 1970s, the Latin American and African debt crises of the 1980s, the Asian financial crisis of the 1990s, and international terrorism in the first decade of the twenty-first century—force planners to alter and adapt development models.

INDUSTRIALIZATION STRATEGIES

Since the time of Britain's industrial revolution, governments have equated industrialization with economic development, economic sovereignty, and military strength. Latin America's largest countries launched their major industrialization drives in the 1930s. Following World War II, a number of newly independent Asian and African countries also developed their industrial capacities. Steel mills and auto plants became symbols of national prestige.

Neoclassical economists frequently criticized industrialization programs in many LDCs, arguing that each country should specialize in economic activities for which it has a "comparative advantage." That is, it should produce and export those goods it can provide most efficiently and cheaply relative to other nations. Based on that argument, neoclassicists maintained that most Third World nations should abandon plans for industrialization and concentrate, instead, on the production and export of raw materials or agricultural products.[51] Rather than manufacture goods such as cars, washing machines, or fertilizers, they insisted, countries such as Sri Lanka or Kenya would be better off increasing tea or coffee exports, where they have a comparative advantage, so that they could use those earnings to import manufactured products. Similarly, they contended that it made little sense for Nigeria to build steel mills or for Uruguay to manufacture refrigerators. Still, many LDCs have been reluctant to depend fully on revenues from the export of "primary goods," in part because agricultural and raw-material prices are so volatile. One possible solution (easier said than done) is to pursue balanced growth, including some industrial development (presumably manufacturing products such as Indonesian wicker furniture, which draw on local natural resources and can be exported), while still stressing primary goods production and export.

Industrializing nations have generally pursued two alternative strategies: import-substituting industrialization (ISI) and export-oriented industrialization (EOI). In the first case, as we have seen, LDCs reduce their dependency on manufactured imports by producing more of them at home. Like Latin America, Asian nations began industrialization by producing for their own consumption. But, unlike Latin American ISI, which focused on consumer goods for the home market, EOI quickly turned to industrial development tied to exports. Although EOI has been most closely associated with East and Southeast Asia, it is a strategy now widely embraced in Latin America and other parts of the Third World. Starting later, Latin American and other developing areas have yet to catch up with Asia's export capabilities. One is much more likely to find shirts, blouses, electronics, or running shoes in American department stores that are manufactured in Singapore, Sri Lanka, Indonesia, or Thailand than similar products from Honduras, Brazil, or Colombia.

Import-Substituting Industrialization (ISI)

National economic policies are partly the product of deliberate choice, partly the result of political and socioeconomic opportunities and constraints. As we have seen, ISI emerged as a development strategy in Latin America during the 1930s as the worldwide depression sharply reduced international trade.[52] Because the industrialized nations of North America and Europe curtailed their consumption of Third World primary goods (Uruguayan wool, Argentinian beef, or Brazilian coffee), Latin America was denied the foreign exchange needed to import manufactured products. But while it was initiated as a response to the international economic crisis, ISI was subsequently transformed into a long-term strategy for industrial development. With substantial unemployment at home and urban populations pressing for economic growth, government leaders faced a political imperative to industrialize. Nationalist presidents such as Argentina's Juan Perón and Brazil's Getúlio Vargas forged populist coalitions of industrialists, blue-collar workers, and the urban middle class, all committed to industrialization.

As we have seen earlier, in order to protect embryonic domestic industries from foreign competition, *consumer* imports were generally limited by protective quotas and tariffs. At the same time, however, planners also wanted to facilitate other types of imports, namely capital equipment (primarily machinery) and raw materials needed by domestic manufacturers. To reduce the cost of those imports, governments overvalued their own currencies.[53] Eventually, most Latin American countries established multiple currency exchange rates, with differing rates for transactions tied to imports, exports, and other financial activities. To further encourage industrial development, governments also offered domestic manufacturers tax incentives, low-interest loans, and direct subsidies.[54]

Because of ISI's impressive record in Latin America from the 1940s into the 1970s, the strategy was emulated in many parts of Africa and Asia, sometimes with comparable success. Turkey, for example, enjoyed strong ISI growth before shifting to EOI during the 1980s.[55] Even East Asia's highly admired industrial export miracle was preceded by a period of ISI. By the 1970s, however, the ISI strategy had begun undermining Latin America's economies. As John Sheahan notes, "It fostered production methods adverse for employment, hurt the poor, blocked the possible growth of industrial exports [and] encouraged high-cost consumer goods industries."[56]

To understand how poorly Latin America's newly industrialized countries (NICs) fared in international trade relative to their East Asia counterparts, it is useful to compare Mexico (one of the region's major industrial powers) with East Asia's "little tigers" (South Korea, Taiwan, Hong Kong, and Singapore). Mexico has a larger population than the other four combined. It also has a considerable geographic advantage over them, being located thousands of miles closer to the United States, the world's largest importer. Yet as of the mid-1980s (prior to NAFTA), the combined value of manufactured exports of all four little tigers was 20 times as high as Mexico's.[57]

Export taxes and overvalued currencies put traditional primary goods exporters at a competitive disadvantage, thereby depriving the country of needed foreign exchange revenues. At the same time, because local consumer-goods manufacturers were allowed to import capital goods cheaply, the region never developed its own capital-goods industry and, instead, imported manufacturing technologies that were inappropriate to local needs. Subsidized imports of machinery and heavy equipment encouraged capital-intensive production (i.e., using relatively advanced technologies and machinery while employing fewer workers) rather than the labor-intensive manufacturing common to Asia. The ISI model of industrialization benefited a small, relatively well-paid "labor elite" (i.e., skilled unionized workers employed in highly mechanized factories). But it failed to provide enough jobs for the region's work force, leaving too many Latin Americans unemployed and underemployed.

Ironically, although ISI was originally designed to make Latin America more economically independent, in the end it merely replaced dependence on consumer-goods imports with dependence on imported capital goods, foreign technologies, and overseas bank credit. Traditional primary exports were allowed to languish, while little was done to develop new manufactured exports. Increased balance of trade deficits contributed to Latin America's spiraling foreign debt, leading eventually to a major debt crisis and an economic depression in the 1980s.[58] That crisis, in stark contrast to East Asia's prosperity at that time, induced Latin American governments to abandon their inwardly oriented economic policies as they tried to emulate East Asia's export-driven model. The North American Free Trade Agreement (NAFTA) between Mexico,

Canada, and the United States is the most dramatic manifestation of that region's move toward EOI.[59] Chile, once among the most inward-looking economies in the hemisphere, has been at the forefront of export manufacturing and free trade.[60]

Export-Oriented Industrialization (EOI)

East Asia's NICs initiated their industrialization drive through import substitution, just as their Latin American counterparts had done years earlier. Soon, however, they diversified into manufacturing for export. Early protectionist measures were phased out, thereby forcing local companies to become more competitive. State planners shaped the market, pressuring manufacturers and offering them incentives to export. By 1980, manufactured goods constituted more than 90 percent of all South Korean and Taiwanese exports but represented only 15 percent of Mexico's and 39 percent of Brazil's.[61] Fueled by their dynamic industrial export sectors, East Asia's booming economies became the envy of the developing world. More recently, India has enjoyed impressive growth stemming from the export of services as well as manufactured goods.

There are a number of explanations for East Asia's decision to stress manufactured exports and for Latin America's initial failure to do the same. For one thing, the East Asian industrialization drive began in the 1960s, a period of unprecedented expansion in world trade, inspired by the GATT, the General Agreement on Trade and Tariffs, and the West's economic boom. The opportunities offered by outwardly oriented growth were more obvious to government policy makers at that time. Conversely, the expansion of Latin American industrialization began during the Great Depression of the 1930s, a period of greatly restricted world trade. Indeed, it was their very inability to export traditional products at that time that inspired Latin American nations to turn initially to ISI. In retrospect, Latin America should have moved to EOI after World War II, but ISI seemed to be working so well until the mid-1970s that there was little incentive to change. Ironically, one reason why East and Southeast Asian countries chose EOI is that their economic opportunities seemed more limited than Latin America's. Because of their smaller populations, Hong Kong, Singapore, and Taiwan (though not South Korea) saw ISI, which relied upon the domestic market, as less feasible for them than for larger countries like Mexico, Argentina, Brazil, and Colombia.[62] Furthermore, with fewer agricultural goods or raw materials to export, East Asians turned a weakness into a strength by emphasizing manufactured exports.

Finally East Asian industrialization policies differed from Latin America's in part because they were more influenced by U.S. economic advisers and because East Asia's government planners were more likely to have received their economic training at American universities. During the decades after World War II, many Latin-American government economic planners were strongly influenced by the United Nations Economic Commission for Latin America (ECLA), a vigorous advocate of ISI. Until the 1980s, Latin American intellectuals remained very committed to economic nationalism and the need to limit U.S. influence. On the other hand, Taiwanese and South Korean military and political dependence on the United States during the postwar decades made their governments more receptive to American policy advisers advocating EOI. Since that time, many East Asian economic planners have received their graduate training at American universities, where they were inculcated with the values of free trade. It was not until the 1970s and 1980s that American-trained economists favoring free trade began to direct economic policy in Latin America.[63]

EAST AND SOUTHEAST ASIA'S ECONOMIC CRISIS

For decades, industrializing countries in East and Southeast Asia seemed to be doing everything right economically. The developmental state and the EOI strategy produced phenomenal growth and comparatively equitable income distribution. China, using a more centrally planned industrialization strategy and far more state ownership, pursued EOI with equal success. But for countries like Indonesia, Malaysia, South Korea, and Thailand, the bubble burst during the financial crisis of the late 1990s. There and elsewhere in Asia, the developmental state seemed in need of fine tuning. For the most part, the region has recovered far more quickly than Latin America did in the 1980s and 1990s, and most East and Southeast Asian economies resumed economic growth by 2001.

The Onset of the Crisis

On July 2, 1997, the Thai government announced that the exchange rate for their national currency, the baht, which had previously been fixed (i.e., the Thai government had guaranteed that its value relative to the dollar would remain constant), henceforth would be allowed to float (its value would now fluctuate based on market forces).

> To the casual observer this was ... hardly worth [much] attention ... But to individuals controlling huge pools of investment resources in Southeast Asia [including foreign investors], this was a flashing red light signaling danger for the entire region.[64]

As the value of the baht fell, investments on the Thai stock exchange and bank accounts held in bahts also lost value. For both the Thai government and private companies that had secured extensive loans in dollars from international banks, this meant that the cost in bahts of repaying those loans climbed precipitously.[65] International banks, in turn, curtailed further dollar loans to Thailand, knowing that it would be difficult for debtors to repay. The Thai private sector reduced its demand for foreign loans for the same reason.

> Panic soon set in. Thai and foreign investors began to unload their stocks on the Bangkok stock market and to sell other liquid securities. As confidence in the baht declined, Thais holding baht bank accounts rushed to convert their holdings into dollars or other hard currencies, thereby further undermining the value of the national currency. Rather than basing their decisions on a reasoned analysis of Thailand's economic capabilities, investors increasingly chose the pure psychology of escape. All controllers of liquid capital ... began behaving like spooked wildebeests on the Serengeti.[66]

For the many Thai businesses with overextended foreign debts, the costs of repayment were becoming overwhelming. Companies that imported consumer goods or manufacturing inputs (machinery, raw materials, technology licenses) found the price of doing business rising sharply as the value of the baht declined. Before long, many companies were closing down and laying off workers. Had the 1997 economic crisis been limited to Thailand, it would have been tragic for the Thai people but would have had little consequence for the world economy. Not surprisingly, however, foreign and domestic investors in other Southeast and East Asian boom economies began to fear that those countries might also be overheated. Plagued by the same fragilities (including excessive external debts) that had undermined Thailand's economy, Indonesia, Malaysia, and later South Korea were all forced to devaluate their currencies and were plunged into deep recessions. During the following year, the economic crisis threatened to spread to Hong Kong and sent chills down the spines of the region's two economic giants, Japan and China. At the same time, however, countries with relatively smaller foreign debts (Taiwan, Singapore, the Philippines, Vietnam, and China) were less vulnerable to capital flight and survived the crisis relatively well.

Causes of the Asian Crisis

What was perhaps most shocking about Asia's sharp economic plunge was how utterly unexpected it had been. Virtually up to the day that Thailand began the crisis by announcing its intention to float the baht, respected financial analysts had portrayed Southeast and East Asian economies as vibrant and growing. Why were the world's investment specialists so taken by surprise? What caused the initial virus in Thailand, and why did it spread so rapidly and insidiously to neighboring countries?

Several previously unnoticed weaknesses in the region's economies set the stage. Precisely because economic performance had been so spectacular for years, both investors and lending agencies had come to see rapid growth as virtually inevitable. Consequently, they threw caution to the wind. Businesses in Thailand, Indonesia, Malaysia, and South Korea had borrowed and invested excessively. From 1992 to 1997 alone, Asian companies (excluding Japan) had borrowed more than $700 billion from the rest of the world. The result was questionable investments, manufacturing overcapacity, and excess construction of new real estate. The downtown business centers of Bangkok, Jakarta (Indonesia), and Seoul (South Korea) were dotted with new, half-occupied office buildings. Not surprisingly, Southeast and East Asia's external debts eventually exceeded their capacity to repay readily.

In truth, economic growth is invariably cyclical, and no country or region can maintain high growth rates indefinitely. In particular, annual growth of the magnitude of 7 to 12 percent is only possible when economies are first taking off, and such rates usually cannot be sustained once these countries become more developed. Another problem was that credit in some countries was often not directed to firms or industries that could most effectively invest it. In Indonesia, "crony capitalism" saw the Suharto dictatorship steering government aid and bank credits to political insiders, most notably the president's children, who became billionaires. Corruption was not as pervasive in

South Korea, but the country's major industrial conglomerates enjoyed a cozy relationship with the government that allowed them ready access to state credit and other forms of government assistance.

These underlying long-term weaknesses were then aggravated by additional short-term problems. For a period of time, several Southeast Asian countries had pegged their currencies to the dollar, meaning that their governments had guaranteed to keep the currencies' values fixed relative to the dollar. The purpose of that arrangement was to assure foreign investors that the value of their investments in the region would not be undermined by devaluation, as it had been in many Latin American countries.[67] But in the mid-1990s, when the dollar strengthened, the region's pegged currencies automatically gained value as well (relative to currencies such as the Japanese yen). As a consequence, the price of Southeast Asia's exports increased while the cost of its imports declined, contributing to a growing trade deficit. This compounded the adverse effects of China's 1994 currency devaluation, which had lowered the price of its exports and enabled it to undersell Southeast Asian products (especially electronics) on the international market. Interestingly, Argentina ran into similar problems when it pegged its currency to the dollar. A four-year recession in that country ended in political and financial meltdown in 2002.

Consequences of the 1997 Crash

While Thailand's decision to devalue the baht was an unavoidable reaction to the country's growing trade deficit, it prompted panic among major portfolio investors elsewhere in Southeast Asia. Before long, as investors pulled out of Indonesia and unloaded its currency, that government was forced to devalue the rupiah. The crisis next spread to Malaysia and South Korea. Ultimately, its implications were even broader, as international financial institutions watched events in Asia and became increasingly concerned about their investments in other LDCs. Asia's sharp currency and stock market declines spread to Russia and caused steep drops in the Argentine, Brazilian, and Chilean stock markets as well. All of these countries suffered economic downturns of two years or longer.

As Asia's financial crisis intensified, the region sank into a deep economic recession, inflicting enormous pain on the population. Unable to pay their debts, many companies were forced into bankruptcy, throwing their employees out of work. Inflation heated up dangerously, and domestic banks, faced with extensive defaults on their loans, declared bankruptcy themselves.

> Along the way, billions of dollars in production and hundreds of millions of jobs [were] lost. ... Since the crisis began [through October 1998], $1 trillion in loans [went] bad, $2 trillion in equity capitalization for the Asian stock markets ... vaporized, and $3 trillion in GDP growth [was] lost.[68]

Implications for East Asia's Growth Model

What does the economic crisis of the late 1990s imply about the viability of East and Southeast Asia's developmental state and its export-led growth model? Is that model now no longer attractive? Conservative critics argue that the crisis shows the dangers of "too much government control."[69] Because investment decisions in the area were influenced by government planners rather than by market forces, these analysts contend, bank loans and government aid too often went to well-connected industries and industrial sectors, rather than to those who could make best use of the assistance. There is certainly some truth to this charge, particularly where crony capitalism prevailed, as in Indonesia and the Philippines. However, it is unlikely that state intervention per se was the major cause of the crisis. After all, China and Vietnam—market-socialist countries with the highest level of state control in the region—suffered no financial crisis, nor did the developmental states in Singapore and Taiwan. Rather, the key causal factor seems to have been external indebtedness. Countries such as Thailand, Indonesia, and South Korea (or, outside the region, Mexico, Brazil, and, more recently, Argentina), which had borrowed abroad excessively, got into trouble. Those that had either exercised restraint (Taiwan and China) or been unable to secure extensive foreign credit (the Philippines and Vietnam) were not badly hurt.

The most important elements of East and Southeast Asia's development model—widespread public education aimed at developing a skilled work force, agrarian reform, equitable income distribution, emphasis on manufactured exports—did not contribute to the crisis and remain the region's strengths. The time has probably come to reduce the role of the developmental state, and most countries in the region have already begun to do so. But the model seems to have served its purpose well in getting those economies off the ground and running.

In the future, Asian governments will probably continue to let their currencies float freely (to continually appreciate or decline in value, according to market forces) rather than allow a pegged currency to become seriously overvalued, thereby forcing the government to devaluate it sharply. Borrowers and lenders also need to be more careful about seeking and extending credit. At the same time, the World Bank and the International Monetary Fund (IMF)—both of which failed to anticipate the Asian crisis, as they had failed earlier with the 1994 Mexican peso crisis—must better monitor the financial health of LDCs and must offer the financial community better advance warning about serious imbalances in currency values. So too must private rating services, such as Standard and Poor's and Moody's, which also failed to alert investors of the problem by lowering Asia's credit ratings. Such advance warning regarding Argentina in 2001 prevented that country's crisis from spreading elsewhere.

None of these flaws, however, calls into question Asia's underlying development model.[70] Indeed, experts such as Joseph Stiglitz, chief economist of the World Bank, and Jeffrey Winters argue that bad private-sector decisions, not the developmental state, caused the crisis. Further, they insist that most East and Southeast Asian economies remain fundamentally sound.[71]

East Asia's Recovery

Whereas the Latin American debt crisis lasted for nearly a decade, most East Asian economies began to recover by 2001, only four years after the start of that crisis. By 2002, the region's economy had rebounded, achieving a growth rate of 6.5 percent or more that year and the one that followed, a rate that most of the other Third World regions could not emulate in the best of times. The Asian Development Bank projected similar rates of growth for 2004 and 2005.[72] While this demonstrates the basic resilience of the East Asian economy, the damaging effects on the poor and middle class of the 1997–2001 crisis still linger. Except for South Korea, standards of living in the region were barely back to 1997 levels. In Indonesia, where the recovery has been slower (partly damaged by a series of Islamist terrorist attacks, which slowed foreign tourism and investment), real per-capita income in 2003 was still 8 percent below 1997.[73]

GROWTH WITH EQUITY

Until this point, our discussion of economic development has focused on measurements of production. Indeed, production is the primary measure of economic development used in popular and scholarly analysis. Typically, economies are thought to be performing well when their Gross National Products (GNP) or Gross Domestic Products (GDP) are growing rapidly. Far less attention has been focused on how that growth is distributed. It is to that important dimension that we now turn.

Early debate on Third World development often pitted mainstream social scientists against left-of-center scholars with the former primarily interested in the prerequisites of growth and the latter more concerned with the equity of economic distribution. For example, while many economists were impressed with Brazil's rapid economic expansion in the late 1960s and early 1970s, critics pointed out that the country's extremely unequal income distribution meant that few benefits of rapid growth managed to reach the poorest half of the population. On the other hand, although left-leaning economists were favorably impressed by Cuba's far-reaching income redistribution and social welfare programs for the poor, conservative critics noted the country's erratic performance in terms of economic growth.

Some market-oriented economists even insisted that increased inequality was a necessary evil in the early stages of economic development because it concentrated capital in the hands of entrepreneurs who could invest in productive activities. Their critics countered that development of that sort did little to help the majority of the people. In many developing nations, they maintained the bottom half of the population would benefit more from meaningful redistribution of wealth and income, even with little growth, than from strong economic growth without redistribution.[74]

In time, however, analysts of varying ideological persuasions have concluded that there is no intrinsic contradiction between these two goals. In fact, a proper development strategy entails growth with equity.[75] One study has shown that since the 1960s, countries with higher levels of income equality have grown faster than those with highly concentrated patterns. East Asia's economic takeoff since the 1970s and 1980s demonstrates that point. For example, Taiwan and South Korea have coupled spectacular economic growth rates with relatively equitable income distributions.[76] Indeed, broadly based purchasing power in both those countries has helped stimulate their economic growth. In South Korea, almost all peasant families own television sets, a feat hardly conceivable in Africa or most of Latin America. During the Korean television industry's takeoff, these domestic purchases supplemented exports in stimulating that industry's growth.

What accounts for the higher level of economic equality in East Asia as compared to Africa or Latin America? One important factor is the pattern of land distribution in the countryside. For a variety of reasons, farm land is generally far more equitably distributed in Asia than in Latin America.[77] While the size of Latin America's largest land holdings has declined in recent decades, estates of several thousand acres were common in the recent past, and today large land owners still dominate the countryside in nations such as Brazil or Colombia. On the other hand, the largest holdings in Asia, where there is much heavier population pressure, are rarely more than one or two hundred acres and are far smaller in countries like South Korea.

Landholding patterns reflect both historical legacies and contemporary government policies. Spanish colonialism established an agrarian structure in Latin America and the Philippines dominated by large *latifundia*. In contrast, Japanese colonial authorities in Korea and Taiwan encouraged smallholder farming. Although European colonial regimes established large export-oriented plantations in Southeast Asia, land ownership there was still never as concentrated as in Latin America. It is surely not coincidental that the Philippines, the East Asian nation with its region's most concentrated land and income distributions, is also the region's only country that shares Latin America's Spanish colonial heritage. In the postcolonial period, South Korean and Taiwanese agrarian reform led to more egalitarian land distribution in those countries, just as American-imposed reform had done in Japan after the war. By reducing rural poverty, land reform contributed to higher overall levels of income equality.

Another major determinant of national income distribution is the relationship between rural and urban living standards. Although city dwellers enjoy higher incomes and greater social services throughout the Third World, the urban-rural gap is particularly marked in Africa and Latin America. Residents of Mexico City, for example, have incomes averaging four to five times higher than in the countryside. There are many reasons for such discrepancies, but government policy often plays an important role. In Chapter 6 we noted that, until recently, African and Latin American governments kept the price of basic food crops below their market value to satisfy urban political constituencies.[78] By contrast, East Asian farmers generally have received the free-market price for their crops or even subsidized prices above market value.

Industrial policy also affects income distribution. Latin America's ISI strategy encouraged the importation of capital equipment for domestic industries. Such capital-intensive development created many relatively well-paid, skilled industrial jobs, but left behind far more poorly paid, unskilled urban workers and rural peasants. Conversely, East Asia's EOI strategy took advantage of that region's large labor force, thereby producing a large number of low-wage jobs.

Initially employing labor-intensive methods that utilized their pools of cheap labor, Hong Kong, Taiwan, and South Korea successfully exported low-tech goods such as textiles and footwear. As increased numbers of workers were employed, two changes took place over time. First, greater demand for labor in export industries caused factory wages to rise; second, rural-to-urban migration due to the lure of factory jobs reduced the supply of rural labor, thereby driving up income levels in the countryside. What had begun as a policy exploiting cheap labor eventually promoted economic growth, higher wages, and greater income equality.[79] As wage levels rose substantially in the four "little tigers," those countries shifted from low-tech products to more sophisticated exports such as electronics, commercial services (most notably Singapore), computer software, computers, and automobiles (South Korea). Production of apparel and other low-wage items was passed on to poorer, low-wage Asian nations such as China, Malaysia, Thailand, Indonesia, Bangladesh, and Sri Lanka. China, which first became an industrial giant by manufacturing lower-priced consumer goods and parts for foreign brands, is now beginning to produce more high-end products, including some under Chinese brand names.

A final factor that distinguishes East Asia from less-developed regions is its relatively high educational level.[80] Table 10.1 offers education data for the United States, four East Asian NICs, four Latin American NICS, and India. The second column presents literacy rates for all adults over the age of 15. The third column indicates the percentage of school-aged youth who are enrolled in school. Finally, the last column (Educational Index) is a composite index of the country's education level. The highest, or best, score that a country can achieve for this index is 1.0, and the lowest possible score is a 0.

Both the East Asian and Latin American NICs presented in this table have literacy rates and education levels that are below the United States (though on some measures the gap is smaller than one might expect) but considerably higher than India, or Africa, the Middle East, and most of South Asia. Not surprisingly, the NICs with the lowest school enrollment and literacy rates, and educational indices, tend to be those with the highest rates of poverty (Colombia, Mexico, Thailand). Surprisingly, Singapore, a prosperous country with fairly equitable income distribution, falls below the group's average for the educational index and adult literacy. But its extremely high current school enrollment ratio (97 percent compared to 95 percent in the United States and 71 percent in Mexico) suggests that future generations will be far more educated.

TABLE 10.1   Comparative National Educational Levels

Country	Adult Literacy	Primary-Tertiary Enrollment Ratios	Educational Index
United States	99.9%	95%	.98
Hong Kong	93.3	63	.83
Singapore	92.1	97	.87
South Korea	97.6	90	.95
Thailand	95.3	60	.84
Argentina	96.7	83	.92
Chile	95.6	80	.90
Colombia	91.5	73	.85
Mexico	91.1	71	.84
India	56.5	56	.56

Source: United Nations Development Programme, *Human Development Report, 2001* (New York: Oxford University Press, 2001), 141–144. Reprinted by permission.

While educational attainment generally correlates with economic development and growth, two countries in the table stand out as exceptions: Argentina—a more affluent Third World country which, until the 1990s, enjoyed more equitable income distribution—ranks second out of the eight NICs for both adult literacy and educational index (trailing only South Korea). Yet its economy has performed erratically for decades. Meanwhile, Hong Kong, one of the Third World's most phenomenal economic performers for the past 40 to 50 years, has a relatively low educational index and a very low enrollment ratio (almost as low as India's). The Argentine anomaly is related to the fact that in the first 30 years of the twentieth century, it used its enormous wheat and beef exports to build an affluent society and a substantial industrial base. In the 1920s, it not only was the richest nation in the Third World, but it had a per-capita income ranked fifth in the entire world, far ahead of Japan and Italy, for example. That early development, combined with a work force largely made up of recent European immigrants, produced high education levels. Since the 1940s, however, despite its strong educational base, Argentina's failure to modernize its agricultural and industrial production has sent it on a downward economic slide. It is also worth noting that its current enrollment ratios, while higher than its Latin American counterparts, are far lower than Singapore or South Korea, indicating that it may be beginning to lose ground. The reasons for Hong Kong's somewhat disappointing educational performance are harder to discern. But it is true that South Korea and the other Asian NICs listed here, with higher educational performances than Hong Kong, also have more equitable distributions of income.

Although Table 10.1 does not indicate *great* differences between the East Asian and Latin American education and literacy rates, earlier data published by the United Nations Development Program do reveal some important differences. Although comparable proportions of the children in both regions attend primary (elementary) school, East Asian students are much more likely to complete their elementary education (97 to 99 percent in Hong Kong, Singapore, and South Korea; 57 to 72 percent in Colombia and Mexico).[81] Another difference concerns how countries allocate their educational resources. The East Asian NICs have concentrated their resources especially on primary and secondary education (K through 12) and, consequently, have higher enrollment ratios than their Latin American counterparts for both those educational levels. On the other hand, Latin American nations are more prone to allocate resources to university and other postsecondary education than their East Asian counterparts. Consequently, they have higher enrollment ratios at that level. Cultural norms limiting women's education have also reduced postsecondary enrollments in East Asia, with the notable exception of South Korea.

While all levels of education are important for a country's economic growth, East Asia's education strategy has produced a more widely educated work force at the mass level. Latin America's allocation of more of its educational resources to postsecondary education reflects, in part, the political influence of the middle-class families whose children attend those schools. Because increased education opens up greater opportunities for upward mobility, national educational levels tend to correspond with income equality.[82] Thus, the most educated populations in Latin America (Cuba, Argentina, Uruguay, Costa Rica) generally also have the most equitable income distributions in the region (though Argentina's income pattern has become much more unequal in the last

10 to 15 years). Conversely, Brazil, with a very poor educational record, has one of the world's poorest income distributions. In general, East Asia's high rate of primary and secondary education has contributed to greater income equity.

ECONOMIC DEVELOPMENT AND THE ENVIRONMENT

Throughout the world, economic development has inevitably caused some degree of environmental degradation. For example, prior to European settlement, the East Coast of the United States was covered with thick forest. Since then, population growth, urban sprawl, and farming have destroyed most of that environment. Today, industrial pollution in the United States and Europe contaminate the surrounding air and water, sometimes affecting areas thousands of miles away. In the LDCs, rapid population growth, combined with economic modernization and industrialization also has brought tremendous environmental damage. In Indonesia, for example, foreign-owned mines and logging firms have dumped health-threatening waste into nearby water systems and harvested vast tracks of jungle timber, bringing birth defects (in mining areas) and flooding (in timber regions) in their wake.[83] Massive dams in China flood archeological treasures, farm land, and vacated villages. Since the 1970s environmental groups in advanced industrialized nations have begun to question the tradeoffs between growth and the conservation of our natural-resource heritage. Some of the more radical environmentalists in the United States and Europe have proposed zero-growth strategies for highly industrialized nations. They suggest limiting population growth and creating a less consumer-oriented society.

But the option of zero growth, or even of reduced economic growth, which has never attracted significant support even in the First World, is unacceptable in the Third World. In countries such as India, Indonesia, Egypt, Nigeria, and Brazil, where a substantial portion of the population lives in poverty, it would be politically suicidal and ethically questionable for government leaders to propose limiting economic growth. Environmental regulations and controls are generally far weaker in the LDCs, because of the urgent need for economic growth and because the "green" (ecology) movement arrived there much later and has not developed the political influence of its counterparts in areas such as Western Europe. Moreover, LDCs often lack the government infrastructure to enforce environmental controls.

The Costs of Growth

The world's industrialized nations continue to be the major consumers of natural resources, the leading polluters of air and water, and the major contributors to global warming, ozone-layer depletion, and other looming ecological disasters. For example, in recent years, developed nations consumed some 80 percent of the world's paper, 80 percent of its iron and steel, and more than 85 percent of its chemicals. Per-capita use of cars in the developed world is more than 25 times as high as in the LDCs, cement consumption is 3.5 times as high, and iron and steel consumption is 13 times as high.[84]

Yet, ironically, it is those same developed countries that now insist that the LDCs become better environmental citizens. In response, Third World leaders complain that the United States, with only 4 percent of the world's population, consumes more than 25 percent of the planet's resources.[85] Hence, many Third World leaders bristle at the suggestion that they make special efforts to protect the environment.[86] Still, because of their more fragile economic and ecological situations, many developing nations do confront some of the world's most pressing environmental challenges. Peasants hungry for firewood in Rwanda, Nepal, and India deplete nearby forests. In African countries such as Sudan, Nigeria, and Burkina Faso, 75 percent or more of all energy is supplied by burning wood. Giant cattle ranchers and poor peasants in Brazil burn vast areas of the Amazonian jungle each year to clear the land for cultivation. In Malaysia and Indonesia, Japanese-owned logging firms cut down large tracts of rain forest to manufacture furniture. Since 1950 alone, more than 25 percent of the earth's tropical rain forests have been destroyed. As a consequence, in regions such as Central America, Indonesia, and Sub-Saharan Africa, rains and waterways wash off topsoil, rainfall patterns shift, and both droughts and floods occur more frequently. In short, in many parts of the Third World, the arable land area is declining and deserts are growing.

Third World cities such as Shanghai, Cairo, New Delhi, Nairobi, and Sao Paulo have grown incredibly in recent decades (Chapter 7), producing enormous quantities of raw sewage, auto emissions, and industrial waste. As streets become choked with cars and buses (few of which have proper emission-control devices), air quality rapidly deteriorates. Elsewhere, mines, oil fields, chemical plants, and factories, operating with few environmental safeguards, pollute their surroundings. The consequences for local populations—ranging from infection to respiratory illnesses, birth defects, and loss of farm land—have often been tragic. Still other environmental costs—destruction of rain forests, global warming—have consequences that extend far beyond the developing world.

Environmental Decay as a Third World Problem

Nowhere is the difficult tradeoff between economic growth and environmental conservation more starkly illustrated than in China, home to more than one-fifth of the world's population. Since the government introduced free-market economic reforms in the 1980s, the country has enjoyed the world's highest rate of economic growth, averaging about 8 percent or more annually. Living standards have tripled, and millions of Chinese citizens have moved out of poverty. The number of people spared from hunger, disease, and early death is undoubtedly staggering. Balanced against those gains, however, are enormous increases in air and water pollution and extensive destruction of the country's farm land, raising the prospect of future famine just when China has finally managed to feed its population adequately. By 1990, China consumed 10 percent of global energy and was responsible for 11 percent of carbon dioxide emissions, a figure that continues to rise as the economy leaps forward.[87]

Attracted by higher urban living standards, millions of peasants have migrated to the cities, often abandoning farms in productive agricultural regions. In addition, substantial quantities of farm land have been paved over for highways, factories, and urban sprawl. Since the late 1950s, China's total arable land has decreased by somewhere between 15 and 55 percent (depending on what estimate one accepts), while population has grown by some 80 percent.

Though China's annual rate of population growth is currently relatively low (1 percent or lower), loss of farmland because of economic development continues to accelerate at an alarming rate. So far, China has averted hunger by farming the remaining land more intensively, and some recent grain harvests have reached record or near-record levels. But this intensive use of fertilizers and pesticides eventually depletes the soil, and a food crunch likely looms in the coming decades. As the country is forced to import increasing amounts of food, prices of grains and other foods are likely to rise worldwide, with serious consequences for the poor throughout the developing world.

Environmental Decay in the LDCs as a Global Problem

The debate over Third World environmental policy is further complicated by the fact that many LDCs are stewards of natural resources that are critical to the entire world. For example, the massive, purposeful burning of the Amazonian rain forest contributes significantly to global warming. Destruction of rain forests there as well as in Africa and Asia deprives the world of many animal species and plant forms that are potentially important ingredients in future lifesaving medicines.[88]

Unfortunately, the very economic development to which Third World people rightfully aspire poses potentially disastrous threats to the environment. It would be unconscionable to tell poor Indians or Egyptians that they should not hope for a higher standard of living. But barring major technological and political breakthroughs, achieving an acceptable standard of living for all Third World people could easily overtax the planet's resources. Invariably, economic development brings greatly increased usage of fossil fuels (coal, petroleum, and natural gas) and a corresponding increase in pollution. Brazil, China, and India already rank third through fifth in the world, behind the United States and the former Soviet Union, in greenhouse gas emissions (carbon dioxide and other fossil-fuel emissions that trap the earth's heat and produce global warming). As China's economy continues its rapid growth, and as India further industrializes, these two Asian giants will surely burn more fossil fuels for their factories and vehicles, thereby accelerating the greenhouse effect on global warming.

THE SEARCH FOR SUSTAINABLE DEVELOPMENT

Discussion of the environmental consequences of economic growth often turns to the objective of *sustainable development*, defined as economic development that "consumes resources to meet [this generation's] needs and aspirations in a way that does not compromise the ability of future generations to meet their needs."[89] Whenever feasible, it involves the use of *renewable resources* (such as wind and water power for generating electricity) in place of resources that cannot be replaced (for example, coal and petroleum), or that are currently being consumed at a faster rate than they can be replaced (such as tropical rain forests, ocean fish such as cod and salmon). It also embraces consumption of resources in ways that least pollutes the environment: limiting auto and industrial emissions, finding sustainable substitutes for pesticides and other agricultural chemicals that pollute the soil and water system, and reducing the use of products that destroy the world's ozone layer.[90]

In theory these are goals to which all nations, rich and poor alike, can aspire. Even here, however, the debate often turns to which countries should take the lead or bear the greatest economic costs. At the groundbreaking 1992 United Nations Conference on Environment and Development (UNCED) in Rio de Janeiro—often called the Earth Summit—signatories made a nonbinding commitment to reduce greenhouse emissions by the year 2000 and developed an action plan for sustainable development into the twenty-first century. The Rio Declaration listed 27 guiding principles on the environment and development, including the LDCs' right to economic development and the alleviation of poverty. Still, as one analyst observed:

> At the Rio Summit, the conflicts between the rich and poor became evident. The Northern [industrialized] countries, which felt vulnerable to global environment problems such as climate change and biodiversity loss, attempted to extract commitments on environmental conservation from the South. However, the South, which felt more vulnerable to perceived underdevelopment, was concerned with extracting [economic] transfers from the North.[91]

The difficult tradeoff between growth and environmental protection was vividly brought home to this author at a meeting in Jamaica with local social scientists. After one U.S. scholar spoke of the importance of preserving the island's ecology, a Jamaican economist sarcastically replied, "You Americans raped your environment in order to develop your country and raise your standard of living. Now we Jamaicans reserve the right to do the same."[92] While such feelings may be counterproductive, they are understandable. Third World leaders note that the already industrialized countries ask NICs such as China and Mexico to reduce smokestack emissions and beseech Thailand and Brazil to sustain their rain forests, but it is First World nations that have wreaked the greatest havoc on the environment and have offered the developing nations little help to defray the costs of environmental controls. The United States in particular has done little to allay Third World doubts. In 1997, worldwide negotiations produced the Kyoto Protocol, which envisioned a global contract that would bind signatories to reduce their emissions of six greenhouse gases by 2010 to 5.2 percent below their 1990 level, an estimated 29 percent below what they were expected to grow to without an accord. The protocol would go into effect once it had been signed by nations that accounted for 55 percent of the world's greenhouse gases. Four years later (2001), 178 nations agreed in Bonn, Germany to meet objections by Japan and other nations by modifying the Kyoto Protocol so as to lower the targeted 5 percent reduction to only 2 percent. Still, the new U.S. president, George Bush, outraged the European Union and much of the world community by announcing that the United States would not ratify the Kyoto agreement. From the Bush administration's perspective— supported by a number of American business organizations and many Congressional Republicans—the dangers of global warming had been overstated and the U.S. government was unwilling to undermine its own economic growth by accepting Kyoto's environmental targets.

By breaking its previous pledge to honor Kyoto (though the protocol had never been ratified by the U.S. Senate), the administration reinforced the belief of Third World nations that they were being held to a double standard when it came to making economic sacrifices for the environment. Most of the international community has been determined to continue pursuing Kyoto's goals. However, since the United States accounts for 25 percent of all greenhouse emissions (the world's largest share), its decision to pull out not only makes it harder to reduce overall levels, but it also made it more difficult to garner the necessary ratification of the proposal by countries accounting for 55 percent of total emissions. In early 2005, following Russian ratification, the Kyoto accord. went into effect without U.S. participation.

Some Signs of Progress

Despite these obstacles, there are some hopeful signs of progress. At the very least, the governments of developing countries and international development agencies have become more conscious of the growth-environmental tradeoff. Together many of them have begun looking for ways to achieve sustainable development that reduces damage to the environment. Many LDCs that previously saw the green movement as a Western conspiracy to keep them under-developed have come to realize that sustainable growth is in their own interest.

One of the most important means of improving living standards and preserving the environment is population control. Other policies can also help: the use of renewable fuels such as solar energy and water power (nuclear energy remains far more controversial); organic farming that replenishes, rather than depletes, the soil; government regulations that discourage, rather than encourage, irrational use of rain forest areas; and stricter antipollution controls. For example, Brazil has revised tax laws (so far with little effect) that had previously encouraged ranchers to clear the Amazonian forest. Also, Mexico City has improved its air quality by relocating local cement plants and oil refineries, replacing city taxis and buses with newer vehicles that have better emission controls, and requiring private cars to stay off the road one day per week.

Ultimately, however, even if strict environmental measures were implemented, they still would not fully reconcile the tension between economic growth and environmental protection. Furthermore, environmental controls are generally expensive and often reduce productivity. If the world's industrial powers want the LDCs to make such sacrifices, they will probably have to underwrite much of the cost. This might involve debt forgiveness, subsidized technology transfers, or direct grants.[93]

Which of the economic models discussed earlier in this chapter is best equipped to handle the environmental challenge? The answer is not clear. It seems certain that preserving the environment requires some active state intervention. Since factory owners cannot be counted on to monitor and limit their own pollution nor will citizens likely volunteer to limit their use of automobiles, state regulation is needed. Consequently, the neoclassical model, which severely limits government economic intervention and depends heavily on free-market mechanisms, seems ill-suited to protect the environment.

In principle, command economies can be particularly suited to defend the environment since the state controls the means of production and can self-regulate. In fact, however, communist governments from the Soviet Union and

Poland to China and North Korea have had very poor environmental records. On the one hand, directives to managers of state enterprises usually demand that they maximize production, with little thought given to environmental consequences. On the other hand, absent a free society and a free mass media, citizens are unable to organize environmental pressure groups or even to know the extent of ecological destruction. Thus, it appears that if developing nations are to have any chance at sustainable development, they must combine an honest, effective, and responsible state with a free democratic society where green activists can mobilize popular support.

FINDING THE RIGHT MIX

Often it has been easier to recognize what has not worked in the Third World than to identify what has. The dependency theorists' assumption that economic liberation required reduced ties to the capitalist core has been shattered by the success of East Asia's export-oriented growth and the failures of protectionism. Similarly, command economies, while often able to reduce economic inequalities, have had poor records of economic growth and modernization. The abject failure of North Korea's communist economy, in stark contrast to South Korea's prosperity, demonstrates that model's failures. On the other hand, the neoclassical minimal state can hardly address the deep inequities, societal cleavages, and looming ecological nightmares plaguing many LDCs. The challenge for Third World economies is to establish a strong and effective, but not overbearing, state—one that can promote growth, equitable distribution, and a healthy environment, while avoiding unwarranted interference in the market, crony capitalism, and authoritarianism.

Many Third World countries have now embraced East Asia's export-oriented industrial model. Beyond the previously mentioned problem of transferability, however, there are at least two other fundamental concerns about universalizing the East Asian experience. The first concerns the extent to which the world economy can continue to absorb growing industrial exports. East Asia launched its EOI strategy during a period of unparalleled economic growth in the First World. International trade was expanding rapidly, and developed countries could absorb a rising tide of industrial exports. Since the 1970s, however, First World economic growth has slowed down due, in part, to factors such as spikes in energy costs (in the 1970s and recently), the transfer of industrial jobs to the NICs and, perhaps, most recently the psychological and economic effects of terrorism. Even should the Japanese and Western European economies recover their former dynamism, some analysts question whether the international market can absorb an ever-enlarging flow of industrial exports, most notably from China, the world's emerging industrial giant, or whether protectionist measures in the First World might place a cap on imports.[94] Supporters of EOI counter that there is no sign of a looming cap on industrial imports, particularly since the larger NICs have become major importers themselves.[95] However, the recent Asian financial crisis demonstrates that even the most sophisticated and apparently successful development models can run into serious difficulties as new challenges develop and hidden weaknesses surface.

CONCLUSION: DEMOCRACY AND ECONOMIC DEVELOPMENT

Earlier in this chapter, we observed that in the second half of the twentieth century the most dynamic Third World economies were typically governed by authoritarian regimes. Almost all of Asia's most impressive economic takeoffs—China, Taiwan, South Korea, Singapore, Thailand, Malaysia, and Indonesia—transpired under authoritarian or semi-authoritarian developmental states or (in the case of China) a modified command economy. Chile initiated Latin America's most successful transition from ISI to export-led growth during General Pinochet's military dictatorship. Some have argued that authoritarian governments are better equipped to control wage demands from labor and to impose development plans on business.

To be sure, economic takeoffs have usually begun under authoritarian regimes of some sort. However, for every authoritarian success story, there have been several economic disasters. Corrupt dictatorships throughout Africa, the Middle East, Central America, and the Caribbean have plundered their country's limited wealth, created inefficient private or state monopolies, and used the economy to reward their political allies. Chile's bureaucratic authoritarian regime performed well economically, but its counterparts in Argentina, Uruguay, and even Brazil were considerably less successful. Overall, statistical analyses of Third World economic growth rates in recent decades reveal that authoritarian governments do not perform any better than democratic ones. And one recent study indicated that dictatorships perform more poorly. Bruce Bueno de Mesquita et al. ranked hundreds of governments worldwide since 1952 and compared the 179 most autocratic governments with the 176 most democratic ones.[96] During that period, democratic rulers achieved an average real annual growth rate (adjusted for inflation) of 3.04 percent, while autocratic governments attained only 1.78 percent, a substantial difference. Moreover, the authors argue convincingly that the difference in performance has a logical explanation. Governments that need to appeal to a broad coalition of voters (democracies), they insist, are more likely to pursue policies that promote broadly based economic growth, while governments that owe their incumbency to a small coalition of strategic allies (dictatorships) are more likely to be corrupt and to pursue policies designed to keep themselves in power no matter what the cost to the national economy. In recent years, the world's most populous democracy, India, has enjoyed an impressive period of sustained economic growth. Of course, the ranks of democratic governments include both strong economic performers and weak ones, as do authoritarian governments. But these findings, along with many others, offer hope that democratic governments and the worldwide movement toward democracy may produce faster economic growth along with greater political justice.

DISCUSSION QUESTIONS

1. What have been the major accomplishments and failures of command economies?
2. Compare the nature of state economic intervention in Latin America to East Asia's developmental state.

3. What are the major arguments presented in the neoclassical development model?
4. What were the major causes of East and Southeast Asia's recent economic crisis? What implications did the crisis have for evaluating the region's economic model?
5. In what ways does economic growth in the Third World contribute to environmental degradation?
6. What evidence is there that authoritarian Third World governments can promote early economic growth better than democracies? What counterevidence do some scholars offer to suggest that democracies have better economic records? In what ways might each one promote economic growth?

NOTES

1. Of course, we have seen that in the short to intermediate term, economic growth can be politically destabilizing. However, if growth can be combined with equitable distribution, the chances of unrest are greatly diminished. In any event, all other factors being equal, in the long run rising living standards should rebound to the regime's political advantage. The potentially destabilizing effects of unequal economic growth were treated elsewhere in this book and will not be discussed in this chapter.

2. Joan M. Nelson, ed., *Economic Crisis and Policy Choice: The Politics of Adjustment in the Third World* (Princeton, NJ: Princeton University Press, 1990); Dharam Ghai, ed., *The IMF and the South: The Social Impact of Crisis and Adjustment* (London: Zed Books, 1991).

3. Martin Staniland, *What Is Political Economy?* (New Haven, CT: Yale University Press, 1985), 6.

4. Ibid., 12.

5. In its original meaning, liberalism (as articulated in the eighteenth century) called for limited government. Today, outside of the United States, the terms "neoliberal policies" or "liberalization" refer to policies that reduce the role of government in the economy (contrary to the way the term *liberal* is used in the United States).

6. Simon Kuznets, *Modern Economic Growth: Rate, Structure and Spread*, 7th ed. (New Haven, CT: Yale University Press, 1976); Hollis Chenery and Moises Syrquin, *Patterns of Development, 1950–1970* (London: Oxford University Press, 1975). Of course, these are general tendencies or trends, not inviolable rules. Thus, East and Southeast Asian countries such as Taiwan, South Korea, and Malaysia have entered or passed through the intermediate stage of development without an appreciable worsening of income distribution.

7. Adapted from Adam Przeworski, *Democracy and the Market* (New York: Cambridge University Press, 1991), 105, fn. 10.

8. Ed A. Hewett, *Reforming the Soviet Economy: Equality versus Efficiency* (Washington, DC: Brookings Institution, 1988), 38.

9. Abraham Bergson, *The Real National Income of Soviet Russia since 1928* (Cambridge, MA: Harvard University Press, 1961), 261.

10. Harry Harding, *China's Second Revolution* (Washington, DC: Brookings Institution, 1987), 30–31.

11. Stephen White, John Gardener, and George Schopflin, *Communist and Postcommunist Political Systems* (New York: St. Martin's Press, 1990), 322; Harding, *China's Second Revolution*, 30.

12. Claes Brundenius, *Revolutionary Cuba: The Challenge of Economic Growth with Equity* (Boulder, CO: Westview Press, 1984); Carmelo Mesa-Lago, *The Economy of Socialist Cuba: A Two-Decade Appraisal* (Albuquerque: University of New Mexico Press, 1981).

13. Erich Wede and Horst Tiefenbach, "Some Recent Explanations of Income Inequality," *International Studies Quarterly* 25 (June 1981): 255–282.

14. An obvious moral and political weakness, not discussed here, is that command economies require government repression. I am taking that very serious flaw as a given and am limiting my discussion in this chapter to the system's economic strengths and weaknesses.

15. Liang Heng and Judith Shapiro, *After the Nightmare* (New York: Collier, 1986).

16. John Sheahan, *Patterns of Development in Latin America* (Princeton, NJ: Princeton University Press, 1987).

17. Ibid., 85.

18. Dale Story, *Industry, the State and Public Policy in Mexico* (Austin: University of Texas Press, 1986), 68.

19. Both those industries were nationalized in the 1930s. Subsequently, the state also took over electricity and telecommunications.

20. Story, *Industry, the State and Public Policy in Mexico,* 21. My statistic is extrapolated from Story's data.

21. Samuel Schmidt, *The Deterioration of the Mexican Presidency: The Years of Luis Echeverría* (Tucson: University of Arizona Press, 1991), 162–164; Elia Marún Espinosa, "Intervencionismo estatal y transformaciones del sector empresa pública en México," in *El Nuevo Estado Mexicano: Estado y Economía,* ed. Jorge Alonso et al. (Mexico City: Nueva Imagen, 1992), 193–240.

22. For startling data on overstaffing and "ghost workers" in Africa, see Richard Sandbrook, *The Politics of Africa's Economic Recovery* (New York: Cambridge University Press, 1993), 43, 61.

23. *New York Times,* December 7, 1993.

24. *New York Times,* November 2, 1993.

25. Ibid.

26. During Mexico's 1994 presidential campaign, I interviewed a major spokesperson for the PRD, the country's principal left opposition party. Though he had once been a Marxist congressman, he readily conceded that President Salinas's economic liberalization program, involving massive layoffs of state workers, had been necessary. That interview took place a week after the peasant uprising in Chiapas that many analysts believed shifted the Mexican political spectrum to the left.

27. Howard Handelman and Werner Baer, eds., *Paying the Costs of Austerity in Latin America* (Boulder, CO: Westview Press, l989); Stephan Haggard and Robert R. Kaufman, eds., *The Politics of Economic Adjustment* (Princeton, NJ: Princeton University Press, 1992).

28. Furthermore, even economic growth, though obviously beneficial, does not necessarily translate immediately into higher living standards for much of the population.

29. Extrapolated from Sinichi Ichimura and James W. Morley, "The Varieties of Asia-Pacific Experience," in *Driven by Growth,* ed. James W. Morley (Armonk, NY: M. E. Sharpe, 1992), 6; and Steven Chan, *East Asian Dynamism* (Boulder, CO: Westview Press, 1990), 8; UNDP, *Human Development Report, 1997* (New York: Oxford University Press, 1997), 21–22.

30. The World Bank, *Engendering Development* (New York and London: Oxford University Press, 2001), 207.

31. Again, China does not fit that model. A large, though rapidly falling, share of its economy continues to be state owned, while another substantial portion is run by cooperatives. State regulation, though reduced, is still formidable. Thus, despite its many changes since the early 1980s, Communist China remains distinct from

the other Asian economies described in this section and will be excluded from the discussion that follows.

32. Milton and Rose Friedman, *Freedom to Choose* (New York: Harcourt Brace Jovanovich, 1980), 57; David Felix, "Review of Economic Structure and Performance: Essays in Honor of Hollis B. Chenery," *Economic Development and Cultural Change* 36, no. 1 (1987): 188–194; Ian Little, "An Economic Reconnaissance," in *Economic Growth and Structural Change in Taiwan,* ed. Walter Galenson (Ithaca, NY: Cornell University Press).

33. Robert Wade, *Governing the Market: Economic Theory and the Role of Government in East Asian Industrialization* (Princeton, NJ: Princeton University Press, 1990); Gary Gereffi and Donald L. Wyman, eds., *Manufacturing Miracles* (Princeton, NJ: Princeton University Press, 1990); Stephan Haggard, *Pathways from the Periphery* (Ithaca, NY: Cornell University Press, 1990); Chalmers Johnson, "Political Institutions and Economic Performance: The Government-Business Relationship in Japan, South Korea and Taiwan," in *The Political Economy of the New Asian Industrialism,* ed. Frederic C. Deyo (Ithaca, NY: Cornell University Press, 1987).

34. Chalmers Johnson, *MITI and the Japanese Miracle* (Stanford, CA: Stanford University Press, 1982).

35. Chan, *East Asian Dynamism,* 47–48.

36. Johnson, "Political Institutions and Economic Performance."

37. Chan, *East Asian Dynamism,* 49.

38. Johnson, "Political Institutions," 159.

39. Haggard, *Pathways from the Periphery.*

40. Robert Wade, "Industrial Policy in Asia: Does It Lead or Follow the Market?" in *Manufacturing Miracles,* 231–266; Wade, *Governing the Market.*

41. Johnson, "Political Institutions."

42. For a criticism of the developmental state concept and its alleged benefits, see Cheng-tian Kuo, *Global Competitiveness and Industrial Growth in Taiwan and the Philippines* (Pittsburgh, PA: University of Pittsburgh Press, 1995).

43. These conglomerates dominate the economy. By the mid-1980s, Korea's 10 largest chaebols produced two-thirds of the nation's GNP. See Wade, *Governing the Market,* 309.

44. Herman Kahn, "The Confucian Ethic and Economic Growth," in *The Gap between Rich and Poor,* ed. Mitchell A. Seligson (Boulder, CO: Westview Press, 1984).

45. Christopher Ellison and Gary Gereffi, "Explaining Strategies and Patterns of Industrial Development," in *Manufacturing Miracles,* 395–396.

46. Neoclassical economics (or the neoclassical approach) is a revised formulation of Adam Smith's classical economic approach.

47. Wade, *Governing the Market*, 11.

48. Alice H. Amsden, *Asia's Next Giant: South Korea and Late Industrialization* (New York: Oxford University Press, 1989); see also the works by Haggard, Wade, and Johnson cited earlier in this chapter.

49. Wade, *Governing the Market*.

50. Richard Albin, "Saving the Environment: The Shrinking Realm of Laissez-Faire," in *International Political Economy*, 2d ed., eds. Jeffrey A. Frieden and David A. Lake (New York: St. Martin's, 1991), 454.

51. Bela Balassa, *The Newly Industrializing Countries in the World Economy* (New York: Pergamon Press, 1981).

52. This section draws heavily on Sheahan, *Patterns of Development in Latin America*, 82–98.

53. For example, if a nation's currency was worth 10 pesos to the dollar in the free market, governments might impose official rates of 5 pesos to the dollar for trade purposes. This would artificially double the value of the peso, thereby halving the number of dollars needed to import a forklift or machine lathe. At the same time, consumer goods produced domestically with the imported machinery would still be protected against import competition by tariffs and quotas.

54. Ibid., 84; Werner Baer, "Import Substitution and Industrialization in Latin America: Experiences and Interpretations," *Latin American Research Review* 7, no. 1 (1972): 95–122.

55. Helen Shapiro and Lance Taylor, "The State and Industrial Strategy," in *The Political Economy of Development and Underdevelopment*, 5th ed., eds. Charles K. Wilber and Kenneth P. Jameson (New York: McGraw-Hill, 1992).

56. Sheahan, *Patterns of Development*, 86–87.

57. Wade, *Governing the Market*, 34, 36.

58. Barbara Stallings and Robert Kaufman, eds., *Debt and Democracy in Latin America* (Boulder, CO: Westview Press, 1989); Handelman and Baer, *Paying the Costs of Austerity*; Haggard and Kaufman, *The Politics of Economic Adjustment*.

59. Haggard, *Pathways from the Periphery*.

60. Chile has had the most success of any Latin American country in pursuing an EOI strategy since the 1970s. Argentina's efforts, however, were sabotaged by the country pegging its peso to the dollar (one peso is always worth one dollar). Consequently, after a boom in the 1990s, Argentina's economy collapsed in the early years of the twenty-first century as its overvalued peso destroyed its export capability.

61. Gary Gereffi, "Paths of Industrialization: An Overview," in *Manufacturing Miracles*, 15. Brazil's proportion grew steadily from 8 percent in 1965 to 45 percent in 1987. Mexico's manufacturing ratio, on the other hand, was quite volatile, falling from 31 percent of exports in 1975 to 15 percent in 1980, only to jump back to 47 percent in 1987. In large part this reflected the shifting price and significance of petroleum exports.

62. Gary Gereffi and Donald Wyman, "Determinants of Development Strategies in Latin America and Asia," in *Pacific Dynamics*, eds. Stephan Haggard and Ching-in Moon (Boulder, CO: Westview Press, 1989), 37. Gereffi and Wyman, however, cite Bela Balassa's research warning against overstating the importance of size.

63. Robert Dore, "Reflections on Culture and Social Change," in *Manufacturing Miracles*, 353–367.

64. Jeffrey A. Winters, "Asia and the 'Magic' of the Marketplace," *Current History* 97 (December 1998): 420.

65. In other words, if the baht had previously been worth $0.10 then a Thai business borrowing $1 million from a U.S. bank would convert that loan into 10 million bahts. But if the decision to float the value of the baht caused its value to fall to $0.05, then the loan of $1 million would cost 20 million bahts to pay back.

66. Ibid. The Serengeti is the African plain famous for its wildlife.

67. In other words, a floating exchange rate presents the possibility that a foreign investor could invest, say, $1 million in the Thai economy (converting it into bahts at, say, 10 bahts per dollar) and then find out the following week that the baht had been devalued to 20 per dollar, thereby reducing the dollar value of the investment by 50 percent.

68. Winters, "Asia and the 'Magic' of the Marketplace," 419.

69. Charles Wolf Jr., "Too Much Government Control," *Wall Street Journal*, February 4, 1998.

70. Meredith Woo-Cumings, "All in the Family: Reforming Corporate Governance in East Asia," *Current History* 97 (December 1998): 426–430.

71. Joseph Stiglitz, "Bad Private-Sector Decisions," *Wall Street Journal* (February 4, 1998).

72. Asian Development Bank (ADB.org), "Asian Development Outlook 2004 : I. Developing Asia and the World" http://www.adb.org/Documents/Books/ADO/2004/part010100.asp; World Bank statistics suggest a slightly lower growth rate of 5.7-6.3 percent for 2004 and 2005. See, The World Bank Group, DevNews Media Center, "East Asia On Solid Ground, Set To Grow

By 6 Percent In 2004," http://web.worldbank. org/WBSITE/EXTERNAL/NEWS/

73. ADB.Org, "East Asia: Six Years After the Crisis, Statement by Tadao Chino, president of the Asian Development Bank. http://www.adb. org/Documents/Speeches/2003/ms2003069.asp

74. Irma Adelman and Cynthia Taft Morris, *Economic Growth and Social Equity in Developing Countries* (Stanford, CA: Stanford University Press, 1973). A similar argument has been made in research by Keith Griffin.

75. Perhaps the seminal work in this area was Hollis Chenery et al., *Redistribution with Growth* (London: Oxford University Press, with World Bank and University of Sussex, 1974). There have been large numbers of World Bank studies supporting this strategy.

76. Richard E. Barrett and Soomi Chin, "Export-Oriented Industrializing States in the Capitalist World System: Similarities and Differences," in *The Political Economy of the New Asian Industrialism*, 28–31; Ward, *Governing the Market*, 38.

77. Howard Handelman, ed., *The Politics of Rural Change in Asia and Latin America* (Bloomington: Indiana University Press, 1981).

78. Robert H. Bates, "Governments and Agricultural Markets in Africa," in *Toward a Political Economy of Development*, ed. Robert H. Bates (Berkeley: University of California Press, 1988); see also Michael J. Lofchie, *The Policy Factor: Agricultural Performance in Kenya and Tanzania* (Boulder, CO: Lynne Rienner Publishers, 1989), 57–59; Charles Harvey, ed., *Agricultural Pricing Policy in Africa* (London: Macmillan, 1988), 2.

79. Sheahan, *Patterns of Development*; Haggard, *Pathways from the Periphery*, chap. 1.

80. I have previously discussed two other influences on distribution that need not be repeated here. First, as Simon Kuznets has demonstrated, countries in the intermediate stage of economic growth tend to have more unequal income distribution than either poor or developed nations. Second, all other factors being held equal, socialist or Marxist regimes have more equal distribution than capitalist ones.

81. UNDP, *Human Development Report, 1993* (New York: Oxford University Press, 1993), 162–163.

82. Haggard, *Pathways from the Periphery*, 239–240. Haggard notes, however, that some research has challenged the widely assumed correlation between education and income equality. See Frederick Harbison, "The Education-Income Connection," *Income Distribution and Growth in Less-Developed Countries*, eds. Charles R. Frank and Richard C. Webb (Washington, DC: Brookings Institution, 1977).

83. The *New York Times* (September 8, 2004).

84. Gareth Porter and Janet Welsh Brown, *Global Environmental Politics* (Boulder, Co: Westview Press, 1996), 113.

85. Bhaskar Nath and Ilkden Talay, "Man, Science, Technology and Sustainable Development," in *Sustainable Development*, eds. Bhaskar Nath, Luc Hens, Dimitri Devuyst (Brussels, Belgium: VUB University Press, 1996), 37.

86. For a general discussion of international environmental debates, see Jacqueline Vaughn Switzer and Gary Bryner, *Environmental Politics: Domestic and Global Dimensions* (New York: St. Martin's Press, 1998), 200–234.

87. Marian A. L. Miller, *The Third World in Global Environmental Politics* (Boulder, CO: Lynne Rienner Publishers, 1995), 43–44.

88. A surprisingly high proportion of advanced, modern medications use ingredients drawn from tropical rain forests.

89. Nath and Talay, "Man, Science," 36.

90. For information on the debate over sustainable development, see Ken Conca, Michael Alberty, and Geoffrey D. Dabelko, eds., *Green Planet Blues: Environmental Politics from Stockholm to Rio* (Boulder, CO: Westview Press, 1995), 205–238.

91. Andrew Blowers and Pieter Leroy, "Environment and Society: Shaping the Future," in *Environmental Policy in an International Context: Prospects*, eds. Andrew Blowers and Pieter Glasbergen (New York: John Wiley & Sons, 1996), 262.

92. Meeting of Oxfam Study-Tour participants with an economist at the University of the West Indies, Kingston, Jamaica.

93. Some environmental experts believe that it will be impossible to maintain sustainable development and that the world faces certain ecological disaster. See Joseph Wayne Smith, Graham Lyons, and Gary Sauer-Thompson, *Healing a Wounded World* (Westport, CT: Praeger Publishers, 1997).

94. Robin Broad and John Cavanagh, "No More NICs," *Foreign Policy* 72 (Fall 1988): 81–103.

95. Communication with Stephan Haggard, April 6, 1994.

96. Bruce Bueno de Mesquita et al., "Political Competition and Economic Growth," *Journal of Democracy* 12, no. 1 (2001): 58–72. Note that they were analyzing the performances of individual governments, not of countries. Hence, over a period of nearly 50 years, during which most countries had multiple governments, there were many hundreds of cases from which they selected their sample of about 355.

Glossary

Afghan Arabs A term used to refer to Arabs who fought as volunteers with the fundamentalist Taliban forces in Afghanistan.

Agrarian reform Distribution of farmland to needy peasants along with the government support programs such as roads, technical assistance, and lines of credit needed to make beneficiaries economically viable.

Ancien régime The old political order. The term is often used to describe a decaying regime threatened or ousted by a revolutionary movement.

Apparatchik A career bureaucrat in the Soviet government. Often used more broadly to refer to a bureaucrat whose primary interest is in protecting his or her authority and perquisites.

Authoritarian system A political system that limits or prohibits opposition groups and otherwise restricts political activity and expression.

Autonomy A substantial amount of self-rule for an ethnic group or region that falls short of full independence.

Baht The Thai national currency.

Barrio A poor urban neighborhood in Latin America or the Philippines.

Bourgeoisie A Marxist term (also used by non-Marxist scholars) for those who own society's productive resources, most notably businesspeople.

Bureaucratic-authoritarian regimes Military dictatorships, found most often in Latin America's more developed countries, that were based on an alliance between the military, government bureaucrats, local business elites, and multinational corporations.

Capital goods (or equipment) Goods such as machinery that are used for production of other goods rather than for consumption.

Capital-intensive production Industrial or agricultural production that relies more heavily on machinery and technology than on human labor.

Caretaker government An interim government (sometimes military) that steps in to restore order but plans to step down relatively quickly.

Caste system A rigid social hierarchy in which individuals are born with a status that they retain regardless of their education or achievement.

Chaebols Powerful industrial conglomerates that dominate the South Korean economy.

Christian (or Ecclesial) Base Communities (CEBs) Small Catholic neighborhood groups in Latin America that discuss religious questions and community problems. Commonly located in poor neighborhoods, many CEBs were politicized or radicalized in the 1960s and 1970s.

Civic action programs Development programs such as road or school construction carried out by the military.

Civil society The network of politically relevant groups that are relatively independent of state control.

Class consciousness A measure of how much a social class (workers, peasants, or the middle class) view themselves as having common goals that are distinct from, and often opposed to, the interests of other classes.

Clientelism The dispensing of public resources by political power holders or seekers who offer them as favors in exchange for votes or other forms of public support.

Collective farming (collectivization) Joint farming activity by a peasant community, state farm, or cooperative of some sort. In communist countries, the government often collectivized farming against the wishes of the rural population.

Colonization Asserting control over a previously independent region. Also used to describe the settlement of tropical forests or other previously uninhabited areas by migrating farmers or large agricultural operations.

Coloreds A South African term coined during the period of White rule to describe people of mixed racial background.

Command economy An economy in which most of the means of production are owned and managed by the state and in which prices and production decisions are determined by state planners.

Commercialization of agriculture The process whereby subsistence farmers (i.e., those raising crops largely for their own family consumption) convert, sometimes unwillingly, to farming for the commercial market.

Communal politics (communalism) Politics that have a strong ethnic base and often involve conflict between ethnicities.

Comparative advantage A country's capacity to engage in economic activity efficiently and cheaply relative to other nations.

Consociationalism A division of political power between formerly antagonistic groups (such as ethnicities) based on power sharing, limited autonomy, and mutual vetoes.

Consolidated democracy Democratic government that is broadly supported by all major political participants and is therefore likely to endure for the foreseeable future.

Consumer subsidies Payments made by the state that allow consumers to purchase goods at prices below their free-market value.

Core nations The richer, industrial nations of the world.

Correlation A tendency of two or more factors (variables) to change in the same direction (e.g., higher income correlates with greater education). Negative correlations move in opposite directions (e.g., alcoholism and education).

Coup d'état (coup) A seizure of political power by the military.

Crony capitalism A corrupt form of capitalist development in which powerful, well-connected businessmen use their government ties to accumulate vast wealth.

Cultural pluralism A diversity of ethnic groups.

Culture of poverty A sense of powerlessness and fatalism allegedly commonly found among the urban poor.

Currency exchange rates The value of a nation's currency relative to major currencies such as the dollar or Euro.

Democratic consolidation The process through which democratic norms (democratic "rules of the game") become accepted by all powerful groups in society, including labor, business, rural landlords, the church, and the military.

Democratic transition The process of moving from an authoritarian regime to a democratic one.

Devaluation (of a nation's currency) Allowing a currency that was previously overvalued relative to the dollar and other "hard" (stable) currencies to decline in value. This is normally done to correct a negative trade balance in which the value of imports exceeds exports.

Developmental state A state that intervenes actively in the economy in order to guide or promote particular economic development goals.

Dirty war The military's mass violation of human rights during its fight against subversive groups in countries such as Argentina and Peru.

Double day The burden facing working women, who continue to perform most of the family's domestic responsibilities (such as cooking and child care) while also working outside the home.

Economic disincentives Economic policies or practices that discourage desired outcomes, such as government-enforced low food prices that discourage agricultural production.

Economies of scale Economic efficiencies achieved through large-scale operations.

Ejido Communal farms in Mexico that were given special status under the country's agrarian reform programs.

Employer of last resort An employer (often the state) that hires people who can find no other employment.

EOI See Export-oriented industrialization.

Ethnicity or ethnic group A group that feels it has common traditions, beliefs, values, and history that unite it and distinguish it from other cultures.

Export-Oriented Industrialization (EOI) An industrialization model heavily tied to exporting manufactured goods.

Federalism A government form that divides power between the national government and smaller governing units.

Fundamentalism A theological doctrine that seeks to preserve a religion's traditional worldview and to resist any efforts by religious liberals to reform it. It also frequently seeks to revive the role of religion in private and public life, including dress, lifestyle, and politics. Used interchangeably with "revivalism."

GDP See Gross Domestic Product.

Gender Development Index (GDI) An index measuring a country's key social indicators (literacy, income, life expectancy) for women as compared to men.

Gender Empowerment Measure (GEM) An index of women's political empowerment based on the proportion of women holding major business positions and national political offices.

Gender gap A systematic difference in social status or achievement between men and women (e.g., a difference in income levels).

Gender quotas A percentage of seats in an elected body such as parliament or on a party's list of candidates for that body that are designated for women.

GNP See Gross National Product.

Great Leap Forward China's effort (1958–1961) to accelerate economic development rapidly by extracting tremendous sacrifices from the population.

Green movement The political movement seeking to preserve the environment.

Green revolution Dramatic increases in grain production due to improved seeds and other technological breakthroughs in the Third World (most notably in Asia).

Greenhouse effect (greenhouse gases) Carbon gases produced by burning fossil fuels that threaten to warm the world's climate dangerously by limiting the dispersion of heat from the atmosphere.

Gross Domestic Product (GDP) A measure of a nation's production that excludes certain financial transfers normally included in GNP.

Gross National Product (GNP) A measure of a nation's total production (see Gross Domestic Product).

Gross Real Domestic Product Gross Domestic Product as measured by purchasing power rather than currency exchange.

Gulags Internment camps for political prisoners. Originating in the Soviet Union, the term is also used to describe other repressive systems.

Hacienda A Latin American agricultural estate that, until recently, often included pre-capitalist labor relations.

HDI See Human Development Index.

Historical dialectic A Marxist term used to describe the ongoing tension between particular forces in history.

Human Development Index (HDI) A composite measure of educational level, life expectancy, and per-capita GDP.

Import-Substituting Industrialization (ISI) A policy of industrial development based on manufacturing goods domestically that were previously imported.

Informal sector The part of the economy that is unregulated by the government while similar activities are regulated and taxed.

Infidel One who does not believe in religion. Often used by Islamic fundamentalists to mean one who does not believe in the Islamic religion.

Infrastructure The underlying structures (including transportation, communication, agricultural irrigation) that are needed for effective production.

Internal warfare Military action aimed at controlling guerrilla unrest or other domestic civil insurrection.

Invisible hand The capitalist notion that the good of society is advanced most effectively when individual actors (businesspeople, workers) seek to maximize their own economic advantage.

Iron rice bowl The Chinese government's policy, now increasingly disregarded, of guaranteeing employment and a basic living standard to its population.

ISI See Import-substituting industrialization.

Islamism Islamic fundamentalism or revivalism A movement designed to bring the Islamic faith to its fundamental, strictly interpreted beliefs and traditions. An Islamist is a believer in Islamism.

Jihad An Islamic holy war.

Khmer Rouge The communist revolutionary movement in Kampuchea (Cambodia).

Koran Divinely revealed law according to the Muslim religion.

Kulaks Wealthier peasants. Originally a term used in Russia but later applied more broadly.

Kurdistan The contiguous regions within Iran, Iraq, Turkey, and Syria that many Kurdish people believe should be their independent national homeland.

Labor-intensive industry Industries that make more extensive use of human labor, as opposed to machinery and technology.

Laissez faire A policy of minimal state intervention in the economy.

Latifundia Large agricultural estates.

LDCs (less developed countries) The term is used synonymously with Third World and developing countries.

Liberal democracy A democracy that not only has free and fair elections but also respects civil liberties and upholds basic freedoms.

Liberalization of the economy Reducing the degree of state intervention in the economy (referring to the eighteenth-century classical liberalism of Adam Smith).

Liberated zones Areas (most notably in the countryside) controlled by the revolutionary army. Used in China and Vietnam.

Liberation theology A reformist interpretation of Catholic doctrine that stresses the emancipation of the poor.

Lost decade The decade of the 1980s during which Africa and Latin America suffered severe economic declines.

Machismo Male chauvinism (used particularly in Latin America).

Macro-economic policy Economic policies that affect society as a whole.

Maquiladoras Assembly plants, most notably in Mexico, that import parts from the United States and re-export assembled goods.

Marginal population People excluded from the mainstream of the nation's political and economic life.

Market socialism A hybrid of Marxist economics and free enterprise that has been adopted by countries such as China.

Mass mobilization The process whereby large segments of the population are activated politically. Governments or revolutionary movements may choose to mobilize the population.

Mestizos Persons of mixed Indian and European cultural heritage (Latin America).

MNC See Multinational corporations.

Moral economy The web of economic and moral obligations that binds a social unit together. Often used in reference to peasant-landlord relations in the countryside.

Mujahideen Islamic "freedom fighters" or guerrillas in a holy war.

Mullah A Muslim cleric.

Multinational corporations Corporations with holdings and operations in a number of countries. Overwhelmingly based in the developed world, many of them exercise considerable economic power in the Third World.

Nationality A population with its own language, cultural traditions, and historical aspirations that frequently claims sovereignty over a particular territory.

Neoclassical economics Economic theory that supports a free market and little state economic intervention.

Neocolonialism Economic or cultural dominance of one sovereign nation over another.

New social movements Grass-roots reformist movements that are free of traditional political party ties or class-based ideologies.

New world order A vision of a more peaceful world order under U.S. leadership that many had expected to follow the collapse of the Soviet bloc and the end of the Cold War.

NIC (newly industrialized country) Countries in East Asia and Latin America (such as Taiwan and Mexico) that have developed a substantial industrial base in recent decades.

Nurturing professions Occupations such as teaching and nursing that are commonly filled by women and that involve roles commonly associated with motherhood.

Parastatals Semi-autonomous, state-run enterprises.

Partial democracies Governments that have some of the elements of liberal democracy, such as competitive elections, but are not totally free.

Patron-client relations Relations between more powerful figures (patrons) and less powerful ones (clients) involving a series of reciprocal obligations that benefit both sides but are more advantageous to the patron.

People's war The term used by Chinese leader Mao Zedong and others to describe mass-based guerrilla struggles.

Perestroika The restructuring of Soviet society (most notably its economy) by President Mikhail Gorbachev.

Periphery Third World countries, commonly seen by dependency theorists as occupying a lesser rank in the international economy.

Pirate settlement Low-income urban settlements whose members have purchased their lots but lack legal title.

Pluralist democracy A form of government that allows a wide variety of groups and viewpoints to flourish and to engage in political activity independent of government control.

Political culture The set of political beliefs and values that underlie a society's political system.

Populism A multi-class, reformist political movement that promises increased welfare programs for the poor and middle class but rejects a basic restructuring of the economic order. Third World populist movements are often led by a charismatic (and sometimes demagogic) political leader.

Praetorian politics Politics lacking in legitimate authority, leaving competing groups in society to use whatever resources they have at their disposal (including violence, bribery).

Private sector The sector of the economy that is owned by individuals or private companies.

Privatization The process of transferring to the private sector portions of the economy formerly owned by the state.

Procedural democracy Standards of democracy based on political procedures (such as free elections) rather than outcomes (such as social justice).

Professionalized military A military whose officers receive a great degree of professional training.

Progressive church The reformist and radical wings of the Catholic Church (primarily in Latin America).

Proletariat The working class (blue-collar workers).

Pseudo-Democracies Governments that have apparently competitive elections and other trappings of democracy but in reality are only partially free and whose elections are not fully free and fair.

Public sector The sector of the economy belonging to the state.

Real wages (income) The true purchasing power of one's wage or income when the effects of inflation are factored in.

Reconciliation approach A more contemporary perspective of modernization theory that holds that it is possible for LDCs to simultaneously attain some development goals that were previously considered contradictory, at least in the short run (such as early economic growth and equitable income distribution).

Relative deprivation The gap between an individual's or group's expectations or desires and their actual achievement.

Reserved seats Seats in a government body such as the national parliament that are specifically set aside for an underrepresented group such as women.

Responsibility system China's policy of transferring collective farmland to peasant owners.

Revivalism Attempts to revive traditional religious practices and, sometimes, to revive the role of religion in politics. See also Fundamentalism.

Rupiah The Indonesian national currency.

Secularization The separation of church and state and, more generally, the removal of religion from politics.

Shantytown A community of poor homes or shacks built by the inhabitants. Unlike slums, they are generally in outlying urban areas rather than the central city.

Sites and services Housing arrangements in which the state sells or gives each inhabitant a legal title to a plot with basic services such as electricity and water, leaving the recipient to build his or her own home.

Smallholders Peasants owning small plots of land.

Social mobility The ability to move from one rank or social class in society to another.

Spontaneous shelter Urban housing built by the occupant.

Squatter settlement Communities built by the poor who illegally or semilegally occupy unused land.

Stabilization programs Government programs, often imposed by the International Monetary Fund (IMF), to cut budget and trade deficits. The purpose is to reduce inflation and stabilize the currency.

Sub-Saharan Africa Countries in Africa below the northern tier of Arab nations. Also called Black Africa.

Subsidized housing Housing provided by the state at prices below their market value.

Substantive democracy Standards of democracy that measure government policy outcomes, such as literacy and health levels or socioeconomic equality, not just democratic procedures (as distinguished from procedural democracy).

Sustainable development Economic development that "consumes resources to meet [this generation's] needs and aspirations in a way that does not compromise the ability of future generations to meet their needs."

Technocrat A government bureaucrat with a substantial degree of technical training.

Theocracy (theocratic state) A state run by religious clergy or their allies. Church and state are joined tightly.

Third wave The widespread transition from authoritarian to democratic government that has taken place in the Third World and Eastern Europe since the mid-1970s.

Third World countries Less developed countries in Africa, Asia, Latin America, and the Middle East.

Traditional society Societies that adhere to long-standing values and customs that have not been extensively transformed by modernization.

Tribe Subnational groups who share a collective identity and language and who believe themselves to hold a common lineage.

Wars of national liberation Wars of independence fought against colonial powers.

Zipper-style quotas A type of quota system for electoral lists of candidates for parliament or other government bodies in which the candidates are ranked and the group that is assigned a quota of candidates (such as women) must be given rankings comparable to the majority group on the candidate list (in this case men).

Index

A

Abidjan, Côte d'Ivoire, 171, 178
Acapulco, Mexico, 178
Acción Democrática, Venezuela, 161, 162
Acción Popular, Peru, 161
Acton, Lord, 256
Addis Ababa, Ethiopia, 171, 172
Adult literacy. *See* Literacy
Afghanistan
  Al Qaeda and Soviet invasion of,
    59–60
  ethnic conflict, 96
  Islamism, 45
  middle class, 34
  modern (Western) values and, 14–15
  revolution, 217
  Taliban government, 46, 51–52, 56,
    59, 61, 115
  UN peacekeeping forces in, 247
  women's status, 115, 139
Afghan Service Bureau (MAK), 60
Africa. *See also* Sub-Saharan Africa;
  specific countries
  adult literacy gender gap, 116
  authoritarian governments, 30
  crop pricing in, 164–165
  democratic transition, 30
  economic development, 244
  ethnic conflict, 78, 84–85, 106–107
  Islam, 47
  military budget, 239, 241
  military regimes, 226
  political development, 8–10
  political instability in, 14
  rural population, 148, 274
  urban population, 170–172, 174,
    182, 274
  women in government, 136
  women's status, 114, 118–119, 120,
    123, 124, 141
African Americans, 79
African National Congress (ANC),
  S. Africa, 87, 134
Agrarian reform, 148–169
  case for, 154–157
  crop pricing and, 164–165

  externally imposed, 157–158
  land ownership patterns, 154
  limits, 162–164
  moderate, 161–162
  peasant politics, 150–153
  politics, 153–157
  revolutionary transformation,
    158–161, 215, 217
  women's economic power and, 119
Albania, 30, 86, 183
Albin, Richard, 265
Algeria
  agrarian reform, 159
  Islamism, 45, 56
  military regime, 223, 233, 234,
    235, 242
  revolution, 199, 200, 217
Algiers, Algeria, 184
al-Jazeera, 63
All-China Women's Federation, 137
Allende, Salvador, 191, 231
Almond, Gabriel, 12, 13
Al Qaeda terrorist network, 15,
  59–63, 69
al-Zawahiri, Ayman Muhammad, 60
Amin Dada, Idi, 96, 105, 232, 237
Amnesty International, 128
Amsden, Alice H., 264
Anglican church, 46
Angola
  democratic transition, 218
  ethnic conflict, 85, 105
  military budget, 239
  revolution, 199, 200, 217
Ankara, Turkey, 177, 184
Annapurna Mahila Mandal of
  Bombay, 125
Apartheid, S. Africa, 86–87
Apter, David, 12
Aquino, Corazón, 23, 52, 130, 131, 224
Arab League, 91, 105
Arab Nations
  social and economic development, 7
  women in government, 131–132, 135
  women's status, 116, 123
Aracajo, Brazil, 178

political economy, 258
revolutionary movement, 152, 213, 217, 219
rural population, 149, 152
urban crime, 182, 183
urban population, 181, 184
women in government, 136
Colonialism, 80–81, 82, 92, 118
Command economies, 254, 255–257, 281–282
Committees for the Defense of the Revolution (CDRs), Cuba, 138, 214–215
Communications. *See also* Mass media
ethnic conflict and, 91–92
Communism, 30–31, 159–160, 217, 218, 255–256
Communist Party, 191, 198, 204, 213, 215, 216, 234
Conflict theory, 14
Confucianism, 36, 37, 46, 47, 48, 71
Congo, Democratic Republic of the (Kinshasa)
ethnic conflict, 77, 79, 85, 100–101
military regime, 223
rural population, 148
urban population, 171
Congo, Republic of (Brazzaville)
military coup in, 234
military regime, 237, 246
Congolese Republic (Brazzaville)
political economy, 257
Congress Party, India, 65, 89
Consociational democracy, 98–99
Contras, Nicaraguan, 161
Convention for a Democratic South Africa (CODESA), 87
Corporate interests, military regimes and, 238–239
Corruption, government, 237–238
Costa Rica
civilian regime, 228
democracy, 31, 248
economic development, 276–277
political development, 9, 14, 17
public policy, 38–40
underdevelopment, 2–3
women in government, 135, 136
women's status, 123, 125

Côte d'Ivoire, 85, 91, 171, 178, 185–186, 246
Council for Economic Planning and Development, Taiwan, 262
Cox, Harvey, 45
Crime, urban, 182–183
Croats, 86
Crony capitalism, 263, 270
Crop pricing, 164–165
Crouch, Harold, 238
Cuba
agrarian reform, 156, 159, 160, 161, 166, 215
economic development, 254, 256, 257, 273, 276–277
ethnic conflict, 93
military regime, 242
public policy, 38–40
revolution, 151, 152, 198, 199, 200, 203, 207, 208, 209, 217
revolutionary regime policies, 214–215, 216, 218
rural population, 151
social development, 5–8
urban population, 178, 179, 192
women in government, 135
women's status, 125, 137, 138–139, 140
Cultural Revolution, China, 159, 199, 216, 256
Cultural values
church–state relationship and, 70–71
modernization theory and, 12–15
women's status and, 137–139
Cutright, Philips, 32
Cyprus, 98, 102
Czechoslovakia, 30

D

Dahl, Robert, 35–36, 38
Dahomey, 226, 237. *See also* Benin
Dalai Lama, 50
Dal Khalsa (Sikh organization), India, 90
Darfur, Sudan, ethnic conflict, 76, 101, 102
das Neves Ceita Baptista de Sousa, Maria, 130

Ethnic conflict (*cont.*)
  settlement through exhaustion, 105
  systematic violence, 96
  toward peaceful resolution of,
    105–106
  tribes and, 83–85
  uneasy balance, 93–94
Ethnic dominance, 94–95
Ethnic harmony, relative, 92–93
Ethnic pluralism, democracy and,
  106–108
Evans, Glynne, 103
Evans, Peter, 16
Everett, Jana, 125, 126
Executive-branch dominance, 40–41
Export-oriented industrialization
  (EOI), 176, 266, 268–269
External influences. *See* Outside
  intervention

F

Fahd, King of Saudi Arabia, 61
Falwell, Jerry, 49
Federalism, 97–98
Feminist groups, 126
"Feminization of Agriculture, The"
  (FAO), 120
Finer, Samuel E., 227
First, Ruth, 234
First World Countries, 2, 3–5, 280
FMLN, El Salvador, 209, 218–219
Food and Agriculture Organization
  (FAO), United Nations, 120
Fox, Vincente, 29
France, 103, 200, 201, 205
Franco, Francisco, 82
Frank, Andre Gunder, 16
Free Countries, 29
Freedom House, 29
Frei, Eduardo, 244
French Canadians, 77, 81, 82, 93, 97–98
Fuerza Armada de Liberación
  Nacional (FALN), Venezuela,
  192, 214
Fujimori, Albert, 22, 41
Full democracies, 24
Fundamentalism, 54–65
  definitions, 55

Hindu, 63–65
Islamic, 54–55, 59–63
radical and conservative, 55–56
western modernization and, 56–59

G

Gandhi, Indira, 64, 90, 130, 131, 137
Gandhi, Rajiv, 90, 102, 130, 137
Gandhi, Sonia, 130
Gautama, Siddhartha, 53
Gender Empowerment Measure
  (GEM), 116–117, 142
Gender quotas, 133–134, 136
  zipper-style, 135, 136
General Agreement on Trade and
  Tariffs (GATT), 268
Georgia, 77
Germany, 34, 37
Ghana
  military in, 223, 234, 238,
    239–240, 246
  urban population, 176, 177
Gilbert, Alan, 190
Global warming, 279, 280–281
Gorbachev, Mikhail, 227, 257
Gorostiaga, Xavier, 66
Government corruption, 237–238,
  270–271
Government policies. *See also*
  Political development
  economic development and, 4–5
  neoclassical (neoliberal), 263–265
  social development and, 6–7
  urban employment and, 175
Grass-roots political activism, women
  and, 125–128
Great Britain, 46, 76, 118, 201. *See also*
  British colonies
Greenhouse effect, 157. *See also* Global
  warming
Greenpeace, 128
Gross Domestic Product (GDP), 3, 6,
  7, 148, 239, 273
Guatemala
  democracy, 24, 25–26
  ethnic dominance, 94–95
  military regime, 246
  political culture, 36